Ottoman Historical Documents

Ottoman Historical Documents

The Institutions of an Empire

V. L. Ménage, edited with additions by Colin Imber

EDINBURGH
University Press

Edinburgh University Press is one of the leading university presses in the UK. We publish academic books and journals in our selected subject areas across the humanities and social sciences, combining cutting-edge scholarship with high editorial and production values to produce academic works of lasting importance. For more information visit our website: edinburghuniversitypress.com

Edinburgh University Press Ltd
The Tun – Holyrood Road
12 (2f) Jackson's Entry
Edinburgh EH8 8PJ

Typeset in 10/12pt Times New Roman by
Servis Filmsetting Ltd, Stockport, Cheshire

A CIP record for this book is available from the British Library

ISBN 978 1 4744 7936 3 (hardback)
ISBN 978 1 4744 7937 0 (paperback)
ISBN 978 1 4744 7938 7 (webready PDF)
ISBN 978 1 4744 7939 4 (epub)

Contents

Note on Transliteration xii
The Islamic Months xiii
The Ottoman Sultans, c1300–1687 xiv
List of Illustrations xvi
Preface xvii
Maps xx
Figures xxii

CHAPTER I The Dynasty: Legitimation and Titulature **1**
Section 1 The Assertions of the Chroniclers 1
1 The voice of the dervishes: the dream of Ertoġrul 2
1a From the Anonymous Chronicles 2
1b From the *Tevārīkh-i Āl-i ʿOṣmān* 2
2 The voice of the *ġāzīs*: how ʿOs̱mān became an independent ruler 3
3 The voice of the *ʿulemā*: how ʿOs̱mān became an independent ruler 4
3a *Kitab-ı Cihan-nüma* about why ʿOs̱mān and his descendants were called *ġāzī* 4
3b *Kitab-ı Cihan-nüma* about how the drum and the standard came to ʿOs̱mān 4
4 Pagan Turkish tradition: the genealogy of the Ottoman sultans 5
4a Yazıcıoğlu ʻAlī on the line of ʿOs̱mān 5
4b Şükrullāh on the line of ʿOs̱mān 6
5 Conflation in the Oxford Anonymous Chronicle 6
Section 2 Titulature: Caliphal Claims 7
1 Inscription of Kayḫosrev II (1236–46) on a tower of the sea walls at Antalya 9
2 Inscription on the tomb of the Aydın-oğlu Muḥammad (d. 1334) at Birgi 9
3 Inscription of 1337 from the Şehadet Mosque in Bursa 9
4 Inscription from a bridge in Ankara, dated 1375 9
5 Other inscriptions referring to Murād I 9
6 Dedicatory notice in a Qurʾān preserved in the mausoleum of Murād I 9
7 Inscription on the tomb of Bāyezīd I, dated 809/1406–7 10
8 Title-page of an almanac (in Persian), dated 824 (1421) 10

9 A reference in Ṭursun Beg's History of Meḥmed II 10
10 A reference in Celālzāde's History of Süleymān I 10
11 Ebu'ṣ-Su'ūd's proemium to his statement on 'state lands' 10
12 The second deposition of Muṣṭafā I, 1623 11
13 *Fatwās* on the Ghalzay Ashraf, 1726 11
14 Süleymān I to Archduke Ferdinand of Austria, 1554 12
Sources 12

CHAPTER II The Dynasty: Princes **14**
Section 1 The Appointment of Princes in the Early Fourteenth Century 14
1 'Os̱mān's sons 14
2 Orḫān's sons 14
3 Orḫān's sons, after the conquest of Nicaea 15
Section 2 Princely Governorships 15
1 Prince Ḳorkud leaves Istanbul for his governorship 15
2 A letter from Prince 'Ālemşāh's mother Gülrūḥ to Bāyezīd II 16
3 A decree of Prince Aḥmed to the *yaya yoldaşlar* 18
4 A decree of Prince Selīm [II] 18
5 A decree of Prince Meḥmed [III] 18
Section 3 Fratricide 19
1 A statement of the former Byzantine Emperor John VI Kantakouzenos (d. 1383) 19
2 The accession of Bāyezīd I, 1389 19
2a From the Anonymous Chronicles 19
2b From Karamanī Mehmed Pasha's historical treatise on the Ottomans 20
3 The civil war (1402–13) 20
4 The accession of Murād II, 1421 20
5 The accession of Bāyezīd II, 1481 20
6 The first accession of Meḥmed II, 1444 21
7 The second accession of Meḥmed II, 1451 21
7a From Michael Doukas's *Historia Turco-Byzantina* 21
7b From Ibn Kemāl's *Tevârih-i Âl-i Osmân* 21
8 Popular criticism of fratricide: the story of the abdication of 'Alī Pasha 22
9 The accession of Meḥmed III, 1595 22
10 The accession of Aḥmed I, 1603 23
Sources 24

CHAPTER III The Dynasty: Recruitment into the Sultan's Service **26**
Section 1 *Pencik* and *Devşirme* 26
1 A decree regulating the *pencik* 26
2 Tolls to be levied on slaves taken across the Bosphorus 28
3 A template decree for levying boys for the *devşirme* 29
4 A Janissary lobbies the sultan on behalf of his family 30
5 Escaping the *devşirme* 31
6 The recovery of a captured novice 31
Section 2 Promotion to the Sultan's Service 31
1 Command to the *ağa* of the Janissaries, 1562/3 32
2 Command to the *ağa* of the Janissaries, 1567/8 32

3 Command to the *aġa* of the Janissaries, 1560/1 32
4 Command to the *aġa* of the Janissaries, 1573/4 32
5 Command to the *aġa* of the Janissaries, 1583 33
6 The pay of palace servants: an account register from 1478 33
Section 3 *Berāts* 34
1 The appointment of a preacher in Bursa 35
2 The appointment of a *beglerbegi* 35
3 The appointment of a *ḳāḍī* 36
4 The appointment of a metropolitan 36
5 The appointment of mountain guards 37
Sources 37

CHAPTER IV The Vizierate and the *Dīvān* **39**
1 The *Āṣaf-nāme* of Luṭfī Paşa 39
2 The *dīvān*: a Venetian account 49
3 Submissions to the sultan 50
3a Submission of the vizier Yemişçi Ḥasan Paşa 50
3b Submission of the vizier Yemişçi Ḥasan Paşa 51
3c Submission of the vizier Yemişçi Ḥasan Paşa 51
3d Submission of the vizier Yemişçi Ḥasan Paşa 52
3e Submission of Yemişçi Ḥasan Paşa 52
3f Submission of the grand vizier Meḥmed Paşa 52
4 The sultan's written instructions 53
5 The death of a grand vizier: the report of Henry Lello, English ambassador, 1597–1607 53
Sources 55

CHAPTER V The Provincial Administration and the *Tīmār* System **56**
1 From the report of Iacopo de Promontorio, c1475–80 57
2 An entry in a *tīmār*-register, with marginal notes 60
2a *Tīmār* of İnebegi and Ḥüseyn, sons of *ser'asker* Ḥasan 60
2b [Possibly relating to the village of Yılınça] 61
2c [possibly relating to the village of Pirvol] 61
3 Two entries from the detailed register of Āmid, 1518 62
3a *Tīmār* of Yemini the Kurd, a *sipāhī* of the *sancaḳ* of Āmid 62
3b *Tīmār* of Sa'du'llāh the *yaṣavul*, a *sipāhī* of the *sancaḳ* of Āmid 62
4 Sundry marginal notes in a summary-register of c1445, Thessaloniki etc. 63
5 Marginal notes in a similar register of 1455, Skopje 64
5a *Tīmār* of Mūsā, retainer (*ḫidmetkār*) of 'Īsā Beg 64
5b *Tīmār* of Yūsuf, kinsman of the *mīr-aḫur* Ḥamza Beg 64
6 Two *tīmār* grants 65
6a Thessaloniki: the *tīmār* of Meḥmed 65
6b Yalaḳabad [in the *sancaḳ* of] Ḳocaeli 65
7 Conversion of privately owned revenue to a *ḫāṣṣ*-estate 65
8 A call for volunteers before the Moldavian campaign, 1484 66
9 Submissions by and to the *sancaḳ begi* of Bosnia, c1512–14 66

9a The *sancaḳ begi* of Işkodra to Yūnus Paşa of Bosnia 66
9b The *sancak begi* of Zvornik to Yūnus 66
9c The *sancaḳbegi* of Bosnia to the *nā'ib* of Visoka 67
9d The *sancaḳ begi* of Bosnia to the Porte 67
9e The *sancaḳbegi* of Bosnia to the Porte 67
9f The *sancaḳbegi* of Bosnia to the Porte 68
9g The *sancaḳbegi* of Bosnia to the Paşa 68
9h The *sancaḳbegi* of Bosnia to the Paşa 68
10 'The good old days' 68
Sources 69

CHAPTER VI The Religio-legal Institution **71**
Section 1 Law and Religious Practice 71
1 Passages on the law of sale from Ḥanafī legal texts 72
1a From *al-Matn* of al-Qudūrī (d. 1037) 72
1b From *al-I<u>kh</u>tiyār fī ta'līl al-Mu<u>kh</u>tār* of al-Mūṣilī (d. 1284) 72
1c From *al-Fatāwā* of Qāḍīkhān (d. 1195) 72
2 A *fatwā* on the application of Shāfi'ī doctrine 72
3 A *fatwā* on acquiring land for a new mosque construction 73
4 A *fatwā* on taxing land occupied by descendants of the Prophet 73
5 A *fatwā* on a *ḳāḍī* granting unauthorised tax exemptions 73
6 A *fatwā* on Rumelian *ḳāḍī*s issuing *ḥüccet*s 73
7 A *fatwā* on *sipāhī*s taking a tithe 74
8 A *fatwā* on Muslim villagers neglecting prayer 74
9 A *fatwā* on money fines for neglecting prayer 74
10 A *fatwā* on executing a repentant heretic *şeyḫ* 75
11 Command to the *sancaḳbegi* of Amasya 75
12 Command to the *sancaḳbegi* of Amasya, İlyās beg 75
13 To the *sancaḳbegi* of Kastamonu and the *ḳāḍī* of Küre 76
14 To the *ḳāḍī* of Niksar 76
Section 2 The Administration of Law 77
1 A *ḥüccet* on repairs to a monastery on Mount Athos 78
2 A *ḥüccet* on returning a defective slave-girl to the vendor 78
3 A *sicill*-entry on the sale of a vacant site by a Muslim to a *<u>dh</u>immī* 79
4 A *sicill*-entry on a debt owed by a *<u>dh</u>immī* to a Muslim 79
5 A *sicill*-entry on a money loan 79
6 A *sicill*-entry on the daughter of a recent convert 79
7 A *sicill*-entry on divorce and the legality of the wife's second marriage 80
8 A *sicill*-entry on cloth measuring short 80
9 A *sicill*-entry on unsatisfactory goods 80
10 A *sicill*-entry on a complaint by the weavers' guild 80
11 A *sicill*-entry on a smith not receiving his dues 80
12 A *sicill*-entry on the payment of tax on a slave-girl 81
13 A *sicill*-entry on the ownership of sheep 81
14 A *sicill*-entry on a burglary 81
15 A *sicill*-entry on a violent argument between father and son 81
16 A *sicill*-entry on a command to the *sancaḳbegi*s and *ḳāḍī*s of Anaṭolı 82

17 A *sicill*-entry on a command to the *ḳāḍī* and the inspector of *muḳāṭaʿa*s 82
18 A *fatwā* on contracting marriage between minors 82
19 A *fatwā* on the validity of contracting marriage without the *ḳāḍī* 83
20 A *fatwā* on re-marrying without intermediate marriage 83
21 A *fatwā* on giving customs money as *zakāt* 83
22 A *fatwā* on giving alms 83
23 A *fatwā* on a preacher's statement about a *ḳāḍī* 83
24 A *fatwā* on the testimony of foreign merchants (*ḥarbī*) against a *dhimmī* 84
25 A *fatwā* on a Christian woman's charitable endowment 84
26 A *fatwā* on the Ottoman conquest of Istanbul and its surroundings 84
27 A *fatwā* on slaves purchasing slaves of their own 85
28 A *fatwā* on the sultan's slaves contracting marriages 85
29 A *fatwā* on a *ḳāḍī* acting outside his jurisdiction 85
30 A *fatwā* on the dismissal of a debauched *ḳāḍī* 85
31 A *fatwā* on the death of a falsely accused person after wrongful torture 86
32 A *fatwā* on extortionate loan transactions 86
33 A *fatwā* on tax income for *sipāhī*s 86
34 A *fatwā* on tax income, including in kind, for *sipāhī*s 86
35 A *fatwā* on *bennāk* tax 87
36 A *fatwā* on capitation tax (*ispençe*), grape tithe and taxes on pigs 87
37 A *fatwā* on a rebellious son of the sultan 87
38 A *fatwā* on those who lead the sultan astray 87
39 A *fatwā* on deposing a sultan who disturbs order by accepting bribery 88
40 A *fatwā* on the legality of killing fomenters of corruption 88
41 A *fatwā* on punishment for a thief stealing from the imperial treasury 88
Sources 88

CHAPTER VII *Ḳānūnnāme*s **91**
1 The 'Kraelitz text' 92
2 The *ḳānūnnāme* of Ḫüdāvendgār, 1487 99
3 Extracts from the 'general' *ḳānūnnāme*, c1500 104
4 The *ḳānūnnāme* of Siverek, 1518 108
5 The *ḳānūnnāme* of Sīs, 1518 109
6 The *ḳānūnnāme* of Nikopol, reign of Süleymān I 110
6a Instructions on dealing with the *tīmār*s of the district 110
6b Exposition of the *ḳānūnnāme* of the *voynuḳ*s 115
7 Extracts from the *ḳānūnnāme* of Egypt, after 1525 117
Sources 119

CHAPTER VIII Taxation and Finance **121**
1 Annual income and expenditure of the Imperial Treasury 122
1a An estimate of treasury income and expenditure, c1475–80 122
1b An estimate of treasury income and expenditure for the years 1527–8 127
2 Customs and *muḳāṭaʿa*s 130
2a Entry from a register of *muḳāṭaʿa*s 130
2b Entry from a register of *muḳāṭaʿa*s 130
2c A decree granting a *muḳāṭaʿa* 130

2d The problems of a tax-farmer 131
2e Demand for the delivery of payment due from a tax-farm 131
2f Tax avoidance 132
2g Tax arrangements in newly conquered fortified towns 133
2h A command written to the *ḳāḍī* and the fortress-commander of Kili 134
3 Silver mines 134
3a Instructions to a farmer of silver mines 134
3b Extract from a register for Bosnia, 1489 135
4 *Jizya* 135
4a Instructions to a *jizya*-collector 135
4b Two extracts from a *jizya* register 137
4c Accounts for the *jizya* of the infidels of the *vilāyet* of Menlik 138
5 Debasement of the coinage 139
5a Debasement under Meḥmed II 139
5b A debasement heralds a mutiny 139
Sources 140

CHAPTER IX *Waqf*s **141**
Section 1 Foundation and Function 141
1 Founding a *waqf* 142
2 A vizieral *waqf* 142
3 A new *waqf* 149
4 *Waqf*s established by conquerors and colonisers 150
4a The *waqf* of Murād I 150
4b The *waqf* of the Ṣaru Şeyẖ 150
4c Note protecting dervishes who descend from the district's conqueror 150
5 The *Waqf* of Mūsā 151
5a A note on the village of Ḳızıl Delü, 1412 151
5b A register entry on the *waqf* of Ḳızıl Delü, sixteenth century 151
5c A renewed *berāt* for Ḳızıl Delü Sultan's *waqf*, 1641/2 151
5d An undated register entry on the *waqf* of Ḳızıl Delü 152
5e Note appended to an undated register entry on the *waqf* of Ḳızıl Delü 152
6 The *Waqf* of Orẖān 152
7 *Waqf*s in decline 153
7a The *Waqf* of Dervīş Bāyezīd in Seydī Kavaġı 153
7b The *Waqf* of Saġrı Ḫatun 153
7c *Waqf* of the *zāviye* of Ḳāḍī Ṣalāḥu'd-Dīn 153
8 The *waqfīya* of Selçük bint ʿAbduʾllāh, freedwoman of Meḥmed 154
Section 2 Problems 154
1 A cash and family *waqf* 155
2 Cash and charitable *waqf*s 155
2a The *Waqf* of charitable donors (*erbāb-i ḫayrāt*) in the quarter 155
2b *Waqf* of charitable donors 155
2c *Waqf* of Ḥāccī Meḥmed in the village of Şeynelü 156
2d The *Waqf* of Ḥāccī Ḥasan b. Ūrūc the Felter 156
3 Cash *waqf*s: Questions of legality 156
3a A question on donating profit from interest 156

3b A question on interest 157
3c A question on using legal devices 157
3d A question on making restitution for not lending out *waqf* moneys 157
Sources 157

CHAPTER X Treaties and Foreign Relations **159**
1 The Genoese treaty with Murād I, 1387 160
2 The Byzantine–Turkish Treaty of 1403 162
3 The peace settlement of 1444 165
3a The sworn statement of Ibrāhīm Beg of Ḳaramān, 1444 165
3b The Treaty of Edirne, 1444 166
4 A grant of peace and of free passage for merchants 167
5 An offer to pay tribute 167
6 The peace terms offered by Süleymān I to Charles V, 1547 168
7 The English capitulations, 1580 169
8 The troubles of an ambassador 172
9 Latin text of the agreement at Zsitva-Torok, 1606 172
Sources 174

Glossary 175
Bibliography 184
Index 196

Note on Transliteration

I have followed Ménage's example in using the modern Turkish alphabet in transliterating Ottoman words, adding diacritical marks to indicate the original form of the word in the Ottoman-Arabic script. Turkish uses the standard Latin alphabet, but the following letters should be noted:

c English *j*, as in *jam*
ç English *ch*, as in *church*
ı roughly as *a* in English *woman*
ö as in French *eu*
ü as in French *lune*

I have not used the modern Turkish ğ. Following Ménage, I have instead indicated the letter used in the Ottoman-Arabic script, thus:

g ك
ġ غ

Latin letters with diacritics represent the following letters in the Ottoman-Arabic script:

ḍ ض
ġ غ
ḥ ح
ḫ خ
ḳ ق
ñ ڭ
s̱ ث
ṣ ص
ṭ ط
ẕ ذ
ẓ ظ
ż ض
ʿ ع
ʾ ء

I have spelled some of the more familiar Arabic terms using the standard Arabic transliteration, rather than the Ottoman – for instance, *jizya*, *waqf* rather than *cizye*, *vaḳıf*.

The Islamic Months

(1) Muḥarram
(2) Ṣafar
(3) Rabīʿ al-awwal (Rabīʿ I)
(4) Rabīʿ al-t͟hānī (Rabīʿ II)
(5) Jumādā al-ūlā (Jumādā I)
(6) Jumādā al-āk͟hir, Jumādā al-t͟hānī (Jumādā II)
(7) Rajab
(8) S͟haʿbān
(9) Ramaḍān
(10) Shawwāl
(11) D͟hūʾl-Qaʿda
(12) D͟hūʾl-ḥijja

The Ottoman Sultans, c1300–1687

ʿOsmān (c1300–c1326)
|
Orhān (c1326–62)
|
Murād I (1362–89)
|
Bāyezīd I (1389–1402)
|
Süleymān (Rūmeli 1402–11) – Mūsā (Rūmeli 1411–13) – Meḥmed [I] (Anatolia 1411–13)[1]
|
Meḥmed I (1413–21)
|
Murād II (1421–44; 1446–51)[2]
|
Meḥmed II (1444–46; 1451–81)
|
Bāyezīd II (1481–1512)
|
Selīm I (1512–20)
|
Süleymān I (1520–66)
|
Selīm II (1566–74)
|
Murād III (1574–95)
|
Meḥmed III (1595–1603)
|
Aḥmed I (1603–17)[3] – Muṣṭafā I (1617–18; 1622–3)
|
ʿOsmān II (1618–22) – Murād IV (1623–40) – Ibrāhīm (1640–8)
|
Meḥmed IV (1648–87)

1. After the defeat and captivity of Bāyezīd I at the battle of Ankara in 1402, his sons fought over the succession to the rulership of the remaining Ottoman territories until the final victory of Mehmed [I] in 1413. The information given here is simplified. See Dimitris Kastritsis, *The Sons of Bayezid: Empire Building and Representation in the Ottoman Civil War of 1402–13*, Leiden (2007).
2. In 1444 Murād II abdicated in favour of his son, Prince Meḥmed. In 1446, he was recalled to the throne and reigned until his death in 1451, when his son ascended the throne as Meḥmed II.
3. Before 1603, the practice of fratricide ensured that the sultanate passed directly from father to son. After 1603, it was, in general, the eldest surviving son who succeeded.

Illustrations

Map 1	Anatolia	xx
Map 2	The Balkan Peninsula	xxi
Figure 1	The palace: plan of the second and third courts	xxii
Figure 2	A firman with the *ṭuġra* of Ahmed I	xxiii

Between pages 38 and 39

Plate 1 The grand vizier
Plate 2 The *şeyḫü'l-islām*
Plate 3 An *içoġlan*, a page of the inner palace
Plate 4 A *ḫāṣṣeki*, an officer of the palace, holding the sultan's parasol
Plate 5 The *re'īsü'l-küttāb*, the chief clerk to the *dīvān*
Plate 6 A *tülbenddār*, maker and keeper of the sultan's turbans
Plate 7 A *siliḥdār* and a *çoḳadār* on horseback
Plate 8 A *samsoncu*, a keeper of the sultan's mastiffs

Between pages 90 and 91

Plate 9 The *ḳāḍī'asker* of Rūmeli on horseback
Plate 10 A Janissary officer with a firearm and powder-horn
Plate 11 A *muḥtesib*, a market inspector with a pair of scales
Plate 12 A butcher publicly shamed for selling short weight
Plate 13 An arsenal guard
Plate 14 The sultan's *sipāhī*s in procession
Plate 15 Armourers (*cebeci*) and *müteferriḳa*s in procession
Plate 16 A *deli* ('madcap'), a volunteer soldier

Preface

V. L. Ménage (1920–2015)[1] – Vic to his friends and colleagues – was lecturer in Turkish and then Professor at the School of Oriental and African Studies, London, from 1955 until his retirement in 1983. Over his years of teaching, he translated a series of Ottoman documents dating largely from the fourteenth to the sixteenth centuries, which formed the basis of his famous course on 'Ottoman Institutions'. Upon his retirement he gave the collection to his SOAS colleague Dr Colin Heywood, with the instruction: 'Do whatever you like with it'. Vic himself never envisaged publication, but Colin immediately recognised its importance for anyone studying or teaching this period of Ottoman history and, with the intention that we should jointly edit and publish the collection, made copies for Dr (later Professor) Michael Ursinus and myself. As it turned out, other commitments soon got in our way and the project was never realised. The idea of editing the documents remained buried somewhere in my subconscious, but it was not until over three decades later that my colleague Dr Georg Christ learned of their existence and at once realised their importance, not only for Ottoman historians, but equally for historians of late medieval and early modern Europe, and especially for students in his own fields of Venetian and Mamluk history. It was Georg who finally prodded me into action. He did not, however, confine himself to stirring my conscience, but immediately set about organising the collection into a useable format and making an electronic copy which rendered the process of editing much simpler. And that was not all. He also arranged for Dr Johannes Lotze to re-type much of the original typescript (including Vic's handwritten notes) in the period between completing his PhD and winning the Royal Asiatic Society's inaugural Bayly Prize for the best thesis on an Asiatic subject. Without Georg's and Johannes' help and continuing encouragement, Vic's document collection would still be slumbering on a shelf. I am also greatly indebted to Dr Kate Fleet for permission to use her translation of the 1387 Ottoman–Genoese treaty and to Dr Christine Woodhead for her fluent translation of a tricky passage from Selānikī's *History*.

When Vic was teaching the course, Ottoman history was still an exotic subject with almost no place in conventional university history departments in Europe or North America. Even in departments offering courses on the Middle East, Turkish and Ottoman studies tended to be

[1] For an obituary and personal appreciation, see Colin Heywood, 'V. L. Ménage (1920–2015): Turcologist and Historian of the Early Ottoman State: A Personal Memoir', *International Journal of Turkish Studies*, 21/1–2 (2015).

marginal. Nor was it a subject in which academic publishers showed much interest. As a result, anyone teaching the subject frequently had to fall back on their own resources for the provision of teaching materials. Another problem that teachers faced, and continue to face, is linguistic in nature. The Ottoman Empire was multi-lingual and, although the language of the court, the government and the literate elite was Turkish, Ottoman Turkish is so far removed from the Turkish of today as to be almost incomprehensible to modern Turks. Furthermore, official documents – and especially legal material – are likely to be written in Arabic, or – especially if they are treasury documents – in Persian. Before the mid-fifteenth century Turkish sources are rare, and Greek, Slavonic, Latin or Italian materials are often more significant. With the emergence of the Ottoman Empire as a great power from the late fifteenth century, the languages of the neighbouring states in Europe and the Middle East also become increasingly important both for records of diplomatic exchanges, and for the accounts of European residents and travellers in Ottoman lands. In brief, the array of languages confronting any aspiring Ottoman historian is bewildering. A solution to the problems facing students as they attempt to hack their way through this linguistic jungle is to provide translations of representative Ottoman and Ottoman-related texts. There has recently been a welcome increase in the number of such translations available, but when Vic was teaching, there was little available. Hence, with characteristic thoroughness, he made his own.

Vic made the collection to accompany his course on 'Ottoman Institutions', with the translated documents in each of the ten chapters illustrating one particular institution or aspect of Ottoman government. The first four chapters concern the organs of central government – that is, the Ottoman dynasty itself and the vizierate. Chapter V deals with provincial government, and Chapters VI and VII with the legal system and the law. Chapter VIII presents documents concerning finance and taxation and Chapter IX the closely related subject of *waqf*s. The collection ends with a series of treaty texts and other documents on foreign relations. In their original format as materials to be handed out and studied in class or in a seminar, the translations did not require an introduction or explanatory notes. I have, however, assumed that readers will usually be working on their own and therefore provided each chapter with a very brief introduction which places the documents in context. I have also added explanatory notes where these seemed necessary, and a glossary of the innumerable technical terms encountered. Vic's typescript also had handwritten annotations, evidently for his own use. Many of these were clearly prompts, pointing to larger issues raised in the text, which could become the subject of a group discussion. Some raised specific problems of interpretation, or queries for further consideration, while others were technical, noting emendations, variant readings and other matters. Most of these I have omitted, often reluctantly, in order to prevent the text becoming too long and unwieldy. Some I have incorporated into my own notes, and some I have incorporated verbatim. These are identified by the siglum 'VLM'.

I have not made any changes to the original translations, and I have presented them in the order in which they appear in the typescript. I could not match the accuracy or elegance of Vic's translations, and any changes in the order would have upset the coherence of each chapter. I have, however, added a few texts and also one or two passages which Vic omitted in the original translations or gave only in summary. In one case I have to confess that I had to substitute my own translation, as I had lost the original. However, more than eighty percent of the text is exactly as Vic left it. There is one omission some Ottomanists might find surprising. This is the so-called *ḳānūnnāme* ('law-book') of Meḥmed II on 'state organisation' which has been a major source of reference for many studies of the Ottoman court and government. Vic himself recognised the difficulties that this text presents, noting in a preamble to his partial translation: 'It is a compilation probably made in the late sixteenth century and fathered on Meḥmed II . . . Thus, though it may contain a nucleus of regulations dating from Meḥmed II's reign, the only safe approach to it now is that *no* statement in it is to be accepted as valid for that reign without independent corroboration'. I agree with this assessment, although I suspect that it dates from the early seventeenth century. Given the many problems surrounding this text, it seemed wiser to omit it. As a substitute, I have included short extracts from the 1525 *ḳānūnnāme* of Egypt.

Vic originally made the collection for student use, and it is primarily with students and teachers of Ottoman history in mind that I have made an edited version. The collection should also be useful for anyone with a serious interest in Ottoman history. Since Vic's retirement in 1983, the study of Ottoman history has expanded beyond recognition: new fields of research have opened up, new journals devoted to Turkish and Ottoman Studies have been founded and new scholars have come into the field. Nonetheless, the translations presented here remain as relevant as ever. Documents and other primary source materials do not go out of date, and the topics covered in the collection remain essential to an understanding of the Ottoman Empire's history between the fourteenth and sixteenth centuries. I hope that readers will find it useful.

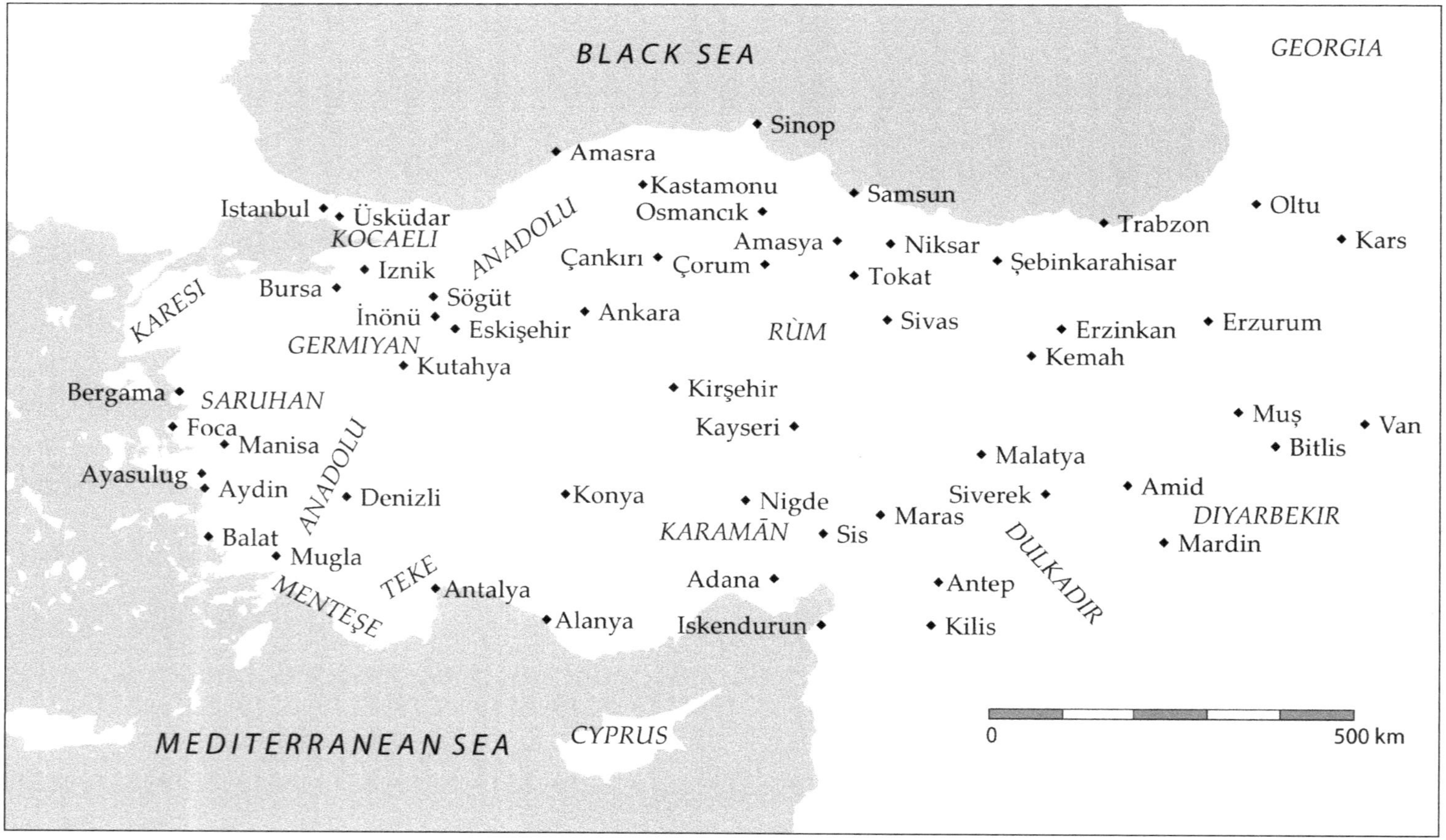

Map 1 Anatolia

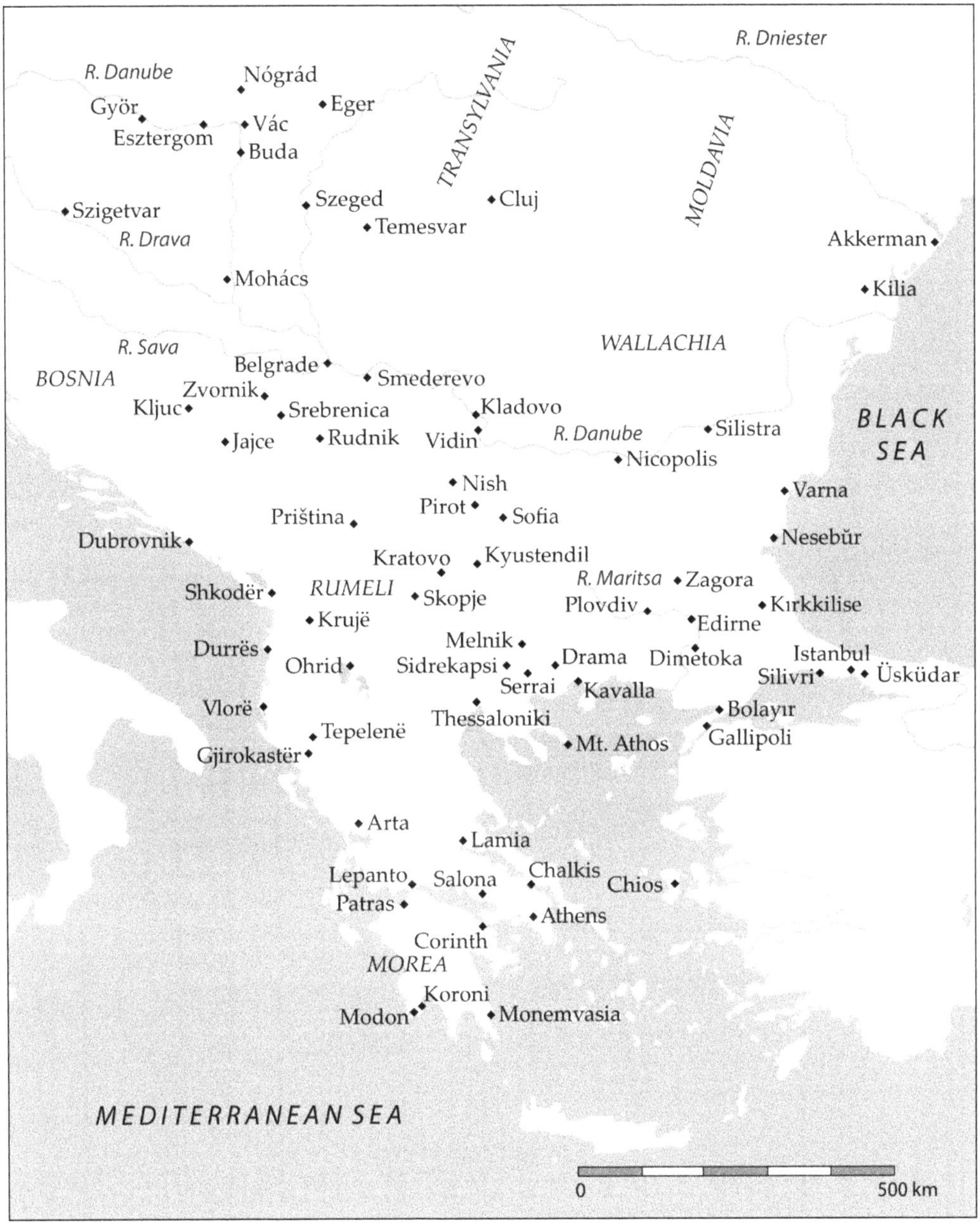

Map 2 The Balkan Peninsula

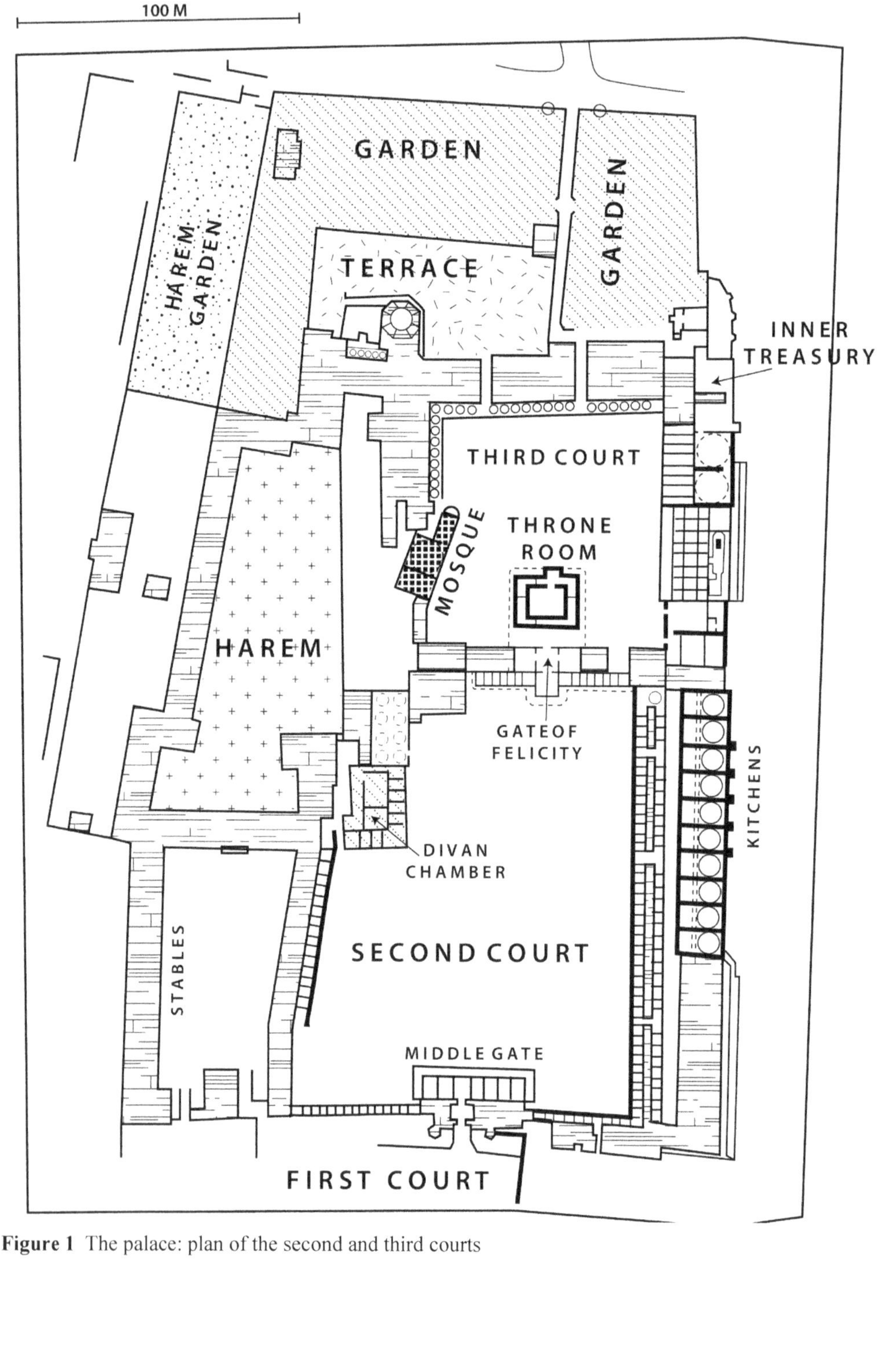

Figure 1 The palace: plan of the second and third courts

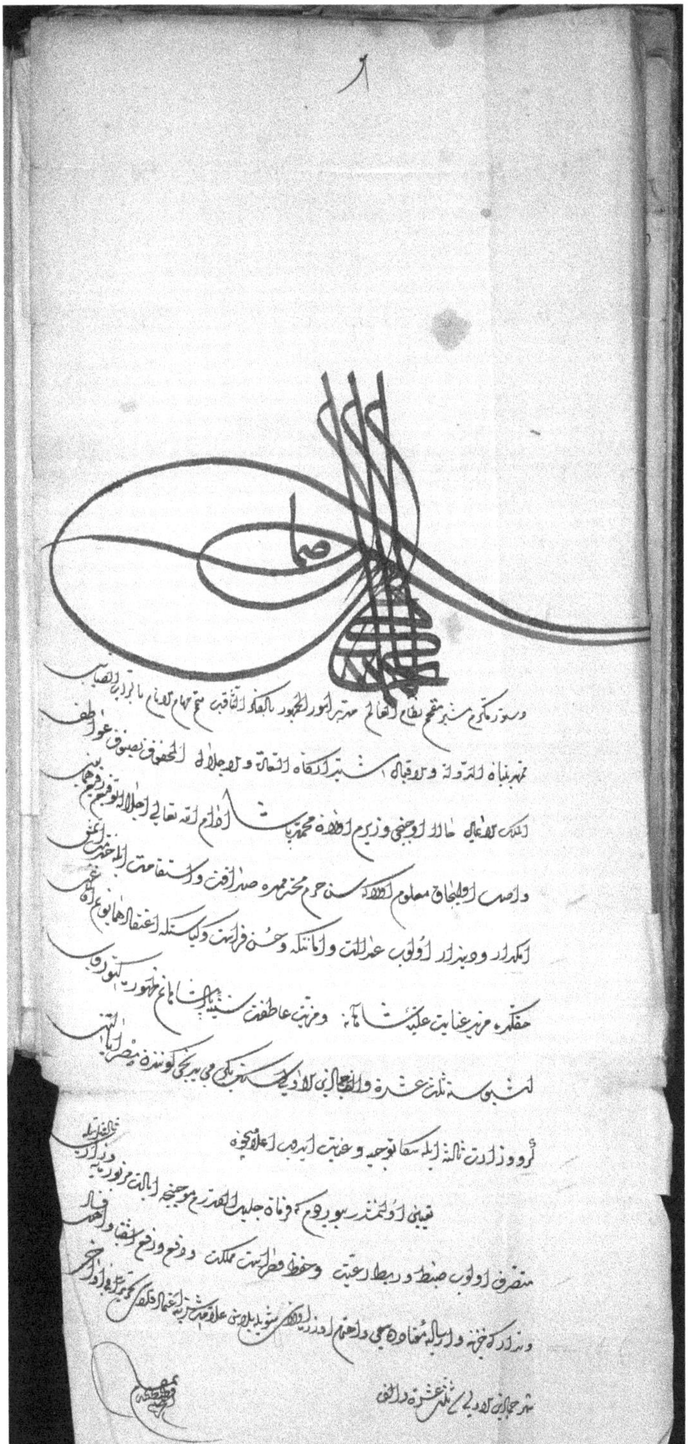

Figure 2 A firman with the *ṭuġra* of Ahmed I

CHAPTER I

The Dynasty: Legitimation and Titulature

SECTION 1 THE ASSERTIONS OF THE CHRONICLERS

The Ottomans, like any other dynasty, needed to legitimise their rule in the eyes of their subjects. The basis of their claims to rightful rulership and superiority over rival dynasties is embedded in the largely mythical accounts of the Empire's origins found in the earliest Ottoman chronicles. These reflect popular oral traditions which circulated in the fifteenth century, and while they share much material in common, the variations between them often reflect the milieu in which they arose.

The anonymous passages **1a** and **1b** reflect the culture of the popular dervish groups that proliferated in the early Ottoman period. They tell how a holy *şeyḫ* interpreted the dream of ʿO̱smān's father, Ertoġrul, as foretelling the greatness of the Ottoman dynasty. By the device of making ʿO̱smān (or, in some versions, Ertoġrul himself) marry the *şeyḫ*'s daughter, the tale links the Ottoman dynasty to the dervishes and provides it with a spiritual lineage

Passage **2** from the chronicle of ʿĀşıḳpaşazāde reflects the culture of active soldiers. In it, ʿO̱smān scornfully rejects the legalistic view that his sovereignty, expressed through the performance of the Friday Prayer in Ḳaraca Ḥiṣār, should be by the licence of the Seljuk sultan: he is a sovereign ruler by right of conquest. To this, Aşıkpaşazade appends additional reasons for giving ʿOsmān the right to rule independently.

Passages **3a** and **3b** from the chronicle of Neşrī, by contrast, reflect the legalistic views of the *ʿulemā*, in making the last Seljuk Sultan ʿAlāʾed-dīn appoint ʿO̱smān as his legal successor and ʿOsmān assume sovereignty only on ʿAlāʾed-dīn's death without progeny.

In passage **4a**, dating from the reign of Murād II (1421–51), Yazıcıoğlu is drawing on pagan Turkish tradition to assert the genealogical claims of the Ottoman dynasty. The sultan, he asserts, is a descendant of Ḳayı, the eldest son of the eldest son of Oġuz Ḫān, the eponymous ancestor the Oġuz, or western Turks. This line of descent gave the Ottoman sultan primacy among all western Turkish and Tatar rulers.

The tale in passage **4b** makes use of this genealogical claim to assert the Ottoman Sultan Murād II's superiority over the Ḳaraḳoyunlu Cihānşāh, his neighbour on his eastern frontier.

The anonymous author of passage **5** conflates all these elements in his account of Osman's achievement of sovereignty.

1 The voice of the dervishes: the dream of Ertoġrul[1]

1a From the Anonymous Chronicles

It is related that one night when Ertoġrul was still alive he dreamed a strange dream. In the morning he pondered the dream and went [from Ankara] to Konya, where there was an interpreter of dreams named ʿAbduʾl-ʿazīz to whom he told his dream. Some have said that the interpreter was a holy *şeyḫ* named Edebali[2] . . . Ertoġrul told him: 'I saw a moon rise from your bosom and enter mine. Then a tree sprang from my navel; there were mountains in its shade, and from them streams flowed to water the land'. The *şeyḫ* said: 'You will have a son named ʿOs̱mān who will fight many *ġazā*s. Your descendants will be *pādişāh*s; your son will marry my daughter, and their line will be *pādişāh*s'. Some time later ʿOs̱mān was born. When he grew up, he married that *şeyḫ*'s daughter, and she bore him a son, Orḫān.

1b From the Tevārīkh-i Āl-i ʿOṣmān

Though Ertoġrul had many concubines (*cāriye*), he had no children and was continually praying to God to send him a son. He married a pious lady, and one night he dreamed a dream. In the morning he rode [from 'Sögütçek'] to Konya and told his dream to a vizier of Sultan ʿAlāʾed-dīn, named ʿAbduʾl-ʿazīz, who was a great astrologer. He said: 'In my dream a spring (*pıñar*) flowed from my hearth (*ocaḳ*) and covered the world like a sea'. ʿAbduʾl-ʿazīz consulted his astrolabe and his books and said: 'God will give you a son whose descendants will rule the world'. Ertoġrul praised God and returned home. A son was born to him and named ʿOs̱mān. ʿOs̱mān succeeded his father after his death; he was an even mightier warrior, with over a thousand followers. The Byzantines (*Rūm ṭāʾifesi*) marched under the son of the Emperor of Constantinople to attack ʿAlāʾed-dīn. ʿOs̱mān divided his warriors into three groups, made a night attack from three sides and defeated them. He took much booty and sent half of it to ʿAlāʾed-dīn. ʿAlāʾed-dīn was astonished at ʿOs̱mān's prowess and sent ʿAbduʾl-ʿazīz to him with gifts of armour from the treasury, fifty files of camels, fifty files of [mules] and the White Standard of the Prophet which he had received from the Sultan of Egypt. ʿAbduʾl-ʿazīz had a beautiful daughter: she too was sent and also a standard and a drum.[3] ʿOṣmān went out to meet ʿAbduʾl-ʿazīz and entertained him. Next morning ʿOs̱mān made the *ġusl*[4] and went out riding with his followers. When they were about to turn back, a cloud of dust was seen. From it emerged an armed infidel *beg* who called: 'Which of you is ʿOs̱mān?' [The *beg* is named Miḫāl. The Prophet, appearing to him in a dream, had given him the name ʿAbduʾllāh and told him to seek out and join his servant ʿOs̱mān, who had the Prophet's White Standard; Miḫāl's descendants would make conquests as far as Hungary. Miḫāl came up and made the profession of faith before ʿOs̱mān. Several days later ʿAbduʾl-ʿazīz returned to ʿAlāʾeddīn and told him

---

[1] For a full discussion of passages 1(a) and 1(b), see V. L. Ménage, 'On the recensions of Uruj's "History of the Ottomans"', *Bulletin of the School of Oriental and African Studies*, 30/2 (1967), 314–22.

[2] The redactor of this account evidently knew of two versions of the story: in this one, the dream is interpreted by a certain ʿAbduʾl-ʿazīz, who lived in Konya; however, the redactor prefers and mainly follows another version in which the interpreter is a *şeyḫ* named Edebali (who, it is implied, also lived in Konya).

[3] The standard and drum were symbols of sovereignty. The purpose of the story is to show that the Seljuk Sultan ʿAlāʾed-Dīn appointed 'Os̱mān as his heir and successor.

[4] This implies that the marriage has taken place. *Ġusl* is the total ritual ablution that would be required after the consummation of the marriage.

what had happened. ʿAlāʾed-dīn sent to ʿOs̱mān the sword of the Caliph ʿOs̱mān, which the Sultan of Egypt had sent him. After ʿOṣmān had married ʿAbduʾl-ʿazīz's daughter Rābiʿa, she bore him a son, Orḫān.]

2 The voice of the *ġāzīs*: how ʿOs̱mān became an independent ruler

When [ʿOs̱mān] took Ḳaraca-ḥiṣār, the houses of the town were left empty. Many men came from the land of the Germiyan-oġlı[5] and other lands and asked for houses, and ʿOs̱mān gave them to them. Within a short time, the city began to flourish. He also gave many churches, which they made into mosques. They also set up a market. These people agreed among themselves and said: 'Let us establish the Friday Prayer, and let us ask for a *ḳāḍī*'.[6] There was a holy man (*ʿazīz*) named Ṭursun *faḳīh*,[7] who acted as *imām*. The people put the matter to him, and he came and told ʿOs̱mān Gāzī's father-in-law Edebalı.[8] While they were still speaking, ʿOs̱mān came and asked [what was afoot] and learned what [the people] wished. He said: 'Do whatever you think right'. Ṭursun *faḳīh* said: 'My Ḫan! For this we need licence and permission from the sultan'. ʿOs̱mān said: '*I took this city with my sword.* What concern (*daḫl*) has the sultan in this, that I should seek permission from him? God, who made him *sultan*, has, through the *ġazā*, given me the rank of *ḫān*. And if the sultan would make a claim on me by virtue of that *sancaḳ*,[9] I carried that standard into battle against the infidel. And if he says: "I am of the line of Seljuk", I say that I am the descendant of Gök Alp.[10] And if he says, "I came to this land before they did", I say that my grandfather Süleymānşah came before he did'. Hearing this, the people were satisfied, and he made Ṭursun *faḳīh ḳāḍī* and *ḫaṭīb*:[11] the *ḫuṭbe* was first recited in Ḳaraca-ḥisār . . .

Once a *ḳāḍī* and a *subaşı* had been appointed and a market had been set up and the *ḫuṭbe* had been recited, then the people asked for a *ḳānūn*.[12] A man came from Germiyan and said: 'Sell the tolls (*bāc*) of this market to me'. The people said, 'Go to the Ḫān'. He did so and made his request. ʿOs̱mān Ġāzī said: 'What is a "toll"?' The man said: 'I take money on whatever comes to the market'. ʿOs̱mān said: 'Fellow, have you any claim on the people coming to this market that you should ask money from them?' The man said, 'My Ḫān! In all countries it is the traditional law and custom (*töre ve ʿādet*) that *pādişāh*s take it'. ʿOs̱mān said: 'Did God command it, or did the rulers introduce it themselves?' The man said: 'It is the custom; it has existed from the beginning'. ʿOs̱mān became truly angry and said: 'Fellow! What a man has gained is his own property. What money did I put with his that I should ask him to pay me? Get out! Do not mention this to me again, or you will suffer for it'. The people said: 'My Ḫān! It is the custom that people should give something to those that look after (*bekle-*) the market'. ʿOs̱mān said: 'Since you say so, let everyone who brings a load and sells it pay 2 *aḳçe*s, but he who

[5] The ruler of Germiyan, the emirate adjoining Ottoman territory.

[6] As part of his address during the congregational prayer on Friday (*khuṭba*/*ḫuṭbe*), the preacher (*khaṭīb*) recites a prayer for the ruler. It is this act, together with the issue of coinage in his name, that establishes the ruler's legitimacy and independence. An established Muslim community also requires a *ḳāḍī* to settle disputes in accordance with Islamic law.

[7] *Faḳīh* (Arabic: 'jurist'): the title indicates a learned man.

[8] The author is following the tradition that makes Edebalı (and not ʿAbduʾl-ʿAziz) ʿOs̱mān's father-in-law (see 1a and 1b above).

[9] That is, the standard which ʿAlāʾed-dīn had sent him.

[10] In one of the genealogies of the Oğuz, Gök Ḫān (here Gök Alp) is the senior son of Oğuz Ḫān.

[11] *Ḫaṭīb* (Arabic): a preacher.

[12] *Ḳānūn*: law, statute. See Chapter VII.

does not sell shall pay nothing. Whoever undoes this *ḳānūn* of mine, may God undo his faith and his worldly welfare. Furthermore, to whomever I give a *tīmār*, it is not to be taken from him without good reason. When he dies, it is given to his son, even if the son is a child: let his servants (*ḫidmetkār*) campaign when there is a campaign until the son is able to go. Whoever infringes this *ḳānūn* of mine, may God be displeased with him. If any of my descendants is caused to lay down any *ḳānūn* but this, may God be displeased with him who lays it down and *with him who causes him* to lay it down'.[13]

3 The voice of the *ʿulemā*: how ʿO̱smān became an independent ruler

3a The Kitab-ı Cihan-nüma *about why ʿO̱smān and his descendants were called* ġāzī

Abaḳa Khān[14] made Masʿūd[15] sultan of Armenia and Sivas . . . but he had no profit or benefit from these territories in any way at all: he possessed nothing but the mere name of sultan . . . After him, the House of Seljuk completely lost dominion, and there was no *ḫuṭbe* and no coinage in their name left on the face of the earth. The people of Rūm[16] became divided, and every group had a king (*malik*) and a coinage and every city a ruler (*emīr*) and a *ḫuṭbe* . . . ʿO̱smān Ġāzī captured Bilecik and Söġüd in 699 (1299/1300). In 700 (1300/1), the caliph in Egypt of the ʿAbbāsid line was al-Ḥākim bi-amriʿllāh . . . In the time of these rulers ʿO̱smān Ġāzī was girded with the sword by Sultan ʿAlāʾed-dīn Kayḳubād b. Farāmurz[17] and devoted himself to the *ġazā*, as his father Ertoġrul had done, and made the good intention (*nīyet-i ḫayr*):[18] 'I shall gain my bread solely from the *ġazā* . . .'[19] And all the mighty sultans and noble kings of his time saw that he possessed sincerity of intention: so they did not object when he took Bilecik from the infidel, but said: 'Whatever he conquers from the infidel, let that be lawful (*ḥalāl*) to him'. And that is why ʿO̱smān and his descendants were called *ġāzī*, for their principle of action was not to bear sway by usurpation over the lands of the Believers, like other kings and sultans, but it was solely the *ġazā* and the *cihād*.

3b The Kitab-ı Cihan-nüma *about how the drum and the standard came to ʿO̱smān*

His mother and his people came out one or two marches in order to welcome ʿO̱smān. It happened that at that juncture, at the time of afternoon prayer, the drum and the standard and the *berāt*[20] and the sword and the royal robe of honour came from Sultan ʿAlāʾed-dīn . . .

[13] At the time when ʿĀşıkpaşazāde was writing in the second half of the fifteenth century, military fiefs (*tīmārs*) were non-hereditary. Here the author is protesting what he sees as the illegal practices of his own day and is implicitly criticising Meḥmed II (1451–81). The tirade against 'him who causes him to lay it down' may refer to Meḥmed II's vizier Ḳaramānī Meḥmed Paşa whom 'Āşıḳpaşazāde blames for making *tīmārs* non-hereditary.

[14] The Ilkhānid ruler (r. 1265–81/2)

[15] The Seljuk sultan, a vassal of the Ilkhānids.

[16] *Rūm*: Anatolia.

[17] Neşrī is identifying the legendary Seljuk Sultan ʿAlāʾed-dīn with the historical Seljuk Sultan ʿAlāʾed-dīn [III] (1301–3) who was, in fact, a contemporary of ʿO̱smān.

[18] In Islamic law, an act of worship (*ʿibāda*), such as prayer, fasting, almsgiving or the waging of holy war must be performed with sincerity of intention (*nīya*) in order to be valid.

[19] Holy War, if performed with sincere intent, is a legitimate means of earning a livelihood.

[20] Or: 'a horse'. The Arabic letters *brāt* may be read as *berāt* ('diploma of appointment') or *bir at* (Turkish: 'a horse').

When the drum and the standard[21] came to ʿOs̱mān, he set aside one fifth of the booty and proposed to go to Konya with limitless gifts, to meet Sultan ʿAlāʾed-dīn, to receive his blessing (*himmet*) and become his heir (*velī ʿahd*), for this sultan had no son and had sent the drum and the standard and the sword because he regarded ʿOs̱mān as his son. And although ʿOs̱mān had some sort of independence (*istiḳlāl*), yet he observed the due courtesies and maintained the *ḫuṭbe* and the coinage in the name of ʿAlāʾed-dīn. But when ʿOs̱mān had made ready to go to the sultan, word came that he had died. Since he had no son, his vizier Ṣāḥib took his place. When ʿOs̱mān heard that, he said: 'It is God who gives the judgment' and at once made Ṭursun *faḳīh* both *ḳāḍī* and *ḫaṭīb* for Ḳaraca-ḥiṣār, for this Ṭursun *faḳīh* was a holy man who acted as *imām*.

4 Pagan Turkish tradition: the genealogy of the Ottoman sultans

4a Yazıcıoğlu ʿAlī on the line of ʿOs̱mān

Our *pādişāh* Sultan Murād[22] b. Sultan Meḥmed Ḫān, the mighty *pādişāh*, lord of the sultans of the Arabs and the Persians, leader of the armies of those who declare God's unity, slayer of the infidels and the polytheists, sultan and son of a sultan, the most noble of the Ottoman line, is most fitted to be *pādişāh*. He is superior in descent and in 'bone' to all the progeny of the other *ḫān*s of the Oğuz, indeed to the progeny of the Jenghizid *Ḫān*s.[23] Thus, it is fitting, both by *şerʿ* and by *ʿörf*,[24] that the *ḫān*s of the Turks and the Tatars should come to his Porte to offer salutation and service. May the Almighty God make him to endure, and may his descendants be world rulers so long as the world lasts!

Near to the time of the Prophet, Ḳorḳut Ata arose from the clan of the Bayat. He was the sage of the Oğuz people. Whatever he foretold took place: he brought news from the unseen world, for the Almighty God would inspire him. He said: 'In the final times the *ḫān*ship will again return to the Ḳayı, from whose hands no-one will take it away'. And what he spoke of was the line of ʿOs̱mān.

In short, the *beg*s and *kedḫudā*s[25] of those lands [on the frontiers of Rūm] gathered and came to ʿOs̱mān Beg. They consulted together and said that 'Ḳayı Ḫān was, after Oğuz himself, the *ağa* and the *ḫān* of all the Oğuz clans . . . According to the *töre* of the Oğuz, the *ḫān*ship and the rank of *pādişāh* belong to the progeny of the *ḫān*s of no other clan so long as the progeny of Ḳayı exists. Henceforward we can expect no help from the Seljuk sultans, for most of their land has been lost to them and the Tatars have overcome them completely. Since the late Sultan ʿAlāʾed-dīn regarded you with favour, do you be *ḫan*, and we will serve you in the *ġazā* here'. ʿOs̱mān accepted; then they all stood up and bowed low three times in the fashion of the Oğuz. (In those days something of the Oğuz *töre* still remained; it was not completely forgotten, as it is now.) They sent for *k.mrān* (?) from the [. . . ?] and offered the goblet to ʿOs̱mān. When he drank, the *çavuşes*[26] called benedictions, saying (shouting?): 'Health and

[21] See note 3 above.
[22] Murād II (1421–51).
[23] Descent from Jenghiz Khan was regarded as bestowing a legitimate claim to rulership.
[24] *Şerʿ* and *ʿörf*: sacred law and customary law.
[25] *Kedḫüdā* (Persian: 'deputy'): presumably a deputy of the lord (*beg*).
[26] *Çavuş*: a herald, an usher in the sultan's court.

wellbeing! May your rule be blessed (*pādişāhlık mübārek olsun*)!'[27] Then they all moved off and advanced against the fortress of Bilecik, in the year 699 (1299/1300).

4b Şükrullāh on the line of ʿOs̱mān

In the year 852 (1448/9) the late Sultan Murād sent me on an embassy to Mīrzā Cihānşāh.[28] After I had performed my duty, one day the *şaġāvul*[29] came and said: 'The *mīrzā* wishes to speak with you privately'. I went to him, and in the course of the conversation he said: 'Sultan Murād is my spiritual brother, and also he is related to me'. I asked what the relationship was. The *mīrzā* ordered them to summon Mawlānā Ismaʿīl, the history-reciter, and to bring the Oġuz histories. Mawlānā Ismaʿīl came and brought a book written in Mongol writing and reported from that book that Oġuz had six sons, Gök Alp,[30] Yer Alp, Deñiz Alp, Gün Alp, Ay Alp and Yıldız Alp [=sky, earth, sea, sun, moon and star]. The *mīrzā* said: 'My brother sultan is descended from Gök Alp the son of Oġuz, with 45 generations between Gök Alp and Ertoġrul: and Ḳara Yūsuf[31] is descended in 41 generations from Deñiz Alp . . . The descent of my brother Sultan Murād is senior to mine, by as far as the sky is higher than the sea'.

5 Conflation in the Oxford Anonymous Chronicle

The laudable qualities of the House of ʿOs̱mān, which have not been found united in other sultans.

The sultans are descended from Ḳayı Ḫān, the descendant of Oġuz Ḫān. Oġuz Ḫān's testament was that Ḳayı should be *ḫān* after himself, and thereafter Ḳayı's descendants . . . For some time, the *ḫān*ship remained in the line of Ḳayı; but later the Seljuks and other Turkish *beg*s became *ḫān*s by force, down to the time of ʿOs̱mān. When calamity overtook the Seljuks, the great *beg*s of the Turks, in accordance with the testament, made ʿOs̱mān Beg *ḫān* over themselves . . . From this it is clear how superior the Ottoman sultanate is to other sultanates.

Moreover, the sultanate of most sultans came about through treachery to their predecessors and through aggression against Muslims, as the Khwārazmshāhs did to the Seljuks, the Seljuks to the Ghaznavids, the Ghaznavids to the Sāmānids, Timür to Emīr Ḥusayn[32] and Ḳara Yūsuf to Sultan Aḥmed.[33] But ʿOs̱mān and his predecessors, although they had no *tīmār* or pay (*ʿulūfe*) from the Seljuks but occupied themselves with the *ġazā* against the infidels on the borders (*uc memleketinde*) and supported themselves with booty (*māl-i ġanīmet*) yet, as long as the Seljuks bore the name of sultan, ʿOs̱mān Beg laid no claim to the sultanate. But when the Seljuks were destroyed through the invasion of the Mongols and the Muslims were left with no *ḫān*, he accepted the *ḫān*ship for the sake of the Muslims at the request of the *begs*, who knew that he was marked for the *ḫān*ship.

He engaged in the *ġazā* and conquered cities and fortresses; and his descendants have

---

[27] The author is here referencing a ceremony in the Ottoman court, where the *çavuşes* in unison called down blessings on the new sultan.
[28] The Ḳaraḳoyunlu ruler Cihānşāh (1436–67).
[29] *Şaġāvul*: an escort, accompanying official visitors.
[30] *Alp* (Turkish): 'hero, warrior', here used as title. Cf. n. 10 above.
[31] Cihānşah's grandfather (d. 1420).
[32] Of Balkh, killed 1370.
[33] Aḥmed Jalāyir, killed 1410.

followed in the same path. Most of their territories are lands conquered by them from the infidels; most of their revenue arises from the *jizya*.[34] And their *ḳul*s,[35] apart from their other troops, number some forty- or fifty-thousand, whereas no other *pādişāh* has possessed ten thousand such *ḳul*s.

But around them were various Muslim rulers (*mülūk*) who were evil and would harm the Well-protected Territories of the Muslims.[36] Whenever there was the slightest disturbance (*fitne*) they would rise and plunder and kill the Muslims[37] and would always urge on the infidels. When the infidels marched against the Muslims, when it was obligatory (*vācib*) upon them [the *mülūk*] to assist the Muslims, they would seize the chance to attack from the other side. Consequently the eradication of these people was obligatory (*vācib*), by the *sharīʿa* (*şerʿ*) and custom (*ʿörf*), by reason (*ʿaḳl*) and transmitted authority (*naḳl*); so they expelled them and became sole rulers in Rūm.

Since their distinguishing qualities were to uphold the Faith and to protect the poor, each succeeding ruler has sought to outdo his predecessor in good works; and their subjects have imitated them. The lands of Rūm, which in the past were mostly *dār al-kufr*,[38] have become *ḳubbat al-islām*:[39] the temples and churches have become dervish-convents and mosques and *medrese*s: no other land of Islam contains so many pious foundations; and the *seyyid*s and *şeyḫ*s and *ʿulemā* and *fuḳarā*[40] and *imām*s and *ḫaṭīb*s and *waqf*-officials (*ehl-i vaḳf*) who receive the alms (*ṣadaḳa*) of the Ottoman rulers number some forty-thousand. May God have mercy on the departed members of this House and support in felicity those who are living, and may He grant all the desires of our Ḫan, Sultan Bāyezīd b. Sultan Meḥmed, the Sultan of the Two Lands and the *Ḫāḳān* of the Two Seas, sultan of the sultans of the world.

SECTION 2 TITULATURE: CALIPHAL CLAIMS

After their conquest of Anatolia in the eleventh and twelfth centuries, the Seljuk sultans who ruled much of formerly Byzantine Anatolia in the twelfth and thirteenth centuries began to adopt titles of sovereignty (**1**) typical of the rulers of the old Islamic world.

These titles in turn passed, with many variations, to the independent emirs ruling in Anatolia in the fourteenth century (**2**) following the collapse of the Seljuk sultanate. Among these emirs were the Ottoman sultans (**3–7**).

These began to use titles proper to the caliph (**Table 1.1**) – in addition to that of sultan, as in passages **9** and **10** – as early as 1421 (**8**), but before the mid-sixteenth century their effect was rhetorical and did not, it seems, signal a serious claim to the caliphate. Promulgation of the idea of the Ottoman sultan as caliph, and therefore as successor to the Prophet and the four Orthodox Caliphs, began in earnest in the 1540s, with Ebū'ssuʿūd's formulation of the claim (**11**).

[34] *Jizya*: in Islamic law, a poll-tax payable by adult non-Muslim males in exchange for legal protection of life, limb and property.

[35] *Ḳul* has the literal sense of 'slave'. Here it might be understood as a 'servant of the sultan'.

[36] That is, the territories of the Ottomans.

[37] Here 'the Muslims' specifically refers to the Ottomans. The implication is that the other rulers in Anatolia are not true Muslims.

[38] *Dār al-kufr* (Arabic: 'the abode of infidelity'): the non-Islamic lands.

[39] *Ḳubbat al-Islām* (Arabic: 'the cupola of Islam'): the city of Basra, a seat of Islamic learning.

[40] *Fuḳarā* (Arabic: 'poor people'; sing: *faḳīr*): dervishes.

In Sunnī theory, the caliphate/*imām*ate is elective and not hereditary, and the caliph/*imām* should be chosen from the Prophet's own tribe, the Quraish. The Ottoman sultanate, however, was hereditary and not elective, and the Ottoman genealogy did not trace the line back to the Quraish and thus, in principle, the sultan could not be caliph. Ebū'ṣ-suʿūd bypassed this problem by asserting that the sultan was 'heir' to the 'great caliphate', implying that the Ottomans were the true successors to the four Orthodox Caliphs and that henceforth the caliphate was hereditary within the Ottoman dynasty.

The political use of the caliphal claim can be seen in (**12**) where the sultan's mental incapacity is invoked as legal grounds for his deposition, and in a fatwa (**13**) where it is used to counter the Afghan Nāder Shāh's claim to territories in Iran and the Caucasus held by the Ottomans.

The preamble to Süleymān I's letter to the Habsburg Archduke Ferdinand [I] (**14**) listing the lands and seas under his rulership is typical of the Ottoman sultans' correspondence with foreign monarchs in the sixteenth century and later. Ferdinand is simply addressed as 'King of Germany' (*Nemçe*). By stating that the Ottoman sultans conquered their lands 'by the sword', the sultan is belittling the Habsburgs who acquired their lands through inheritance and dynastic marriages.

Table 1.1

Titles adopted by the Ottoman sultans

Arabic	Turkish	Persian	Ottoman
amīr		*mīr*	*mīr*
			emīr
	beg		*beg*
malik			*melik*
		khudāwandgār	*ḫudāvendgār (> ḫünkār)*
sulṭān			*sulṭān*
khān	*ḫān*		*ḫān*
khāḳān	*ḫaġan*		*ḫāḳān*
		shāh	*ṣāh*
		shāhānshāh	*ṣehinṣāh*
		pādishāh	*pādiṣāh*

Caliphal titles

khalīfa
amīr al-muʾminīn
imām

Greek
αὐθέντης, whence Turkish *efendi*, Italian *(Grand) Signor*

1 Inscription of Kayḫosrev II (1236–46) on a tower of the sea walls at Antalya

Has ordered the construction of this blessed tower the supreme sultan (*al-sulṭān al-aʿẓam*), the exalted <u>*sh*</u>*āhin*<u>*sh*</u>*āh* (<u>*sh*</u>*āhin*<u>*sh*</u>*āh al-muʿaẓẓam*),[41] the master of the necks of the peoples, sultan of the sultans of the world, lord of the kings of the Arabs and the Persians, margrave of the horizons (*marzbān al-āfāḳ*), Ġiyāth al-Dunyā waʾl-Dīn, glory (*ʿalāʾ*) of Islam and of the Muslims, the shadow of God in the lands, Abūʾl-Fatḥ, Kayḫosrev b. Kayḳobād b. Kayḫosrev, partner (*qasīm*) of the Commander of the Faithful, in the year 641 (1244/5).

2 Inscription on the tomb of the Aydın-oğlu Muḥammad (d. 1334) at Birgi

This tomb has been built for the great *emīr* (*al-amīr al-kabīr*), the learned (*al-ʿālim*), the fighter in the holy war (*al-mujāhid*), the margrave (*al-murābiṭ*), the founder of pious works (*abūʾl-khayrāt*), the sultan of the *ġāzī*s (*sulṭān al-ġuzāt*), Mubāriz al-Dawla waʾl-Dīn Muḥammad b. Aydın . . .

3 Inscription of 1337 from the Şehadet Mosque in Bursa

. . . the great *emīr*, the exalted (*al-muʿaẓẓam*), the fighter in the holy war, sultan, son of the sultan of the *ġāzī*s, *ġāzī* son of the *ġāzī*, Shujāʿ al-Dawla waʾl-Dīn, margrave of the horizons (*marzbān al-āfāq*), hero of the world (*bahlavān*[?]*-i jihān*), Orḫān b. ʿOthmān . . .[42]

4 Inscription from a bridge in Ankara, dated 1375

In the days of the rule of the just king (*al-malik al-ʿādil*), the *ġāzī*, the supreme (*al-aʿzam*) sultan Ġiyāth al-Dunyā waʾl-Dīn, Abūʾl-Fatḥ, Murād Ḫān b. Orḫān . . .

5 Other inscriptions referring to Murād I

. . . al-malik al-kabīr . . . Murād Beg . . . (1378, Iznik)
. . . al-malik al-muʿaẓẓam waʾl-khāḳān al-aʿẓam . . . sulṭān ibn sulṭān, Murād . . . (1385, Gallipoli)
. . . al-malik al-muʿaẓẓam al-khāḳān al-mukarram, sulṭān ibn sulṭān, Murād . . . (1388, Iznik)

6 Dedicatory notice in a Qurʾān preserved in the mausoleum of Murād I

Waqf of our lord, the supreme Sultan al-Malik al-Ẓāhir Abū Saʿīd Barqūq[43] (may God make eternal his rule), ruler (*ḥākim*) of the lands of Egypt and Syria and the Ḥijaz, to the tomb of

[41] The grammar in this phrase is faulty.
[42] The date, reading and authenticity of this inscription have been much discussed. See R. C. Jennings, 'Some thoughts on the Gazi-Thesis', *Wiener Zeitschrift für die Kunde des Morgenlandes*, 86 (1986), 151–61; Heath W. Lowry, *The Nature of the Early Ottoman State*, Albany: SUNY Press (2003), 33–44; Colin Heywood, 'The 1337 Bursa inscription and its interpreters', *Turcica*, 36 (2004), 215–31; reprinted in Colin Heywood, *Ottomanica and Meta-Ottomanica*, Istanbul: Isis Press (2013), no. 6. For further references, see Heywood, *Ottomanica*.
[43] Mamlūk sultan, reigned 1382–99.

the deceased (*al-marḥūm*), the martyr (*al-shahīd*), Murād Beg b. Orḫān b. ʿOthmān (may God sanctify his spirit and illuminate his tomb).

7 Inscription on the tomb of Bāyezīd I, dated 809/1406–7

This is the tomb of the felicitous and deceased sultan, Bāyezīd Ḫān b. Murād Ḫān: it was constructed by the supreme sultan, the lord of the kings of the Arabs and the Persians, Süleymān Ḫān[44] b. Bāyezīd Ḫān . . .

8 Title-page of an almanac (in Persian), dated 824 (1421)

For the perusal of the most glorious sultan and mighty *s̲h̲āhins̲h̲āh*, possessor of the necks of the peoples and lord of the kings of the Arabs and the Persians . . . glory of the *ġāzīs* and of the fighters of the *jihād*, subduer of the infidels and the refractory, the shadow of God over the worlds, the caliph (*ḫalīfa*) of God in the lands . . . the sultan, son of the sultan, Sultan Meḥmed b. Bāyezīd b. Murād Ḫān . . .

9 A reference in Ṭursun Beg's History of Meḥmed II

Sultan of the two lands, *ḫāḳān* of the two seas, *amīr al-muʾminīn*, conqueror of the infidels and the polytheists, the sultan son of the sultan, Meḥmed Ḫān b. Murād Ḫān . . .

10 A reference in Celālzāde's History of Süleymān I

. . . sultan of the *ġāzīs* and *mujāhid*s, proof of the rulers and the cloistered, shadow of God on the two earths, sword of Islam and the Muslims, killer of infidels and polytheists, extirpator of rebels and the obstinate, conqueror of fortresses and taker of castles . . . the most mighty sultan and mighty *ḫāḳān*, lord of the kings of the Arabs and the Persians, proof of the men of the sword and of the pen, king of the two lands and the two seas . . . His Excellency Sultan Süleymān Ḫān son of Selīm Ḫān son of Bāyezīd Ḫān (may God make eternal the shadow of his sovereignty and make everlasting the glory of his majesty).

11 Ebuʾs-Suʿūd's proemium to his statement on 'state lands'

[When] the *ḫāḳān* of the face of the earth, the *ḫalīfa* (caliph) of the Apostle of the Lord of the Worlds,[45] the one who prepares the path (*mumahhid*) for the ordinances of the manifest *sharīʿa*, upholder of the foundations of the firm Faith, manifestation of the Exalted Word, raising aloft the standards of religion to the extremities of distant lands, possessor (*mālik*) of the kingdoms of the world, the shadow of God over all the peoples, conqueror of the lands of the East and the West through God's glorious assistance and His conquering army, leader of holy campaigns celebrated among the people and mighty battles (*waqāʾiʿ*) recorded on the pages of epics, the possessor of the Supreme Imāmate (*ḥāʾiz al-imāma al-ʿuzmā*), resplendent

[44] Süleymān was Bāyezīd I's eldest son.
[45] The Prophet Muḥammad.

sultan, heir of the Great Caliphate[46] (*wārith al-ḫilafat al-kubrā*) from generation to generation, the promulgator (*nāshir*) of the sultanic *ḳānūn*s, the tenth of the Ottoman *ḫāḳān*s, breaker of Caesars,[47] conqueror of princes, sultan of the Arabs, Persians and Romans (*sulṭān al-ʿarab waʾl-ʿajam waʾl-rūm*), the protector of the holy ground of the Two Sacred Sanctuaries[48] . . . the sultan, son of the sultan, Sultan Süleymān Ḫān . . .

12 The second deposition of Muṣṭafā I, 1623

The *ʿulemā* sent word to the *pādişāh*'s mother, saying: 'Tomorrow, as your son, our *pādişāh* Sultan Muṣṭafā is sitting on his throne, we have, according to the *sharīʿa*, questions to put to him: first, "What is your name?", then: "Whose son are you?" and "What day is it today?" If he can reply to these, then he is *amīr al-muʾminīn*[49] and our *pādişāh* and may whoever looks at him askance be struck blind! But if not, then his imāmate is not licit (*cāʾiz*) according to the *sharīʿa*. The imāmate of a child is not licit, nor is that of a lunatic'.

13 *Fatwās* on the Ghalzay Ashraf, 1726

Question: Is it permissible for the Muslims to offer the *bayʿa*[50] to two *imām*s at the same time?

Answer: It is agreed (*icmāʿ*) that two *imām*s cannot exist at the same time, unless they are separated by a great obstruction like the Indian Ocean,[51] so that the one cannot extend protection over the territories of the other.

Question: If after all the Muslims have paid the *bayʿa* to and have appointed as *imām* the Sultan of the Two Lands and the Two Seas, the Servitor of the Two Noble Sanctuaries, Sultan Aḥmed Ḫān,[52] whose glorious ancestors were rulers and *imāms* (*mülūk ve eʾimme*); if then Zeyd, on the ground that he has conquered by his sword territory in the vicinity of Isfahan, claims the position of *imām* and sultan for himself . . .?

Answer: Zeyd is a rebel (*bāġī*).[53] If he abandons his presumptions and submits to the Shadow of God upon earth, well and good: if not, then his fate is expressed in the words: '. . . if one party wrongs the other, fight the one that does wrong until it returns to Allah's command'[54] and in the *ḥadīth*:[55] 'If the *bayʿa* has been paid to two Caliphs, then kill the second of them'.

---

[46] 'Imāmate' and 'Caliphate' are synonyms here. The reference is to the Four Rightly Guided Caliphs who succeeded the Prophet.

[47] Probably a reference to Süleymān's victories over the Habsburgs. 'Caesar' (*Kaiser*) was a title of Charles V as Holy Roman Emperor.

[48] Mecca and Medina.

[49] 'Commander of the faithful', the title of the Caliph.

[50] *Bayʿa* (Arabic): in sunnī dogma, the oath of allegiance offered by the 'men of loosing and binding' to the newly elected caliph.

[51] In sunnī dogma there can be more than one caliph only if 'a great sea' separates them.

[52] Aḥmed III (1703–30).

[53] *Bāġī*: a person who rebels against the legitimate Muslim sovereign, but without renouncing Islam.

[54] Qurʾān 49:9.

[55] *Ḥadīth*: a reported saying or deed of the Prophet.

14 Süleymān I to Archduke Ferdinand of Austria, 1554

I who am the sultan of sultans, the proof (*burhān*) of the *ḫāḳān*s, granter of crowns to the kings of the earth, shadow of God over the earth, *pādişāh* of the White Sea,[56] the Black Sea, Rūmeli, Anaṭolı, Rūm, Ḳaramān, Erżurūm, Diyārbekir, Kurdistan, Lūristān, Georgia, Ẕū'l-ḳadriyye, Damascus, Egypt, Aleppo, Mecca and Medina and Jerusalem, and the whole land of Arabia, Baghdad, Jāzān, Yemen, Ṣan'a, Aden, Basra and Algiers, of the lands of the Tatars and the Qipchak plain (*dasht*), and of the throne of Budin,[57] and the places belonging to it, and of many other lands conquered by my sword – I, Sultan Süleymān-şāh, son of Sultan Selīm-şāh Ḫān: you King Ferdinand, who are king of the land of Nemçe[58] and the places belonging to it, have sent a letter . . .

SOURCES

Section 1

1a F. Giese (ed.), *Die Altosmanischen Anonymen Chroniken*, Breslau (1922), 6–7.
1b Anonymous, *Tevārīkh-i Āl-i 'Oṣmān*, MS Aya Sofya 2705, 69v–71v.
2 'Aşiḳpaşazāde, ed. Ç. N. Atsız, *Tevārīḫ-i Āl-i 'Osmān*, in *Osmanlı Tarihleri*, Istanbul (1949), 103, 104
3a and 3b Neşrī, ed. F. R. Unat and M. A. Köymen, *Kitab-ı Cihan-nüma*, vol. 1, Ankara (1949) 48–52, 106–8.
4a Yazıcı-oğlu 'Alī, quoted by Paul Wittek, in 'Yazījīoghlu 'Alī on the Christian Turks of the Dobruja', *Bulletin of the School of Oriental and African Studies*, 14 (1952), 647, n. 2 & n. 3.
4b Şükrullāh, MS Nuruosmaniye 3059, f. 158v; Turkish translation in Ç. N. Atsız, *Osmanlı Tarihleri*, 51.
5 Anonymous Chronicle, Bodleian Lib., MS Marsh 313, ff. 5r.–7v. The passage is also translated in Dimitri J. Kastritsis, *An Early Ottoman History: The Oxford Anonymous Chronicle*, Liverpool (2017), 52–4.

Section 2

1 Rudolph Meyer Riefstahl and Paul Wittek, *Turkish Architecture in South-Western Anatolia*, Cambridge (1931), 50.
2 Riefstahl and Wittek, *Turkish Architecture*, 105.
3 Paul Wittek, *The Rise of the Ottoman Empire*, London (1938), n. 27.
4 Paul Wittek, 'Zu einigen frühosmanischen Urkunden', *Wiener Zeitschrift für die Kunde des Morgenlandes*, 55 (1959), 132–3.
5 Paul Wittek, 'Notes sur la tughra ottomane', *Byzantion*, XX (1950), 280.
6 Ahmed Tevhid, 'İlk altı pādişāhımızın Brusada kā'in türbelerinden Ḫüdāvendgâr Sulṭān Murād Ḫān-i Evvelin türbesi', *Tarih-i Osmani Encümeni Mecmuası*, 3/13–18 (1328/1910), 1048.
7 Ahmed Tevhid, 'İlk altı padişāhımızın', 1051.
8 Ç. N. Atsız, *Osmanlı Tarihine Ait Takvimler*, Istanbul (1961), 3.
9 Tursun Bey, ed. Mertol Tulum, *Târîh-i Ebü'l-Feth*, Istanbul (1977), 33.
10 Celālzāde Muṣṭafā, ed. Petra Kappert, *Geschichte Sultan Süleymān Ḳānūnīs*, Wiesbaden (1981), 5b–6a.
11 Ömer Lütfi Barkan, *Kanunlar*, Istanbul (1943), 296–7 and plate 55 (autograph); Ahmet Akgündüz, *Osmanlı Kanûnnâmeleri*, 5, Istanbul (1992), 268.

---

[56] The Mediterranean.
[57] Budin (Slavonic: Budim): Buda, the capital of the old Kingdom of Hungary.
[58] Nemçe (Slavonic: Nemets): Germany.

12 Tuği, ed. Midhat Sertoğlu, 'İbretnüma', *Belleten*, 11/43 (1947), 513.
13 Yenişehirli Abdullah, *Behçetü'l-Fetāvā*, Istanbul (1849), 195.
14 A. C. Schaendlinger, *Die Schreiben Süleymāns des Prächtigen an Karl V., Ferdinand I. und Maximilian II.*, Vienna (1983), 47.

CHAPTER II

The Dynasty: Princes

SECTION 1 THE APPOINTMENT OF PRINCES IN THE EARLY FOURTEENTH CENTURY ACCORDING TO THE ANONYMOUS CHRONICLES

In the early decades of the Ottoman Empire's existence, princes played an important role in the expansion and government of the nascent polity. Passages **1**, **2** and **3** from the fifteenth-century Anonymous Chronicles suggest that the first Ottoman rulers, ʿOs̲mān and Orḫān, distributed newly conquered territories in north-western Anatolia among their sons and followers. Orḫān's son, Murād, who succeeded his father as ruler, is remembered by the epithet 'Ḫüdavendgār' ('ruler'), and the *sancaḳ* of Bursa which his father bestowed on him, as shown in passage **3**, came to be known as the '*sancaḳ* of Ḫüdavendgār' in the succeeding centuries.

1 ʿOs̲mān's sons

When ʿOs̲mān gave out (*baḫṣ-et-*) the regions which he had taken, he gave the *sancaḳ* of Ḳaraḥiṣār, which is called İnöñi, to his son Orḫān; he gave the post of *subaşı*[1] there to his brother Alp-Gündüz . . . He gave Aynegöl to Ṭurġut Alp; even now the name of that worthy (*ʿazīz*) is remembered: there are villages in that region called Ṭurġut-eli. To his father-in-law Şeyḫ Edebalı he gave the revenues (*ḥāṣıl*) of Bilecik . . . He had another son named ʿAlī Paşa: him he kept by his side.

2 Orḫān's sons

Orḫān gave [the newly conquered border region] with its *sancaḳ* to his son Süleymān Paşa: he gave the *sancaḳ*[2] of İnöñi to his son Murād Ḫān Ġāzī, his younger son.

---

[1] Literally 'army commander'.

[2] *Sancaḳ* has the sense of a sub-province. The troops in a *sancaḳ* fought under the banner (*sancaḳ*) of the *sancaḳ* governor.

3 Orhān's sons, after the conquest of Nicaea

After conquering Nicaea, [Orhān] gave Nicomedia to his son Süleymān Paşa . . . He gave the *sancak* of Bursa to his son Murād Hān Ġāzī, while Orhān supervised (*nāẓır*) the whole land.

SECTION 2 PRINCELY GOVERNORSHIPS

The practice of appointing princes to provincial governorships continued after Orhan's death, but they were no longer sent to newly conquered territories. From the reign of Murād I until the late sixteenth century it was the custom to send princes, on reaching puberty, to governorships in Anatolia where, under the guidance of their mother (as evident from passages **1** and **2**) and their tutor (*lala*), they established their own court. Passage **1** records the income assigned to Bāyezīd II's son Ḳorḳud (b. 1470), and the retinue and equipment that accompanied him as he set out for his seat of government in Manisa in 1483. Although always remaining under the supervision of their mothers and tutors, the princely governors had the right to issue decrees relating to their province in their own name, as demonstrated in passages **3**, **4** and **5**).

1 Prince Ḳorkud leaves Istanbul for his governorship

A. Details of the accoutrement bestowed on Ḳorḳud Çelebi[3] on 30 Dhū'l-Qaʿda 888 (30 December 1483).

Cash: 100,000 *aḳçe*s.
Gold *üsküf*[4] with its red cap and white *tuġ*.[5]
1 cloak, with rich gold, of red Frankish velvet.
1 standard-finial of silver.
14 *arşun* by Bursa measure of taffeta for the standard.
Robes of honour: 20 (of red silk 10; of one-coloured silk 10).
Select saddles: 5 (inlaid overall 1; gold inlay 4).
Silverware: 1 dish, 1 tray, 2 candlesticks, 1 basin, 1 ewer.
Copper vessels: 10 dishes, 20 trays, 20 plates, 20 cups, 4 cauldrons, 3 [. . . ?].
Stables: 3 strings of horses, 5 files of mules, 10 files of camels.

B. Income enjoyed by Ḳorḳud Çelebi when he was living in the houses of İsḥāḳ Paşa[6] before he went out to the *sancaḳ*:

To the Çelebi Sultan: daily stipend of 100 *aḳçe*
His mother: per day 50

---

[3] *Çelebi* was a title for princes in this era.
[4] *Üsküf*: a tall bonnet with silver thread.
[5] *Tuġ*: a horsetail standard, here to be attached to the prince's headgear.
[6] Isḥāḳ Pasha was the vizier responsible for placing Ḳorḳud on the throne in the interregnum between the death of Meḥmed II and the accession of Bāyezīd II in 1481.

His governess (*dāye*): per day 50
His nurse (*dadı*): per day 5
His tutor (*lālā*) Ibrāhīm Aġa: per day 50
The Aġa of his Porte: per day 5
6 pages (*oġlan*) at 2 per day: 12
3 doorkeepers at 3 per day: 9
His *ḫoca*[7] per month: 1,000
Food per month: 5,000

Total per month: 13,140 per day: 298[8] [x 30] per month: 7,140
Payments by the month: 6,000

C. Suite of Ḳorḳud Çelebi

*Sipāhī-oġlan*s: 14
*Siliḥdār*s: 14
*ʿUlūfeci*s:[9] 20
Tent-pitchers: 3
Cooks: 5
The rest will be supplied from the daybook (*rūznāme*), as the need arises.

D. Gifts given to him five days later

2 *amīraḫūrī*[10] *ḳaftan*s of Bursa velvet with gold thread and red buttons.
2 more *dolama*s[11] of Yazdī silk.
To his mother 10,000 *aḳçe* in cash.

2 A letter from Prince ʿĀlemşāh's mother Gülrūḫ to Bāyezīd II

May God the Blessed and Exalted, give my fortunate and felicitous sultan many years of life and, for so long as heaven and earth survive, may he be the sultan of jinn and men! May your armies be victorious and your enemies crushed! Amen, O Lord of the Worlds!

What follows: I, a weak woman and your slave, was at [your] service, rubbing my face in the dust at your feet, and free of all grief and care in the shadow of your good fortune. When at last, at the *pādişāh*'s command, I set out into a strange land, my sultan commanded: 'You should discipline my son in accordance with the command of God Most High and the *sharīʿa* of the Prophet'. From then until now, through the grace of God Most High and the good fortune of my sultan, I have looked after him and disciplined him and now – praise be to God – in the days of my sultan, he has become a young man.

Now, my sultan, in these days of his youth, he needs a benevolent Muslim tutor who will

[7] *Ḫoca* (Persian: *ḫᵛāja*): a religious teacher.
[8] Read: 238.
[9] The *sipahi-oġlan*s ('cavalrymen'), *siliḥdar*s ('weapon-bearers') and *ʿulufeci*s ('salarymen') were the names of three of the Six Divisions (*altı bölük*) of the Household Cavalry serving the sultan.
[10] The reading is uncertain. The kaftans may have been the livery of the prince's head stableman.
[11] A *dolama* is a jacket of fine wool or silk, worn beneath an over-garment.

nurture his spiritual and worldly well-being, always guide him to goodness and drive away the mischief-makers from his Porte. He now has a tutor who is the leader in depravity and in league with all kinds of mischief-makers. He not only ignores the command of God Most High and the *sharīʿa* of the Prophet, he only ever follows his own fancies and leads my dear son astray. When he wanted to get him to satisfy his wishes, which were contrary to both the *sharīʿa* and custom, and my son, your slave, did not accept, his tutor, together with that intriguer, his religious instructor and that hypocrite, the doctor, encouraged him to drink wine. And what drinking! They led him with all the members of his Porte out into the open country, with two double drums each, kettledrums and other instruments. They presented [him] with things like this, and when my son, your slave, was drunk, he did all sorts of things exactly as they wished.

Here is one of them. The people came and complained about a member of his Porte, the *subaşı*[12] called Iskender. Because several people spoke of Iskender's ill-treatment of the people and his embezzling my son your slave's money [saying] 'Let us take 20,000 *aḳçe*s as a *muḳāṭaʿa*,'[13] they seized the men who made this [complaint], clapped them in irons, and tortured the Muslims by leaving them out in the August sun. [. . .]

My fortunate sultan, by God! Numerous things like this are going on. They cannot even be described . . . It does not stop with their making him drink in the city. For a whole month they took him and forced him to drink until he became sick. He was ill for a month and, my *pādişāh*, when he recovered, only God knows what we suffered . . . The tutor himself committed all kinds of mischief. He incited my son your slave to do things like this, so that most of the time he would be in a stupor and he could get him to do whatever he wanted . . . My fortunate sultan! I, your weak slave, can no longer put up with the depravity of these mischief-makers . . . Up until now income has never covered expenditure. I, his mother, have not received my salary for a year. Others are in the same position. We sent to him to complain that he had increased expenditure, because one day he had had fifty kaftans distributed in a gathering. The other outgoings are all like this. They felt insulted because I said this, and when I previously sent to them to say that the longer the tutor perpetrates mischief, the more he does things like this, inciting my son [to commit] acts harmful to his spiritual and worldly welfare, and causing a deficit in my accounts, they said that our slave, the *aġa* of the Porte had taught [me] to say this. The *dīvān* also denounced [him], and a few evil-doers spread the word. They made it understood that what I, your slave, had said came from him. By God, my *pādişāh*! What they said about him is a lie. There is no more faithful slave than him, he is a true Muslim . . .

Now my son is the slave of my fortunate sultan and the fruit of my life. I am terrified that these mischief-makers may suddenly, at their leisure, destroy him and deceive me. My fortunate sultan! Answer my cries and, by the majesty of God Most High and by the soul of the Prophet, and [for the sake of this] lady, your slave, remove his tutor, his religious teacher and his doctor, who are workers of sedition. My sultan has many slaves and learned men. Send a slave and a learned man who will further his spiritual and worldly welfare by acting as his tutor and religious teacher . . .

The insignificant one, the mother of ʿĀlemşāh[14]

---

[12] *Subaşı* ('army chief'): the holder of large fief, usually responsible for maintaining order in a district.

[13] *Muḳāṭaʿa*: usually, a bundle of revenues sold as a tax farm. That does not seem to be the meaning here.

[14] Prince ʿĀlemşāh died in 1503.

3 A decree of Prince Aḥmed to the *yaya yoldaşlar*[15]

When the exalted sign[16] arrives, you are to know that heretofore I found it necessary to go to the borders of the land. Now, reposing my trust in God, I have returned and come to Amasya, on my way to that direction [where the addressees are]. Now my brother [Selīm]'s true situation is known to you, and since I have had full confidence in you from of old, it is my full intention to show you due favour. I am not annoyed with you at all. If some malicious person has misrepresented what I said, do not believe it; for by God, I am not annoyed with you, but pleased with you. When by God's grace I attain my desire [the throne], I will give to the *yaya-başıs* fine flowered velvets (*ağır çatma*) and make their pay 25 *aḳçe*: and I will make my gift always an *ağır çatma*, not permitting any treasurer's charge (*ḫazīnedārlıḳ*). Those of you who are due for promotion to the *bölük*[17] I will promote to the *bölük*s of the *sipāhīs* and the *siliḥdār*s,[18] giving the first 20 *aḳçe* a day each, and the second 18. To those going out to a *tīmār*, I will give a *tīmār* of 15,000 *akçe*. For those not going to the *bölük* or to a *tīmār*, I will make their pay 10 *aḳçe* . . . By God the High the Great, by God the Mighty the Ancient, I will not break this compact (*ʿahd ü peymān*) . . . After you have sent, by a man whom you trust, the reply to this noble compact (*ʿahdnāme*), keep me informed of how things are with you . . . 11 Shawwāl 918 (20 December 1512).

4 A decree of Prince Selīm [II]

A command should be written to the *ḳāḍī* of Kastamonu:

My imperial household (*ḫāṣṣa-i hümāyūnum*) is in need of some copper vessels. Copper should be bought from Küre the Prosperous.[19] Each of the ewers has been described exactly and marked. My slave [. . .] has been sent, and when he arrives you should set the craftsmen there to work on them very rapidly and send them to my Porte by hired pack-animal. You should record individually how and for how much each type [of vessel] is produced, sign the record and send it with [the vessels], recording [also the cost of] hiring [the pack-animals].

This matter is important. You should not allow any delay but make them work rapidly.

Written on 5 Jumādā I 954 (23 June 1547).

5 A decree of Prince Meḥmed [III]

Tuesday, 20 Şaʿbān the Mighty 999 (13 June 1591).

It was proven according to the *sharīʿa* that the brigand called Ḥāccī Muṣṭafā from the *ḳażā* of Ortapare attacked Selver, the wife of someone called ʿĪsā from the village called Kuyucak, with the intention of committing a vile act, and that the Muslims rescued her from him. When a copy of the court record was submitted, he was condemned to the galleys, and a noble command was sent to the [*sancaḳ*]*begi* of Sığla.

---

[15] Literally, 'companions on foot'. Presumably the Janissaries.

[16] 'The exalted sign' (*nişān*) refers to the prince's cipher (*tuğra*) at the head of the decree, guaranteeing its authenticity.

[17] *Bölük* refers to one of the six divisions of the sultan's household cavalry.

[18] The *sipāhīs* and the *siliḥdār*s were the two superior *bölüks*.

[19] The copper-mining district of Anatolia.

SECTION 3 FRATRICIDE

When a sultan died, there was no rule as to which prince should inherit the throne. Instead, any male member of the Ottoman dynasty in the paternal line was entitled to succeed the deceased sultan, and the succession went to whichever prince had eliminated his rivals – normally, but not invariably, his brothers. The practice of fratricide was known already in the fourteenth century and is recorded by the former Byzantine Emperor John VI Kantakouzenos (d. 1383), as can be seen in passage **1**. The first Ottoman ruler to eliminate his brothers was possibly Murad I (r. 1362–89), but the first clearly recorded instance was the assassination of Bāyezīd I's brother Yaʿḳūb in 1389, as shown in passages **2a** and **2b**). Passage **3** indicates that, following the passing of Bāyezīd I (r. 1389–1402), his sons Süleymān, Mūsā and Meḥmed fought to the death rather than accept joint rulership. The death of a sultan was often the signal for a period of anarchy, and it was for this reason that the sultan's entourage would attempt to conceal news of his death until the succession was decided, as passages **4** and **7** show.

In 1482, Bāyezīd II ordered the killing of his nephew, the son of his brother Cem (**5**) who, after his defeat in battle, had fled to Rhodes, and in 1522 Süleymān I executed a son of Prince Cem whom he found still living on the island. When there was more than one adult prince to contest the succession, the throne went to the one who succeeded in defeating and killing his rivals in war. Passage **3** in **Section 2** above presents the decree from Prince Aḥmed, which is an attempt to buy the Janissaries' adherence to his cause in the war over the succession with his brother Selīm [I] in 1512. (As for the distribution of gifts in a bid to secure allegiance, passage **6** describes how, during the succession from Murad II to Mehmed II, the abdicating sultan himself saw it fit to show various favours to his viziers.)

That fratricide within the dynasty never gained popular acceptance is clear from the justificatory language which the literary chroniclers felt obliged to use when describing the practice, as seen in passages **2b** and **7b**. Popular chroniclers were more forthright, using the story of Orḫān's fictitious brother ʿAlī Paşa as a vehicle to express their disgust in passage **8**. Fratricide as normal practice ended after the accession of Meḥmed III in 1595; passage **9** describes how the new sultan executed the nineteen brothers that he found in the palace, provoking an outcry in the capital. It was the courtiers of the Inner Palace that fixed the bloodless accession of his son, Aḥmed I, in 1603, as evident in passage **10**.

1 A statement of the former Byzantine Emperor John VI Kantakouzenos (d. 1383)

For they have a barbaric law to kill everyone who disputes for rule, and to spare neither for age nor kinship . . . for it is their custom to act thus not only towards those of other tribes but towards those of the same tribe also.

2 The accession of Bāyezīd I, 1389

2a From the Anonymous Chronicles

An infidel came unexpectedly and martyred Ġāzī Murād. On learning of this, the *begs* consulted together and as a result summoned Yaʿḳūb Çelebi, saying: 'Come, your father wants you'. They took him to the tent and attended to him: they placed Bāyezīd on the throne (*taḫt*) and made him *pādişāh.*

2b From Karamanī Mehmed Pasha's historical treatise on the Ottomans

Thus, the sultan entered the ranks of the martyrs . . . This was in the year 791 (1389). The length of his reign was thirty years. In that year the throne of the sultanate was mounted by his felicitous son, his rightly-guided successor, upheld by the support of Him Who is praised and glorious, Sultan Bāyezīd Ḫān. He was a just man and valiant, a friend to the *ʿulemā* and the dervishes, showing mercy to the rich and concern for the ascetics and the pious. To him mighty monarchs turned their faces 'from every remote path' and towards him learned *ʿulemā* made their way from every distant station. He had a brother named Yaʿḳūb Çelebi, in whose survival lay great possibilities and mischiefs (*mafāsid*), which are not hidden from him who possesses sound intelligence. Hence, the sultan dealt with him as was necessary: 'necessity justifies what is forbidden' (*al-ḍarūrāt tubīḥ al-maḥẓūrāt*). Thus, the inherited state remained under the hand of the valiant and generous and excellent sultan, without the rivalry of a rival or the contention of a contender.

3 The civil war (1402–13)

Since the coming of Tīmūr Beg to fight with Bāyezīd Beg and the defeat of Bāyezīd Beg and the accession of his son Süleymān Beg and the seizing of the country of Rūmeli is nineteen years.

Since the death of Emīr Süleymān Beg at the hand of his brother Emīr Mūsā and the accession of Mūsā b. Bāyezīd Beg is twelve years.

Since the death of Emīr Mūsā at the hand of his brother and the accession of the Sultan of Islam and the Muslims . . . Sultan Meḥmed . . . is eight years.

4 The accession of Murād II, 1421

Before Sultan Meḥmed died [at Edirne], they sent the Çāşnigīr-başı[20] Elvān Beg to Rūm,[21] to fetch Sultan Murād. Sultan Meḥmed had four sons and seven daughters. Before he died, he had made the testamentary declaration (*vaṣīyet*): 'Put Sultan Murād on the throne'. When they had sent off the *Çāşnigīr-başı*, the viziers Ḥāccī ʿIvaż Paşa and Bāyezīd Paşa and Ibrāhīm Paşa met together and consulted. They sent the Janissaries into Anatolia, telling them: 'There is a campaign.' By the time Sulṭān Murād had been informed and had come to Bursa, they had concealed Sultan Meḥmed's death for forty days, not letting anyone know; then they sent the body to Bursa.

5 The accession of Bāyezīd II, 1481

My slave Iskender: when this letter (*biti*) reaches you, you are to know that I have killed Gedik [Aḥmed Paşa].[22] It is necessary that you, without delay, have Cem's son strangled. This is

---

[20] *Çāşnigīr başı*: the chief taster.

[21] Anatolia.

[22] Bāyezīd suspected the vizier Gedik Aḥmed Paşa of loyalty to Prince Cem.

most urgent – but no-one is to know about it. Thus you are to know: you are to place reliance upon the Noble Sign. Written in the third decade of Shawwāl of the year 887 (January 1482).

In the residence of Edirne.[23]

6 The first accession of Meḥmed II, 1444

The *pādişāh* [Murād II] spent some days in Bursa, then arose and encamped in the plain of Mihaliç. He summoned the *aġa* of the Janissaries, Ḫıżr Aġa, and the other *begs*, showed them favours (*iltifāt*) according to their ranks, clad them with garments (*libās*) and said: 'Look, *begs* and pashas. Until this moment, it is I who have been your *pādişāh*. From today, your *pādişāh* is my son. Now show me how you get on together and how you manage things and how you apply yourselves to every task! For I have given all my crown and throne and my title (*ʿunvān*) entirely to my son. Now you are to recognise my son as *pādişāh*.' Saying 'It is for the Ḫünkār to command', they all placed their heads to the ground.

7 The second accession of Meḥmed II, 1451

[Murād II] lay ill for three days, and on the fourth day they sent a messenger to his son, who came on the thirteenth day. For thirteen days they concealed his corpse, and the pashas told no-one that he had died: they held *dīvāns*[24] and allocated *tīmārs*, and the physicians pretended to carry out treatment and to give potions. Thirteen days after his death, his son, Sultan Meḥmed Ḫān, came to Edirne and sat on the throne: then the people realised that Murād was dead. Meḥmed at once sent his father's body to Bursa. He had a tiny brother, born of the daughter of Isfendiyār. Him too he sent to his place.

7a From Michael Doukas's Historia Turco-Byzantina

Then finding a son of his father, eight months old, born of the daughter of Isfendiyār, the lord of Sinop, his legal wife (while he himself [Meḥmed] was born of a slave), the mother of the child, who was his own [Meḥmed's] step-mother, being on that day in the palace to offer condolences to the ruler, he sent one of the commanders from among the sons of Evrenos, named ʿAlī, who was at that time chief doorkeeper (*protoostiarios*); and he strangled the child in the apartment of the aforesaid lady. The next day [Meḥmed] killed ʿAlī, too, and gave the child's mother, all unwilling, in marriage to his father's slave Isḥāḳ.

7b From Ibn Kemāl's Tevârih-i Âl-i Osmân

As has been set out before, Sultan Murād Ḫān had an infant son named Aḥmed, by the daughter of Isfendiyār . . . Although he was brother to the *pādişāh*, he was a foe to kingship (*milk*) and a burning coal on the threshing-floor of the realm (*mülk*). The ancient *ḥadīth* has been transmitted: 'Kingship is childless, and pregnant like the night'. It is an accepted report that 'Two lions cannot dwell together in one thicket nor two stallions share one mare. Two swords cannot fit into one scabbard, nor two lions rest in one lair'. Though he was still an immature

---

[23] This decree of Bāyezīd II appears to be an autograph.

[24] *Dīvāns*: councils.

child, yet action was taken by the counsel of experienced elders . . . and it was seen to be the better course (*mustaḥsen*) to root up the sapling of mischief (*fesād*) before it put forth leaves and branches and to extinguish the sparks of the fire of tumults (*fiten*) before they burst into flame . . .

8 Popular criticism of fratricide: the story of the abdication of ʿAlī Pasha

When Orḫān Ġāzī became a sovereign *pādişāh* in the whole land, his brother ʿAlī Pasha left his position as *beglerbegi* and became a dervish . . . In those days *pādişāh*s and lords took counsel with their brothers. They honoured and respected one another, right up to the time of Yıldırım Ḫan.[25] Brother killing brother began in the time of Yıldırım Ḫan.

9 The accession of Meḥmed III, 1595

Thus on Friday 27 January, at the ninth hour and a quarter of the day, the new king Sultan Meḥmed arrived in Constantinople . . . He disembarked in public near the gate called 'of the Jews',[26] at the *köşk* or new pavilion that was made recently on the shore near the Great Palace . . . He entered on foot, not wishing to mount a horse (although one was brought for him), in company with his *lālā* . . . and the *bostāncı-başı*[27] . . . He went in straightaway to see the queen his mother, whom he had not seen for twelve years, and the king his father [lying] dead, and then he entered the royal-chamber and sat in the royal seat (*sedia*). All of the viziers arrived by the public gate of the Great Palace to kiss his hand. Meanwhile the death of Sultan Murād [III] and the accession of the new sultan were announced by public proclamation in all the markets and public places of the city, and guards of Janissaries were posted in them . . .

At the time when the *ikindi*[28] was called from the towers,[29] that is, at the 22nd hour, they carried the dead king from the Great Palace in a cypress coffin entirely covered with a cloth of silk and gold, written all over with Turkish letters, which the Turks regard with great reverence since it had come from Mecca and had covered the tomb of their prophet, and with a turban made in the fashion which he used to wear when alive, with a *sorguç* in it (which is various feathers with jewels, which the Grand Signiors are accustomed to wear). There went before the noble viziers of the Porte, namely [. . .], and nearer the body Ibrāhīm Paşa and Ḫalīl Paşa, his sons-in-law. The *ağa*s and other principal lords of the court carried him on their hands, all dressed in black cloth; and on their turbans, which they wore small out of mourning, some had black veils (*veli*) and others were wearing *şemle*s, which are turbans made of woven wool, as a sign of mourning . . . That night there were led before the new king Sultan Meḥmed's nineteen brothers who remained alive, born to his father of various mothers (and not one of them of his own mother), to kiss his hand and so that he might see them alive, according to their age, the eldest being eleven. The king their brother told them not to be afraid, for he did not wish to harm them but only to have them circumcised after their custom. This was a thing that none of his predecessors had ever done. As soon as they had kissed his hand they were circumcised and led aside and dexterously strangled with handkerchiefs by

---

[25] Yıldırım means 'thunderbolt' in Turkish and refers here to Bāyezīd I.

[26] Çıfut Kapı.

[27] *Bostāncı başı*: head gardener.

[28] The afternoon prayer.

[29] The minarets.

a mute. This is a matter certainly worthy of amazement and full of cruelty, except that the custom of this realm mitigates it and makes it not seem so unusual. On Saturday these innocent princes were washed and made ready in their fashion, one after the other, according to their ages, and all placed in cypress coffins and in the same order laid out facing (*dinanzi*) the court of the *dīvān*[30] and shown to the king dead, for it is the custom that he should see them first alive and then also dead, and that he should strengthen the first foundations of his reign with his brothers' blood.

10 The accession of Aḥmed I, 1603

On 18 Rajab 2012 (22 December 1603) the *ḳāʾimmaḳām*[31] for the grand vizierate, the vizier Ḳāsim Paşa, after performing the dawn prayer, set out for the *dīvān* as usual and took his place beneath the dome. Before complainants were admitted and while the viziers were still on their own and had not begun to discuss affairs, Ḥüseyn Aġa, who at that time was the *ketḫüdā* of the doorkeepers, was summoned in haste to the *bāb-i saʿādet*,[32] and the *aġa* of the *bāb-i saʿādet* came out and gave him a note wrapped in a napkin, saying 'Give this *ḫaṭṭ-i hümāyūn*[33] to the *ḳāʾimmaḳām*'. Ḥüseyn delivered it to Ḳāsim Paşa, who opened and looked at it, but could not read it. He asked Ḥüseyn: 'What sort of a note is this? Who gave it to you?' Ḥüseyn explained that the *ḳapu aġası* had given it, saying that it was a *ḫaṭṭ-i humāyūn*. The *paşa* then said: 'This writing is illegible and not like the *pādişāh*'s hand. It has the word "my father", but our *pādişāh*'s father is no longer alive'. He then showed it to me, saying: 'I cannot read it. Perhaps you can'. I came up close to the *paşa*'s ear and read out the extraordinary missive secretly. It said: 'You, Ḳāsim Paşa: my father has died at God's command, and I have seated myself on the throne. Control the city firmly.[34] If there is any trouble, I will cut off your head'. When Ḳāsim Paşa understood what it said, he was very distressed and thoroughly perplexed, for there had been no word that Sultan Meḥmed was ill. At last he sent a note to the *aġa* of the *bāb-i saʿādet*, ʿAbduʾr-rezzāḳ, saying 'They have brought me a strange Noble Rescript, but I cannot understand what it means. Is the intention to try me, or does it mean what it says?' The *ketḫüdā* of the gatekeepers was sent out, and Ḳāsim Paşa was invited alone into the *ʿarż odası*.[35] He arrived there alone and in a hurry, but when he saw Sultan Aḥmed Ḫān in person seated upon the throne, he trusted [what he saw] and returned to the *dīvān*. He sent the *çavuş başı*[36] with a sealed note summoning the *muftī*. Then the *miʿmār aġa*[37] was ordered to attend to the funeral arrangements, while the *aġa* of the Janissaries and the others who were present at the *dīvān* were warned not to go away. The place where the imperial throne was to be set up was prepared, and then the felicitous imperial throne itself was brought out. Everyone had

[30] The second court in the palace. The council chamber where the imperial council (*dīvān*) met is situated in this court.
[31] *Ḳāʾimmaḳām* ('deputy'): the vizier appointed to deputise for the grand vizier.
[32] *Bāb-i saʿādet* ('the gate of felicity'): the gate leading from the second court of the palace to the third court.
[33] *Ḫaṭṭ-i hümāyūn* ('imperial rescript'): an order of the sultan written in his own hand.
[34] The interregnum between the death of a sultan and the enthronement of his successor was often the signal for rioting, especially by the Janissaries, hence the need to conceal the sultan's death and to maintain control of Istanbul.
[35] *Arż odası* ('chamber of petitions'): the throne-room between the second and third courts of the palace where the sultan received petitions.
[36] *Çavuş başı*: the head *çavuş* in the palace.
[37] *Miʿmār aġa*: the sultan's chief architect.

their own guess as to what was going on, [all] imagining that Sulṭān Meḥmed would appear. Not a single person was aware of what had happened. When the *muftī*, Muṣṭafā Efendi, came to the *dīvān*, he emerged with the viziers and stood with them in line beside the throne, while the other dignitaries and people stood opposite. Then a felicitous youth of about fourteen came out, wearing a *şemle* and with a Yūsufī turban on his head. Making salutations (*selām*) to left and right he approached the throne and took his place on it. The people of the world were in shock: some wept, and some were overcome. After the *çavuşes* had shouted the acclamation (*gülbāng*), and prayers had been performed and praise given, first the *muftī* and the viziers and then the other people present at the *dīvān*, in these strange circumstances, in turn made the *bayʿa*. When no-one was left, the *pādişāh* gave a salutation and went into the inner palace, and the heaven-like throne was removed.

SOURCES

Section 1

1 *Anonymous Chronicles*, MS E, fol. 5v.
2 *Anonymous Chronicles*, MS E, fol. 8r.
3 *Anonymous Chronicles*, MS E, fol. 9r.

Section 2

1 Şahabettin Tekindağ, 'Korkud Çelebi ile ilgili iki belge', *Belgelerle Türk Tarihi Dergisi*, 17 (1969), 37–9; İbrahim Hakkı Uzunçarşılı, 'Sancağa çıkarılan Osmanlı şehzadeleri', *Belleten*, 39 (1975), 680–2, pl. 11.
2 M. Çağatay Uluçay, *Haremden Mektuplar*, Istanbul (1956, repr. 2012), 36–9.
3 Zarif Orgun, 'Şehzade Ahmed'in yayalara verdiği ahidname', *Tarih Vesikaları*, 2/9 (1942), 166–7.
4 Feridun M. Emecen, Zekai Mete and Arif Bilgin, *Şehzâde Dîvânı Defterleri: Manisa Şehzâde Sarayı Defterleri*, Ankara (2017), 176.
5 Feridun M. Emecen et al., *Şehzâde Dîvânı Defterleri*, 629.

Section 3

1 John Cantacuzenus, ed. Ludwig Schopen, *Ioannis Cantacuzeni Eximperatoris Historiarum Libri IV*, Bonn (1832), vol. III, 111.
2a *Anonymous Chronicles*, MS E, fol. 17r.
2b Karamanī Mehmed Pasha, *Risāla fī al-Tawārīkh al-Salāṭīn al-ʿUthmāniyya*, trans. İbrahim Hakkı Konyalı in Ç. N. Atsız (ed.), *Osmanlı Tarihleri*, Istanbul (1949), 347.
3 Almanac of 1421, in Ç. N. Atsız (ed.), *Osmanlı Tarihine Ait Takvimler*, Istanbul (1961), 26.
4 *Anonymous Chronicles*, MS E, fol. 31r.
5 Suha Umur, *Osmanlı Padişahları Tuğraları*, Istanbul (1980), 120.
6 Halil İnalcık and Mevlûd Oğuz (eds.), *Gazavât-i Sultân Murâd b Mehemmed Hân*, Ankara (1978), 36–7.
7 ʿĀşıḳpaşazāde, *Tevârîh-i Âl-i Osmân*, ch. 122.
7a Michal Ducas, ed. Vasile Grecu, *Historia-Turco Byzantina (1341–1462)*, Bucharest (1958), 287; this passage is also translated in Doukas, tr. Harry J. Magoulias, *Decline and Fall of Byzantium to the Ottoman Turks*, Detroit (1975), 190.
7b Ibn Kemāl, ed. Şerafettin Turan, *Tevârih-i Âl-i Osmân*, vol. VII, Ankara (1957), 9–10.
8 Oruç b. ʿĀdil, ed. Franz Babinger, *Tevārīḫ-i Āl-i Os̱mān*, Hanover (1925), 15–16.

9 Report to Barton, H. G. Rosedale, *Queen Elizabeth and the Levant Company*, London (1904), plates 6–8. The English ambassador Barton received this report from the Portuguese Jew Salomon Usque, who had probably heard it from Esperanza Malchi, the agent (*kira*) of Meḥmed III's mother Ṣafiye.

10 Ḥasan Beyzāde Aḥmed Paşa, ed. Şevki Nezihi Aykut, *Hasan Bey-zâde Târîhi*, vol. III, Istanbul (2004), 797–804.

CHAPTER III

The Dynasty: Recruitment into the Sultan's Service

SECTION 1 *PENCIK*[1] AND *DEVŞİRME*

In the fifteenth and sixteenth centuries most members of the sultan's household – whether as troops, palace servants or as members of the political elite – entered imperial service by one of two routes. The first of these was as prisoners taken in frontier raids and wars in Europe, as described in passage **1**. While most prisoners-of-war remained the property of their captors, to be sold in the market as slaves, the sultan took a certain proportion – nominally one-fifth – for his own use, to be brought up in his service. In addition to his share of the captives, the sultan also secured an income from prisoners-of-war by levying a toll on each captive ferried across the Straits from Europe to Anatolia via the ports of Istanbul and Gallipoli, as described in passage **2**. The regulations from the time of Bayezid II (r. 1481–1512) laid out in passage **1** show that, among other legislative efforts of this reign, there was an attempt to systematise and control this practice.

The second route into the sultan's service was through the *devşirme* ('collection'). This was the levy of Christian boys made primarily, although not exclusively, in the Balkan provinces of the Ottoman Empire. Passage **3** is a template providing a model for commands to local authorities to carry out the levy and laying out the procedures to be followed. Since the levy was a gateway to a career in the sultan's service and a regular income, and since it also provided opportunities for the recruits to petition the sultan on behalf of their original families and communities, as evident in passage **4**, it was not necessarily unpopular. Passages **5** and **6** nonetheless make it clear that some of the boys raised in this way tried to abscond.

1 A decree regulating the *pencik*

The command conveyed by the imperial sign[2] is this:

Various texts (*naṣṣ*) in the Ancient Word of the Wise Sovereign offer decisive proofs that

---

[1] *Pencik* (from Persian *panjyak*; 'one-fifth'): the levy of – nominally – one-fifth of the prisoners-of-war for the sultan's service.

[2] The 'imperial sign' is the *ṭuġra*, the sultan's cipher which was affixed to sultanic decrees to guarantee their authenticity.

the *ġāzīs* and the fighters of the *jihād* enjoy a near approach to God and an exalted rank. Hence it has been the noble practice of my illustrious forefathers and mighty ancestors, from their first origin to the present day, to root out infidelity and sin and to destroy the foundations of the temples of the idolaters, and thus to acquire religious merit. And now, since I too have followed in their path so that the gate of the *ġazā* and the *jihād*[3] lies open, and since the *pencikçi-başı*[4] Yūsuf has sent a man to my lofty Porte requesting a *ḳānūnnāme*,[5] I have given him this *ḳānūnnāme* and have commanded as follows:

If the *uc begi*s[6] assemble the *aḳıncı*s[7] and the other young warriors and make an incursion into the *dārü'l-ḥarb*,[8] that is an *aḳın*; and if the *ucbegi*s do not campaign themselves but put the *aḳıncı*s and the other young warriors under the command of their deputies and send them into the *dārü'l-ḥarb*, so that they number one hundred or more, that is a *ḥarāmīlik*; and from these two types of expedition, the *pencik* is to be taken. If the *ucbegi*s do not campaign but send their deputies so that the number campaigning is less than one hundred, that is a *çete*, and of this the *pencik* is not to be taken. Henceforth this practice is to be followed, and no other.

On the matter of rewards to the *ucbegi*s and the *pencikçi*s and the *ṭovıca*s,[9] I have commanded: When there is an *aḳın* or a *ḥarāmīlik*, all the lads brought in on that *aḳın* or *ḥarāmīlik* – all those in the possession of the commanders of the *aḳın*, of the *pencikçi*s, of the *ṭovıca*s, of the *aḳıncı*s and of the other young warriors – are to be assembled and registered under the supervision of the *pencikçi-başı*. The commander of the *aḳın* is to be rewarded with twenty of the lads whom he brought in by his own efforts, the *pencikçi*s with five each of those whom they won themselves, the higher-ranking *ṭovıca*s with one each of those whom they won themselves, and the lower-ranking *ṭovıcas* with one between two of those whom they won themselves. The rest, from the age of ten to seventeen, are to be taken [by Yūsuf]. If some of those over the age of seventeen show signs of being suitable, they too are to be taken, the owner being paid for each lad 300 *aḳçe*s from the Treasury. The lads taken must not be crippled or sick, or show signs of reaching puberty, or have begun to grow a beard.

When the *pencik* lads are due to be taken, the *sancaḳbegi*[10] and the *ṭovıcas* are to assist. No one is to raise objections in this matter. If anyone refuses obedience, the *sancaḳbegi* is to punish him; if anyone persists in obstinacy, the matter is to be reported to me in writing, for me to punish him.

Further, I have commanded that when, of the lads brought in from the *aḳın*s and *ḥarāmīlik*s, those to be taken for the state (*beglik*) have been taken and the levy is completed, the *ṭovıcas* are to offer assistance until they reach pacified territory (*ellik*), guarding them where necessary and conducting them where necessary. If it happens that *ṭovıca*s are bringing lads out of hostile territory (*yaġı*), the matter is to be reported to me and action taken as I command.

Further, I have commanded that, in whatever way a person is to be rewarded, he is to be

[3] *Ġazā* and *jihād* both have the general sense of 'holy war'. *Jihād* refers to the activity in general; *ġazā* refers to a single campaign.
[4] The commander of the *pencikçi*s: the officials charged with organising and administering the *pencik*.
[5] *Ḳānūnnāme*: a code of sultanic laws. See Chapter VII.
[6] *Uc begi*s ('frontier lords'): the hereditary governors of *sancaḳ*s on the frontiers of the Ottoman Empire in Europe.
[7] *Aḳıncı*s ('raiders'): the cavalry stationed on the frontiers of the empire in Europe, charged with making raids into enemy territory.
[8] *Dārü'l-ḥarb* (Arabic: 'the Abode of War'): the territory outside the realms of Islam.
[9] *Ṭovıca* (Mongol): an officer of the *aḳıncı*s.
[10] The *sancaḳbegi* is involved as the chief officer of the area where the selection is taking place.

rewarded from what he has won by his own efforts: he is not to transfer to his own name the prisoner (*esīr*) of somebody else.

Further, I have commanded that when the *pencikçi*s are going to assemble the *pencik* lads, they are to do it with the co-operation of the commander who led the raid. One register of all the lads assembled is to be written by the *pencikçi-başı* and one by the commander of the raid. When the *pencik* lads are brought to my lofty Porte, the register and a representative of each[11] is to come with them. If the commander of the raid is not present in person, the lads are to be assembled and registered under the supervision of his deputy; when later the lads come to my Porte, the representative of this deputy, with the deputy's register, and the representative of the *pencikçi* with the *pencikçi*'s register are to come and hand over the registers together.

Further, I have commanded that on the matter of the gifts of animals won on raids, whatever regulation and custom (*ḳānūn ve ʿādet*) has been followed from of old up to the present is to be followed.

Further, I have commanded that the *uc begi*s and the *pencikçi*s and the *ṭovıca*s are to regard this *ḳānūn* as incontestable and established. They are to act according to its tenor, making no alteration and offering no opposition. If anyone alters or opposes it, he will be punished. Thus they are to know. Written in the first decade of Shawwāl 898 (16–25 July 1493).

2 Tolls to be levied on slaves taken across the Bosphorus

To the *ḳāḍī* of Istanbul and the *emīn*[12] for the *pencik*.

When the exalted sign[13] arrives, be it known that: You the *emīn* have sent a letter to my Porte and requested a *ḳānūnnāme* on the matter of the *pencik* of the prisoners[14] who come to the quay (*iskele*) . . . Now the ancient *ḳānūn*[15] on the *pencik* is this:

on a baby at the breast and up to the age of three, 10–30 *aḳçe* are taken;
from ages three to eight, 100 *aḳçe*: these are called 'children' (*beçe*);
from ages eight to twelve, 120–200 *aḳçe*: these are called 'lads' (*ġulāmçe*);
from a *ġulām*[16] who is of age (*bāliġ*) 250–280 *aḳçe*;
from a bearded *kāfir*,[17] 200–270 *aḳçe*;
from an old (*pīr*) *kāfir*, 150–200 *aḳçe*, but if he is senile (*fertūt*) 130–50.
If a *ġulām* or *kāfir* lacks an eye or a hand, 130–50 *aḳçe* are taken.
For a slave-girl who is an *umm walad*,[18] 120–50 *aḳçe* are taken.
If [a female prisoner] is fully-grown (?), elderly, a young girl or an infant; has a defect [that would affect her market-price]; is ill or crippled, or lacks a hand or an eye, [the toll] should be taken in accordance with what is given above.

[11] That is, of the *pencikçi-başı* and the commander.
[12] *Emīn*: a salaried official administering an enterprise.
[13] A reference to the *tuġra*, the sultan's cipher, authenticating the document as coming from the sultan.
[14] *Esīr* ('prisoner'): here in the sense of 'slave'.
[15] *Ḳānūn*: a law or regulation issued by or ratified by the sultan; sultanic law in general.
[16] *Ġulām*: a young man.
[17] *Kāfir*: an infidel.
[18] *Umm walad* ('mother of a child'): a female slave who has given birth to her master's child, which he has recognised as his.

Now I have commanded that, when the felicitous command arrives, you are to act according to this *ḳānūnnāme* and to collect the *pencik* as set out; and you are to write down each person separately, class by class, in detail noting beneath the name of each the money collected, and to make a detailed register, leaving nothing out. You are to show all zeal in this matter and to collect the imperial moneys (*māl-i pādişāhī*).

You who are the *ḳāḍī* are to register the copy of this *ḳānūnāme* in the *sicillāt*:[19] it is not to be lost but always followed; and after you have seen this decree, you are to leave it in the possession of the *emīn*, and whoever becomes *emīn* [later] is to retain it . . . 6 Shawwāl 916 (6 January 1511).

3 A template decree for levying boys for the *devşirme*

The command of this noble sign is this:

Since it has from of old been the *ḳānūn* and the custom in my well-protected territories to take lads for the Janissaries, I have ordered that in the *ḳāḍīlık*[20] of X, embracing x households, and in that of Y, embracing y households, a and b lads respectively, a total of c, be collected, at the rate of one lad per forty households: and having full confidence in the trustworthiness and probity of [. . .], I have appointed him *emīn*, and I have given this order to [. . .] one of the *yayabaşı*s[21] of my exalted court, and I have commanded that he is to go without delay to these *ḳāḍīlık*s, to warn the people by proclamation in each *ḳāḍīlık*, and, without omitting a single village, to gather all the sons of the infidels and of the *a'yān*,[22] together with their fathers, and have them brought before him and to inspect them personally. If any infidel has several sons, he is to register and take and detain one good one for the Janissary service, of the age of fourteen or fifteen, or at the most seventeen or eighteen; but he is not to take the son of a man not having several sons,[23] and after taking one he is to send the others back to their father, without any injustice (*ḥayf u ta'arruż*).

Having taken and registered one lad according to my command, he is not [thereafter] to exchange him.[24] The name of every boy taken, his father's name, the names of the villages and of the father's *sipāhī*,[25] and the description of the boy are to be registered in detail, so that if the boy disappears, reference to the register will show who he is and where he comes from, and he can easily be recovered. It is reported that when such collections are made, *levend*s[26] from outside are included by deception: no such person is to be included, but the [bearer] is to collect from the sons of settled *ra'īyet*[27] infidels, being on guard against trickery.

And I have commanded that when the Janissary boys have been collected to the number of 100 or 150, [the bearer] is to put his trusted agent in charge of them, handing over the register, too. Each *ḳāḍī*[28] also is to attach his own trusted agent [to the consignment], together with a

---

19 *Sicillāt* (plural of *sicill*): a *ḳāḍī*'s registers.
20 *Ḳāḍīlik*: a *ḳażā*, the judicial and administrative district of a *ḳāḍī*.
21 *Yayabaşı*: an officer of the Janissaries.
22 *A'yān*: the local notables.
23 Otherwise his farm would lack labour for cultivation, thereby reducing revenue.
24 That is, he should not exchange him for an inferior one.
25 *Sipāhī* ('cavalryman'): a cavalryman occupying a fief (*timar*).
26 *Levend*: a ruffian, sometimes serving as an auxiliary in the army.
27 *Ra'īyet* (pl. *re'āyā*): a member of the tax-paying peasantry.
28 *Ḳāḍī*: a legal official, combining the functions of judge, notary and administrator.

sufficient number of *voynuḳ*s[29] (in places where there are *voynuḳ*s) or (where there are not) of *müsellem*s[30] and men of the *sipāhī*s [to act as escort], and so send them to the *aġa* of the Janissaries in Istanbul. They are to be strictly guarded on the way, so that there is no chance of one escaping or disappearing. The person registering the Janissary boys is to make two registers, one remaining with himself and the other sent on with the man by whom he sends the Janissary boys; the latter is to deliver the boys, together with that register, to the *aġa* of the Janissaries: and later the two registers are to be compared, so that there is no possibility of making substitutions among the Janissary boys.

And I have commanded that [the bearer] is to warn the man by whom he sends the boys on ahead that, as he is taking them to Istanbul, he is not to delay or to take one *aḳçe* from anybody or to permit any exactions, but to bring them by the direct route. He is not to confuse the halting places, so that they lodge overnight twice in any one village, to save the villagers from excessive hardship in feeding the Janissary boys and taking them into their houses and keeping them in custody.

The *ḳāḍī*s of those [two] *ḳāḍīlık*s and the *nā'ib*s[31] and the *subaşı*s[32] and their representatives and the village *ketḫüda*s[33] are to offer all assistance in this matter, and are to present before [the bearer] all the boys in the villages and districts under their jurisdictions: nobody's son is to be kept back in his house or concealed or smuggled away – every precaution is to be taken against any sort of deception.

In this matter, the bearer and his men and other people engaged in this business are absolutely forbidden to take one *aḳçe* from anyone. If anyone hides away a boy on his *tīmār*[34] or in his house or in his village and does not show him to the bearer, or helps a boy escape, or introduces a *levend* by trickery, or shows any negligence or indulgence, I will grant no latitude at all but will cause him to suffer *siyāset.*[35] Let them realise this . . .

(undated; early sixteenth century?)

4 A Janissary lobbies the sultan on behalf of his family

A command is to be written to the *ḳāḍī* of Tepedelen:[36]

At this present time, my slave (*ḳul*) Ḥasan, one of the Janissaries of my Porte, has come to my Porte and stated: 'I used to live in the village of Toskoş, belonging to the *ḳażā* of Tepedelen, my infidel name being Lagalik, and when I was taken as an *'acemī-oġlan* the 30 *aḳçe* entered against me in the *ḫarāc*[37]-register was not deleted, so that year by year the *ḫarāc*-collectors demand from my relations there the *ḫarāc* imposed upon me. This is unfair (*ḥayf*)'.[38]

Now, I have commanded that when my noble command arrives you are to investigate

[29] *Voynuḳ*: a Serbian auxiliary soldier. See Chapter VII.
[30] *Müsellem*: one of a group exempted from certain taxes in exchange for auxiliary military service.
[31] *Nā'ib*: a *ḳāḍī*'s deputy.
[32] *Subaşı*: an officer commanding a division of provincial *sipāhī*s, and also having police functions in his district.
[33] *Ketḫüdā* ('deputy'): here, a headman representing his village to the government.
[34] *Tīmār*: a *sipāhī*'s fief. See Chapter V.
[35] *Siyāset*: capital punishment.
[36] Tepelenë in southern Albania.
[37] *Ḫarāc*: the *jizya*, the head-tax imposed on non-Muslims, in Ottoman practice often referred to as *ḫarāc*. See Chapter VIII.
[38] The boy's statement to the *dīvān* shows that he remained in touch with his family after he had been taken as a *devşirme* and drafted into the Janissaries. This must have been a common experience.

(*teftīş*), with the cognizance of the *ḫarāc*-collectors, whether this man is indeed the one who was taken from this village as *ʿacemī-oġlan*. If it is proven and evident according to the noble *sharīʿa* that he is, you are to make an entry against his name so that the *ḫarāc* in question is not, contrary to the noble *sharīʿa*, to be demanded from his relations . . . 980 (1572)

5 Escaping the *devşirme*

Command to the *beg* and the *ḳāḍī* of Sīs:[39]

You the *ḳāḍī* have sent a letter and reported: 'Heretofore the *yaya-başı* Dāvūd, who had come for the collection of *ʿacemī-oġlans*,[40] took seven boys from the village of Meki and brought them to the *aġa*: after initiating (*telḳīn*) them [into Islam], he took them to Istanbul and changed their garments;[41] then some *dhimmī*s,[42] the relatives of those boys, stole them away and brought them to the aforementioned village; they put them in the church and are initiating them according to their vain rites'.[43] I have commanded that when my noble command arrives you are to investigate, and if the matter is proven to be as has been submitted, you are to seize these boys and the infidels who led them astray and send them all to my exalted court, taking care that they do not abscond. Thus you are to know. 972 (1564/5).

6 The recovery of a captured novice

Command to the *beglerbegi* of the Archipelago:[44]

The *aġa* of the Janissaries has sent a memorandum [stating the following]: 'The *ʿacemī-oġlan* named Ḫıżr, whom ʿAlī, the *aġa* of Anaṭolı collected (*devşir-*) to be a Janissary boy in the year 977 (1569/70) from the village named Mecne in the *ḳażā* of Lemnos, and whose name before he became a Muslim was Sotiri, his father's name being Yorgi (tall, fair, blue-eyed, brown eyebrows, scar over his right eyebrow, moles on his right ear and his right hand, at present about seventeen), and who was earlier taken prisoner by the infidels in the battle of the Imperial Fleet,[45] has been found at the oar in the infidel ship which the *beg* of Rhodes captured; he is Greek by birth, and is still only learning Turkish . . .'

SECTION 2 PROMOTION TO THE SULTAN'S SERVICE

The destiny of most of the *devşirme* recruits, or *ʿacemī oġlan*s ('foreign boys'), was to serve in the Janissary Corps or other military units, as shown in passage **1**. The first stage in their training was to serve as labourers for Turkish farmers in Anatolia, where they learned Turkish and the rudiments of Islam (see passage **2**) and became accustomed to hardship. The second stage was to learn a craft (such as gardening, as in passage

---

[39] Present day Kozan, near Adana. Sīs was the seat of an Armenian Catholicos.

[40] *ʿAcemī oġlan*: a boy levied through the *pencik* (*q. v.*) or the *devşirme* (*q. v.*), in training before his admission to palace service or the Janissary corps.

[41] The change of clothes signified conversion to Islam.

[42] *Dhimmī*: a Christian or Jewish subject of a Muslim sovereign. In this case the *dhimmī*s are Armenians.

[43] That is, baptism.

[44] The Grand Admiral. The admiral was *beglerbegi* of the province of the Archipelago, consisting of the Greek islands and the *sancaḳ*s adjoining the coasts of Greece and Anatolia.

[45] The battle of Lepanto, 7 October 1571.

2), serving on building projects (see passages **3** and **4**), in the naval arsenals or other enterprises, acquiring skills which could be useful in a military context. It was after this period that they graduated – 'went out to the Porte', as passages **3**, **4** and **5** call it – to serve the sultan in the Janissary Corps.

While anyone recruited into the sultan's service either through the *devşirme* or as a prisoner-of-war had the status as a 'slave' (*ḳul*) or 'slave of the Porte' (*ḳapı ḳulu*), one group directly served the sultan in person. These were the lads who, after their arrival in Istanbul, were taken directly into the palace and trained in the palace schools. Upon graduation they served as officers and pages in the different departments of the palace and, as passage **5** shows, from a senior position could be 'sent out' as members of one of the six divisions of household cavalry, or to governorships or senior posts in the provinces.

The great majority of staff in the palace was non-Muslim in origin. That palace servants could make a good living regardless of their origins is clear from passage **6**, a register detailing the pay of palace staff in 1478, the year when the New Palace – the present-day Topkapı Palace – was completed.

1 Command to the *aġa* of the Janissaries, 1562/3

Since Pīrī, the chief of the artillerymen at my exalted court, has reported that he needs artillerymen, having ordered that twenty-five *ʿacemī-oġlan*s be given [to him] to be apprentices for the artillerymen, I have commanded that, in accordance with my order, you should nominate twenty-five *ʿacemī-oġlan*s from those who are 'with the Turks' (*Türk üzerinde*) to become artillery apprentices, list them with their names, and deliver them to the aforementioned. 970 (1562/3).

2 Command to the *aġa* of the Janissaries, 1567/8

Since lads are needed for the garden of Edirne, having ordered thirty lads to be supplied from those who have really (*biʾl-fiʿl*) embraced Islam, I have commanded that when [. . .] arrives you are to list thirty lads, capable of serving in the gardens, from those who have now embraced Islam. 975 (1567–8).

3 Command to the *aġa* of the Janissaries, 1560/1

Having ordered that twenty-three of the *ʿacemī-oġlan*s serving on the aqueduct leading into Istanbul should 'go out to the Porte' (*ḳapuya çık-*) and having sent you the list of their names, I have commanded that when [. . .] arrives you should, in accordance with my noble order, 'send out (*çıḳar-*) to the Porte' those named. 968 (1560/1)

4 Command to the *aġa* of the Janissaries, 1573/4

Since Sinān, the chief of my court architects, has sent a letter saying: 'Of the *ʿacemī-oġlans* who are engaged in smith's work on the noble mosque which is being built at Edirne,[46] seven,

[46] The Selimiye mosque.

who were working on the ironwork for the windows, have completed their service' and has requested that they should be 'sent out to the Porte.' Their names have been noted and a decree has been sent [to Sinān], and I have commanded that when [. . .] arrives you are to 'send out to the Porte' according to their *ḳānūn* the seven *ʿacemī-oġlan*s noted in the memorandum (*tezkire*) sent [herewith] and cause [the transfer] to be noted in the register. 981 (1573/4)

5 Command to the *aġa* of the Janissaries, 1583

Since at this present time, some of the Janissaries of my exalted court are at Demirḳapu, and some are on the campaign in the East, and some are in Egypt, and some are serving with the fleet, and some are in the Bender area, and some are serving in garrisons at the frontiers, so that few Janissaries are left in attendance (*mülāzemet*) at my court of felicity, having ordered that 200 lads should 'go out to the Porte', I have commanded that when [. . .] arrives you are to 'send out (*iḫrāc*) to the Porte', according to the traditional custom and *ḳānūn*, 200 from among the fit and senior and experienced *ʿacemī-oġlan*s and to send the register of them to the checking office (*muḳābele ḳalemi*). 991 (1583)

6 The pay of palace servants: an account register from 1478

Pay of those attached to the court, for Ṣafar and the two Rabīʿs of the year 883 (4 May–31 July 1478)[47]

Section (*bölük*) of the [Privy] Chamber (*oda*):			
Baḫşāyiş 4 Maḥmūd 2 Iskender 2			
Aḥmed 2 Ismāʿīl 1 ʿAlī 1			
	[total]	per day	12
Section of the Pantry: [4 names, at 1 or 2]		per day	6
Section of the Treasury: [3 names, at 1 or 2]		per day	5
Section of the Falconers of the *enderūn*:[48]			
The *aġa*: 10 [and 8 names, at 1-7]		per day	38
Section of the *rikābī*s[49] under Yaʿḳūb Aġa:			
The *aġa*: 50 [and 22 names, including 2 mutes, an *imām* and 2 *müʾezzin*s at 1-10]		per day	132
Group (*cemāʿat*) of the *ġulām*s of the *enderūn* who have been sent out (*iḫrāc*): [9 names, at 1 or 5]		per day	18
Group of the *müteferriḳa*s:[50]			
Ḥasan Beg, *zaʿīm* of the *yürük*s[51] 50			
ʿAlī Beg, former head of the *rikābī*s 50			

[47] Pay was distributed every three months.
[48] *Enderūn*: the Inner Palace, the sultan's private residence.
[49] *Rikābī* (*rikāb* is Arabic for 'stirrup'): an officer of the palace entitled to accompany the sultan when he was on horseback.
[50] *Müteferriḳa* (Arabic: 'miscellaneous') A miscellaneous group of palace servants, entitled to escort the sultan on horseback.
[51] *Yürük*s: semi-nomadic Turkish tribesmen in Anatolia and the Balkans. Groups of *yürük*s provided auxiliary military services.

Sinān Beg, former head of the Tasters	47		
[etc: 65 names, from 50 down to 3, among them a lutist, a *nedīm*,[52] an astrologer, and several pensioners]		per day	551
Section of the gardeners: [3 names, at ½ to 5]		per day	8½
Group of the *sipāhī-oġlans*[53] under ʿAlī Beg: [71 names, from 18 to 5, beginning with *kethudā* at 17 and ending with a *kātib* at 10]		per day	654
Group of the *siliḥdārs* under Turġud Beg: [63 names, from 16 to 6]		per day	496
Group of the ʿ*ulūfecis* under Aḥmed Beg: [53 names, from 7 to 1]		per day	250½
Group of the *ġarībs* under Mūsā Beg: [35 names, from 20 to 1, including six noted as 'Ḳarāmānī']		per day	236
Group of the door-keepers [50]			144
Group of the *çavuşes* under Süleymān Beg [7]			65
Group of the tent-pitchers under Ḥasan Beg [38]			100

[plus tasters 12 – per day 152; bakers 9 – per day 20; cooks 24 – per day 66; *solaḳs*[54] 20 – per day 63; keepers of hounds 15 – per day 58; houndsmen 12 – per day 29; tailors 23 – per day 86; armourers 13 – per day 67; falconers: keepers of peregrine falcons 33 – per day 85, keepers of goshawks 13 – per day 51, keepers of sparrowhawks 11 – per day 53; staff of the Imperial Stable: superintendant, clerk, deputy 3 – per day 44, saddlers 13 – per day 58, grooms 28 – per day 77, farriers, water carriers and coachmen 13 – per day 49, group of muleteers 16 – per day 51, group of donkeymen 2 – per day 8, group of keepers of female camels 22 – per day 68, keepers of male camels 18 – per day 56, group of keepers of breeding camels 11 – per day 28]

SECTION 3 *BERĀTS*

Any holder of public office in the Ottoman Empire occupied his position by virtue of a *berāt*. This was a warrant, issued in the sultan's name and cast in the form of a decree addressed to the public at large, appointing the nominee to office and laying out the terms of service. Passage **1** below records the appointment of a preacher to the mosque of Murad I in Bursa; passage **2** the appointment of a governor-general (*beglerbegi*) of the province of Anaṭolı (western Anatolia); passage **3** the appointment of a *ḳāḍī*; passage **4** the appointment of a Greek Metropolitan; and passage **5** the confirmation of the appointment of guardians on a mountain-pass in Bulgaria.

[52] *Nedīm*: a companion of the sultan.

[53] *Sipāhī-oġlans* ('cavalry lads'), *siliḥdārs* (weapon-bearers'), ʿ*ulūfecis* ('salarymen') 'of the left' and 'of the right', and *ġarībs* ('strangers') 'of the left' and 'of the right' made up the Six Divisions (*altı bölük*) of the household cavalry. The designations 'of the left' and 'of the right' indicate whether they rode on the left or right of the sultan in processions.

[54] *Ṣolaḳs*: the Janissaries serving as the personal bodyguard of the sultan.

1 The appointment of a preacher in Bursa

My command is this: to the bearer of the cipher (*tevḳīʿ*) of this mandate (*misāl*) . . . Ḥāccī Paşa Faḳīh I have assigned the post of preacher (*ḫaṭīb*) of the mosque (*cāmiʿ*) which my grandfather Ġāzī Ḫüdāvendgār[55] built in the town of Bursa, and I have commanded that he is to go there and recite the *ḫuṭbe*[56] every Friday and receive his stipend (*vaẓīfe*) from the *mütevellī*[57] according to the founder's stipulation, and he is to pray for the soul of the founder and for the continuance of my prosperity (*devām-i devlet*). Those who see my decree are to put their trust in it and not act counter to it. Written in the first decade of the month of Dhūʾl-Qaʿda 823 (November 1420), in the residence of Edirne.

2 The appointment of a *beglerbegi*

The reason for the writing of the mandate (*mis̱āl*) . . . is this:

To every person who through his laudable character regards it as an obligation (*farż*) upon himself to expend the currency of his life, night and day, in rendering due service at the Porte of *pādişāhs*, divine inspiration binds mighty sultans to entrust affairs within their capabilities, and so to favour them that, while spending their time in the discharge of great duties, they may live in prosperous comfort.

Therefore, upon the *emīr* of my threshold, the bearer of the exalted cipher . . ., the *emīrüʾl-ümera*[58] . . . ʿĪsā Beg . . . who has served uprightly at my court . . ., I have conferred (*taḳlīd*) the duty of *beglerbegi* of Anaṭolı, regarding him as fit to hold it, as Ḳaraca Beg[59] did hitherto, so that from today it is to be under his authority (*yed*) and he is to exercise (*muta-ṣarrıf*) it. No-one is to object or interfere. The *sancaḳbegi*s, *ḳāḍī*s, *subaşı*s, *nāʾib*s, *sipāhī*s, *keṯhudā*s, dignitaries (*aʿyān*) and *reʿāyā* and the other inhabitants [of Anaṭolı], low and high, are to recognise him as their magistrate and governor (*ḥākim ve vālī*), to present themselves at the place which he orders and to show no remissness in paying him all possible honour . . . And in all *umūr-i dīvānīye*[60] and matters (*ḳażāyā*) which pertain to the office of *beglerbegi* they are to have recourse to him; they are not to act counter to his orders and prohibitions. He is to apply himself duly to carrying out (?) administrative matters (*umūr-i siyāset*)[61] and sultanic commands (*aḥkām*) . . . In making decisions (*faṣl-i ḥukūmet*) and resolving dissensions (*ḳaṭʿ-i ḫuṣūmet*) he is not to discriminate between strong and weak, noble and base. He is always to care for the oppressed and put down the evil of the oppressors, so acting that the land be prosperous . . . and no-one suffers injustice. Wherever he learns that there are rebels (*bāġī*) and criminals (*ḥarāmī*) and [fomenters of] sedition (*fesād*), he is to put them down and seize them, so that the people are well-guarded and preserved from pillage and the fear of enemies and may be assiduous in prayer for the continuance of the victorious state (*devlet-i ḳāhire*). Whenever the occasion arises, he is to present himself with the troops of Anaṭolı . . . and fulfil

---

[55] Murād I (1362–89).

[56] *Ḫuṭbe*: the sermon delivered during the Friday prayer, which includes a prayer for the ruler.

[57] *Mütevellī*: the administrator of a *waqf*. See Chapter IX.

[58] *Emīrüʾl-ümerā* (Arabic: 'commander of commanders'): *beglerbegi*.

[59] Ḳaraca Beg lost his life at the battle of Varna in 1444.

[60] Matters falling outside the scope of the *sharīʿa* that would come before the *beglerbegi* rather than the *ḳāḍī*.

[61] *Siyāset* sometimes has the sense of 'capital punishment', suggesting that the sultan is conferring the power to impose the death penalty.

his due service in my victorious army. Whatever domains (*ḫavāṣṣ*) and other [. . .] perquisites (*müteveccehāt*) Ḳaraca Beg enjoyed hitherto, he is to enjoy the same. Those who see this are to put their confidence in the world-conquering sign.[62] Written on 7 Rajab 855 (5 August 1451), in the residence of Edirne.

3 The appointment of a *kāḍī*

The command . . . is this:

Inasmuch as . . . the *ḳāḍī*s and magistrates are the reason for the strengthening of the divine laws and the cause for the well-being of human affairs and the means for promoting good order, to the bearer of this exalted cipher . . . Mevlānā Bedreddīn . . . I have entrusted and conferred and given, on 15 Dhū'l-Ḥijja 952 (17 February 1546) the *ḳāḍī*ship of Budin,[63] which with its dependencies is written in the sultanic register at 130 *aḳçe* a day, and I have commanded that he is to go and be *ḳāḍī* and magistrate in that *ḳażā*. Holding fast to the implementation of the commands of the *sharīʿa* . . . he is not to diverge from its straight path. In questions that arise he is to investigate the various dicta of the Ḥanafī *imām*s and find the most valid course and act upon it. He is to deal with the writing of *sicill*-entries and legal documents (*ṣukūk*), the giving in marriage of young boys and girls, the contracting of marriages, the implementation of testaments, the division of the estates of the *reʿāyā*,[64] the custody of the goods of orphans and of missing persons, the dismissal and appointment of guardians and *nāʾib*s, and all other *şerʿī*[65] affairs . . . All the people of that region are to recognise him as their *ḳāḍī* and his judgment as effective, and in all *şerʿī* affairs they are to have recourse to him and not diverge from his orders (*emr*). If he fulfils this duty in lawful fashion, he is to have the use (*mutaṣarrıf*) of whatever the former *ḳāḍī*s had, and he is to occupy himself with prayer for the continuance of my prosperity . . . Thus they are to know . . . Written in the first decade of Rabīʿü'l-awwal 953 (May 1546)

4 The appointment of a metropolitan

The command . . . is this:

The bearer of the noble mandate, the priest . . ., having paid to my imperial treasury a gift (*pīşkeş*) of . . . ducats, I have given him the metropolitanate of . . . and I have commanded that as from today he is to be metropolitan there, and in accordance with 'leave them to practice what they profess', he may carry out all their rites and ceremonies: and [he is to exercise his office] in the same fashion as former metropolitans exercised it over the priests and monks and other Christians of that district, and he is to have the use of whatever churches and vineyards and orchards and fields [his predecessors] had. Like the former metropolitans, he is to be exempt from courier[-corvée] (*ulaḳ*) and *cereḫor*[66] and poll-tax (*ḫarāc*) and other impositions (*ʿavāriż ve tekālīf-i dīvānī*). The priests and monks and other Christians of that place are to

---

[62] A reference to the *ṭuġra*.

[63] Buda.

[64] It was a duty of the *ḳāḍī* to oversee the division of the inheritances of the *reʿāyā*, the term here referring to all members of the tax-paying class. The inheritances of the *ʿaskerī* (military) class came under a separate jurisdiction.

[65] *Şerʿī*: relating to the *sharīʿa*.

[66] Labour service in support of the army.

recognise him as metropolitan over them and to have recourse to him in matters pertaining to the office of metropolitan. (Late fifteenth century)

5 The appointment of mountain guards

The command . . . is this:

Heretofore my late father, to ensure the guarding of the pass on the road which goes to Puranlu, a dependency of Menlik in Kostandin-ili,[67] gave to twenty infidels[68] a command that they should guard it night and day. Now they have brought it and submitted it, and I for my part have accepted it[69] and have given them this noble command, and I have commanded that the twenty infidels are to go and guard that pass, as they have done before, by night and day against thieves and bandits. When they find a wrongdoer or a bandit they are to seize and bind him and inform my Porte. They are so to exert themselves that there shall at that pass be no loss or damage to anyone's life or limb, Muslim or *dhimmī*; if there is, they are to bear the *ġarāmet*[70] for it. After these twenty infidels guard that pass as set out, they are to be secure (*emīn*) from *ḫarāc* and *ispence*[71] and sheep-tax (*ʿādet*) and billeting (*ḳonaḳ*) and fortress-building and courier[-corvée] and forced labour (*suḫra*); no-one is to take food and fodder from them by force, but buy it for cash. Thus they are to know . . . Written on 11 Jumādā II 860 (17 May 1456), in the camp at Sofia.[72]

SOURCES

Section 1

1 İbrahim Hakkı Uzunçarşılı, *Osmanlı Devleti Teşkilâtından Kapukulu Ocakları*, Ankara (1943), 1, 87–9; Irène Beldiceanu-Steinherr, 'En marge d'un acte concernant le penğyek et les aqınğı', *Revue des Études Islamiques*, XXXVII/1 (1969), 45–7.
2 Uzunçarşılı, *Kapukulu Ocakları*, 1, 89.
3 Uzunçarşılı, *Kapukulu Ocakları*, 1, 92–4; Ahmet Akgündüz, *Osmanlı Kanûnnâmeleri*, 2, Istanbul (1990), 123–5.
4 Uzunçarşılı, *Kapukulu Ocakları*, 1, 27–8.
5 Uzunçarşılı, *Kapukulu Ocakları*, 1, 126.
6 Uzunçarşılı, *Kapukulu Ocakları*, 1, 23n; remainder of the text and its date not quoted.

Section 2

1 Uzunçarşılı, *Kapukulu Ocakları*, 1, 115–16.
2 Uzunçarşılı, *Kapukulu Ocakları*, 1, 116.
3 Uzunçarşılı, *Kapukulu Ocakları*, 1, 132.
4 Uzunçarşılı, *Kapukulu Ocakları*, 1, 134.

[67] Modern Kyustendil, Bulgaria.
[68] Probably the local bandits [VLM].
[69] The *berāt* is valid for the sultan's lifetime only
[70] The payment due as compensation for homicide, injury to the person or loss of property.
[71] *İspence*: a poll-tax levied on non-Muslims, in lieu of *çift*-tax on their tenements.
[72] The document was issued at Sofia in 1456, when the sultan was on his way to besiege Belgrade, in response to a petition presented to him in the army camp.

5 Uzunçarşılı, *Kapukulu Ocakları*, 1, 135.
6 Ahmed Refik, 'Fātiḥ devrine ʿāʾid vesīḳalar', *Taʾrīḫ-i ʿOsmânî Encümeni Mecmûʿası*, 26–49 (1335–7/ 1916–8), 5–23.

Section 3

1 Feridun Beg, *Münşeʾātüʾs-selāṭīn*, Istanbul (1274/1857), 1, 166.
2 Feridun Beg, *Münşeʾātüʾs-selāṭīn*, Istanbul, 1, 269. The date of this document is incorrect. See Halil İnalcık, *Fatih Devri üzerinde Tetkikler ve Vesikalar*, Ankara (1954), 77n.
3 İbrahim Hakkı Uzunçarşılı, *Osmanlı Devletinin İlmiye Teşkilatı*, Ankara (1965), 92–3.
4 Robert Anhegger and Halil İnalcık, *Kanunname-i Sultani ber Muceb-i Örf-i Osmani*, Ankara (1956), 65; Ahmed Akgündüz, *Osmanlı Kanunnameleri*, 1, Istanbul (1990), 407; French translation: Nicoara Beldiceanu, *Les Actes des Premiers Sultan*, Paris, The Hague (1960), 137.
5 Halil İnalcık, *Fatih Devri Üzerinde Tetkikler ve Vesikalar*, Ankara (1954), Document X.

Plate 1 The grand vizier (JRL1118969)

Plate 2 The şeyḫü'l-islām (JRL1118965)

Plate 3 An *içoğlan*, a page of the inner palace (JRL1118972)

Plate 4 A *ḫāṣṣeki*, an officer of the palace, holding the sultan's parasol (JRL111973)

Plate 5 The *re'īsü'l-küttāb*, the chief clerk to the *dīvān* (JRL1118974)

Plate 6 A *tülbenddār*, maker and keeper of the sultan's turbans (JRL1118975)

Plate 7 A *siliḥdār* and a *çoḳadār* on horseback (JRL1118978)

Plate 8 A *samsoncu*, a keeper of the sultan’s mastiffs (JRL1119045)

CHAPTER IV

The Vizierate and the *Dīvān*

The *dīvān-i hümāyūn* ('Imperial Council') was the senior executive and judicial body in the Ottoman Empire, meeting in the second court of the palace under the presidency of the grand vizier, as described in passages **1** and **2**. Its membership represented the four branches of government. The viziers, who would normally reach their position after serving as provincial governors, as seen in passage **1**, represented the political-military establishment. The *ḳāḍī ʿasker*s of Rūmeli and Anaṭolı were the senior *ḳāḍī*s of the empire, responsible for judicial affairs in the European and Asiatic provinces, respectively. The *defterdār*s were responsible for financial affairs, and the *nişāncı* for the scribal service. Apart from its executive function, the *dīvān* acted as a court, hearing petitions from members of the public, either in person or by proxy (see passage **2**) and, from the reign of Bāyezīd II (r. 1481–1512) onwards, also cases involving members of the military (*ʿaskerī*) class. Until the last decades of the sixteenth century, either the grand vizier or the *dīvān* collectively reported on the day's deliberations to the sultan: all decrees or other documents emanating from the *dīvān* were issued in the sultan's name. From the late sixteenth century on, it seems to have become more common for the grand vizier to make submissions in writing and to receive the sultan's written reply, as can be observed in passages **3a–f**. Passages **1**, **4** and **5** demonstrate that, while the grand vizier held the highest political office after the sultan himself, his appointment, dismissal and, at times, execution was entirely at the discretion of the sultan, who could be guided in his decision by his family or courtiers of the inner palace (see passage **5**).

1 The *Āṣaf-nāme* of Luṭfī Paşa[1]

In the name of God, the Merciful, the Compassionate.

Laud and praise that matchless Provider who has no like or peer, and who is a sultan without a vizier; and prayers and salutations upon that leader of the Prophets and commander of the pure, who is the bringer of good tidings and the warner; and also upon his family and his companions, each of whom was a prudent manager for the promotion of the Faith. May the

[1] Luṭfī Paşa wrote his *Āṣafnāme*, a book of advice for grand viziers, in retirement after his dismissal from the vizierate in 1541. VLM used to describe Luṭfī Paşa as a 'well-meaning but thick Albanian'.

commendation of God be upon him and his family and his companions so long as the heavens and the earths endure. Thereafter:

The author of this treatise, the weakest of God's servants, Luṭfī Paşa b. ʿAbduʾl-Muʿīn[2] was brought up, enjoying the sultanic bounty, in the private apartments (*ḥarem-i ḫāṣṣ*) from the reign of the late Sultan Bāyezīd Ḫān as a devoted servant of this Ottoman Porte: and while in the private apartments I studied various branches of learning. Upon the accession of Sultan Selīm Ḫān, being then *çoḳadār*, I 'went out' [from the palace] to the post of *müteferrıḳa*[3] at 50 *akçe* [per day]. I was then granted [in succession] the posts of *çāşnigīr-başı*, *ḳapucı-başı*, *mīr-ʿalem*, *sancaḳbegi* of Ḳastamonı, *beglerbegi* of Ḳaraman, [*beglerbegi* of Anaṭolı,] and vizier.[4] After 'going out', this humble creature, full of faults, consorted with numerous *ʿulemā* and poets and men of culture, and so far as I could I improved myself through the study of the various branches of learning.

When our present *pādişāh* Sultan Süleymān Ḫān – the greatest of the sultans and the most noble of the *ḫāḳān*s, the aider of the servants of God and the protector of God's domains, the fighter along the path of God, the servitor of the Two Noble Sanctuaries,[5] the ruler of the two lands and the two seas (may God prolong his glory!) commanded that I should assume the post of grand vizier,[6] I found various procedures and principles and *ḳānūns* of the imperial *dīvān* to be at variance with what I had observed earlier and to be in disorder. Therefore, as a memento to my brethren who will assume the duty of the grand vizierate, I have composed this treatise, inserting in it the proper procedures relating to the grand vizierate and the main points necessary to that post, and I have entitled it 'The *Āṣafnāme*',[7] so that when it is seen by my brethren who receive the favour of appointment to the vizierate they may utter a prayer for me. I have arranged it in four chapters . . .

When I came to the post of vizier, I had found the affairs of the exalted *dīvān* in considerable confusion. Over seven years [1534(?)–41], by prudent management, I set them in order so far as was possible. Then various self-interested double-dealers 'in whose hearts there is a disease'[8] slandered me to the felicitous *pādişāh*. To avoid being subjected to women in respect of various matters relating to my private life (*ḥarem*) and to make myself secure from their wiles, [I considered it better to renounce] the grand vizierate. So I gave it up and went to my estate (*çiftlik*) at Edirne, and there in the nook of seclusion I devoted myself with peace of mind to prayer to the Glorious God. I realised that the prosperity of this transient world rapidly declines and easily departs. It is better for the wise man, not being heedless, to find tranquillity in the corner of abnegation and in the contemplation of gardens and meadows. It is God

[2] The patronymic ʿAbduʾl-Muʿīn, like ʿAbduʾllah, shows that Luṭfī Paşa was of non-Muslim descent.

[3] *Müteferriḳa* (Arabic: 'miscellaneous'): A miscellaneous group of palace servants, entitled to escort the sultan on horseback.

[4] While omitting all details of his Albanian background, Luṭfī Paşa lists the posts which he occupied during his ascent to the vizierate. In the inner palace, he served in the sultan's privy chamber and as 'keeper of linen' (*çokadar*). On the accession of Selīm I in 1512, he graduated to service in the outer palace, as *müteferriḳa*, head taster (*çāşnigīr başı*), head gatekeeper (*kapucı başı*) and keeper of the sultan's standards (*mīr-ʿalem*). From service in the palace, he graduated to posts in the provinces as *sancaḳ*-governor (*sancaḳbegi*) and governor-general (*beglerbegi*). He was appointed third vizier in c1536, second vizier in 1538 and grand vizier in July 1539. He was dismissed in May 1541. He married the sultan's sister Şāh Sulṭān, and it was reportedly a violent quarrel with his wife that led to his dismissal. According to contemporary gossip, she objected to his sleeping with boys.

[5] Mecca and Medina.

[6] In July 1539.

[7] 'The book of Āṣaf'. Āṣaf was the legendary vizier of King Solomon.

[8] Qur'ān 2:10.

to whom we turn for help and in whom we trust. May God, Glorious and Exalted, protect the practices and procedures of the Ottoman House from the fears and dangers of the time and from the malevolent eye of enemies. Amen.

Chapter One sets out what the moral qualities and rules of conduct of the grand vizier should be, and how he should behave in his dealings with the *pādişāh.*

Firstly, the grand vizier should be free of personal ambition, dealing with every matter [solely] for the sake of God's service, for there is no further office higher than his to which he may attain, and he should speak the truth to the *pādişāh* without embarrassment, calling the dignitaries to testify to God [that he has done so(?)].

The confidential matters which he transacts with the *pādişāh* should be kept secret, not merely from outsiders but even from the other viziers. Once, in the reign of the late Sultan Selīm (who was the most eminent of the sultans in justice and martial valour, in talent and generosity, the tiger who with head uplifted paced the arena of the sultanate) the late Pīrī Paşa, who had been granted the grand vizierate by the sultan because of his confidence in his intellect and his grasp of affairs while serving as *defterdār*,[9] went to see the *pādişāh* during the afternoon to consult over a certain confidential matter: and on that felicitous occasion he and the *pādişāh* had long discussions. In the *dīvān* [the next day] the vizier Mesīḥ Paşa asked: 'What did you discuss yesterday?' In consequence Pīrī Paşa made a recommendation (*telḫīṣ*) that he should be disgraced and dismissed: but with difficulty, and thanks to the intercession of several people, he was saved.[10]

The *pādişāh* should not mix overmuch with favourites (*nedīm*). True, monarchs must always have favourites and companions, but the favourite and the companion, although he is granted largesse and honorific robes, should not interfere in public affairs.

The grand vizier should ensure that the *pādişāh* sees most of his submissions (*ʿarż*) and not let him conceal himself behind the veil of seclusion; and matters on which the grand vizier has made submissions to the *pādişāh* should not be altered.

The grand vizier should, in the privacy of the night, enquire from his intimates, men free of ambition, about poor and weak men who are deserving of office and grant them office and set them on their feet; for a vizier is like a prudent physician and should help men lacking strength to recover from the disease of poverty and indigence. As a man possessing the ability to do so, he should be apt at offering employment, [in peacetime and] in time of war.

A vizier should not grant *zeʿāmet*s[11] to his own dependants (*tevābiʿ*) but should satisfy them by granting them *tīmār*s;[12] and if he does grant *tīmār*s, they should be few; and he should not combine two or three *kılıç*es,[13] unless they are on the *ḫāṣṣ*[-estates][14] of a *defterdār* or a *nişāncı.*[15]

---

[9] *Defterdār* ('book-keeper'): controller of finance.

[10] Pīrī Pasha was Grand Vizier from 1517 to 1523 and served as *defterdār* from late in the reign of Bāyezīd II (1481–1512). The vizier Mesīḥ Paşa died in 1501. The incident described cannot therefore have occurred between these two men.

[11] *Zeʿāmet*: a fief worth more than 20,000 *aḳçe* per year.

[12] *Tīmār*: a fief worth between 2,000 and 20,000 *aḳçe* per year.

[13] *Kılıç* ('sword'): the indivisible core of a *tīmār*. In this passage, Luṭfī Paşa warns that grand viziers should themselves support their own followers and dependants, or at least not give them large fiefs. Nor should they dodge the restriction by combining lower value fiefs into a single unit, as this would reduce the number of troops available for military service.

[14] *Ḫāṣṣ*: a fief worth more than 100,000 *akçe* per year.

[15] *Nişancı* ('chancellor'), the officer responsible for overseeing the production of documents issued in the sultan's name.

He should not issue firmans for couriers (*ulaḳ*) on any trivial pretext. There is in the Ottoman territories no burden so inequitable as the courier. Courier-orders should be issued only in matters of the first importance when there is the risk of harm in state affairs; they are not justified in trivial matters. During my vizierate, in order to liberate the helpless subjects from this, I stationed post-horses at various points.[16]

The vizier should restrain the *pādişāh* from the inclination to amass wealth and from falling into sin through the desire for wealth. Whenever money fell in [the Treasury] as *beytü'l-māl*,[17] I caused it to be held in trust at the Porte until the heirs should present themselves, and our just Sultan Süleymān Ḫān commanded that it should be held in trust at the Porte for seven years and, if within seven years no heir came to light, either by report or otherwise, [only then] should it be credited to the treasury (*ḫazīne*); for if the money (*māl*) of the people is made to accrue without [proper] cause to the money of the *pādişāh*, this is an indication that the state is approaching dissolution.

The grand vizier should exert himself to see appointed efficient and strict persons as *aġa* over the Janissaries (*ḳul ṭā'ifesi*) and men of intellect with a grasp of affairs as their secretary (*kātib*). So long as the Janissaries are not under discipline (*mażbūṭ*), the grand vizier can have no peace of mind.[18]

The grand vizier should without hesitation report to the *pādişāh* whatever is necessary relating to the affairs of religion and state (*dīn ü devlet*). He should not feel over-apprehensive of being dismissed: it is better to enjoy good repute among the people through being dismissed than to carry out an inequitable policy.

The grand vizier should perform the five daily prayers in company (*cemā'at*) in his residence; and his door should be open so that access to him is easy. He should, without compromising his honour, strive to conciliate people so far as possible. He should beware of releasing, in return for gifts, any wrongdoers and criminals who are discovered. To officers of the state (*aṣḥāb-i devlet*) bribery (*rüşvet*) is a disease that admits of no cure – except that it is admissible to accept gifts from one's friends, or from those who customarily offer gifts, or from people of means who do not stand in need [of any recompense]. Beyond that, beware, beware of bribery! God preserve us from it!

The grand vizier has a *ḫāṣṣ* to the [nominal] value of 1,200,000 *akçe*. If the *ḫāṣṣ* produces [in fact] one and a half [times] its book value (*yazu*), [the revenue] approaches two million. If there comes in a further two or three hundred thousand in the form of precious stuffs and horses[19] from the *emīr*s of the Kurds and [other] powerful *emīr*s round about, the total must come to 2,400,000 *akçe*. Praise be to God the Exalted, in the Ottoman state this recompense is sufficient – anyway, I used to lay out 1,500,000 *aḳçe* per year on the expenses of my kitchen and my retinue (*ḳul*) and 500,000 *aḳçe* on alms (*taṣadduḳāt*), so that four or five hundred thousand remained in my treasury. A considerable sum [too] had been saved up from booty won on campaigns (*ġazā*) and from tithes and taxes (*a'şar ve rüsūm*) regarded as licit (*ḥelāl*) which had accrued to me in the posts of *beglerbegi* which I had held: this I expended on alms and good works (*ḥasenāt*). 'Praise be to God Who has been bountiful to us and favoured us.'

---

16 On couriers, see Colin Heywood, 'The evolution of the courier order (*ulaḳ ḥükmi*) in Ottoman chancery practice', in J. Zimmermann, C. Herzog, R. Motika, *Osmanische Welten: Quellen und Fallstudien. Festschrift für Michael Ursinus*, Bamberg (2016), 269–312.

17 *Beytü'l-māl* ('treasury'): money or goods coming to the treasury when there are no apparent heirs.

18 Janissary rebellions and mutinies were as much a threat to the sultan as they were to the grand vizier.

19 Presumably as gifts and perquisites.

Greed is a base course to follow, with no limit to it, whereas contentment is a treasure that does not waste away, with many benefits in it.

The grand vizier should spend his time on state affairs (*mühimmāt-i salṭanat*). It is not fitting that he should devote his attention to debauchery or musical parties or merrymaking. After he has attained that post, what is fitting is quietude and piety. He should exert himself to reforming his own character and to putting the world to rights so far as is possible.

The grand vizier should, by the favour and attentions he shows them, bring before the public eye office-holders who are members of the *dīvān* and learned members of the *ʿulemā* and thus win their support. No-one but him should sentence office-holders and members of the *dīvān*. The *müderris*es[20] and the [other] members of the *ʿulemā* class (*ṭāʾife*) are all jealous of one another, [so] he should not believe what they say about one another but should consult with those who are the heads (*reʾīs*) of the *ʿulemā* and make investigations and take soundings over [appointments to] posts among the *ʿulemā*. As for posts in the bureaucracy (*manāṣib-i küttāb*) – whether it concerns the *rūznāme*[21] [department] or the *muḳābele*[22] [department] or any other – he should be careful not to let them fall to incompetents (*nā-ehl*) knowing nothing of office-management (*aḥvāl-i ḳalem*).

The grand vizier should on two days a week have a meal specially prepared for the sake of the noble soul of the Prophet . . . and invite [to it] many people from among the pious and the wise, and by that means inform himself of numerous matters [by learning] from various wise men – this, at least, is what I did during my grand vizierate.

The grand vizier should know the precedence of the office-holders when they attend to him, understanding each one's rank. Firstly, *beglerbegi*s are below viziers – nobody takes precedence over them. *Defterdār*s of the finances (*māl defterdārları*) take precedence over *sancaḳbegi*s and *aġa*s of the stirrup. The head of the *aġa*s of the stirrup is the *aġa* of the Janissaries; then comes the *mīr-ʿalem*, then the *ḳapucı-başı*, then the *mīr-aḫur*,[23] then the *çāḳırcı-başı*[24] and the *çāşnigīr-başı* and the *aġa*s of the *bölük*s.[25] The *defterdār*s take precedence over the *nişāncı*, unless the *nişāncı* is a former *defterdār*. The *defterdār*s of the finances and the *nişāncı* rank with the *ḳāḍī*s of the capitals (*taḫt ḳāḍīleri*),[26] taking precedence over all *müderris*es, both 'of fifty' and 'of sixty'.[27] The chief *defterdār* ranks with the *ḳāḍī*s of the Three Towns.[28] The *ketḫüdā*[29] of the *defterdār* takes precedence over a *müteferrıḳa* and a *çāşnigīr*: *müderris*es of the Ṣaḥn[30] take precedence over him. One day during the reign of the late sultan Selīm Ḫān the *çavuş*es[31] and the *kātib*s[32] were disputing [this question]. When it was submitted [for decision] to the sultan, he ruled: 'The *kātib* should be given precedence,

---

20 *Müderris*: a teacher in a *medrese*.

21 *Rūznāme* ('day-book'): The office maintaining a daily account of the income and expenditure of the treasury.

22 *Muḳābele*: ('collating'): The office checking payments and grants against centrally held registers.

23 *Mīr-āḫur*: master of the sultan's stables.

24 *Çaḳırcı-başı*: head falconer.

25 The six divisions (*altı bölük*) of household cavalry.

26 The *ḳāḍī*s of Istanbul, Bursa and Edirne,

27 The reference is to the daily income of the *müderris*es in *aḳçe*. This determined their status.

28 The *ḳāḍī*s of Istanbul, Üsküdar and Eyüp.

29 *Ketḫüdā*; deputy.

30 *Ṣaḥn* (Arabic: 'courtyard'): abbreviation of Ṣaḥn-i S̱emān ('the court of eight'), the eight *medreses* adjoining the Mosque of Meḥmed II in Istanbul, which at this time were the superior *medrese*s in the Ottoman Empire.

31 *Çavuş*: ('herald, marshal') one of a corps within the palace, responsible for ceremonial, conveying ambassadors, carrying orders and messages, and – occasionally – carrying out executions.

32 *Kātib*: scribe, secretary.

for the *kātib*'s service concerns the secret affairs of the state, but that of the *çavuş* concerns affairs which are public'. Among the *kātib*s, the highest-ranking are the *kātib* of the Janissaries and the *rūznāmeci*.[33] The post of *müteferrıḳa* with stipend should not be given to a man from outside [the Palace service] unless he has 'gone out' from the *ḥarem-i ḫāṣṣ*[34] or is the son of a *beglerbegi* or of a *defterdār*.

A man who does not have a *ze'āmet* of 80,000 *aḳçe* is not eligible for a *sancaḳ*. The upper limit (*nihāyet*) of a *sancaḳ* is 400,000 *aḳçe*. If a *defterdār* of the finances goes out to a *sancaḳ*, he is appointed at 400,000 *aḳçe*, while an *aġa* of the stirrup is appointed at 350,000. It is the *ḳānūn* that viziers should rise to their feet for a *za'īm*.[35] The upper limit of a *ze'āmet* to which a *kātib* is appointed is some 50,000 *aḳçe*, and for a *çavuş* some 40,000. It is permissible to conflate [holdings], but too much conflation leads to a shortage of *ḳılıç*[-holdings], so one should be wary of conflating.

The grand vizier should say, in most of his interviews with the *pādişāh*: 'My *pādişāh*, I have removed the burden from my neck; I have spoken the truth of the matter; henceforth it is you that shall give answer on the Day of Recompense'.

He should be attentive to give hearing personally to complaints in the *dīvān*.

If an ambassador arrives from round about, guards should be set over him so that he does not learn too much of what is going on, and they should be ordered not to let him move around much.

The condition of the price-tariff (*narḫ*)[36] is a matter of the very greatest importance, and the grand vizier should be most attentive to it. It is not permissible that some officeholders should be rice-merchants or that the residences of others should be druggists' shops.[37] The price-tariff concerns the interests of the poor.

Officeholders should not be dismissed because of just one or two complainants. If there are on one or two occasions complaints against a *sancaḳbegi* or a *ḳāḍī*, the grand vizier should send him a letter of advice and admonish him; but if he does not take heed from this and there are again complainants against him, then he should be dismissed.

The grand vizier should know people's capacities. He should know each man's capability, whether it consists in personal qualities or learning or service rendered [and for what office he is suited] and should make appointments accordingly.

He should stand firm on the matter of appointing as *sipāhī*[38] a man who belongs to the *re'āyā*[39] and is not the son and grandson of *sipāhī*s. Once that door is opened, perforce everyone will escape from the status of *ra'īyet* and become a *sipāhī*; and when there are no *ra'īyet*s left, the *pādişāh*'s revenues will perforce be small.

It is God who knows best. 'Blessed is He in whose hand is the kingdom: and He has power over all things'.[40]

---

[33] *Rūznāmeci*: the official responsible for maintaining the *rūznāme*.

[34] The sultan's private apartments.

[35] The holder of a *ze'āmet*.

[36] *Narḫ*: the daily fixed price of goods in the market.

[37] That is, because they are speculating.

[38] *Sipāhī*: a cavalryman holding a *tīmār* in exchange for military service.

[39] *Re'āyā* (sing.: *ra'īyet*): the tax-paying, rural subjects of the sultan.

[40] Qur'ān, 67:1.

Chapter Two sets out the organization of military campaigns.

Firstly, in the areas where a campaign is necessary, one of the viziers or one of the *beglerbegi*s must be appointed *serdār*;[41] it is customary that in some areas a *sancaḳbegi* too should be *serdār*. One should arrange (*tedārük*) beforehand the amount of cash and provisions that are necessary for that campaign and [only] then set out.

If it is necessary that the *pādişāh* himself should set out, the grand vizier should convene the *defterdār*[s][42] and the other members of the *dīvān* and arrange how much cash is necessary and how many troops (*ʿasker*), and where stocks of provisions should be deposited, and he should settle with the *mīr-aḫur*[43] the questions concerning the camels and mules and horses which the *pādişāh* will need, and he should also take along a carriage for the use of the *pādişāh*.

When camp is made, the grand vizier should encamp at some distance from the *pādişāh*. The *pādişāh* should encamp in the middle with the [palace] troops (*ʿasker*) encamped all around him and the ordinary soldiers (*ḫalḳ*) at a distance of about a mile from the tent (*ḫayme*) of the *pādişāh*. The treasury tent (*ḫazīne çadırı*) should be erected in front of the pavilion (*oṭaḳ*) of the pādişāh, and the *defterdār* should hold *dīvān* there. It is the *ḳānūn* that camels should be given to the viziers and the *ḳāḍīʿasker*s[44] and the *nişāncı* and the *defter emīni*;[45] so it is set down in the register for Sultan Selīm Ḫān's Çaldıran campaign.[46]

On the march, the grand vizier should approach the sultan on horseback whenever he wishes, and other viziers and members (*erkān*) of the *dīvān* may approach when they are summoned, as may *sancaḳbegi*s out of office.

Each night, one *sancaḳbegi* should perform picket-duty (*ḳaravul*), and one *bölük aġası*[47] should stand guard before the [sultan's] tent (*oṭaḳ*). On one occasion during the reign of the late Sultan Selīm, on the way to the conquest of Diyārbekir, a number of scoundrelly spies, sent by Shāh Ismāʿīl, had come up to before the [sultan's] tent with the intention of setting it on fire and then, when the *pādişāh* started up and came out, stabbing him with daggers. They were detected and punished; but since that time it has been commanded that one of the *aġa*s of the *bölük*s should stand guard in turn.

The army should have an honest (*müstaḳīm*) commissary-general (*nüzl emīni*). The *ḳānūn* is that the *pādişāh* should present six days' provisions to the Janissaries and the *sipāhī*s: Sultan Selīm Ḫān provided this for three days on entering the frontier region (*serḥadd*) and for three days on leaving it.

If victory is won, the *pādişāh*'s hand is kissed as on feast-days (*ʿīd*), and the viziers and the *ḳāḍīʿasker*s and the *defterdār*s are vested with *ḳaftan*s; officeholders in the provinces (*ṭaşra*) too, both the *beglerbegi*s and the *sancaḳbegi*s, are vested with *ḳaftan*s.

Ḳānūn concerning armed retainers (*cebelü*): a holder of a *tīmār* of 6,000 *aḳçe* provides two; of 10,000 *aḳçe*, three; a holder of a *zeʿāmet* of 20,000 *aḳçe* provides four.

The holder of a *tīmār* must be present on a campaign in person, unless he is a young lad or is sick.

---

41 *Serdār*: 'commander'.

42 The manuscripts are at variance.

43 *Mīr-aḫur*: master of the sultan's stables.

44 *Ḳāḍīʿasker* ('military judge'): one of the two chief justices of the Ottoman Empire.

45 *Defter emīni* ('superintendent of the register'): head of the office responsible for registers recording assignments of *tīmār*s, *zeʿāmet*s and *ḫāṣṣ*, and therefore of military obligations.

46 The campaign of 1514 against the Safavid Shah Ismaʿīl I (1501–24).

47 *Bölük aġası* ('commander of a division'): commander of one of the Six Divisions (*altı bölük*) of the household cavalry.

The cash taken on campaign [when] with the *pādişāh* should be doubled, for largesse (*baḫşiş*) may be necessary.

Before one sets out, the frontiers should be entrusted to efficient governors and strengthened. Victories should be announced to the frontier regions.

As important as affairs by land are, maritime affairs are even more important. One day the late Sultan Selīm Ḫān – the noblest of the sultans in wisdom and percipience, in justice and generosity, the fortunate ruler who achieved the felicity of becoming Servitor of the Two Sanctuaries[48] and succeeded in becoming ʿAzīz-i Mıṣr[49] – said to the late Kemālpaşazāde:[50] 'I wish to increase the Arsenal to 300 [berths], so that it reaches from the fortress of Galata as far as Kāġıdḫāne.[51] My intention is to conquer the Franks'.[52] The late *mollā* replied: 'My *pādişāh*, you dwell in a city whose benefactor is the sea. If the sea is not secure, ships will not come; and if ships do not come, Istanbul cannot prosper'. The sun of the life of Sultan Selīm was then near to sinking, so that the plans in his noble mind were not carried through. But now our *pādişāh* Sultan Süleymān Ḫān, the just and generous, has also paid close attention to maritime affairs, and his attention and his supervising eye are directed to ensuring that our affairs at sea are well regulated and that the sea-going *ġāzī*s are victorious over the infidel. Indeed, this humble individual was the reason that many governors were appointed over the sea[53] from among the independent *beg*s and sea-captains.[54] I really made great exertions, thinking: 'The sea is one wing of the Ottoman sultanate and state: let it receive due attention (*maʿmūr olsun*)'. This is the gist of the submission which I made to my *pādişāh* Sultan Süleymān Ḫān: 'Among the sultans of the past there were many who ruled the land, but few who ruled the sea. In the organisation of naval campaigns, the infidels are superior to us. We must become victorious over them'. When I made this submission, he said: 'What you say is true. So it must be'. And I caused an *emīn*[55] for naval expenses to be appointed by the *pādişāh*.

On the matter of campaigns, the upshot of my words and the pith of my remarks is this: both affairs relating to land and matters concerning the sea, and the good order and proper disposition of the viziers and the *emīr*s are occasions for the grand vizier to enjoy honourable renown and for men to utter his name with gratitude. He should exert himself to the degree that is necessary.

Chapter Three sets out the management of the treasury.

Firstly, the management of the treasury is a most important matter. The sultanate exists through the treasury, and the treasury through good management (*tedbīr*), not through oppression (*ẓulm*). When I became grand vizier I found the treasury in confusion and deficit. At the time of the accession of Sultan Süleymān Ḫān, income (*īrād*) had been equal to expenditure (*maṣraf*). Income sometimes fell short, and then funds were provided from the old treasury

[48] Mecca and Medina.

[49] Ruler of Egypt. The term is derived from Qurʾān 12 and was sometimes used to denote the Mamlūk sultans. The reference is to Selīm I's defeat of the Mamlūks in 1517, which gave him control of Egypt and the Hejaz, including Mecca and Medina.

[50] Kemālpaşazāde (1468–1536): an Ottoman scholar, jurist and statesman.

[51] That is, Selīm intended the naval arsenal to stretch the entire length of the Golden Horn in Istanbul.

[52] *İfrenc*: a literary term denoting the West or westerners. Selīm's intention was probably the conquest of Rhodes.

[53] The reference is to the establishment of locally based naval flotillas in coastal districts.

[54] That is, corsairs.

[55] *Emīn*: superintendent.

outside [the palace]. But this procedure leads to disorder: income must *exceed* expenditure. I so managed affairs that no deficiency affected the institutions (*āyīn*) of the sultanate.

The grand vizier should first of all investigate each year the amount of the income and the expenditure and see that the income exceeds the expenditure. He should be on his guard against increasing the numbers of the Janissaries (*ḳul ṭa'ifesi*): troops should be few but good. All the nominal rolls (*defter*) of the troops should be kept in proper order; all the troops should be actually present; and their names should tally with those in the nominal rolls. Fifteen thousand stipendiary (*'ulūfeli*) troops represent a large force: to produce the pay for 15,000 men, year in and out, without falling short, is a heroic task. Whether it be the income of the treasury, or [allocations for] the pay of the troops (*ḳul*) or [for] supplies for the palace or for the kitchens or for the stables – [in each case income] should be sufficient [to cover expenditure] and indeed leave a small balance.

The grand vizier should introduce into the *dīvān* as *defterdārs* prudent and intelligent and serious-minded men who are experienced in the raising of revenue (*taḥṣīl-i emvāl*); he should give them liberty of action and entrust matters freely to their hands. But they, for their part, should not be carried away by their own notions or personal fancies but be most diligent in attending to the finances of the *pādişāh*. In the reign of our present *pādişāh*, Ibrāhīm Paşa[56] and Iskender Çelebi[57] were the most prominent men of the age through [the sultan's] favour and [bestowal of] titles: the *pādişāh* himself would visit their mansions and their pleasure-gardens, and they had become the cynosure of the eyes of the whole world. Finally, however, at the time of the conquest of Baghdad, both were exposed to [the sultan's] wrath, the one because of various imputations made when he became *serdār*, the other because of his deficiencies in his management of the [campaign-]treasury and of supplies.

In the management of the treasury, a particular effort should be made that increase of wages (*mevācib*) is not encouraged overmuch, and care should be shown in granting pensions (*teḳā'üd*). If a pension becomes necessary, then the rate has been for a *beglerbegi* 160 *aḳçe* [a day], for a *ḳāḍī'asker* 150, for a *defterdār* 80, for a *ḳāḍī* of a capital 80, for a vizier 250 or 200, and for a *sancaḳbegi* 70. If [such an officer] retires with a *ze'āmet*, then a grand vizier is granted one of [an annual revenue of] 200,000 *aḳçe*, a vizier one of 120,000, a *beglerbegi* one of 80,000, a *defterdār* one of 60,000 and a *sancaḳbegi* one of 50,000. These are given [only] to the deserving among them, who have rendered long service and are incapable of continuing.

It is preferable to allot *muḳāṭa'as*[58] by *emānet*[59] rather than by *iltizām*.[60] It is the *defterdār* who should recommend (*'arż*) [to the sultan the assignment of] *muḳāṭa'as* to fit persons.

The tribute (*ḫazīne*) of Egypt, which amounts to 150,000 gold pieces per annum, is reserved for the *pādişāh*, for his personal expenses.

To sum up, what I have to say regarding Treasury affairs is that the income and the expenditure should be checked every year and the appropriate action should be taken.

---

[56] Ibrahim Paşa, grand vizier from 1523 to 1536, executed after the 'campaign of the Two Iraqs' of 1533–6, against the Safavid Shah Tahmāsb (1524–76).

[57] Iskender Çelebi, *defterdār* from 1525 to 1534, executed in Baghdad in 1535, during the 'Campaign of the Two Iraqs'.

[58] *Muḳāṭa'a*: the exploitation of a source of revenue; a tax-farm.

[59] *Emānet*: management by a salaried treasury agent.

[60] *Iltizām*: management by a tax-farmer.

Chapter Four sets out matters pertaining to the *re'āyā*.
Firstly, it is necessary that *eşkinci*s[61] and *ellici*s[62] and *aḳıncı*s[63] be [raised] from the *re'āyā*, for although the Tatars [of the Crimea] owe allegiance to the Ottoman Porte, yet they are a refractory people, and it does not do to get them to serve on campaigns. The *aḳıncı*s have been designated foragers (*ḳara-ḳulluḳçı*) to the army for [obtaining] provisions.

The registers relating to the *re'āyā* should be kept in the register-office (*defterḫāne*) of the *dīvān*. A survey (*taḥrīr*) should be made every thirty years: the dead and the incapacitated (*marīż*) should be struck out and a new register made. This should be compared with the old register, and the [numbers of the] *re'āyā* [in the new one] should not fall short from [those in] the old register. If the *re'āyā* of a district, fleeing from oppression, go to another district, the authorities (*ḥākim*) of that [second] district should send them back, so that the land (*memleket*) may not be left uncultivated.

The levying of *'avārıż*[64] from the *re'āyā*, at the rate of 20 *aḳçe* once every four or five years, has been introduced. This was collected once in the reign of Sultan Selīm Ḫān; thereafter it has been collected at the rate of 20 *akçe* once every four or five years. It was envisaged as money paid in return for the tranquillity which the *re'āyā* enjoyed, and for the provision of ship-biscuits to the warriors. But it is not a reasonable (*ma'ḳūl*) thing, and it should not be taken every year, so that it may not cause discontent.

It is the customary practice [to levy] oarsmen for the ships. Fit and young men are sent in the proportion of one oarsman to four households (*ḫāne*), and if they serve for some months, they are paid ten *aḳçe* a day from the Treasury.

If one of the *re'āyā*, having by outstanding service shown himself worthy of a *tīmār*, as a special mark of favour becomes a *sipāhī*, his relatives and his father and mother should not enjoy protection (*ṣıyānet*); or if [one of the *re'āyā*] becomes a *dānişmend*,[65] he himself escapes from the statute of *ra'īyet*, but his relations still remain *re'āyā*.

As to the class of the noble *seyyids*[66] – that is, the pure Hāshimite line – many outsiders have entered it. A *naḳībü's-sādāt*[67] has been appointed over them, and those persons who do not appear in their ancient registers, called the *şecere-i ṭayyibe*,[68] should be expelled.

The *re'āyā* should not be given too much latitude. If one of the *re'āyā* is wealthy, he should not be molested; but [at the same time] he should not be permitted to deck himself out like a *sipāhī* in his clothes and apparel, by riding a horse, by the style of his house, or by carrying fire-arms.

This humble creature, full of faults, wrote this treatise in accordance with what I saw and heard as the practice of the noble sultans of old, each of whom modelled himself in piety and justice upon the great *mujtahids*,[69] and in accordance with what I learned during my grand vizierate. It is the glorious and exalted God Who makes easy what is difficult and inspires men to [follow] the right course. May He lead each servant of His to the performance of good deeds and cause him to be remembered for his excellence of character.

---

[61] *Eşkinci*: an auxiliary soldier.
[62] *Ellici*: one of a group of peasants in the service of the military. The role of *ellici*s is unclear.
[63] *Aḳıncı*: a raider based on the Ottoman frontier in Europe.
[64] *'Avārıż*: an extra-ordinary tax, originally levied in times of war or emergency.
[65] *Dānişmend*: a student in a *medrese*.
[66] A descendant of the Prophet.
[67] *Naḳībü's-sādāt*: 'chief of the *seyyids*'.
[68] *Şecere-i ṭayyibe*: 'the pure genealogy'.
[69] *Mujtahid*: an authoritative interpreter of Islamic law.

2 The *dīvān*: a Venetian account

In the second court of the palace there is a very beautiful *loggia*, with a portico before it, exactly like a chapter-house for monks, before which is their cloister. Here sit the four *paşa*s[70] and the secretaries of the Grand Turk,[71] the three *ḳāḍī'asker*s, the *beglerbegi* of Greece,[72] which means the lord of the lords of Greece; it is his business to decide (*mozare*) and conclude matters relating to war; he gives tasks to the troops and increases and decreases their pay, and the Grand Turk together with the *paşa*s ratifies it. There attends also Barbarossa, as *beglerbegi* of the Sea, that is, captain-general of the Sea.[73] Also present is Yūnus Beg, the chief *dragomanno*, that is, interpreter, of the Signior,[74] a Greek from Modon, who has excellent Turkish, Greek and Italian . . .

The Grand Turk never takes part in this public audience, but he has a square window, covered with black silk hangings, which projects above the place where the *paşa*s sit, where he can go, without being seen by anyone, by a certain covered passage. These lords of the audience do not know when the Signior is there or not, so that this doubt makes them all the more attentive in matters relating to justice. This audience is attended also by the *cancellieri*[75] and other noble Turks, and to it on the day appointed anyone, man or woman, of whatever nation, may enter. Those on horseback dismount at the second gate of the palace . . . Those on foot all enter as far as the *loggia* of audience; and if the Janissaries who stand on guard wish to obstruct them, they say 'maslahadumuar',[76] that is, 'I have business', and they are immediately permitted to enter . . .

[In the *dīvān*] people stand in the greatest silence, nor does anyone dare to make any sort of noise, for he would be immediately beaten, and at every audience someone is beaten, in the oddest fashion ever heard (as will be said later). The *paşa*s hear first the most important cases (*cause*), and then all the others, of the poor as well as of the rich, so that no-one departs without being heard and having his case settled. Here they employ neither attorneys nor advocates, but each speaks to his affairs for himself as best he can, and anyone who lacks the language[77] makes use of the *dragomanno*, that is, the interpreter: there are a number of these paid by the Grand Turk. If anyone in advancing his case does not speak respectfully (*molestamente*) or utters any nonsense (*sciocchezze*), he is immediately sent away or beaten.

The *ḳāḍī'asker*s are the chiefs of the doctors of the law, and it is they who judge local cases and matters of conscience and all the appeals which come from the cities outside; for in every city and fortress, and also in the large towns, there is a *ḳāḍī*, and many people appeal from their verdicts (*sentenza*) to the court (*corte*) of Constantinople, where they are reviewed and settled by them, as will be explained more fully. Barbarossa too . . . when he is there hears matters concerning the sea . . .

The *paşa*s rise from this audience or (as they call it) *dīvān* after midday in the summer and

---

[70] The viziers.

[71] The sultan.

[72] Rūmeli. The *beglerbegi* of Rūmeli was a member of the *dīvān* from 1535.

[73] Ḫayrü'd-Dīn Barbarossa (d. 1546) was appointed admiral, with the rank of *beglerbegi* in 1534. A new province – the Province of the Archipelago – comprising the islands of the Aegean and the *sancaḳ*s on the adjoining mainland was created for him.

[74] The sultan.

[75] The *defterdār*s.

[76] Turkish: 'maṣlaḥatım var'.

[77] That is, Turkish.

in winter after the *ikindi*, that is, vespers. Before departing, they eat in this *loggia* three times, once in the morning at dawn, as soon as they arrive, again at the sixth hour, and the third time when they have finished giving audience . . . When they have finished eating and giving audience as has been said, they all go off to the Grand Turk, all the *paşa*s and all the other lords of the audience, and they refer (*referiscono*) to him all that has been done, firstly the doctors of the law, the *ḳāḍī ʿasker*s, the most highly honoured of whom speaks while the others keep silence. The chief secretary[78] has a list (*lista*) on which are the records (*memoriali*) of all the matters dealt with in the audience which need to be referred (*riferirle*) to the Grand Turk, and that memorandum (*nota*) which they make as a record is called *ʿarż*. Then one of the four *paşa*s reports, that is to say, the one who holds the seal of the Grand Turk[79] . . . The decisions (*risolutioni*) and permissions (*grazie*) are all made by the Grand Turk; they [the *paşa*s and so on] merely recommend (*riferiscono*), as do the [Papal] *referendarii in signatura* in Rome, and relate the facts, and the Grand Turk decides (*fa la signatura*), in matters both civil and criminal. So too the *beglerbegi* of Grecia makes recommendation, since he of Anatolia remains for the most of the time at his post: but if he is in Constantinople, he too takes part and states his opinion on matters relating to war, together with the *aġa* of the Janissaries. Finally, when he is there, Barbarossa reports and states his opinion on naval expeditions: but he is not greatly esteemed in Constantinople: although the Grand Turk shows him great favour, because of the need he has of him, yet he does not trust him much, and this is made clear because the Grand Turk always wants to have with him Barbarossa's eldest son, both in time of war and all the time, holding him as it were as a hostage. He does the same with a son of the king of Lesser Tartary[80] and others of his vassals (*suditi*). He recently asked the King of France[81] for a son (so it is said), as a guarantee for himself and in accordance with their custom, but the King, not wishing to give him one, courteously declined (*s'iscusò bellamente*).

3 Submissions to the sultan

3a Submission of the vizier Yemişçi Hasan Paşa[82]

The *ʿarż* of the powerless slave is this: Your Majesty, the principal prop of a campaign is gunpowder. Your Majesty knows that no campaign is possible without gunpowder, as has been many times reported (*ʿarż*) to the imperial stirrup. This year's gunpowder should have been provided last year, and next year's gunpowder should be provided this year. When last year I was at the Porte, the *sancaḳ* of Oltu[83] was granted on the condition of sending 700 *ḳanṭār*[84] of gunpowder a year: and one person was appointed supervisor (*nāẓır*) with the obligation to send 2,700 *ḳanṭār* a year from Ḳaramān. But now, while we were expecting that gunpowder would come from those areas, Ḥasan Paşa,[85] who is in command (*serdār*) against the *celālī*s,[86] has obstructed this and granted the *sancaḳ* and the post of *nāẓır* to other people, so that not one

---

[78] The *re'īsü'l-küttāb*, the chief clerk of the *dīvān*.
[79] The grand vizier. The seal was a symbol of office.
[80] The *ḫān* of the Crimea.
[81] François I (r. 1515–47). François I and Süleymān I were allies against the Habsburg Charles V.
[82] Yemişçi Ḥasan Paşa: grand vizier, 1601–3.
[83] A *sancaḳ* in the province of Erzurum.
[84] *Ḳanṭār*: a measure of weight, about 56.5 kg.
[85] Ṣoḳolluzāde Ḥasan Paşa: commander of the force sent against the *celālī* rebel Ḳara Yazıcı.
[86] *Celālī*: the term applied to rebels in Anatolia.

pound of gunpowder has come from here . . . There is absolutely no gunpowder left here,[87] nor in the frontier fortresses,[88] so that appeals come from them daily, saying 'Help! Send gunpowder', but we have none to send. Not to send gunpowder to them is as much as to say: 'Let the infidels take over straight away'. Gunpowder is not like other things; if provision is not made beforehand to supply it, then, when the time of shortage comes, to produce even 100,000 ducats is useless. All the gold and silver of the world will not supply the place of gunpowder. Fortresses are defended and battles are fought with gunpowder . . . last year only 1000 *ḳanṭār*s came from Egypt, and that is not enough even for eye-shadow. I sent a competent *ḳapucı-başı* to Egypt, and the *beglerbegi* there did not merely refuse to send gunpowder – he would not even let my agent into Egypt . . . Orders are not obeyed, words are not heeded. What use is it for me to be grand vizier when the *beglerbegi* of Egypt ignores what I say and Ḥasan Paşa . . . cancels my arrangements and does the opposite? Can the office of grand vizier be carried out under these circumstances? Your Majesty, the *beglerbegi* of Egypt[89] is still a youngster (*tāze*): you sent him out blindfolded from your imperial *ḥarem* and made him a vizier straightaway, and it is difficult for a man to bear up under so great a favour from Your Majesty. Having been made governor of a province like Egypt and shown such great favour, is he going to pay attention to what a grand vizier says? Your Majesty, this procedure has destroyed the good order of the world: no-one obeys his superior, but does just what he fancies, and so matters have come to this state . . .

3b Submission of the vizier Yemişçi Ḥasan Paşa

Your Majesty, when I reported that 600,000 ducats were necessary for the pay of the *ḳul*s on campaign, you granted 400,000. Your Majesty the pay of the *ḳapu ḳullari*[90] . . . under Nūḥ Paşa, who is commander in Anatolia, amounts to 13,600,000 *aḳçe*.[91] If that amount is sent there, only 300 ducats can go to the Hungarian front, and this cannot be sufficient for the pay of the *ḳul*s serving in Hungary. Your Majesty, if I do not report the facts to Your Majesty, I sin in the eyes of God. What is the commander to do? . . .

3c Submission of the vizier Yemişçi Ḥasan Paşa

Your Majesty, today in the *dīvān* the matter of the pay of the *ḳul*s[92] was submitted to you in detail, and now your *ḫaṭṭ-i hümāyūn*[93] has come, saying: 'Raise money for the pay from the merchants and by selling the effects of Ḥasan Paşa and ʿAlī Aġa,[94] who have been executed. Collect money from here and there and give them their pay'. Your Majesty, by God and the Prophet, I have not been neglectful in the slightest degree over the raising of funds and other state affairs. Had it been possible to obtain cash for this pay-issue by borrowing from the merchants and by casting around here and there and by selling these people's effects, I should not have troubled you . . . It is impossible to borrow from anyone without using torture . . . The

[87] 'Here' probably means Istanbul.
[88] A reference in particular to fortresses in Hungary.
[89] Malḳoç ʿAlī Paşa.
[90] *Ḳapu ḳulları* ('slaves of the Porte'): the Janissaries.
[91] This values the *aḳçe* at 136 *aḳçe* to the gold ducat. See Chapter VIII.
[92] *Ḳul*s ('slaves'): the Janissaries.
[93] *Ḫaṭṭ-i hümāyūn* ('imperial writing'): an order or other document in the sultan's own hand.
[94] The vizier Ṭırnakçı Ḥasan Paşa and the *aġa* of the Janissaries, ʿAlī Aġa, were executed on the orders of Yemişçi Ḥasan Paşa.

*ḳul*s will most certainly demand their pay this Tuesday. This pay has always been paid each year in full, and four or five days before the *bayram*;[95] they are prepared to wait on other pay-days, but not on this one, as Your Majesty knows . . . If they are not paid, they will certainly cause trouble. Your Majesty, this is an extremely critical time. The *ḳul*s are now being ordered for service. Please grant 320 *yüks*[96] for this pay-issue. When the money mentioned comes in, it will be paid into the inner treasury.[97] This is the only solution.

Reply: Raise the money immediately from the outside. It is not possible to give it from inside.[98] Realise that.

3d Submission of the vizier Yemişçi Ḥasan Paşa

This is the petition of the former chief *defterdār* Maḥmūd: When it was proposed to the imperial stirrup that I should be chief *defterdār*, the imperial command was: 'I will grant it, provided that he does not ask for money from the inner treasury'. It is for the *pādişāh* to command. But if the money of which he speaks is the pay for the *ḳul*s and the costs of campaigning, money for these purposes cannot be raised from outside. When campaigns went on for so long a time in the reign of the late Sultan Süleymān, money was regularly supplied from the inner treasury. To raise so much money from outside in these times of disturbances[99] is beyond human power. However, I will exert myself . . . Your Majesty, this man is a competent servant of yours. Grant him the post of *defterdār* . . .

Reply: Why propose to me a *defterdār* like this man? Does he treat my treasury as his *tīmār*? Wages from the inner treasury, campaign expenses from the inner treasury – what use is a *defterdār* like this? It seems that *I* am to be the *defterdār*. There is another Maḥmūd. Summon him and ask him.

3e Submission of Yemişçi Ḥasan Paşa

Your Majesty, when the matter of the post of *defterdār* was submitted to you, you replied: 'I grant him the post on the condition that if he asks for money from the inner treasury, I shall cut off his head'. Your Majesty, no-one wants the post on that condition, for there is no-one who can refrain from asking from the inner treasury, and who can raise money from outside, unless he is capable of working miracles or persuades Gabriel to come down . . . ?

3f Submission of the grand vizier Meḥmed Paşa[100]

Your Majesty. A firman has been written and is about to be sent to the governor of Egypt instructing him to send 3,000 *ḳul*s from the *ḳul*s of Egypt to the campaign in the East,[101] with

[95] *Bayram* ('festival'): here the Feast of Sacrifice, falling in the month of Dhū'l-Ḥijja.

[96] *Yük* ('load'): a sum of 100,000 *akçe*.

[97] Inner treasury: the sultan's private treasury.

[98] That is, from the inner treasury.

[99] During the vizierate of Yemişçi Ḥasan Paşa, the Ottoman Empire was fighting an unsuccessful war in Hungary, attempting unsuccessfully to suppress the *celālī* rebellions in Anatolia and facing a Janissary rebellion. The last year of his vizierate saw the outbreak of war with Safavid Iran. The four petitions from Yemişçi Ḥasan were directed to Meḥmed III (1595–1603).

[100] Lala Meḥmed Paşa: grand vizier, 1604–6. His petition was directed to Aḥmed I (1603–17).

[101] The campaign of Ciğalazāde Sinān Paşa against Shah ʿAbbās in 1604–5.

ten *sancakbegi*s, one of whom is to be in command. On the matter of an exalted indication upon this noble command through the blessed noble rescript (*ḫaṭṭ*) in the words '*mūcibi ile ʿamel olına*',[102] it is for my glorious *pādişāh* to command.[103]

Reply: Done.

4 The sultan's written instructions

When the felicitous *pādişāh* Sultan Meḥmed Ḫān performed the *çıḳma*[104] for the pages, the *ḫaṭṭ-i hümāyūn* was written in these words and was read in all the chambers and the palaces, in 1009 (1600/1). It took place after *bayram* in the month of Dhūʿl-Ḥijja (3 June–2 July), and that is when the *siliḥdar* ʿAlī Aġa went to Egypt as *beglerbegi*. 'Be it known as follows: My *ḳul*s, I have determined for you to go out with honour. This is my admonition to you, that when you go out you should act as is pleasing to God. Let your partiality and affection always be directed this way. If you follow this command of mine, may you be happy in both abodes. If you depart from my command, you will not be happy in this world and the next. Beware of my curse; strive to win my blessing'.

5 The death of a grand vizier: the report of Henry Lello, English ambassador, 1597–1607

After this all was quiett, this Emisgee[105] attending all he could to make a peace with the Emperor, as alike to pacifie the Rebellion in Asia, to the end he might stay at home & enjoy his new married lady:[106] and whyle he attended these busines, an other incident hapned wch gave the G.S.[107] greate disturbe, for that his Shackzadee,[108] to say his eldeste sonne, beinge betwen 18 & 19 yeeres of Age, begane to grieve & murmur to see how his father was altogether led by the old Sultana[109] his Grand mother & the state went to Ruyne, she respecting nothing but her owne desire to gett money, & often Lamented thereof to his mother the young Sultana his fathers weif, not favoured of the Queene mother, who grieved likewise but could not remedie it. Yet she thought wth her self that she would send to a wiseman or fortune teller (for they are very supstitious) to knowe yf her sonne should be the succeeding king & how longe her husband the Emperor should live. aunsweare whereof was retorned her in writing. The Messenger fayling in his messadge delivrd it to the old Sultana in steed of the yong Sultana, who, opening the same, findeth it was directed to her daughter in lawe, wherein was sette downe that within six monethes her sonne should be Emperor not shewing how whether b. the death or deprivacon of his father, wch the Q. mother presentlie comprehended was a plot of Trechery & therewth incensed her sonne the Emperor, who conceaved noe les (& where they ha. any Ielosie they have noe mercie) called his sonne, examined him hereof, who indeede knewe nothing of his mothers action therein. He was layed downe & beaten upon the feete &

102 'Action is to be taken in accordance with what is required'.

103 That is, 'Please write on it'.

104 *Çıḳma* ('going out'): the ceremonies performed when pages left the palace for service outside.

105 Yemişçi Ḥasan Paşa.

106 In 1601, Yemişçi Ḥasan Paşa married Meḥmed III's sister, ʿĀʾişe Sulṭān.

107 *Gran Signior* (Italian): the sultan.

108 *Shāhzāde* ('prince'), in this case Prince Maḥmūd, son of Meḥmed III.

109 Ṣāfīye Sulṭān, mother of Meḥmed III.

bellie, as there faishon is, to make him confess; kept him in Close prison & after two daies was beaten aga., having evy time 200 blowes, & could gett nothing from him. Then the mother was called in question & examined, who confessed she did send unto a wiseman to know her sonnes fortune, but wth no intention of hurte or thought of the depriv. of her husband, whom she tendered so much with many ptestacons of love to him, wch would not satisfie him, espially the Q. mother, but was psentlie that nighte, with 30 more of her followers wch they supposed to be interessed in the busins, shutt up a lyve into sacks & so throwne into the sea. Then he held a councell what he was to do wth his sonne, but to the same called non but only Emisgee & the Muftie,[110] doubting yf all the others should be called & the matter known, the souldiers would rise and deprive him, for they loved the sonne, being a very pper youth & of greate hope, & hated the father for his basenes & cowardlines, suffering him self as a very child to be govned by his mother. In this councell the Muftie was of opinion that by there lawe wthout witnesses he could not be put to death: yet pceav. that nothing but his death would satisfie the father condiscended & gave sentence that [it were better] the sonne were deprived of his lief then the father to live in feare & ielosie of his lief; whereupon the sonne was strangled & most basely & obscurely buryed; yet after his fathers death this psent Turke his brother[111] honored him where he was buryed wth a goodly tombe or monument.

After all this the Q. mother thought she nor her sonne had noe other enemies now to trouble them but that she might goe one in her wonted manner to Rule & govne as she would, & that Emisgee would not (being her Creature, pferrd both to his place & wief by her meanes) any way contradict or crosse her. But contrary to her expecon, he when he sawe (his part & charge being greate) that the Q. mother Reaped the whole benefitt of his place into her cofers, led her sonne after her humor to the greate hurte & piudice of the state & him self not able to mainteyne his porte, secreetely complained to the kinge of the Q. mother, shewing how piudiciall & dishonorable her Councell and advice was to him self & his Empier, she workinge all for her owne ends & purposes, & were she not banished his courts from him, he should shortly see the daunger of it. This advice & Complaint the silly Emperor could not conceale from his mother, but acquanted her, & pceaving Emisgee his drifte & ingratitude towards her, she psently construed it in this manner to her sonne that he had much dishonored him to say he was led by her & that suerlie his drifte was to rise some mischeffe against him . . . The Emperor . . . by her psuasion psent. deprived him of his place wth command to gett him self out of the Citty of Constantinople, wch he did. Yet was not this a full satisfaction to the Q. mother, for she doubted that in contynuance of tyme, by the intercession of her daughter his wief to her brother, he might be receaved againe into grace & so remember her. Therefore she followed her sonne with many calumnacons against him, & left him not untill her sonne se. a comand to strangle him. The *Bustangee-bassa,*[112] accompanied wth some 200 *Iemy-oglans*,[113] coming to the place where he lay to execute the Emperors comand, Emisgee, having advice of it before there comeing, shut his gates & kept th. oute. Then they mounted the walls wth ladders, wherein divs of them were hurte & shott into the bodies with arrowes by him & his people in resisting them, & could not enter his pallace wthout more help . . . In the tyme of this hurly burly, his wief dispatched a way a post wth her letters to her mother & brother, wthall prayer and instance that for her sake he would pdon her husband, vowing that he & she both would

[110] Ebū'l-Meyāmin Muṣṭafā Efendi.

[111] Aḥmed I.

[112] *Bostāncı-başı* ('head gardener'). An occasional duty of the *bostāncı-başı* was to carry out executions.

[113] *ʿAcemī oġlans*.

dpate to the Mecca wthout any further charge or trouble to them & lyve as poore pilgrims. All would not serve, & aunsweare was sent that yf she did trouble them any further in his behalf she should accompany him wth the same death that was appointed to him.

And seeinge no remedy could be had, he yelded & called for the executioner, desiring him only to say his prayers & then do his office; wch he did, stripping him self into his shurte, psenting his garments to his pages; & as the Executioner entered upon him, his first strake him wth one blowe to the ground, then the rest entered & so strangled him wth a corde wch they have for that purpose. His body was comanded to be throwne into a stinking ditch & not to be buryed among muslemen, & this was the fowle end of that greate man.

SOURCES

1 Luṭfī Paşa, ed. Rudolf Tschudi, *Das Asafname des Lutfi Pascha*, Leipzig, (1910). The translation does not follow Tschudi's edition of the text exactly. In some places, VLM has preferred a variant reading recorded in the apparatus.

2 Luigi Bassano, *Costumi, et i Modi Particolari de la Vita de Turchi*, Rome (1545), ch. XX; reprint Franz Babinger (1963), 55–9.

3a Cengiz Orhonlu, *Osmanlı Tarihine Âid Belgeler: Telhisler*, Istanbul (1970), no. 21.

3b Orhonlu, *Telhisler*, no. 33.

3c Orhonlu, *Telhisler*, no. 41.

3d Orhonlu, *Telhisler*, no. 42.

3e Orhonlu, *Telhisler*, no. 93.

3f Orhonlu, *Telhisler*, no. 134.

4 Orhonlu, *Telhisler*, no. 10.

5 Orhan Burian, *The Report of Lello: Third English Ambassador to the Sublime Porte*, Ankara (1952), 14–16.

CHAPTER V

The Provincial Administration and the *Tīmār* System

The earliest detailed description of Ottoman provincial administration appears in the account, dating from the late 1470s, of Ottoman history and institutions by Iacopo de Promontorio, a Genoese merchant in the service of Meḥmed II (r. 1451–81). In passage **1**, he enumerated the *sancaḳ*s in the European and Asian provinces of the Ottoman Empire and calculated the number of troops each 'captain' or *sancaḳbegi* was obliged to bring to war. Most of the revenues in each *sancaḳ* were distributed among the *sipāhī*s, holders of military fiefs (*tīmār*s), who each were obliged to bring to war horses, weapons, armour, tents and armed retainers in proportion to the size of their *tīmār*-income, as described in passage **2a**. Passages **2–6** indicate that, typically, each *tīmār* consisted of a village or villages, where the *tīmār*-holding *sipāhī* resided and from which he drew his income.

Passage **3** demonstrates how the government maintained control of *tīmār*s by making periodic surveys of each *sancaḳ*, recording the names of all adult male taxpayers (although the the *sancaḳ*s in Europe also included widows) and their fiscal obligations, as well as all sources of revenue and how the revenue was distributed. From the detailed registers emerging from each survey, exemplified in passage **3**, the administration was able to draw up summary registers, omitting the names of individual taxpayers, but showing the distribution of *tīmār*s and the obligations of their holders (see also passage **2a**). Surveys were made in newly conquered areas and at certain intervals – nominally every thirty years – thereafter. Passages **2, 3, 4** and **5** show that, as the original registers went out of date, marginal notes were added to record changes in the occupancy of *tīmār*s and the distribution of revenues. Particularly major battles would result in many deaths, and the re-allocations of *tīmār*s would always be made in their immediate aftermath, as evident in passage **6**. Since revenues belonging to private individuals were not available to the treasury for distribution as *tīmār*s or as *ḫāṣṣ* assigned to the sultan, viziers or governors, the seizure of private property was a means for the sultan to increase his available resources: Meḥmed II in particular became notorious for his confiscations, described in passage 7.

While the *tīmār*-holding cavalry made up the bulk of the Ottoman army before the end of the sixteenth century, the sultans also drew on other troops, including the *aḳıncı*s (the raiders on the European frontier), the *ʿazab*s (infantry raised through a levy on urban youth, see passage **1**) and volunteers attracted by the prospect of booty or the award of a *tīmār* (see passage **8**). When there was no campaign, the *sipāhī*s resided on their *tīmār*s, where they also had a role in maintaining order in the locality. Passage **9** indicates that in some provinces on the frontier, warfare was continuous, with raids, counter-raids and sieges a daily and year-round reality. Yet, great fortunes could be made, as passage **10** shows.

1 From the report of Iacopo de Promontorio, c1475–80

Greece[1]

The *beglerbegi* of Grecia, the captain-general over all the captains, *subaşı*s[2] and *ḳāḍī*s,[3] has under him seventeen captains,[4] each with a following (*conducta*) for himself as set out below; and beyond this he has particularly under himself 1,500 fighting men (*armigeri*), with their own pay, whom he pays from his own funds. He has as income in Grecia of 32,000 ducats, through various benefices (*beneficii*),[5] and furthermore very profitable perquisites (*regalie*), principally 4,000 ducats from the said captains and similarly from the abundance of other less important offices which he grants to whomever he wishes. Yet he is obliged in time of war to bring with him at his own expense the said fighting men, all mounted, one third of them with bow, arrows, cuirass (*corazei*), coat of mail (*panziere*), shield, sword, lance and iron mace, with 150 horses in horse-armour (*imbardati*), all in good order; the rest with bow, arrows, sword, shield, mace and lance, apart from those to whom the Signior[6] sometimes grants cuirasses, helmets, bows and coats of mail.

He holds court and palace in style, like the Grand Turk,[7] according to his own rank. He imposes sentences of death and of all other matters to all the inhabitants of Grecia and its provinces *de jure* and *de facto*, and everything that he does is approved by the Signior without any protest. He maintains by him two *subaşı*s . . . and two *ḳāḍī*s as deputies to administer justice; they have 4,000 ducats of maintenance among the four of them, together with profitable perquisites, but they are obliged, like all others, in time of war and whenever the Signior requires, to lead 50 men, *videlicet* the *subaşı*s 50 each and the *ḳāḍī*s 100 each, who go armed only with bow, arrows, sword, shield and mace.

This *beglerbegi*, when he goes with the army, always travels with all his captains and the army of Grecia one day's march or more in front of the Signior; and thus he forms his own city of pavilions duly arranged as does the Signior. He maintains for his transport 500 camels and 500 mules. When he assumes office, every household (*casa*) in all Grecia is obliged to give him one *aḳçe* (*aspro*). And not that the Grand Turk does not give him any part of these 32,000 ducats from his own [resources], but he is provided from the fees (*staglie*) of Greeks, together with various benefices.

The seventeen captains of war

---

[1] Greece (Italian: 'Grecia'): the Ottoman province of Rūmeli.

[2] *Subaşı* (Turkish: 'army head'): an officer in a *sancaḳ* in possession of a *ze'āmet*, responsible for law and order in his district and, on campaigns, acting as an officer of the *tīmār*-holding cavalrymen.

[3] *Ḳāḍī*: a judge in a Muslim court, acting as both judge and notary.

[4] *Sancaḳbegi*s.

[5] That is, *ḫāṣṣ*.

[6] The sultan.

[7] The sultan.

First, the captain of Constantinople. His captaincy reaches as far as Varna, towards the Black Sea, and in the other direction as far as Panidos on the way to Gallipoli. He has as income of 60,000 [sic!] ducats a year and has beneath him one *subaşı* and one *ḳāḍī*. He has the income of his province, that is, from every household of Greeks 10 *aḳçe* and of Turks 20 *akçe*. But he is obliged, whenever the army . . . sets out, to bring with him 1,200 men, all on horseback . . .

[Summary of military obligations]

Captain		*Income*	*Bards*[8]	*Men*
1.	Constantinopoli	60,000 ducats	50	1,200
2.	Galipoli	11,000	nil?	1,100
3.	Adrianopoli[9]	9,000	60	1,300
4.	Nicopoli and Zagora[10]	12,000	70	1,500
5.	Vidin	6,000	50	1,100
6.	Sophia	10,000	55	1,300
7.	Ceruia Lazari[11]	8,000	—	900
8.	Ceruia Dispoti[12]	5,000	50	1,000
9.	Vardarii[13]	12,000	100	1,500

. . . a great captain, formerly ʿAlī Beg son of Evrenos, a great lord . . . [of the 1,500 men] the majority are his slaves.

10.	Scopia[14]	13,000	150	1,600
11.	Albania Schenderbei[15]	? 20	800	
12.	Boxina Regno[16]	5,000	25	900
13.	L'altra Boxina[17]	4,000	?	600
14.	Albania Araniti[18]	5,000	25	1,000
15.	Larta, Loxitoni, and Cetines[19]	7,000	40	1,200
16.	Moree[20]	10,000	60	1,300
17.	Monastirij[21]	12,000	50	1,000

[8] Bards (Italian: *barde*): horse-armour. Iacopo is recording the numbers of heavy cavalrymen that each *sancaḳbegi* is required to bring to war.
[9] Edirne.
[10] Nikopol and Stara Zagora.
[11] Serbia. The land of Lazar Branković (d. 1458).
[12] Serbia. Probably the land of Lazar's brother, Gregor Branković (d. 1459).
[13] The Vardar Valley, the hereditary territory of the Evrenos family.
[14] Skopje.
[15] The territory of Skanderbeg (d. 1468), around Krujë, Albania.
[16] Royal Bosnia. The territory of the former Kingdom of Bosnia.
[17] Hercegovina, the former territory of count Stephen Vukčić.
[18] Southern Albania, territory of the Arianit clan.
[19] Arta, Lamía, Athens.
[20] The Morea, the Peloponnese.
[21] Bitola.

. . . These are about 22,000 men, not costing the Signior anything as regular payment, although it is true that he makes various gifts to them: he even gives arms sometimes to some who are not well armed.[22]

The akıncıs

When the Signior wishes to assemble an army (*perforzo*), there always stand ready in Grecia in all provinces Turks, 8,000 men, all horsemen, called *aḳıncı*s (*achengi*), who have the privilege of sowing[23] on the holdings (*tenitorio*) of the Signior as much as two or three pairs of oxen can plough without paying tithe. They are nothing but corsairs by land, living in the villages of subject Christians. They are obliged at the behest of the Signior to ride wherever he commands at their own cost . . . Of the 8,000, only 6,000 go, the other 2,000 remaining to guard against enemies on the frontiers; that is: **6,000.**

The ʿazabs

Similarly, when he wishes to undertake a campaign, he causes to be selected for war-service in various populous places Turkish craftsmen and peasants called *ʿazab*s (*azappi*), and they number some 6,000. Each of them when in the field has 2 *aḳçe* a day, and no more; their captain has 12. When it comes to an engagement, they are sent ahead like pigs without any mercy, and they die in great numbers; they are cowardly (*poltroni*), going on foot, and they turn their backs – with bow, arrows, sword, cuirass and wooden mace; that is: **6,000.**

The lord *beglerbegi* of Turchia, captain-general over other captains and lords of Turchia, resides in Amasya . . . He has under him 15 captains of provinces, who . . . in time of war lead (the captain-general included) about 17,000 men, although some few remain on the coasts for protection against enemies. He has as income 22,000 ducats in some provinces near to his residence from various perquisites belonging to his office, and from hearth-taxes (*focagij*), 20 *aḳçe* for each household, once a year, from Turks only; and furthermore he has taxes (*gabelle*) and imposts (*datij*) belonging to himself . . . In time of war . . . 300 *barde* and 1,200 men.

[Summary of military obligations]

Captain		*Income*	*Bards*	*Men*
1–2.	Tocati et Amazia[24]	27,000	1,000 4,000	(10,000)

. . . The eldest son[25] of the Grand Turk holds two captaincies . . . he is about 35 years old, the son of an Albanian slave-girl . . . He maintains an army of 10,000 warriors at his own expense, all mounted, with about 1,000 *barde*. But because he is near to Tamburlano,[26] he does not depart; when the Signior asks, he sends to the *beglerbegi* 4,000 of the aforesaid 10,000 . . .

[22] In fact, 20,800, but *perhaps* the contingents of the *subaşı*s and *ḳāḍī*s are to be counted in [VLM].
[23] In a reprise of this passage (p. 61), Iacopo adds 'by the hands of their slaves' [VLM].
[24] Tokat and Amasya.
[25] Prince Bāyezīd.
[26] This does not refer to Timur (Tamburlaine) but, as Iacopo explains, to the son of the Aḳḳoyunlu sultan Uzun Ḥasan (d. 1478), possibly Uğurlu Muḥammad, or Uzun Ḥasan's successor, Yaʿḳūb.

3–4.	Canderone[27]	8,000	— 650	(1,650)

. . . He maintains 1,650 men . . . In time of war he sends into the field to the Signior 650 men, without bards. The remaining 1,000 stay on the frontiers as protection against the Soldano[28] and Ḳaraman . . .

5.	Saltarea[29]	15,000	100	1,400
6–8.	Salcan, Aidin and Mentexe[30]	19,000	300	3,500

. . . The second son, called Çelebi,[31] holds three captaincies . . . If this son were not there, these captaincies would be distributed to three persons.

9.	Belgamo[32]	6,000	25	700

. . . A land largely depopulated for fear of corsairs in the time of the father of this present Turk . . .

10.	Bursia[33]	12,000	80	1,700
11–12.	Angori[34]	25,000	100	1,800
13.	Ottomangic[35]	7,000	30	900
14–15.	Castamina[36]	14,000	120	2,550

. . . It consists of two captaincies, sometimes given to two, sometimes to one. At present, the third son of the Signior[37] is appointed captain . . .

2 An entry in a *tīmār*-register, with marginal notes

2a Tīmār *of İnebegi and Ḥüseyn, sons of* serʿasker *Ḥasan*

themselves in coats of mail	one lad each	one *tenktür*-tent[38] for each two men[39]

[27] Alanya.
[28] The Mamlūk sultan.
[29] Antalya?
[30] Saruḫan, Aydın and Menteşe.
[31] Prince Muṣṭafā. 'Çelebi' means 'prince'.
[32] Bergama.
[33] Bursa.
[34] Ankara.
[35] Osmancık.
[36] Kastamonu.
[37] Prince Cem, third son of Meḥmed II. He held this *sancaḳ* from 1469 to 1474.
[38] Apparently, a small tent, brought on campaign by holders of lower-value *tīmārs*.
[39] The 'men-and-tent' notes in *tīmār*-registers show the number of retainers, the armour and the tents that the holder of the *tīmār* was required to bring on campaign.

Tīmār of İnebegi and Ḥüseyn, sons of *ser'asker* Ḥasan
They hold a *berāt* of the sultan

1. [İnebegi] died. Transferred to Oḳçu Ḳaraca. 1st decade of Rabīʿ I 851 (17–26 May 1447). Edirne.
2. Died. Share of this Oḳçu Ḳaraca given to Yūsuf son of Ṣūfī Sāmī of Şehirköy.[40] I Dhū'l-Qaʿda 852 (January 1449). Edirne.

Village of Yılınça	Village of Pirvol
households: 21	households: 7
revenue: 1,475 [*akçe*]	widows: 1
	revenue: 771

2b [Possibly relating to the village of Yılınça]

At present this village has been given by transfer from Yūsuf son of Ṣūfī Sāmī to Delü Ḫıżr; he holds it and serves. Last decade of Jumādā I 857 (29 May–7 June 1453). The camp at Istanbul.[41]

2c [possibly relating to the village of Pirvol]

At present this village has been given as supplement to ʿAlī, the *çeri-başı*[42] of Sofia. Second decade of Shawwāl 857 (24 October–3 November 1453). Filibe.[43]

Village of
Ponor

households: 48
widows: 2
revenue: 3013

[In total]

villages: 3	households: 76	widows: 3	revenue: 5,259

[40] Pirot.
[41] This entry in the register was made immediately after the fall of Constantinople, in the sultan's camp.
[42] *Çeri-başı* ('troop-commander'): an officer commanding a division of *tīmār*-holding cavalry from a *sancaḳ*.
[43] Plovdiv.

3 Two entries from the detailed register of Āmid, 1518[44]

3a Tīmār *of Yemini the Kurd, a* sipāhī *of the* sancaḳ *of Āmid*

The village of Ḥāne Ḳabrān, *tīmār* of the aforenamed

Şāh Ḳulı, son of Cān Ḳulı: 1 *çift*[45]	Ḥüseyn, son of Cān Ḳulı: 1 *çift*	Ḥüseyn, son of Pīr Ḳulı: 1 *çift*	Ḫüdāvirdi, son of Tañrıvirdi: 1 *çift*
Ḳara Seydī, son of ʿAlī: 1 *çift*			

Total: 5 households

Çift-tax	*Nāʾibcik & vālīcik* tax[46]	*Bevvābī*-tax[47]
5 *çift*s at 24	Grain – 10 *kiles*[48]	at the same rate – 10 *kiles*
120	70	70

Dehnīm-tax[49]	Fodder-tax	Cattle-tax	Irregular taxes
Cash	Cash	at 2 *akçe* per head	55
17	50	15	

$^1/_5$ of wheat	$^1/_5$ of barley produce
250 *kile*	90 kiles
2,000	450

Total: 2,937 [sic!] [Registered on] 1 Ramaḍān 924 (6 September 1518)

3b Tīmār *of Saʿduʾllāh the* yaṣavul,[50] *a* sipāhī *of the* sancaḳ *of Āmid*

The village of Altunaḳar, *tīmār* of the aforenamed

ʿİzzü'd-Dīn, son of Ḥāccī Aḥmed: 1 *çift*	Celāl, son of ʿAlī: 1 *çift*	Bayram, son of Caʿfer: 1 *çift*

[44] The 1518 register of the *sancaḳ* of Āmid was the first to be made after the Ottoman conquest of the district. The taxes recorded here are identical to those levied under Aḳḳoyunlu rule, although their value is expressed in Ottoman *akçe*. The Ottoman system of taxation was applied throughout the *sancaḳ* after the second survey in 1540.

[45] *Çift*: a peasant tenement, nominally the amount of land a family could cultivate with one yoke of oxen.

[46] In origin, possibly a tax for the maintenance of the governor (*vālī*) and his deputy (*nāʾib*).

[47] Possibly a tax in lieu of tolls paid at the city gates.

[48] *Kile*: a measure of grain, in Āmid c.12.8 kg.

[49] *Dehnīm* ('five percent'): apparently a tax on poultry.

[50] *Yaṣavul*: here perhaps a sergeant responsible for ordering the ranks in battle. Probably a position held under the Aḳḳoyunlu regime before the Ottoman conquest of Āmid in 1516.

Meḥmed, son of the Arab: ½ *çift*	ʿĀlī, son of the Arab: ½ *çift*	Ḳāsim the Kurd: ½ *çift*	Yūsuf the Armenian: ½ *çift*

ʿÖmer the Kurd
Total: 8 households

Çift-tax	*Nāʾibcik & vālīcik*- tax	*Bevvābī*- tax
5 *çift*s	Grain – 10 *kīle*s	at the same rate – 10 *kīle*s
120 [*aḳçe*]	70	70

Dehnīm-tax	Fodder-tax	Cattle tax	Irregular taxes
Cash	@ 100 bundles per *çift*	10 a*ḳçe*	53
17	50		

1/5 of wheat	1/5 of barley and millet
250 *kīle*s	130 *kīle*s
2,000	780

Total: 3,170 [*aḳçe*]

Arable land [with] derelict dwellings
Empty plots: 4 *çift*s
Estimated yield: 500 *aḳçe*

4 Sundry marginal notes in a summary-register of c1445, Thessaloniki etc.

Tīmār of the Lagator Rayko.

[note] Died. Hanged as he was proved to be a brigand. Transferred to his son Kraso. July 1451. Sofia.

[note to a village] Given to the infidel named Yavan. One of those who fled from Belgrade and came in. October 1453. Filibe.

Village of Ḳaraḳoç. Boatmen. They run boats on the Vardar, at the transit-point of Vilkat within the boundaries of ʿAvretḥiṣarı.[51] The boats are royal *waqf.* The boatmen hold decrees of the late Emīr Süleymān Beg[52] and the sultan,[53] exempting them from all imposts (*ʿavārıż*).
Households of Muslims: 8 of Christians: 2

Tīmār of Ḳāsim and Aḥmed, sons of Ḳul Ḥamza; they hold it jointly and serve by turns. [note] Since it was reported of this Ḳāsim that he fled from before Istanbul, his share was taken away and given to Ḫıżr, the *ḳul* of Sāmlu ʿAlī Beg, in addition to the *mezraʿa*[54] named Yanaki which he already holds. He and Aḥmed serve by turns, except that when the *pādişāh* or the *beglerbegi* of Rūmeli goes on campaign, they are both to serve. December 1453. Edirne.

[51] Kilkis.
[52] The eldest son of Bāyezīd I. Ruled in Rūmeli from 1402 to 1411.
[53] This is probably a reference to Meḥmed I (1413–21) whom sources often refer to as 'the Sultan'.
[54] *Mezraʿa*: an area of arable land without habitations.

[note to a village] At present it has been taken and given to the *voivode* Dan-oğlu,[55] who presented a noble *tevḳī*ʿ,[56] in exchange for the village of Gostomenos, which has been given to the emperor (*tekfur*) of Istanbul. July 1451. Sofia.'

5 Marginal notes in a similar register of 1455, Skopje

5a Tīmār *of Mūsā, retainer (*ḫidmetkār*) of ʿĪsā Beg*

[note 1] Given to the Janissary Yūsuf of Stanimaka: he renders service to the fortress. 16 July 1463. Camp at Kaçanik.

[note 2] Since this Yūsuf of Stanimaka committed homicide, this *tīmār* has been taken away and given to the doorkeeper (*kapucı*) Ḳırık Mūsā, slave of the sultan (*ġulām-i mīr*) . . . August 1466. Camp at Prilep.

[later entry] Village of Mavrova. Not in the register. Since nobody held it, it was given to two infidels, Dimitri and Oliver, one of them to serve, *cebelü*,[57] each year. 23 December 1462.[58] Istanbul.

households: 12 revenue: 624 copied from the document.

[note] After this Oliver became a Muslim by the name Süleymān, the *tīmār* of ʿAlī, listed two folios below, was added to this *tīmār*, and the whole of the *tīmār* was confirmed to this Süleyman. Date noted there.

5b Tīmār *of Yūsuf, kinsman of the* mīr-aḫur[59] *Ḥamza Beg (value: 1,453)*

[note 1] Given with his consent to his son ʿAlī. 11 July 1463. Camp near Ras.

[note 2] Since he [ʿAlī] committed banditry, it was given to the new Muslim Süleymān, mentioned two folios above. August 1466. Iştip.[60]

[later entry] *Mezraʿa*[61] of Yelov Dol. Not in the register. Since nobody held it, it was given, by the document (*mektūb*) of Umūr Beg, to the infidels Giorg and Miladin, because they undertook to bring it into cultivation, to guard that pass (*derbend*), and to serve annually by turns. 23 December 1462. Istanbul.

[note 1] At present this village, together with the village of Botoçane below and Hotule (?) two pages on and Zormişte one village down, have been given to ʿO̱smān of Ḳastamonı. 29 June 1462. Edirne.

55 Vladislav II, *voivode* of Wallachia (1447–56), son of Dan II (1422–31).
56 A firman verifying his claim.
57 *Cebelü* ('armoured'). That is, he is to serve with the armour and weapons specified in the *tīmār*-register; or, he is to bring one armed retainer.
58 Date given according to the Julian calendar.
59 *Mīr-āḫur*: master of the sultan's stables.
60 Štip.
61 *Mezraʿa*: an area of cultivated land without dwellings.

[note 2] *Mezra'a* of Yelov Dol, eighteen folios down, given to this 'Osmān as a supplement. Date noted there.

6 Two *tīmār* grants[62]

6a Thessaloniki: the tīmār *of Meḥmed [comprising] the village İspere Kelb (?) [worth] 4,100 [*akçe *per annum]*

Bayraḳdār[63] Meḥmed, the standard-bearer of the *beglerbegi* of the province of the Archipelago,[64] 'Alī Paşa,[65] has stated that the above named has died. He bears a command [entitling him] to a *tīmār* in Rūmeli with an initial value of 3,000 *aḳçe*s. Since he recently performed outstanding services in the fleet under the aforenamed and has requested [that he be given the vacant *tīmār*], it has been decreed [that it be given to him] with the surplus value.

6b Yalaḳabad [in the sancaḳ *of] Ḳocaeli: the* tīmār *of Ivaz [comprising] the village of Ḥarmanlı and others [worth] 5,000 [*akçe *per annum]*

Da'ūd (?), who holds a *tīmār* worth 3,000 *aḳçe* in the aforementioned *sancaḳ* and is entitled to a *tīmār* of 7,000 *aḳçe*, has petitioned that the above-named is dead and his *tīmār* vacant and has requested [that it be given to himself]. This has been decreed, with the 1,000 *aḳçe*s surplus.
[Both dated first decade of Jumādā II 979 (21–30 October 1571)]

7 Conversion of privately owned revenue to a *ḫāṣṣ*-estate

To the *ḳāḍī* of Serres:
When the felicitous *tevḳī'*[66] arrives, be it known that: Heretofore I sent to you a noble decree with the order: 'I have made the *mülk*[67]-village of Glamovik-oğlu, dependent on Serres, into *ḫāṣṣ*. You are to lease it out (*muḳāṭa'aya ver-*) and inform my Porte [what arrangements you have made]'. Now I have assigned (*ta'yīn*) 10,000 *aḳçe* from the income of that *mülk* to the orphan son of that Glamovik as a *tīmār*, for him to serve with my victorious army. Therefore, I have commanded that: if the orphan son of this Glamovik-oğlu himself accepts this *muḳāṭa'a*[68] and undertakes (*iltizām*) to hand over to my Porte the excess over and above 10,000 *aḳçe*, you are to grant [the *muḳāṭa'a*] to him, and inform [me] in writing at what price you have granted it. If he does not undertake this, you are to grant the *muḳāṭa'a* to someone else, and at the revenue time (*ḥāṣıl vaḳti*) this Glamovik-oğlu is to take the 10,000 *aḳçe* which I have ordered and is to serve with my victorious army. Thus you are to know . . . [October 1472]
      In the camp of
      Beşiktaş

---

[62] Both grants were made following the battle of Lepanto (1571), when deaths in the battle left many *tīmār*s vacant.
[63] *Bayraḳdār*: standard-bearer.
[64] The admiral (*ḳapudan paşa*) was *beglerbegi* of the [Aegean] Archipelago.
[65] This could refer either to the Admiral Mü'ezzinzāde 'Alī Paşa, who lost his life in the battle, or to his successor Uluç 'Alī Paşa.
[66] The *tuğra* at the head of the document, guaranteeing its authenticity.
[67] *Mülk*: private property; land, the revenues of which are privately owned.
[68] *Muḳāṭa'a*: a bundle of revenues leased out as a tax-farm.

8 A call for volunteers before the Moldavian campaign, 1484

To all the *ḳāḍīs*:

When the exalted *tevḳī*ʿ arrives, be it known that: Seeking assistance from God and from the Prophet, I have embarked on a great *ġazā*, which, God willing, will end in victory.[69] Now each of you is to cause a proclamation to be made in the places under your jurisdiction that persons who are eager for the *ġazā* and the *jihād*, persons who seek booty, persons who are good fighters earning their bread by the sword, persons seeking to gain a *tīmār* by their service (*yoldaşlıḳ*) should come with their weapons and gear and join me on this blessed *ġazā*, so winning the merit of the *jihād* and gaining plunder and booty. Each man who serves will enjoy my favour according to service, a *tīmār* and *dirlik*[70] for him who wants a *tīmār* . . . and *pencik* will not be taken on what such people have won . . . First decade of Rabīᶜu'l-awwal 889 (29 March–7 April 1484).

In the camp of
Devletlü Kabaaġaç

9 Submissions by and to the *sancak begi* of Bosnia, c1512–14[71]

9a The sancaḳ begi *of Işkodra*[72] *to Yūnus Paşa of Bosnia*

A noble command has reached me from the Porte, saying: 'Since the Hungarians are massing and their objective is Bosnia, I have commanded that you are to go and join Yūnus Paşa with your *subaşı*s and your *sipāhī*s'. In obedience to the exalted order, we have set out. I request you to send word by the bearer to tell me what the situation is with regard to that quarter and where you wish me to go. If the matter is urgent, I will make all haste, in order to have the sooner the pleasure of joining you.

Your sincere friend (*muḥibbuhü'l-muḫliṣ*).
Ḫüsrev

9b The sancak begi *of Zvornik to Yūnus*

Your Excellency, my Mighty Sultan: My humble submission is that on Monday 30 Rajab we found an occasion against the fortress of Srebrenica and seized it. We rallied the cavalry and infantry of this area and, under the auspices of the felicitous *ḫüdāvendgār*[73] and of your lordship, the fortress has been taken. The bearer ʿAlīşīr has been sent to your lordship with this good news.

The weak servant (*bende-i naḥīf*)
Muṣṭafā b. ʿĪsā

---

[69] The call is for volunteers for the campaign to take Kiliya and Akkerman in 1484.

[70] *Dirlik* ('a living'): a fief.

[71] The introductory and closing honorifics have been omitted.

[72] Shkodër.

[73] The sultan.

9c The sancaḳbegi *of Bosnia to the* nā'ib *of Visoka*

Mounted *beşlüs*[74] have been appointed from the Porte to the fortress of Kamengrad, and provisions and fodder must be sent to them. When my friendly letter arrives, you are to assist the bearer, the *beşlü-başı* Caʿfer Beg, to buy with his own money as much fodder as he needs at the fixed price. This matter is important and urgent. Shawwāl, 917 (December 1512).

9d The sancaḳ begi *of Bosnia to the Porte*

On the road leading to Kluč and Kamengrad, which are fortresses of the *pādişāh* lying four days' journey within enemy territory, there is a strong fortress named Sokol,[75] which was in the hands of the infidels. They would cut the communications, so that supplies had to be taken through, with much danger, by two- or three-thousand men. They often attacked the supply-columns, killing many men and imprisoning others. Near this fortress are the graves of many famous *subaşıs* and *ġāzīs*, including Gürz Ilyās, Güzel Tursun and Mü'min Ḫoca, each of whom was a *ġāzī* of *subaşı* rank leading a force of two- or three-hundred campaigners (*yoldaş*): they were killed near this fortress and their graves are still places of pilgrimage (*ziyāretgāh*). When recently the supplies for the *beşlüs* of Kamengrad were sent off under my officer with a force of *beşlüs* and *akıncıs*, the infidels set an ambush near Sokol and attacked the column. The *ġāzīs* fought back, and there was much fighting; but finally, under the good auspices of the *pādişāh*, the infidels were defeated and scattered: some took refuge in Gölḥiṣār, some fled to Sokol. The *ġāzīs* pursued them and entered the fortress [Sokol] before they could shut the gates. They killed some and captured others, and the fortress has been taken. On 1 Dhū'l-Ḳaʿda a garrison was put in. So I report.

Near Sokol are mines, like those of Srebrenica which are called *ḫāṣṣ*; they could quickly be put into production and would supply the wages for all the fortresses of Bosnia. To travel to the imperial fortresses would become easy, so that one could go from the Well-Protected Territories to Sokol with just one or two men, and then on to Kluč and Kamengrad. Thus the troops and all the *reʿāyā* in that region would live in tranquillity, praying for the welfare of the *pādişāh*.

The circumstances have been submitted (*ʿarż*) accurately to the *bāb-i saʿādet*.[76] Beyond that (*bāḳī*), the command belongs to the exalted Porte.

9e The sancaḳbegi *of Bosnia to the Porte*

The bearers, the *bölük-başı*[77] Süleymān and Ḫıżr of Manastır, having brought [me] a letter (*mektūb*) from the garrison commander of Vinçac (?) requesting a request (*ʿarż-dāşt*) for the quarterly pay of the troops of that fortress; the matter is reported to the *bāb-i saʿādet*. This fortress being in the immediate vicinity of Jajce,[78] they cannot engage in agriculture at all, and their only support is from their salaries (*ʿulūfe*). It is requested that this fortress be treated as a

---

[74] *Beşlü* (Turkish: 'fiver'): a fortress guard levied from a village.

[75] Sokolovići.

[76] *Bāb-i saʿādet* ('gate of felicity'): the gate between the inner and outer palace where the sultan held audience; by extension, the sultan; the sultan's government.

[77] *Bölük-başı* (Turkish: 'head of a division'): an officer in the Janissaries.

[78] Jajce was in the hands of the Hungarians.

special case; that the wages be transferred (*ḥavāle*) from some source near at hand; and that an exalted decree [to that effect] be granted to the two bearers.

9f The sancaḳbegi *of Bosnia to the Porte*

I have received a letter from the garrison-commander of Sokol, saying 'Since this fortress was 'written',[79] Selāniklü Ilyās has not shown up: but the fortress is in the *dārü'l-ḥarb*,[80] and we must have men (*yoldaş*)'. Therefore he has granted (*tevcīh*) the vacancy (*gedük*) to the bearer, the able campaigner (*yarar yoldaş*) Ḥüseyn of Aḳḥiṣār, who has served and stood guard in the fortress since it was taken and has requested an *'arż-dāşt* [from me] reporting the matter. The matter is therefore reported to the *bāb-i sa'ādet* with the request that this vacancy be granted to the afore-mentioned . . .

9g The sancaḳbegi *of Bosnia to the Paşa*[81]

The *tīmār* of Dolna Luca in the *nāḥiye* of Brod, formerly held by Şīrmerd of Filibe, a member of the garrison of Zvornik, was given some time ago to the bearer, Ketḫüdā-oġlı Meḥmed, also a member of the garrison. Meḥmed has been constant in his service and has in fact been in possession of the *tīmār*; but his *berāt* has been lost, and he has requested an *'arż-daşt* for the renewal of his *berāt*. The matter is therefore reported to your excellency by this dutiful note, and it is requested . . .

9h The sancaḳbegi *of Bosnia to the Paşa*

I have received a letter from the garrison-commander of Voynitsa saying that the two brothers Ḥasan and Meḥmed, who hold a share of the village . . ., hold jointly one fortress-vacancy (*ḥiṣar gedügi*); but they both have families and cannot manage on one vacancy, so Ḥasan has given up his half-vacancy and departed. The commander has requested an *'arż-daşt* reporting the matter, in the hope that the vacancy can be consolidated in favour of the bearer Meḥmed, who holds the other half. The matter is therefore reported to your excellency . . .

10 'The good old days'

On this glorious *ġazā*[82] my grandfather, the *alay-begi*[83] of Bosnia, was present, as was my late father with his seven brothers – all valiant warriors, whose homes in the *nāḥiye* of Bīḫa (?) near Sarajevo are still known to the inhabitants as belonging to 'the sons of the *alay-begi*'. Thus [because I am going to give their testimony on the battle] I must make some mention of them: if any of their connections sees this, I ask them to utter a prayer for them and other learned [readers] to accept my apologies [for speaking of my family]. Well then, in the year 877 (1463) the pre-eminent *ġāzī*-sultan . . . Meḥmed [II] conquered most of Bosnia; seeing that it was necessary to appoint a *sancaḳbegi* of Bosnia, he gave the post first to Minnet-Begoġlı

---

[79] That is, since all receipts and expenditures on the fortress were recorded.
[80] *Dārü'l-ḥarb* ('abode of war'): territory controlled by non-Muslims.
[81] Presumably the *beglerbegi* of Rūmeli.
[82] The campaign of Mohács in 1526.
[83] The holder of a *ze'āmet*, serving as an officer of the *tīmār*-holding cavalry.

Meḥmed Beg. My great-grandfather Ḳara Dāvūd Aġa, then being the *siliḥdār*[84] of the sultan, probably through his relationship to Meḥmed Beg or for some other reason, became *alay begi* of Bosnia with a *ze'āmet* of 50,000 *aḳçe*, and so left (*çıḳ-*) the *ḥarem*.[85] Indeed he [later] received by *berāt* the *ze'āmet* of Yaḥyā-Paşazāde Küçük Bālī Beg, who had led the vanguard in a battle in the reign of Sultan Bāyezīd [II]. That *berāt* is still in my possession and I was thinking of putting it, word for word, into this compilation – I may do so later. Let no-one think, by comparison with the present day, that for a *siliḥdār* to 'go out' with a *ze'āmet* is somehow discreditable: the status of a *ze'āmet* of 50,000 *akçe* in those days was several times higher than that of a vizier nowadays.

I frequently heard my father say: 'We did great things in Bosnia in the days of Ḳara Malḳoç Beg. The *ġāzī*s won such booty that I alone, with my one retainer (*ḫidmetkār*), gained booty worth 60,000 *aḳçe*. Malḳoç Beg sent fully armoured prisoners (*dil*)[86] and heads to the Porte, with a recommendation that my father be given an increase (*teraḳḳī*) and I be given an 'induction' (*ibtidā*),[87] saying: 'The *alay begi* was solely responsible for this [successful] *ġazā*'. My father as *alay begi* was given an increase of 500 *aḳçe*, but my *ibtidā* was made dependent on service in one further campaign. I then went on the 'Irāḳeyn campaign[88] [and rendered service] at the Pass of Karakan. Then, 'because the *alay-begi*'s son has campaigned without an appointment (*ma'zūl*)', I was granted an induction-*tīmār*. God knows that I could not have come home more happily if they had given me the whole *sancaḳ* of Bosnia!' So he would say, pointing out the comparison for those who in later days despised an order for an *ibtidā*.

SOURCES

1 Franz Babinger (ed.), *Die Aufzeichnungen des Genuesen Iacopo de Promontorio de Campis über den Osmanenstaat um 1475*, Munich (1967), 48–60.
2 Nikolaj Todorov and Boris Nedkov (eds), *Turski izvori za balgarskata istoriya*, Sofia (1964), 358 (text), 291–2 (facsimile).
3 M. M. İlhan, *Amid (Diyarbakır): 1518 Tarihli Defter-i Mufassal*, Ankara (2000), 340 (text), 103 (facsimile); 344 (text), 105 (facsimile).
4 Todorov and Nedkov, *Turski izvori*, 366, 384, 406, 406, 420.
5 H. Šabanović, *Krajište Isa-bega Ishakovića*, Sarajevo (1964), 31, 97, 98, 100, 84.
6 Başbakanlık Ottoman Archives, Istanbul, Kâmil Kepeçi 223.
7 Halil İnalcık, *Fatih Devri Üzerinde Tetkikler ve Vesikalar*, Ankara (1954), 169–70, pl. X.
8 Kâmil Kepeçi, 'Bursa'da şer'î mahkeme sicillerinden ve muhtelif arşiv kayıtlarından toplanan tarihi bilgiler ve vesikalar', *Vakıflar Dergisi*, 2 (1942), 406, document II.
9a British Museum, MS Or. 11194, D 13.
9b British Museum, MS Or. 11194, D 17.
9c British Museum, MS Or. 11194, C 12.
9d British Museum, MS Or. 11194, C 13.
9e British Museum, MS Or. 11194, C 17.

---

[84] *Siliḥdār* ('weapons bearer'): a member of the corps of *siliḥdār*s, one of the six divisions (*altı bölük*) of the sultan's household cavalry.

[85] That is, service in the palace.

[86] Dil ('tongue'): a prisoner retained as an informant.

[87] *Ibtidā* ('beginning'): an initial grant of a *tīmār*.

[88] The campaign of the Two 'Irāqs (1534–6).

9f British Museum, MS Or. 11194, C 18.
9g British Museum, MS Or. 11194, C 22.
9h British Museum, MS Or. 11194, C 23.
10 İbrāhīm Peçevī, *Tarīḫi Peçevī*, Istanbul (1283/1866), 1, 87–8, writing in his old age in 1640.

CHAPTER VI

The Religio-legal Institution

SECTION 1 LAW AND RELIGIOUS PRACTICE

Sunnī Islam recognises four schools of law: the Ḥanafī, Shāfiʿī, Mālikī and Ḥanbalī. While the doctrines of each school do not differ widely one from the other, each school developed its own juristic tradition with legal practitioners basing their judgements on the works of authoritative figures within the tradition of the school to which they belonged. There were adherents of all four schools in the various provinces of the empire, but the Ottomans always gave precedence to the Ḥanafī. Passages **1a, b** and **c** represent three genres of Ḥanafī juristic writing: an abridgement (*mukhtaṣar*), a commentary (*sharḥ*) and a textbook arranging and presenting the law in the form of cases (*fatāwā*), respectively.[1] Such texts would form the basis of legal education in a *medrese*.

The primacy of the Ḥanafī School became firmly established during the reign of Süleymān I (r. 1520–66). He went to the extent of forbidding *ḳāḍī*s in Anatolia and Rumelia from giving judgements that follow *shāfiʿī* rules, even in cases where Ḥanafī jurists specifically allow the practice, as seen in passage **2**.The prohibition mirrors a general movement in the mid-sixteenth century to impose uniformity and orthodoxy in law and religious practice. Like his predecessor Kemālpaşazāde (in office 1526–34), the *muftī* of Istanbul Ebū's-suʿūd (in office 1545–74) attempted to explain Ottoman land-tenure and taxation in Islamic terms, as demonstrated in passages **3, 4** and **5**. He also used legal fictions to prevent the political and social upheaval which an over-strict interpretation of the *sharīʿa* might have caused, as evident in passages **6** and **7**. At the same time, passages **8, 9** and **10** indicate that there was a parallel movement towards the establishment of conformity in religious belief and practice.

This had become a vital issue since the rise of the Safavid dynasty in Iran early in the century. The Safavid shahs were heads of a religious order that claimed many adherents among the sultan's subjects. Known as *ḳızılbaş* ('red-heads') from their distinctive head-gear, these maintained contact with the shah through their local leaders (*ḫalīfe*s), and the Ottoman authorities sought to control them by maintaining a network of informers and actively persecuting their communities, as evident from passages **11, 12, 13** and **14**.

[1] *Fatāwā* is the plural form of *fatwā*. However, as an element in the title of a formal juristic work (for instance, *Fatāwā Qāḍīkhān*, *Fatāwā Hindīya*) the term indicates the format of the book, and not that it is a collection of *fatwās*.

1 Passages on the law of sale from Ḥanafī legal texts

1a From al-Matn *of al-Qudūrī (d. 1037)*

Sale is contracted by an offer and acceptance when both are expressed in the past tense. When one of the contracting parties accepts, the other has the choice: he may accept it in the session, or he may reject it. If either of them leaves before the acceptance, the offer is invalid. If either of them leaves the session, the offer is nullified. When there has been both an offer and an acceptance, the sale is binding and neither party has the option to retract, unless there is a defect [in the goods] or [the purchaser] has not seen them.

1b From al-Ikhtiyār fī taʿlīl al-Mukhtār *of al-Mūṣilī (d. 1284)*

[Sale] in law is the exchange of goods with a market-value against goods with a market-value, [with one party] transferring ownership [and the other party] taking possession. If [the transfer of the property] is the transfer [not of ownership but] of the benefits, only then it is lease or marriage [and not sale]; if it is gratuitous, it is a gift . . . (Sale is contracted with two expressions in the past tense [such as when] one says: 'I have bought' and [the other] says: 'I have sold'),[2] because it is a declaration (*inshāʾ*), and in all contracts the law regards notification (*ikhbār*) as a declaration, by which a contract is concluded. The past tense [is also used] because it implies an offer and its conclusion, whereas [the use of the present or] future tense [may imply] a readiness, a command or delegation. [Sale] is therefore concluded [using] the past tense . . .

1c From al-Fatāwā *of Qāḍīkhān (d. 1195)*

(a) If [a person] sells a stone as a ruby when it is glass; or points to a slave and says: 'I have sold you this male slave' and it is a female slave, the sale is void, because they are different categories, so this is a sale of [something that is] non-existent. Similarly, if [a person] buys something from a man against a debt which [the vendor] owes him, and they know that he does not owe him a debt, then [the sale] is void . . .

(b) A man sells something in a lawful sale and defers payment until after the harvest and threshing. In the opinion of Abū Ḥanīfa, the sale is defective. But in the opinion of Muḥammad [al-Shaybānī], the deferral is valid, because postponement after the sale was voluntary. [The vendor] accepted the deferral for an unspecified period. It is as if the purchaser were a guarantor for a certain sum until the harvest or threshing . . .

2 A *fatwā* on the application of Shāfiʿī doctrine

If Hind, whose husband has disappeared and has no means of sustenance, appeals to Shāfiʿī doctrine, and if a Shāfiʿī *ḳāḍī* separates (*tefrīḳ*) her and allows her to marry another husband, and if Zeyd then re-appears, can he take her back as his wife?

---

[2] The passage in parentheses is a quotation from the author's own work, *al-Mukhtār*, on which *al-Ikhtiyār* is a commentary.

Answer: No (Aḥmed).[3]

Another answer: A prohibition has been made by the sultan: 'Shāfiʿī doctrine is not to be current in the lands of Rūm'[4] (Ebūʾs-suʿūd).

3 A *fatwā* on acquiring land for a new mosque construction

If the old mosque in a town falls into ruin, and if Zeyd seeks permission to build another in its place, and if, after permission is granted, Zeyd wishes to build a larger one because the population is more numerous but the old site is too small, may Zeyd build on another site near it?

Answer: Not without the sultan's permission. But if the old site is too small because there are houses around it, it is legal (*meşrūʿ*) to make a compulsory purchase of those houses for their [proper] price.

4 A *fatwā* on taxing land occupied by descendants of the Prophet

Is it legally essential that descendants of the Prophet[5] should, like other *reʿāyā*, pay the *çiftlik*-taxes[6] for the land which they occupy?

Answer: Yes. Those taxes appertain to the land, not to the person who occupies it.

5 A *fatwā* on a *kāḍī* granting unauthorised tax exemptions

If the *ḳāḍī* Zeyd, who is carrying out a survey of a district (*vilāyet*) at the sultan's command, and is not authorised to enregister various *dhimmī*s as exempt (*müsellem*), nevertheless enregisters some of them as exempt from *jizya* and *ʿavārıż-i ʿörfiye*[7] and gives them a certificate (*temessük*) to this effect, what must be done to Zeyd?

Answer: If they are not crippled or poor, he must be dismissed; but if they are, he has acted according to the *sharīʿa* and nothing is to be done.[8]

6 A *fatwā* on Rumelian *kāḍī*s issuing *hüccet*s

*Ḳāḍī*s in Rūmeli issue *ḥüccet*s [confirming] the validity of the sale, purchase, deposit, loan, pre-emption and exchange of land in the possession of *reʿāyā* there and enter [the transactions] in their *sicill*s. Does this accord with the noble *sharīʿa*?

---

[3] 'Aḥmed' is the *şeyḫüʾl-Islām* Kemālpaşazāde (d. 1536) who issued the original *fatwā*. The supplementary answer is by Ebūʾs-suʿūd.

[4] Although Ḥanafī law did not permit a deserted wife to seek a legal separation from her husband, Ḥanafī jurists permitted her to go to a Shāfiʿī *ḳāḍī* to seek a separation. However, in a decree from the early 1540s, Sultan Süleymān removed the right of his Ḥanafī subjects to have recourse to a Shāfiʿī *ḳāḍī*, hence Ebūʾl-Suʿūd's answer. 'The lands of Rūm' refer to Anatolia and Rumelia.

[5] Persons claiming descent from the Prophet (*seyyid*s) could claim fiscal and other privileges. The government was anxious to prevent the proliferation of such claims and of the privileges that attended them.

[6] *Çift*[*lik*]-tax: the annual tax due on a peasant tenement (*çift*[*lik*]).

[7] A *dhimmī* is a non-Muslim subject of an Islamic sovereign, paying a poll-tax (*jizya*) in return for legal protection of life, limb and property. *ʿAvārıż-i ʿörfiye* ('customary incidentals') are extraordinary taxes, levied originally in times of war.

[8] The disabled and the elderly were exempt from taxation.

Answer: It is contrary [to the *sharīʿa*]. The only thing that is taken into account (*iʿtibār*) is the *sipāhī*s' granting [the land] by *ṭapu*. For *ḳāḍī*s to write 'sale' and 'purchase' is erroneous. They must write: 'Zeyd, having assigned (*tefvīż*) to ʿAmr the possession (*taṣarruf*) of the fields of which he has possession, and having received the sum of so much in return, and having ceded [his claim], the *sipāhī* Bekr received a [*ṭapu*] tax (*resm*) of so much and gave it to ʿAmr'.[9]

7 A *fatwā* on *sipāhī*s taking a tithe

If the *sipāhī* Zeyd takes 2 *kīle* in 15 as tithe (ʿ*öşr*) is that *ḥalāl* by the *sharīʿa*?

Answer: To call what the *sipāhī* takes 'ʿ*öşr*' arises from ignorance. If it were ʿ*öşr* it would be given to the poor. It is *ḫarāc-i muḳāseme*, which does not have to be taken at one in ten; it is imposed according to the productivity of the land, and it is permissible for it to be up to the half.[10]

8 A *fatwā* on Muslim villagers neglecting prayer

If, in some Muslim villages, there is no mosque at all and the inhabitants do not pray as a congregation, must the *ḳāḍī* force them to build mosques and punish (*taʿzīr*) those who [then] neglect the prayer?

Answer: Yes. Strict commands (*ḥükm*) were written in the year 944 (1537–8) to the governors (*vülāt*) of the Well-protected Domains to oblige the inhabitants of such villages to build mosques and to attend prayer regularly, and action must be taken in accordance with the command.[11]

9 A *fatwā* on money fines for neglecting prayer

If a *ḳāḍī* punishes with a fine (*taʿzīr biʾl-māl*) those who neglect the prayer, is the money which he takes licit (*ḥalāl*) to the *ḳāḍī*?

Answer: No. After some time, when [the culprit] has resumed attending the prayer, the money must be given back to him.[12]

---

[9] In the Ottoman Empire, land could not be held as private property. The normal way to gain a title (*ṭapu*) to the land was by payment of *ṭapu*-tax to the *sipāhī*. Nonetheless, peasants and others did buy and sell land among themselves, and Ebūʾs-suʿūd was trying to regularise the practice. In recording such 'sales', the *ḳāḍī*s were forbidden to use any term denoting sale or purchase, but instead ordered to use the term 'consignment' (*tefvīż*), and the transaction was complete only after the new occupant of the land had paid the *ṭapu*-tax to the *sipāhī*.

[10] The question is whether a tithe (ʿ*öşr*) is legal when it is levied at a rate of more than 10 percent. The answer justifies taking the tax at a higher rate on the grounds that what the Ottomans called ʿ*öşr* was not to be equated with the tithe (ʿ*ushr*) of Islamic law, but rather the Islamic *ḫarāc-i muḳāseme*, a tax on crops levied at a rate of up to 50 percent according to the productivity of the soil.

[11] Non-attendance at prayer would identify a person as a heretic, and specifically as a *ḳızılbaş*. Compulsory attendance at congregational prayers in a mosque would help maintain the outward forms of orthodox Muslim worship.

[12] In Ḥanafī doctrine, the term *taʿzīr* has the sense of 'discretionary punishment', understood as strokes of the lash. Ḥanafī jurists were very reluctant to admit to the legality of money fines (*taʿzīr biʾl-māl*). When they do so, they require the money to be returned after the culprit has reformed. Ebūʾs-Suʿūd is here following the prescription of Ḥanafī jurists rather than common Ottoman practice.

10 A *fatwā* on executing a repentant heretic *şeyh*

[From a series of answers to a persistent questioner on the legal reasons for executing a heretic (*zindīḳ*) *şeyḫ* who had repented:]

Answer: The repentance of a heretic is acceptable if he repented before he was arrested . . . It is true that, according to Abū Ḥanīfa, the obligation to kill him lapses, but according to the other *imāms*[13] he remains [even after repentance] exactly as he was. The *ḳāḍī*s of the Well-Protected Domains are ordered and authorised[14] to pay no regard to the repentance of those who show contempt in matters of religion, but to sentence them to death in accordance with the rulings of the other *imāms* . . . [But the *ḳāḍī* is a Ḥanafī . . .] According to Abū Ḥanīfa, what lapses through repentance is the obligation to kill him, not the lawfulness of killing him.

11 Command to the *sancakbegi* of Amasya

It has been reported that: 'In the *ḳażā* of Budaḳözi the man known as Süleymān Faḳīh is one of the *ḫalīfe*s[15] from 'up there':[16] he co-operates and mixes with various heretics (*mülḥid*) and trouble-makers (*müfsid*), who are so-called *ḫalīfe*s, and persistently leads the people astray'. I have commanded that you are secretly to track down this Süleymān and his followers, and if indeed they are *ḫalife*s from up there and are people of *küfr* and *ilḥād*[17] and are behaving contrary to the *sharī'a*, then, with the cognizance of the local *ḳāḍī*, you adroitly are to seize them: without revealing it to anyone,[18] you are to take them secretly to the Ḳızıl Irmaḳ and drown them. Alternatively, if it is appropriate to do so, charge them with theft and banditry and punish them. 22 Rabī' I 976 (14 September 1568)

12 Command to the *sancakbegi* of Amasya, İlyās beg

You have reported as follows: 'In accordance with the decree, something was proven against those belonging to 'up there': they were seized and dealt with by night, without anyone knowing about it . . . Some mischief-makers have fled to other *sancaḳ*s; the sending of decrees is requested, ordering the *beg*s and *ḳāḍī*s to surrender them when asked and to search for them if they have disappeared . . . Now I have every confidence in your uprightness. You have shown great shrewdness in dealing with these troublemakers. You have done well . . . Decrees have been sent to the *sancaḳbegi*s and *ḳāḍī*s of Çorum, Kastamonu and Kanġırı,[19] for them to hand over, without argument, bandits who have fled to other *sancaḳ*s. I have commanded that you are to attend to this in person. If in your *sancaḳ* there are people against whom it is proven

---

[13] Although the opinions of Abū Ḥanīfa were, in principle, the most authoritative, the Ḥanafī school recognised the validity of alternative views attributed to other jurists within the school. This gave the executive authorities a range of opinions from which to choose. The answer here is deliberately vague in not stating which of the Ḥanafī *imams* did not recognise the repentance of heretics.

[14] That is, ordered by the sultan.

[15] *Ḫalīfe* ('follower'): here, a representative of the Safavid shah.

[16] 'Up there' (*yuḳarı cānib*): the territory of the Safavid dynasty, Iran.

[17] *Küfr*: unbelief; *ilḥād*: heresy.

[18] That is, the *ḳāḍī* is not to enter the case into his *sicill*.

[19] Çankırı.

according to the *sharīʿa* that, being heretics, they have caused *fesād*,[20] you are to seize and punish them according to the *sharīʿa* . . . You are to act with discretion and not disturb people who are causing no trouble. This is a matter of the first importance, and you are to waste no time. 13 Jumādā II 976 (3 November 1568).

13 To the *sancakbegi* of Kastamonu and the *kāḍī* of Küre

You have reported: 'The preacher (*ḫaṭīb*) Meḥmed, known as Etmekçi-oğlı, is a notorious heretic, outside the *madhhab*[21] of Islam, who denies the Four Friends.[22] He speaks improperly of the Qur'ān . . . The *ʿulemā* and *imām*s and *ḫaṭīb*s and the populace of Küre in general have lodged this complaint: 'He is notorious for heresy. He has been registered frequently. The [local] *muftī* has given a *fatwā* sanctioning his killing. He must be done away with. The *çavuş* [. . .] has been sent to make an investigation. I have commanded that you are to attend to this personally . . . If it is proven according to the *sharīʿa* that this *ḫaṭīb* indeed spoke as has been reported, you are to imprison him and to send a written report, together with copies of the register entries. Then you are to act in accordance with the orders which you will receive. 11 Rabīʿu'l-awwal 976 (3 September 1576).

14 To the *kāḍī* of Niksar

My *ḳāḍīʿasker*[23] has made this submission: You sent to the *dīvān* by the hand of Mevlānā[24] Seyyid Muṣṭafā a letter and a legal decision (*ḥükm*) stating that Erdivan, the *şeyḫ* of the *zāviye* of Matayı in your *ḳażā*, Çıraḳ, ʿAlī and others are *ḳızılbaş* and *rāfiżī*s:[25] a decree was sent ordering an investigation, but when they were summoned to the court they disappeared: because the Erzman brothers were already listed in the register of *ḳızılbaş*, the *beglerbegi* executed them: and disinterested Muslims have reported that these others have disappeared. Having ordered that 'the appropriate authorities should find them and they be sent to the galleys',[26] I have commanded that you should make those whose duty it is to find them, find and arrest them, and you should carefully and with justice examine their cases. If what you have reported is proven and evident according to the noble *sharīʿa*, you should send them, together with a copy of the *sicill*s recording the case, to my threshold of felicity,[27] in the custody of trustworthy men, so that they may be placed in the galleys. You should give a strong warning to the men in whose custody you are sending them, to be careful not to allow them to escape. However, the

[20] *Fesād*: trouble; corruption.

[21] *Madhab*: doctrine.

[22] 'Four Friends': the four Orthodox Caliphs, the successors to the Prophet Muhammad. The *ḳızılbaş* did not recognise the caliphates of the first three Orthodox Caliphs, Abū Bakr, ʿUmar and ʿUthmān.

[23] *Ḳāḍīʿasker* (Arabic: 'military judge'): one of the two senior *ḳāḍī*s in the Ottoman Empire. The *ḳāḍīʿasker*s of Rumelia and Anatolia each had a seat in the imperial *dīvān* and dealt with the legal affairs of the European and Asian provinces, respectively.

[24] *Mevlānā* (Arabic: 'our lord'): a title of a *ḳāḍī*.

[25] *Rāfiżī* (Arabic): a heretic.

[26] Service on the galleys was imposed on 'those guilty of a serious crime, but not meriting capital punishment'. The number of criminals sent to the galleys depended on the requirements of the fleet at any one time. This order was issued during the war of Cyprus (1570–3) which created a heavy demand for galley service.

[27] That is, Istanbul.

investigation is to be strictly proper (*tamām ḥaḳḳ üzre*), and you are to be very careful not to act in any way contrary to the *sharīʿa*. 24 Shaʿbān 980 (30 December 1572).

SECTION 2 THE ADMINISTRATION OF LAW

Although Christians and Jews in the Ottoman Empire enjoyed some legal autonomy in intra-communal affairs, Islamic law applied to all subjects of the Ottoman Empire. Passages **1** and **2** give witness that the Islamic courts were open to both Muslims and non-Muslims, and their use was compulsory in cases involving both a Muslim and a Christian or Jew, as is clear from passages **3** and **4**. As in other Islamic realms, the two figures most essential to the administration and enforcement of the law were the *ḳāḍī* and the *mufti*, as is evident throughout the extracted text passages.

*Ḳāḍī*s were appointees of the ruler, from whom they derived their authority, and acted both as judges in disputed cases and as notaries, recording each transaction in their *sicill*s as it occurred.[28] *Sicill*-entries reflect many aspects of socio-economic life in the Ottoman Empire, including financial transactions (see passages **3**, **4** and **5**), family matters (see passages **6** and **7**), complaints about goods (see passages **8**, **9** and **10**), payment of dues and taxes (see passages **11** and **12**) and ownership claims (see passage **13**). Passages **14** and **15** demonstrate that, in criminal cases and cases of affray, the *ḳāḍī*s shared their duties with the secular authorities – particularly *sancaḳbegi*s and *subaşıs* – who were responsible for administering punishments after the *ḳāḍī* had established and recorded the facts of the case. Parties to litigation or notarial transactions would receive a written record (*ḥüccet*) of the proceedings, as exemplified in passages **1** and **2**. In addition to their judicial and notarial duties, Ottoman *ḳāḍī*s also functioned as administrators in their judicial district, usually acting in response to sultanic decrees, copies of which appear in their *sicill*s, like in passages **16** and **17**.

In contrast to the judgements issued by *ḳāḍī*s, which carried the authority both of the *sharīʿa* and of the sultan, the *fatwā*s issued by *muftī*s were not decrees: for a *fatwā* to come into effect, it required enforcement by a *ḳāḍī* or other executive authority. A *muftī* is simply a recognised expert in the law, and a *fatwā* is an authoritative answer to any question put to the *muftī*, who is supposedly independent of any secular power and responds to queries solely on the basis of the *sharīʿa*. The power of *fatwā*s, therefore, derives from the authority of the *sharīʿa* and the standing of the *muftī*. In much of the Islamic world recognition as a *muftī* was an informal matter, and *muftī*s had no official status as such.

While this may be true of some provincial *muftī*s in the Ottoman Empire, during the course of the sixteenth century the *muftī* of Istanbul – known from late in the century as the *şeyḫü'l-islām* – became the head of the Ottoman *ʿulemā* and, in practice, a senior figure in the government. The growing importance of the office owed much to the abilities, long tenure and closeness to the sultan of Ebū's-suʿūd (in office 1545–74) (see passages **2–10 in SECTION 1** above, as well as **18–37** below). It was open to anyone, from the humblest members of the public to the sultan himself to ask questions of the

[28] *Sicill* (Latin: *sigillum*, via Arabic; *sijill*) in Ottoman usage can refer either to a *ḳāḍī*'s register, or to a single entry in such a register.

şeyḫü'l-islām, and the subject matter of his *fatwā*s ranges from the mundane to matters of state, as one can observe in passages **37–41**. However, as *fatwā*s supposedly had universal validity, their protagonists – even if well-known in reality – are always cloaked in anonymity.

1 A *hüccet* on repairs to a monastery on Mount Athos

He![29]

[note 1] This business was transacted before me. Signed: the humble Seyyid Velī b. Meḥmed, *mevlā*[30] in the *ḳażā*[31] of Sidrekapsı.[32]

[note 2] The matter is as it is set out and the affair as it is written. Signed: the humblest of God's servants Meḥmed b. Ḳāsim el-Cemālī, *ḳāḍī* in the city of Selānik,[33] authorised by the command of the bearer of authority (may his Caliphate be eternal) to supervise the *waqf* estates (?).

[note 3] When this document was presented to me, I found it consonant with the *sharī'a*, so I read it over and signed it. I, the humble ʿAbdü'l-Ḳādir b. Bahā'ü'd-Dīn . . . *mevlā* in the *ḳażā* of Sidrekapsı.

The reason for the writing of the document is this, that the monks Alexi and Papa-Maximo of the monastery Dionysiou, one of the monasteries of Mount Athos, came and said: 'The tower before the door of this monastery has become very ruinous and is very dangerous to our monastery. Grant permission (*icāzet*) for its repair'. Therefore, I went in person and inspected it and saw that it is indeed extremely dangerous. Permission has been granted for it to be rebuilt on the old site to a length of 15 *ḳulaç*[34] and a breadth of 5½ *ḳulaç*, in five storeys. At their request, this certificate has been written and given to them, for them to produce as evidence (*iḥticāc*) in time of need. This business was transacted and [the document] written on 1 Rabīʿ I 926 (20 February 1520).

Witnesses:
Meḥmed Çelebi b. Sinān, the *emīn* and Ḫoca Şīrmerd b. ʿAbdullāh and Ibrāhīm b. Ḫıżr and Rüstem b. ʿAbdullāh and Muṣṭafā b. Ilyās

2 A *hüccet* on returning a defective slave-girl to the vendor

El-Ḥācc Aḥmed son of ʿAbdu'llāh made a statement of [his] plaint in the court of the noble *sharī'a*, in the presence of [Şaʿbān]: 'A month before the date of [this] document I bought from the said Şaʿbān for 31 gold ducats, on condition that she be free from all defects, this slave-girl of medium height, so-and-so. I paid the said sum against payment and receipt. I have now noticed that the said slave-girl has two molar teeth missing, [one] on the right and [one]

[29] 'He!' (Arabic: *huwa*): God. This invocation of the Almighty appears at the head of Ottoman documents.
[30] *Mevlā* ('lord'): title used by *ḳāḍī*s.
[31] *Ḳażā*: a *ḳāḍī*'s judicial and administrative district.
[32] The mine and mint to the east of Thessaloniki. Greek: Siderokaúsia.
[33] Salonica, Thessaloniki.
[34] *Ḳulaç*: fathom. A measure of depth, probably about 1.83m.

on the left of her bottom jaw. This must have happened before I purchased her. If this should cause a reduction in market-price, I seek her return on account of the defect'.[35]

When the said Şaʿbān was examined, he replied: 'I did, in fact, sell this slave-girl to the said plaintiff with the aforementioned defect, for 31 gold ducats and received payment. Furthermore, he saw and accepted her with that defect'. He acknowledged that the said slave-girl was already disfigured with the aforementioned defect when she was with him.

The said El-Ḥācc Aḥmed denied in his presence that he had accepted [her] with the aforementioned blemish. Evidence was then sought conformable to his plaint against the said vendor. When [the defendant] acknowledged that he was incapable of producing definitive evidence, [the plaintiff] demanded that he swear an oath. When the said purchaser had also sworn by God that, at the time of purchase, he neither saw the blemish nor accepted her with it, an obligation arose and a warning was given that the said slave-girl be returned to the aforenamed vendor and the above mentioned sum be returned to the aforenamed customer.[36]

[Before 1625].

3 A *sicill*-entry on the sale of a vacant site by a Muslim to a *dhimmī*

The same Ḥasan stated, in the presence of the *dhimmī*[37] Sarkis: 'I have given him for *ṭapu* the vacant site of some two paces [in breadth] adjoining his house in the quarter of Behlūl and have received 10 *ṣāhīs*[38] as *resm-i ṭapu*.[39] Sarkis confirmed this. Noted.

4 A *sicill*-entry on a debt owed by a *dhimmī* to a Muslim

Creditor: Riḍvān b.ʿAbdullāh: debtor: the *dhimmī* Baḫşī b. Ḫūbyārī: sum: 115. So acknowledged by the debtor.

5 A *sicill*-entry on a money loan

Ḥāccī Ḥasan Çelebi summoned Bālī b. Ḫıżr, saying: 'He borrowed 15 *ṣāhī* from me: now I demand this money'. Bālī replied that Ḥasan had been paid and said: 'Let him swear that he has not received it'. Ḥasan refused to take the oath.[40]

6 A *sicill*-entry on the daughter of a recent convert

Mariam, the daughter of Şāhbula who recently embraced Islam, was brought to the court, she not having reached puberty. When she was asked, she said that she was not aware of having

---

[35] In Ḥanafī law, the buyer is entitled to return the goods and recover the price, if the goods do not conform to the vendor's description at the time of the sale.

[36] Definitive proof would have required two eyewitnesses to the sale. In the absence of such proof, the vendor swears an oath that he is telling the truth. The purchaser does the same, so the case is deadlocked. The *ḳāḍī*'s solution is to dissolve the sale.

[37] *Dhimmī*: a non-Muslim resident in the realms of Islam, enjoying the protection of the law.

[38] *Ṣāhī*: a large silver coin, worth 6–8 *aḳçe*, in use in the eastern provinces of the Ottoman Empire.

[39] *Ṭapu*: title to land or property. *Resm-i ṭapu*: *ṭapu*-tax, the fee payable to acquire title. The term *ṭapu* is often used by itself to refer to the fee.

[40] With his refusal to take the oath, Ḥasan lost the case.

reached puberty, so judgement was given that she was a Muslim by reason of dependence on her mother.

7 A *sicill*-entry on divorce and the legality of the wife's second marriage

Bālī b. Bāyezīd from the village of Saraycıḳ complained in the presence of Timūr b. Mūsā: 'Some time ago, I was stricken with leprosy. This Timūr took away my wife Ḳutlu, together with goods of mine worth 30 ducats'. When Timūr was asked, he said: 'Bālī divorced her, and when her *ʿidda*[41] was completed, I married her'. This has been noted. Muṣṭafā b. Ḫalīl and Ḥüseyn b. Muṣṭafā attended as witnesses and gave legal testimony, saying: 'Bālī divorced Ḳutlu and, when her *ʿidda* was completed, she was married to Timūr: she is now his legal wife'. Entered upon request.

8 A *sicill*-entry on cloth measuring short

Muṣṭafā, the market-inspector (*muḥtesib*) of Anḳara, summoned the *yürük* Ḥāccī Bālī b. Menteşe saying: 'This man's homespun (*ʿabā*) measures 11 *arşuns*,[42] whereas it has from of old been the custom that it be 12'. It was measured, and indeed it proved to be 11. Entered upon request.[43]

9 A *sicill*-entry on unsatisfactory goods

The baker Süleymān's bread [is] under-baked. The grocer Receb's weight [is] short. The fruit-seller Ḥasan's 300-*dirhem* weight [is] 10 *dirhem* short . . . Ḥāccī Aḥmed's soap [is] declared, with the cognizance of Muslims, to be no good. Caʿfer's buns [are] undercooked and short of fat . . .[44]

10 A *sicill*-entry on a complaint by the weavers' guild

Şāh Meḥmed and Ḥāccī Meḥmed and other members of the guild (*ṭāʾife*) of weavers summoned Naṣūḥ b. Saḳā and complained: 'Whenever cotton thread comes [on the market], Naṣūḥ pays a higher price and buys it, leaving the other weavers without thread. From of old, when thread came, we would all buy it together and divide it up. We object to his action, which is contrary to the ancient custom'. Naṣūḥ was warned that when thread comes, he is not to buy it just for himself, but it should be divided among them. He undertook to do this. So noted.

11 A *sicill*-entry on a smith not receiving his dues

The smith Muṣṭafā b. Meḥmed summoned his father Meḥmed and said: 'My father employed me, and I performed a lot of work for him, but he won't pay me my due'. Meḥmed denied that he had employed him. When Meḥmed was asked: 'For how much a day do you engage such a

---

[41] *ʿIdda*: the period of three menstrual cycles during which a woman may not marry following a divorce.
[42] *Arşun*: a unit of length, probably c68 cm.
[43] That is, entered at the request of the *muḥtesib* Muṣṭafā, in case of a repeated offence.
[44] A summary of the *muḥtesib*'s report.

person?' he replied on oath: 'Three *akçe* a day, or at the most four; not more'. Judgement was given for nine months' pay.

12 A *sicill*-entry on the payment of tax on a slave-girl

The reason for the writing of this text is that Şaʿbān, who came by the ship of Mūsā Reʾīs, has paid the tax[45] on the Russian girl who is his slave (description: space between eyebrows, dark blue eyes, gaps in upper teeth), and so has been given this certificate (*temessük*).

13 A *sicill*-entry on the ownership of sheep

Ḥasan *subaşı*, *emīn*[46] for strays (*yava*) and *beytü'l-māl*,[47] summoned Meḥmed b. Ḳara from the village of Maʿcūn, saying: 'Some time ago, a certain man went off, leaving a number of sheep in Meḥmed's care. The man has not shown up for a long time, and I claim those sheep'. When Meḥmed was asked, he said: 'Ḫıżr had only 2 sheep, and I bought these for 80 *akçe* each. They number 17, for they bred, but this was after the sale so that the extra ones are mine, too'.

14 A *sicill*-entry on a burglary

Ḥasan b. Receb of Anḳara town came to the court as a plaintiff, saying: 'Muṣṭafā b. Ustād ʿAlī entered my house last night and stole my property. As he was leaving, we heard him and got up and tied him up. He is still in my house, tied up. Let people come and see'. So Durmuş, the deputy (*ketḫüdā*) of the *sancaḳbegi*, and a number of disinterested Muslims went to Ḥasan's house, and indeed Muṣṭafā was lying there tied up, with various objects wrapped up in a rug beside him. This has been noted at the plaintiff's request. Later, when Muṣṭafā was asked about this, he replied: 'This Ḥasan and Ḳaramānī Ḥasan, with their associates, seized me outside in the street and tied me up and forced me into the house'. When he was asked: 'What about these objects [in the rug]?' he replied: 'They put them there'. Since a record of the evidence was requested, this has been noted.

With regard to the Muṣṭafā mentioned in the above entry (*sicill*), it has been noted at the request of the *ketḫüdā*, that Muṣṭafā was drunk and that his breath smelt of liquor.

15 A *sicill*-entry on a violent argument between father and son

Meḥmed b. ʿAbduʾllāh summoned his son Muṣṭafā, saying: 'My son beat me and tore my beard' and produced some hairs of his beard. When Muṣṭafā denied this, Ḥāccī Ḥüsām and Ḳazancıoğlu Muṣṭafā, appearing as witnesses,[48] stated: 'We saw them tearing at each other's beards'.

---

[45] The *pencik* tax for bringing her into Anatolia, probably via Sinop. As a Russian, the girl had probably been captured by Tatar raiders and sold in the Crimea.

[46] *Emīn*: a salaried manager of an enterprise.

[47] *Beytü'l-māl* ('public treasury'): here, unclaimed inheritances.

[48] The testimony of two male eyewitnesses is the normal standard of evidence. In this case, their evidence will override Muṣṭafā's denial.

16 A *sicill*-entry of a command to the *sancakbegi*s and *ḳāḍī*s of Anaṭolı (abridged)[49]

In the time of my late father,[50] a *ḳānūn* was issued, saying: 'When a slave flees from the copper-mines, the reward (*müjdegānī*), wherever he may be caught, is to go to the man who catches him, and the slave is to be handed back; the *yavacı*s and the *beytülmālcı*s[51] are not to intervene. The maximum reward is 100 *aḳçe*: 30 for one day's journey, 60 for two, 90 for three, and for any longer time, no more than 100.[52] Even if, because of the cost of maintenance, the slave is sold when the due time is up, the sale is to be declared void, and the slave is to be returned, for the slaves in the mine belong to me. If this regulation is disobeyed, I shall not stop short of dismissing you . . .' Now Maḥmūd Ketḫüdā, who is on the staff of the mines, has come to my Porte and produced that noble command, and so I have commanded that, as before, when a slave . . .

17 A *sicill*-entry of a command to the *ḳāḍī* and the inspector of *muḳāṭaʿa*s[53]

You reported that the citadel is in disrepair and that you, with expert builders, had inspected it and estimated the cost of repair at 30,000 *aḳçe*: you requested my command [to proceed]. This was submitted to the foot of my Throne on [. . .] and I ordered the repair at that cost. Therefore, I have commanded that you should have the citadel repaired to its former state, taking the estimated cost from the *muḳāṭaʿa*s there. When the work is completed, you are to draw up the accounts and sign and seal them and send them to the Porte: and you are to give to the *emīn* of the *muḳāṭaʿa* from which the money was taken a certificate (*temessük*), so that the sum will be credited when he has to give his account. You are to take every precaution against extravagance, and to complete the work for less than the estimate if that is possible.

18 A *fatwā* on contracting marriage between minors

If Hind, without the permission of the *ḳāḍī*, states in the presence of several persons: 'I have given my daughter Zeyneb, who is not of age, to my brother ʿAmr's son Bekr, who is [also] not of age', and if ʿAmr says: 'I accept Zeyneb as a wife for Bekr', has a marriage been contracted?

Answer: It has been ordered that it should be by permission of the judge (*ḥākim*).[54]

---

[49] This and the following passage reproduce the texts of decrees received by the *ḳāḍī* and entered in his *sicill*.

[50] Selīm II.

[51] The *yavacı* and the *beytülmālcı* are the officials responsible for escaped slaves and unclaimed inheritances, respectively.

[52] The rule that the reward for returning an escaped slave to his or her owner depended on the distance, measured in days, of the journey undertaken to return the slave derives from the *sharīʿa*.

[53] *Muḳāṭaʿa*: a specified bundle of revenues administered as a tax-farm.

[54] The Ḥanafī law of marriage requires a woman or an underage male to have the consent of a male guardian (*walī*), usually their father. Here, however, the girl's guardian is her mother, hence the requirement for the judge to give his permission to the marriage. The judge is acting as the guardian in giving or withholding his consent.

19 A *fatwā* on the validity of contracting marriage without the *ḳāḍī*

Zeyd, without the cognizance of the *ḳāḍī*, marries his underage daughter to ʿAmr's underage son in the presence of witnesses, and ʿAmr accepts. Is the said marriage valid?

Answer: They are fully competent guardians. The *ḳāḍī* cannot fail to accept it.

20 A *fatwā* on re-marrying without intermediate marriage

What, according to the *sharīʿa*, should happen to people who know that Zeyd took [his divorced wife] Hind without an intermediate marriage (*ḥulla*), but kept silence?

Answer: It should be reported to the authorities (*vülāt-i emr*).[55]

21 A *fatwā* on giving customs money as *zakāt*

If the merchants give the money called 'customs' (*gümrük*) with the intention that it is *zakāt*, does it count as *zakāt*?

Answer: Yes.[56]

22 A *fatwā* on giving alms

Given that Zeyd should give *zakāt* on his sheep, does the money that is taken in respect of them by the *mīrī*[57] count as *zakāt* on the sheep?

Answer: If he gives it with that intention, yes.

23 A *fatwā* on a preacher's statement about a *ḳāḍī*

If the preacher says: 'A *ḳāḍī* cannot be a Muslim, and a Muslim cannot be a *ḳāḍī*,' is his preaching permissible?

Answer: If he is referring specifically to the unjust *ḳāḍī*s, yes: if he is referring to *ḳāḍī*s in general, no.[58]

---

[55] If a man divorces his wife with an irrevocable divorce, he may not re-marry her until she has contracted, consummated and been divorced from an intermediate marriage (*ḥulla*). The term which Ebūʾ-Suʿūd uses to denote the authorities echoes the Qurʾānic injunction: 'Oh ye who believe, obey God and obey the Apostle and those in authority (*ūlūʾl-amr*) from among you' (Qurʾān 4:62/59).

[56] *Zakāt* ('alms tax') is a canonical tax, the proceeds of which are for the support of the poor. The payment of *zakāt*, like prayer or fasting, is classified as an 'act of worship' (*ʿibāda*) and, to be valid as such in the eyes of God, must be made with 'sincere intention' (*niyya*). In practice, *zakāt* was never actually levied and to describe customs as *zakāt* is a legal fiction. The revenues from customs (Turkish: *gümrük*, from Greek: *kommerkion*) were not destined to the poor and were clearly not *zakāt*, but by saying that their payment was given with 'sincere intention', the merchants could claim that what they paid was indeed *zakāt*.

[57] *Mīrī* ('pertaining to the ruler'): the treasury.

[58] In insulting *ḳāḍī*s, who administered the *sharīʿa*, a person is insulting Islam itself. In doing so, he becomes an infidel and, to return to Islam, must undergo a ceremony of 'renewal of faith'. A preacher who had become an infidel in this way could not continue to preach.

24 A *fatwā* on the testimony of foreign merchants (*ḥarbī*) against a *dhimmī*

If *ḥarbī*s[59] who have come with *amān*[60] testify on a certain matter against the *dhimmī* ʿAmr, and if they have certificates from the sultan stating that the testimony of *ḥarbī*s against *dhimmī*s is not to be heard, is their testimony acceptable?

Answer: Certainly not. It was ignorant clerks who wrote that clause into their *ʿahdnames*.[61] There can be no decree of the sultan ordering something that is illegal according to the *sharīʿa*.

25 A *fatwā* on a Christian woman's charitable endowment

If the Christian woman Hind, being in sound health, has made an endowment (*waqf*) of her house and garden, which she owned, to the monks of a church for them to recite the Gospel, and if she has handed over [the property] to an administrator and has had the endowment legally registered [by the *ḳāḍī*] and the deed of endowment (*waqfīya*) has been written and [the terms of the endowment] are being carried out; and if then after ten years her heirs, who had been in another place, present themselves and refuse to accept the *waqf*, can they annul it?

Answer: If the monks are all poor, a *waqf* for their benefit is valid. The condition of reciting the Gospel is a nullity (*laġv*). If they are not poor, it is not valid, and the registration was illegal: the heirs may annul it and divide [the estate among themselves].[62]

26 A *fatwā* on the Ottoman conquest of Istanbul and its surroundings

Did the late Sultan Meḥmed [II] conquer Istanbul and the villages around it by force (*ʿanwatan*)?

Answer: It is generally accepted that he did. But the fact that the old churches were allowed to remain indicates conquest by composition (*ṣulḥ*). This matter was investigated in the year 945 (1538/9). A man aged 117 and another one aged 130 were found, and they testified before the investigating commissioner: The Jews and Christians made a secret agreement with Sultan Meḥmed that they would not assist the [Byzantine] Emperor and Sultan Meḥmed did not enslave them but left them as they were, and that is how the city was conquered'. In view of this testimony, the old churches have remained as they were.[63]

---

[59] A *ḥarbī* is a non-Muslim normally resident in the *dārü'l-ḥarb* ('the abode of war'), the lands outside the realms of Islam. Here it certainly refers to foreign merchants bringing a claim against a non-Muslim resident of the Ottoman Empire. A *dhimmī* is a non-Muslim resident in the realms of Islam, enjoying the protection of the law.

[60] *Amān*: here, 'safe-conduct'.

[61] *ʿAhdnāme*: a treaty, letter of agreement bestowing a privilege.

[62] A *waqf* in support of a 'false religion' – here, Christianity – is invalid. However, a *waqf* in support of 'the poor' of any religion is valid. The woman must therefore prove that the monks she is supporting are 'poor' and that the *waqf* is not intended to support the recitation of the Gospel.

[63] Islamic jurists made a distinction between places which the Muslim conquerors had taken by force (*ʿanwatan*) and those which they had taken by composition (*ṣulḥan*). In the second case, non-Muslims were permitted to retain their places of worship; in the first case they were not. This rule had never been observed in practice, but, in the late 1530s, Çivizāde Muḥīyü'd-Dīn Meḥmed who assumed the office of *şeyḫü'l-islām* in 1539 attempted to impose a regime of strict orthodoxy in this and other matters. By producing two 'eyewitnesses' to the conquest of Istanbul in 1453, Ebūʾs-suʿūd was able to 'prove' that the city had been conquered by composition and that the churches and synagogues in the city could therefore legally remain as they were.

27 A *fatwā* on slaves purchasing slaves of their own

When the sultan, without manumitting him, sends his slave (*ʿabd-i memlūk*) Zeyd out of the palace with a stipend, is it permissible for Zeyd to purchase a slave-girl and enjoy (*taṣarruf*) her?

Answer: It is not possible.[64]

28 A *fatwā* on the sultan's slaves contracting marriages

Can the slaves (*ḳul*) whom the Sultan of the Muslims has taken for *pencik*[65] contract a valid marriage without the sultan's permission?

Answer: No.[66]

29 A *fatwā* on a *ḳāḍī* acting outside his jurisdiction

If a *ḳāḍī* who, in accordance with [the sultan's] order acting as an inspector (*müfettiş*) in another *ḳażā*,[67] hears and adjudicates matters other than those prescribed in the order, is his decision valid?

Answer: No.

30 A *fatwā* on the dismissal of a debauched *ḳāḍī*

If the *ḳāḍī* Zeyd goes to a musical wedding and sits down with debauchees at an immoral party; and if ʿAmr seeks a *fatwā* asking: 'What must be done to the *ḳāḍī* Zeyd?' and the answer is: 'Such a man is not fit to be *ḳāḍī*'; and if ʿAmr shows Zeyd the *fatwā* and Zeyd holds on to it and refuses to give it back and says: 'I am a *ḳāḍī* not on the strength of a *fatwā* but by the *berāt*[68] of the sultan', and so shows contempt for the *fatwā*, what must be done according to the *sharīʿa*?

Answer: By his earlier behaviour he is dismissed and his decisions have no validity; he was granted the sultan's *berāt* in the belief that he was of good character (*ʿādil*); when later his debauched behaviour became apparent, he loses his office. Even if his evil behaviour had been known beforehand and the *berāt* had nonetheless been granted, though he were not dismissed, he would deserve it. But by his contempt of a legal decision (*ḥükm-i şerʿī*), he becomes an infidel; and if he does not return to Islam, he is to be killed.[69]

---

[64] A slave cannot own property and therefore cannot buy another slave. Anything a slave purchases is technically the property of that slave's owner. Here the questioner equates a salaried slave (*ḳul*) of the sultan with a slave (*ʿabd*), as defined in Islamic law.

[65] *Pencik*: the share of prisoner-of-war coming to the sultan. See Chapter III.

[66] Slaves require the permission of their owners to marry.

[67] A *ḳażā* is a *ḳāḍī*'s judicial district.

[68] *Berāt*: a diploma of appointment by the sultan. See Chapter III.

[69] Not to recognise the authority of a *fatwā* amounts to a repudiation of the authority of the *sharīʿa*, making the *ḳāḍī* an infidel. His debauched behaviour, in itself, is not legal grounds for his dismissal. However, as an infidel, if he wishes to avoid being executed, he must undergo the procedure for a 'renewal of faith'.

31 A *fatwā* on the death of a falsely accused person after wrongful torture

If the Jew Zeyd, alleging that ʿAmr has stolen his property, gets the *sancaḳbegi* to torture (*ʿörf*) ʿAmr, and if ʿAmr dies a week or so later, and if then those who really stole the property are discovered, what must be done to Zeyd and [the torturer] Bekr?

Answer: The torturer must pay blood-money (*diyet*), and Zeyd must suffer severe *taʿzīr* and long imprisonment.[70]

32 A *fatwā* on extortionate loan transactions

If Zeyd carries out [loan] 'transactions' at 12 or 13 or more for 10,[71] and if testimony is given that: 'In our day the sultan's command and the *fatwās* of the *şeyḫüʾl-islāms* are to the effect that money is not to be lent at more than 11½ for 10', and if he pays no heed but persists, what must be done?[72]

Answer: Severe *taʿzīr* and long imprisonment. He can be released when his repentance is manifest.

33 A *fatwā* on tax income for *sipāhīs*

Are the eighths which the *sipāhīs* take from the produce of *arż-i mīrī*[73] and the money they take under the name of '*çift*-tax' and the tax on bachelors and on sheep and on bees and the *ṭapu*-tax licit [income] (*ḥalāl*) for *sipāhīs*?

Answer: The sheep-tax is the *zakāt* on sheep, and it is not forbidden (*ḥarām*) to a person not possessing 200 *dirhems*. The bee-tax is the tithe on honey, and that too is not *ḥarām* to a poor man. Except for what is taken from a Muslim who has no land, they are not *ḥarām* to a rich man either.[74]

34 A *fatwā* on tax income, including in kind, for *sipāhīs*

Are the 5 *kīle* in 40 of the crops of the *reʿāyā*, and the *çift*-tax of 22 *aḳçe*, and the 6 *aḳçe* from bachelors and the 9 from married men, and the tithe on hives and the bride-tax, all of which Zeyd the *sipāhī* takes, licit?

Answer: When one-eighth has customarily been taken from of old, it is licit (*ḥalāl*). *Çift*-money of 22 *aḳçe* is also *ḥalāl*: in some places the rate is 57. If a bachelor or a married man

[70] In Ḥanafī law, in cases of homicide or injury, it is the person who is the immediate cause of the death or injury – in this case, the torturer – who pays the blood-money. However, in cases where the person was acting under orders, the authorities may, at their discretion, impose a punishment (*taʿzīr*) on the person who gave the order, hence the *taʿzīr* imposed on Zeyd.

[71] That is, at 20 or 30 percent.

[72] A sultanic decree had fixed the interest on loans at a maximum of 15 percent. Even though forbidden by Islamic law, lending money at interest was commonplace in the Ottoman Empire. This was a point of dispute between Çivizāde and Ebūʾs-suʿūd. See Chapter IX.

[73] *Arż-i mīrī*: land under the full control of the sultan, the revenues of which did not belong to private owners or *waqfs*.

[74] In this and the following queries, the questioner is concerned as to whether the taxes levied by *sipāhīs* on their *tīmārs* are licit according to the *sharīʿa*.

has no land, little or much, then there is no basis in the *sharīʿa* for what is taken from them: that is the position with bride-tax, too. The giving of tithe on honey produced on tithe-land (*ʿöşrī yerde*) is obligatory (*lāzim*).

35 A *fatwā* on *bennāk* tax

Can an *emīn* take *bennāk*[75][tax] from the people of a village exempted by noble command from *tekālif-i ʿörfiye*?

Answer: If *bennāk*-money forms part of the *tekālif-i ʿörfiye*, no.[76]

36 A *fatwā* on capitation tax (*ispençe*), grape tithe and taxes on pigs

Is the money called *ispençe*[77] which the *sipāhī* Zeyd takes from his *reʿāyā ḥalāl*? And if, when the grapes are tithed, he takes one measure in seven, and if when they eat their pigs, he takes one *aḳçe* on two pigs, is that *ḥalāl*?

Answer: What is taken on pigs is illegal (*nā-meşrūʿ*).[78] But if the others have customarily been taken from of old, they are not to be changed.

37 A *fatwā* on a rebellious son of the sultan

If one of the sons of a just sultan departs from obedience and takes certain fortresses, laying imposts on the people by force and, if there being no other means to put down that fighting, people begin to fight against them, is it *ḥalāl* by the *sharīʿa* to fight against them until their assembly is defeated and dispersed?

Answer: It is *ḥalāl*. This is clearly established by Qurʾānic text. It is the command of the *sharīʿa*, and the consensus of the Companions[79] supports it. It is obligatory to strive to put down *fitne* and *fesād* by fighting (for those who are capable of fighting) and (for those not capable) by recitations and prayers.[80]

38 A *fatwā* on those who lead the sultan astray

What, according to the *sharīʿa*, must be done to those who lead the *pādişāh* of Islam astray, cause the *beytüʾl-māl* to be squandered and, when it is not necessary for a *pādişāh* to make a Pilgrimage, provoke much *fitne*?

Answer: They who stir up *fitne* must be killed.[81]

---

[75] *Bennāk*: a peasant possessing less than half a *çift* of land.
[76] *Tekālif-i ʿörfiye* ('customary obligations'): extra-ordinary taxes.
[77] *İspençe*: a capitation tax on adult males in Christian households, levied in lieu of *çift*-tax.
[78] Pigs are forbidden to Muslims and therefore of no commercial value. For this reason, the pig-tax contravened the *sharīʿa*. This prohibition was never observed in practice.
[79] The Companions of the Prophet.
[80] This *fatwā* justifies Süleymān I's war against his rebel son Bāyezīd in 1558. *Fitne* has the sense of 'schism, dissension, chaos'; *fesād* has the sense of 'corruption'. Ebūʾs-suʿūd is invoking Qurʾān 2:191, 2:217 ('*Fitna* is more grievous than killing') and Qurān 5:32 ('The reward of those who wage war against God and his Apostle and strive to act corruptly upon earth is that they shall be killed . . .').
[81] *Fatwā* of the *şeyḫüʾl-islām* Esʿad Efendi legitimising the execution of the grand vizier Dilāver Pasha in 1622, on

39 A *fatwā* on deposing a sultan who disturbs order by accepting bribery

If a *pādişāh* has disturbed the good order of the world (*niẓām-i ʿālem*) by granting posts in the learned and military professions not to the proper persons but, through bribery, to the unfitting, is it permissible (*cāʾiz*) to depose (*ḥalʿ*) him and remove (*izāle*) him?

Answer: Yes.[82]

40 A *fatwā* on the legality of killing fomenters of corruption

If Zeyd, who has been granted the post of *sancaḳbegi* by the sultan, and ʿAmr who has undertaken service for the treasury, having been strictly warned by the *pādişāh* of Islam: 'Do not oppress (*ẓulm*) the *reʿāyā*', pay no heed but seize the property of the *reʿāyā* so that it is proven according to the *sharīʿa* that they are fomenters of corruption (*sāʿī biʾl-fasād*), is it legal for them to be killed by the order of the ruler (*velīyüʾl-emr*)?

Answer: It is.

41 A *fatwā* on punishment for a thief stealing from the imperial treasury

What should be done to Zeyd who was caught filing through the bars of the imperial treasury of the *pādişāh* of Islam in the attempt to steal from it?

Answer: A person attempting to steal from a place of custody[83] but seized before he actually stole must be punished with a severe chastisement (*taʿzīr-i şedīd*). The upper limit for *taʿzīr* is 79 strokes; but, according to one report, Abū Yūsuf permitted more than 100. And *taʿzīr-i şedīd* may take the form of long imprisonment, 'until the offender's repentance and reformation are evident'. Or it may take the form of both beating and imprisonment. What form the *taʿzīr* of such an offender should take is left to (*müfevvaż*) to the discretion (*reʾy*) of the *pādişāh* of Islam. And there is no objection (*beʾs*) if, to punish the corruption (*fesād*) of such an offender and as a warning to others, he is put to death by administrative action (*siyāseten*).

SOURCES

Section 1

1a Al-Qudūrī, *al-Matn*, Cairo (1957), 33.
1b Al-Mūṣilī, *al-Ikhtiyār fī taʿlīl al-Mukhtār*, Beirut: [n. d.], vol. 2, 4.
1c Qāḍīkhān, *al-Fatāwā*, in the margin of *al-Fatāwā al-Hindīya*, Beirut (1892–3), 134, 143.

the demand of the rebels who were to depose and murder Sultan ʿOsmān II.

[82] *Fatwā* justifying the deposition and execution of Sultan Ibrāhīm in 1648.

[83] The punishment for theft (*sariḳa*) is amputation of the hand. However, the definition of *sariḳa* is so tightly restrictive that the punishment cannot in practice be applied. Among many other qualifications, the goods have to be removed from custody by the thief in person, and here the miscreant did not remove the goods. The options available are therefore discretionary punishment (*taʿzīr*), as defined in the *sharīʿa*, or *siyāset*, defined as punitive action outside the *sharīʿa* for the maintenance of good order. The concept of 'corruption' (*fesād*) is invoked here to justify the use of *siyāset*.

2 M. E. Düzdağ, *Şeyhülislâm Ebussuud Efendi Fetvaları Işığında 16. Asır Türk Hayatı*, Istanbul (1972), no. 79.
3 Düzdağ, *Şeyhülislâm Ebussuud Efendi Fetvaları*, no. 285.
4 Düzdağ, *Şeyhülislâm Ebussuud Efendi Fetvaları*, no. 333.
5 Düzdağ, *Şeyhülislâm Ebussuud Efendi Fetvaları*, no. 417.
6 Düzdağ, *Şeyhülislâm Ebussuud Efendi Fetvaları*, no. 827.
7 Düzdağ, *Şeyhülislâm Ebussuud Efendi Fetvaları*, no. 845.
8 Düzdağ, *Şeyhülislâm Ebussuud Efendi Fetvaları*, no. 282.
9 Düzdağ, *Şeyhülislâm Ebussuud Efendi Fetvaları*, no. 188.
10 Düzdağ, *Şeyhülislâm Ebussuud Efendi Fetvaları*, nos 972–6.
11 Ahmet Refik [Altınay], *On Altıncı Asırda Rafizîlik ve Bektaşilik*, Istanbul (1932), no. 29.
12 Refik [Altınay], *On Altıncı Asırda Rafizîlik ve Bektaşilik*, no. 31.
13 Refik [Altınay], *On Altıncı Asırda Rafizîlik ve Bektaşilik*, no. 30.
14 Refik [Altınay], *On Altıncı Asırda Rafizîlik ve Bektaşilik*, no. 39.

Section 2

1 Elizabeth A. Zachariadou, 'Ottoman documents from the archives of Dionysiou (Mount Athos)', *Südost-Forschungen*, 30 (1971), document 13.
2 Colin Imber, 'Four documents from John Rylands Turkish MS. No. 145', *Tarih Dergisi*, 32 (1979), 173–86, document 4.
3 Halit Ongan, *Ankara'nın 1 Numaralı Şer'iye Sicili: 14 Mayıs 1583–12 Şubat 1584*, Ankara (1958), no. 31.
4 Ongan, *Ankara'nın 1 Numaralı Şer'iye Sicili*, no. 44.
5 Ongan, *Ankara'nın 1 Numaralı Şer'iye Sicili*, no. 45.
6 Ongan, *Ankara'nın 1 Numaralı Şer'iye Sicili*, no. 41.
7 Ongan, *Ankara'nın 1 Numaralı Şer'iye Sicili*, nos 13–14.
8 Ongan, *Ankara'nın 1 Numaralı Şer'iye Sicili*, no. 18.
9 Ongan, *Ankara'nın 1 Numaralı Şer'iye Sicili*, no. 20.
10 Ongan, *Ankara'nın 1 Numaralı Şer'iye Sicili*, no. 26.
11 Ongan, *Ankara'nın 1 Numaralı Şer'iye Sicili*, no. 27.
12 Ongan, *Ankara'nın 1 Numaralı Şer'iye Sicili*, no. 43.
13 Ongan, *Ankara'nın 1 Numaralı Şer'iye Sicili*, no. 30.
14 Ongan, *Ankara'nın 1 Numaralı Şer'iye Sicili*, nos 8–10.
15 Ongan, *Ankara'nın 1 Numaralı Şer'iye Sicili*, no. 12.
16 Ongan, *Ankara'nın 1 Numaralı Şer'iye Sicili*, no. 32.
17 Ongan, *Ankara'nın 1 Numaralı Şer'iye Sicili*, no. 34.
18 Düzdağ, *Şeyhülislâm Ebussuud Efendi Fetvaları*, no. 37.
19 Düzdağ, *Şeyhülislâm Ebussuud Efendi Fetvaları*, no. 38.
20 Düzdağ, *Şeyhülislâm Ebussuud Efendi Fetvaları*, no. 131.
21 Düzdağ, *Şeyhülislâm Ebussuud Efendi Fetvaları*, no. 216.
22 Düzdağ, *Şeyhülislâm Ebussuud Efendi Fetvaları*, no. 217.
23 Düzdağ, *Şeyhülislâm Ebussuud Efendi Fetvaları*, no. 272.
24 Düzdağ, *Şeyhülislâm Ebussuud Efendi Fetvaları*, no. 422.
25 Düzdağ, *Şeyhülislâm Ebussuud Efendi Fetvaları*, no. 454.
26 Düzdağ, *Şeyhülislâm Ebussuud Efendi Fetvaları*, no. 456.
27 Düzdağ, *Şeyhülislâm Ebussuud Efendi Fetvaları*, no. 552.
28 Düzdağ, *Şeyhülislâm Ebussuud Efendi Fetvaları*, no. 553.
29 Düzdağ, *Şeyhülislâm Ebussuud Efendi Fetvaları*, no. 625.
30 Düzdağ, *Şeyhülislâm Ebussuud Efendi Fetvaları*, no. 634.
31 Düzdağ, *Şeyhülislâm Ebussuud Efendi Fetvaları*, no. 665.
32 Düzdağ, *Şeyhülislâm Ebussuud Efendi Fetvaları*, no. 796.
33 Düzdağ, *Şeyhülislâm Ebussuud Efendi Fetvaları*, no. 835.

34 Düzdağ, *Şeyhülislâm Ebussuud Efendi Fetvaları*, no. 838.
35 Düzdağ, *Şeyhülislâm Ebussuud Efendi Fetvaları*, no. 843.
36 Düzdağ, *Şeyhülislâm Ebussuud Efendi Fetvaları*, no. 844.
37 Düzdağ, *Şeyhülislâm Ebussuud Efendi Fetvaları*, no. 964.
38 Şeyḫü'l-Islām Esʿad Efendi (in office 1615–22 and 1623–5), as quoted in Tūġī, ed. Midhat Sertoğlu, 'İbretnüma', *Belleten*, 11 (1947), 494.
39 *Şeyḫü'l-Islām* Ḥāccī ʿAbdü'r-Raḥīm (in office 1647–9), quoted in Naʿīmā, *Taʾrīḫ-i Naʿīmā*, 4, Istanbul (1280/1863–4), 325.
40 *Şeyḫü'l-Islām* Meḥmed Ṣādıḳ (in office 1694–5 and 1708–9), as quoted in Ahmet Mumcu, *Osmanlı Devletinde Siyaseten Katl*, Ankara (1963), doc. 12.
41 *Şeyḫü'l-Islām* ʿAbdü'r-Raḥīm (in office 1715–16), as quoted in *Topkapı Sarayı Müzesi Arşivi Kılavuzu* 2, Istanbul (1940), doc. 22.

Plate 9 The *ḳāḍīʿasker* of Rūmeli on horseback (JRL1119064)

Plate 10 A Janissary officer with a firearm and powder-horn (JRL1119017)

Plate 11 A *muḥtesib*, a market inspector with a pair of scales (JRL1119025)

Plate 12 A butcher publicly shamed for selling short weight (JRL1119069)

Plate 13 An arsenal guard (JRL1119074)

Plate 14 The sultan's *sipāhīs* in procession (JRL20020701)

Plate 15 Armourers (*cebeci*) and *müteferriḳa*s in procession (JRL20020709)

Plate 16 A *deli* ('madcap'), a volunteer soldier (1119090)

CHAPTER VII

*Ḳānūnnāme*s

A *ḳānūn* is a 'law' and a *ḳānūnnāme* a 'code of laws'. The term *ḳānūn*, however, is restricted to laws which fell in areas of public law where the ordinances of the *sharīʿa* were either non-existent or too impractical to enforce. This meant that *ḳānūn* was concerned overwhelmingly with the closely interlinked topics of criminal sanctions, land tenure and taxation. In particular, it was *ḳānūn* that underpinned the *tīmār*-system, determining the conditions on which both the *tīmār*-holders and the peasant-cultivators could occupy the land; the military obligations of the *tīmār*-holders; and the taxes which *tīmār*-holders, *subaşı*s and *sancaḳbegi*s were entitled to collect. Passages **1; 2 (xxviii xxx); 3 ch. 1** show that it was also the *tīmār*-holders, *subaşı*s and *sancaḳbegi*s who were responsible for law and order in their district, administering punishments and pocketing fines: hence the criminal statutes included in *ḳānūnnāme*s.

The systematic compilation of *ḳānūnnūme*s began under the aegis of Bāyezīd II (r. 1481 1512). To judge from the archaism of the language, the earliest *ḳānūn* texts seem to be found in a compilation assembled in or immediately after 1488, from a tariff of strokes and fines for criminal offences, a list of taxes and tolls for an unidentified European province and other miscellaneous items, as exemplified here in passage **1**. A recension of the criminal statutes in this compilation forms the criminal code that opens Bāyezīd II's 'general' *ḳānūnnāme* of c1500 (passage **3**) which aimed, as far as possible, to standardise *ḳānūn* throughout the sultan's realms. The earliest properly systematic compilation of *ḳānūn*s is, however, the *ḳānūnnāme* for the *sancaḳ* of Ḫüdāvendgār (Bursa) of 1487, as found in passage **2**. Although evidently modelled on an earlier *ḳānūnnāme* for Kütahya, which survives only in a recension of 1528, it became a model for the development of *ḳānūn*. Many of its clauses were copied verbatim into Bāyezīd II's 'general' *ḳānūnnāme* and, with the introduction of Ottoman law into recently conquered districts during the course of the sixteenth century, was a main source of reference for the compilers of new *ḳānūnnāme*s for these areas.

The introduction of Ottoman law was, however, a gradual process. Passages **4** and **5** present *kānūnnāme*s for newly conquered areas, which usually are summaries of pre-Ottoman taxes, with notes as to whether these had been retained or abolished after the conquest. The full introduction of Ottoman *ḳānūn* in the conquered lands, with the Ḫüdāvengār *ḳānūnnāme* as a source of reference, came about when the areas were re-surveyed in the decades after the conquest. While it is clear that, from the reign of

Bāyezīd II onwards, there was an effort to standardise *ḳānūn*, the differences in the economies, customs and social structures between – and within – different areas of the Ottoman Empire meant that complete uniformity was impossible.

In particular, groups such as gypsies, *yürük*s (see passage **1**, Chapter VI therein), Vlachs or *voynuḳ*s (see passage **6b**), which were either non-sedentary or else co-opted for military or other duties for the sultan, were subject to special statutes. *Ḳānūnnāme*s for *sancaḳ*s were compiled when the *sancaḳ* in question was re-surveyed and, in areas where the Ottoman *ḳānūn* had long been in force, the *ḳānūnnāmes* tend not to dwell on statements of general principle, which were well known; rather, as seen in passage **6a**, they concentrate on special cases and on righting abuses which the surveyors had uncovered.

The practice of making land-and-tax surveys of each *sancaḳ* continued until 1592, the demise of the system reflecting the fiscal and military changes that occurred from the late sixteenth century onwards. The *New Ḳānūnnāme*, compiled in the 1670s and in force until 1858, consolidated the laws of land tenure, including the modifications made from the mid-sixteenth century onwards, into a single legal code.

1 The 'Kraelitz text'[1]

This is the copy of the Imperial *ḳānūn* of Sultan Meḥmed b. Murād Ḫān.

Chapter I. On fornication.

Chapter II. On brawls, altercations and homicide.

Chapter III. On wine-drinking, theft and false denunciation.[2]

(xi) As ground-*ṭapu*[3] for the ground on which a house stands, at the most 50 *aḳçe* is to be taken, below that 40 or 30, and if [the man] is poor, 20 or 10.[4]

(xii) Bride-chamber-tax (*gerdek degüri*) at the highest 60; if [the person] is in medium circumstances 40 or 30 *aḳçe* is to be taken; if he is poor, 20 or 10.

(xiii) When sheep-tax is taken, 1 *aḳçe* is to be taken for 3 sheep.

(xiv) If a *su eri*[5] drives his *ra'īyet*[6] from his land by force, when [the *ra'īyet*] returns [the *su eri*] is not to take *ṭapu*; but if [the *ra'īyet*] abandons it by choice or leaves his land unoccupied

[1] The text was discovered, edited and translated into German by Friedrich Kraelitz-Greifenhorst.

[2] For a translation of the later recensions of Chapters I, II, III on criminal law, see Uriel Heyd (ed. V. L. Ménage), *Studies in Old Ottoman Criminal Law*, Oxford (1973), 62–131. For a Concordance, see Heyd, *Studies*, 159.

[3] *Ṭapu*: title to land; (by extension) the entry-fee giving title to the land.

[4] Clauses (xi)–(xv) appear under Chapter III ('On wine-drinking, theft and false denunciation'), but are evidently misplaced.

[5] *Su eri* (Turkish: 'army man'): a *tīmār*-holding *sipāhī*, timariot. It has been customary to transliterate this term as *süvārī* (Persian: 'cavalryman'), as an equivalent of *sipāhī* (Persian: 'cavalryman'). However, *su eri*, as a counterpart to *su başı* (Turkish: 'army head') seems more probable. The term appears to be a calque of the Byzantine στρατιώτης ('soldier, man of the army'). The replacement of Turkish *su eri* with the Persian *sipāhī* would be an example of the shift in the late fifteenth century from Turkish to Arabic/Persian vocabulary.

[6] *Ra'īyet*: a member of the tax-paying peasantry in the countryside. He would pay taxes to the *su eri*/*sipāhī* on whose tīmār he resided.

for one year, the *su eri* is free to act [as he prefers]. If the *ra'īyet* departs of his own will, his house and the yard are to belong to the *su eri*, but if the *su eri* expels him, they are to belong to the *ra'īyet*.

(xv) The *su eri* is not to hold more land than his [own] *çiftlik*,[7] but is to give *ra'īyet*-land to the *ra'īyets*. Without the permission of the *pādişāh*, [a *su eri*] making [for himself] a *çiftlik* shall not in the future take land from peasant-land (*türk yeri*) or unploughed land. If in the future he does hold *ra'īyet*-land, he is to give the local (?) due (*il ḥaḳḳı*) to the 'poor'.[8]

Chapter IV.

(i–iii) One *çift* is to give annually [3] 'services' (*ḫidmet*) [or] 3 *aḳçe*, [and] one 'sickle' and one 'flail' and one cart-load of firewood, and as yoke-tax 2 *aḳçe*. If money is taken in respect of these seven 'services' (*ḳulluḳ*), 22 *aḳçe* is to be taken.[9]

(iv) From a *benlāk*,[10] 3 ['services'] are to be taken, or 6 or 9 *aḳçe*.

(v) In towns and in the countryside, a tithe (*onda*) is to be taken from vineyards (*bāġ*).

(vi) From the income of carpenters (*taḫtacı*) and foresters (*aġaççı*),[11] 1 *aḳçe* in 20 is to be taken per year.

(vii) A wage-earner and a carter whose trade is carting and who gives up his *çift* and does not sow [a minimum of ?] 2 *müdd*[12] per year, [but] transports salt and other things is to give his *su eri* 50 *aḳçe* a year. If he does not give up his *çift* and does sow 2 *müdd* [per year] as before, they are not to take anything [extra] on the ground that 'You are earning a wage', but he is to give only as before, according to custom (*'ādet*), the tithe [of the produce] and the *ra'īyet*-tax. But a person engaged in carting in a town is, like [other] tradespeople, to pay nothing.

If a person gives up his *çift* because he is weakened by illness or old age or because through extreme poverty he cannot manage it, he is not to be harassed[13] on the ground that 'You are earning a [labourer's] wage' or 'You are a carter' or 'You are a carpenter'; his *su eri* is to take his land from him and give it to someone else, and from him [only] the *benlāk*-tax is to be taken.

(viii) This custom (*'ādet*) does not apply to Tatars and *yürüks*, because they are 'campaigners' (*eşkünci*).

(ix) If a person earns his living from pack-animals, he is to pay 10 *aḳçe* a year; but if in a town, nothing.

---

[7] *Çift[lik]*: an agricultural holding. Fief-holders were entitled to cultivate a plot of land on their *tīmār* for their own use.

[8] The term is *yoḳsul* (Turkish: 'poor, indigent'). Here, and in other texts, it seems to function as the archaic term for *ra'īyet*. The term seems to be a calque of the Byzantine πτωχός ('poor man, peasant').

[9] In 1458, the standard rate of *çift*-tax was raised from 22 *aḳçe* per year to 32 *aḳçe*, suggesting that this clause dates from before 1458. The rate of *çift*-tax was not, however, uniform.

[10] *Benlāk*: a peasant cultivating less than half a *çift*.

[11] This seems to refer to the semi-nomadic groups in the forested areas of western and southern Anatolia, earning a living as foresters and carpenters.

[12] *Müdd* (from Greek: μόδιος): a measure of capacity. The *müdd* of Bursa was c112 litres.

[13] That is, harassed for the payment of *çift-tax*.

(x) The *su eri*'s share (*degür*)[14] is one sheep in 50; half of it belongs to the *subaşı*.

(xi) From cereals, tithe (*ʿöşr*) is to be taken, and *sālārlıḳ*[15] at 5 [*kīle*][16] per 10 *müdd.*

(xii) From flax, 10 sheaves in 100 are to be taken as tithe (*onda*) and 3 as *sālārlık*, and the fifth of it (?);[17] but they are to soften it [first].

(xiii) The *ʿöşr* on cotton: on 100 *lidra,*[18] 10 are to be taken as *onda* and 2½ as *sālārlıḳ*.

(xiv) A rice-grower (*çeltükçi*) who has a *çift* is not, like the [other] settled [peasantry] (*yerlü*), to give seven services; the *su eri* is to exact [only] three, [or] if [the rice-grower] does not present himself [for the labour] (*bulunmazsa*), [the *su eri*] is to take 6 or 9 *akçe.*

(xv) From that member of a *ḳoyun-eri* [group][19] who serves on campaign, *sālārlıḳ* is not to be taken, [but] it is to be taken from his 'associates' (*yamaḳ*).

(xvi) From a Tatar holding a *çift* there is to be taken for 3 services, and tithe and *sālārlıḳ* on his cereals: but there is no [obligation of] service on one without a *çift.*

(xvii) On a fine collected from the *raʿīyet* of a *su eri,*[20] the *subaşı*[21] takes half and the *su eri* half.

(xviii) But the *su eri* is to take all the bride-chamber-tax (*gerdek degüri*). If the daughter of a *su eri* 'comes out' [to be married], the *subaşı* is to take all the bride-chamber-tax.

(xix) The old *ḳara müsellems* and the present-day *müsellems* and those *yaya* who are *raʿīyet,*[22] these too are [subject] to this tax (*resm*).[23]

(xx) The villages attached (*tevābiʿ*) to a town are to bring their tithe to the town if the *su eri* lives in the town; but if he is in the village, to his barn.

(xxi) Tithe is to be taken from fruit (*yemiş*) and small fruit (*meyvece*) and [silk] cocoons and saffron, but not *sālārlıḳ*.[24]

(xxii) In a place where there are reed-beds and meadows (*ot*), [the practice] is to be as it has regularly been in the past.

(xxiii) Tithe on hives: one in ten is to be taken, good [from good] and bad [from bad].

---

[14] *Süvār degüri*: the meaning is unclear. Perhaps to be read as *süri degüri* ('flock tax').
[15] A tax on grain at 2½ percent, paid in addition to the tithe, originally to provide fodder for the *sipāhī/su eri*'s horse.
[16] *Kīle*: a measure of capacity, probably c28 litres.
[17] *Ve ḫumsin/ḫamsīn*: the meaning is not clear.
[18] *Lidra* (Greek: λίτρα): a pound, a unit of weight.
[19] *Ḳoyun eri* ('sheep man'): member of a para-military group, perhaps originally involved with the supply of meat and yoghurt on campaign.
[20] That is, the holder of the *tīmār*.
[21] The holder of a *zeʿāmet*, with policing duties in his area.
[22] *Müsellem* (Arabic: 'exempted'), *yaya* (Turkish: 'footman'): the names of two auxiliary corps, performing services in the army in return for some tax-exemptions.
[23] Kraelitz translates thus. Possibly to be translated: 'are to be treated in this way' [VLM].
[24] This rule reflects the origin of *sālārlıḳ* as a levy of barley or other crop to feed the *su eri/sipāhī*'s horse on campaign.

(xxiv) For each 'eye' of a water-mill one *müdd* of grain, [measured] by the *müdd* of Edirne, is to be taken, half wheat and half barley; for each 'eye' of a *ḳaraca*[25] mill, from one that works all the year, one *müdd*; from one that works for six months, half a *müdd*; and from one that works less than that at this rate – half wheat and half barley, [that is,] in equal quantities, [measured] by the *müdd* of Edirne. A windmill is to give half a *müdd* per year, half in wheat, half in barley, [that is,] in equal quantities, [measured] by the *müdd* of Edirne.

(xxv) A Tatar *ra'īyet* who has land gives (it is reported) each year one 'service'[26] and one 'sickle' and one cartload of firewood, but not the 'campaigners' among them; [the practice] is to be confirmed according to that *ḳānūn*.

(xxvi) A 'settled' [peasant] with sheep or a *yürük*[27] is not to pay summer-grazing-due and wintering-due.

(xxvii) If a *ra'īyet* who has land leaves uncultivated the land he holds and raises crops on the land of another *su eri*, he is to pay two tithes (*onda*), one in respect of the land he is cultivating and one in respect of the land he has abandoned; but if the *su eri* has no land to give to the *ra'īyet* and [for that reason] the *ra'īyet* raises crops elsewhere, he is to pay tithe according to the custom (*'ādet*) only to [the *su eri*] providing him with land (*yerlisi*).

The *ra'īyet*s are to build a house for their *su eri* only once. If that *su eri* goes, however many other *su eri*s may come in, they are to have the house which that departing *su eri* caused to be built; [the newcomer] is not to get them to build a house again.

(xxviii) Tradespeople living in villages – weavers, tailors, shoemakers, smiths, charcoal-burners and the like – are to give 3 services a year or 3 *aḳçe*: they are not to be obliged to do further work on the ground that they are tradespeople, and they are not to have anything taken from them by force, unless they consent at the rate of the local tariff (*narḫ*) and do the work willingly.

(xxix) To sum up, after their dues have been taken from the 'poor' (*yoḳsullar*)[28] in accordance with the *ḳānūnnāme* as is set out, their horses and carts should not be seized by force for courier-service (*ulaḳ*), nor should they be forced to work.

[Chapter V.] On the matter of tolls.

(i) If a Muslim comes from outside, bringing horsecloths, cloaks, leather, honey, oil and all such things and sells them, 1 *aḳçe* in 40 is to be taken,

(ii) From a load of cloth, or if anything such as linen, thread, broadcloth, brocade, sturgeon, tin or lead arrives and is sold, 2 *aḳçe* should be taken per load.

(iii) From a load of early fruit, 1 *aḳçe*, and when the fruit is plentiful, 1 *aḳçe* on 2 or 3 loads.

(iv) When a *segbān*[29] or a *ḳul*[30] or a falconer or an ostler (*at oğlanı*) or a messenger (*elçi*) or

[25] The meaning of *ḳaraca* is unclear.

[26] Reading *ḫidmet* instead of *çift* [VLM].

[27] *Yürük*: a nomadic or semi-nomadic Turkish tribesman.

[28] Here 'the poor' has the sense of tax-paying peasants (*re'āyā*). See n. 7 above.

[29] *Segbān*: 'keeper of [the sultan's] hounds', which may be its meaning here. The sultan's *segbān*s also served as a military force. From the mid-fifteenth century onwards, they were incorporated into the Janissary corps.

[30] *Ḳul* (Turkish: 'slave'), here probably a Janissary.

other [official] passes through, they are to see whether he is carrying an imperial command[31] (*ḥükm-i hümāyūn*) and give him whatever is [there] commanded in the way of fodder and food and riding-animals (*ulaḳ*) and so on; [the official] is not to exact more. If nothing is ordered, they are to give him only accommodation,[32] and whatever else he needs he is to buy from his own purse (*yan*). [The officials] are not to harass anyone or do anything beyond what is ordered; if they do [the local authorities] are to report it to my Exalted Court, so that they may be punished. They are not to do anything to anybody.

(v) If a person's horse or ox or mare enters a corn-field, he is to be fined 5 *aḳçe* and receive 5 strokes; if a calf, 1 *aḳçe* and 1 stroke; if sheep, 1 *aḳçe* and 1 stroke for every 2 sheep. But first [the authorities] are to issue a warning (?) (*ḥüccet*), and if hereafter people pay no heed and do not look after their animals, so that they are found in the crops and the crop is damaged, they are to be fined and beaten in this way and are to pay compensation and be warned to look after the animals and not let them damage the crops.

(vi) If corn is [growing] in the vicinity of a village or within villages or at, or on the way to a watering-place for animals, that is, [at a place] where animals [regularly] come, a hedge is to be made around such crops.

No-one is to act otherwise. Anyone, whoever he may be, who infringes on this *ḳānūn* will deserve punishment and becomes culpable and has committed an offence. Thus they (*sic*) are to know: you (*sic*) are to recognise this *ḳānūn* as conclusive (*muḥaḳḳaḳ*).[33]

[Chapter VI.] Ḳānūn of the *yürük*s.

Of 24 men, 1 is to be a 'campaigner' (*eşkünci*), 3 are to be reserves (?) (*çatal*) and 20 'associates' (*yamaḳ*). The campaigner is to be fully equipped, himself wearing a cuirass (*cebelü*), and with no defect in his lance-blade, his arrow-flights, his arrows, his bow, his shield or his sword. Ten campaigners are to have one baggage-horse among them and one [small] tent (*tenktür*). Campaigners, reserves and associates among the *yürük*s are not to be subject to levies of barley and straw, to [the corvée] of fortress-building or to other emergency impositions (*ʿavārıż*); and the one who campaigns is not to pay *sālārlıḳ* in respect of that year. Thus you are to know.[34]

[Chapter VII.] *Ḳānūn* for the married infidels.

(i) Every married infidel is to give his *su eri* 25 *aḳçe* [a year] for *ispençe*,[35] and also for his son who qualifies to pay poll-tax (*ḫarāc*) the full *ispençe*. From a widow with no land, 6 *aḳçe* a year; the *su eri* is not to set her to work in his house or make her spin, unless he employs her for a wage.

(ii) If there is a *beglik*[36] vineyard, he may make his *raʿīyet*s work on it for three days in the year.

---

31 That is, a command from the sultan.

32 'Accommodation': reading *oda* ('room') instead of *onda* (tithe) [VLM].

33 The formula that ends this clause ('Thus . . . conclusive') is patently the end of a *firman*, indicating that a sultanic decree has been incorporated into the text.

34 Again, this clause clearly reproduces the text of a *firman*.

35 *İspençe*: a tax payable by adult male non-Muslims in lieu of *çift*-tax.

36 *Beglik*: assets reserved for the use of the sultan. Here it denotes a vineyard set aside for the personal use of the *tīmār*-holder as an appointee of the sultan.

If he receives [a tithe ?] from a vineyard, in a place where grape-juice is produced, whether in a town or in a village, the *subaşı* or the *su eri* is to hold *monapolye*[37] for two months and sell the wine (*süçi*) [but] he is not to force it on the infidels at more than the fixed price (*narḫ*). While the *subaşı* or the *su eri* is selling his wine, no infidel is to sell or broach[38] his own wine: [the infidels'] casks and jars are to be sealed, and no-one's wine is to be sold until the wine of the *subaşı* or the *su eri* is sold. He may hold the two months' *monapolye* in whatever months of the year he chooses, and in those months he may sell the tithe (*onda*) which he received from the infidels. If he has wine left over, he is not to force the infidels to buy it, but to sell it only if the infidels agree at the local fixed price.

[From the grape-juice,] both in towns and villages, 10 *medre* in 100 are to be taken as tithe (*onda*) and 3 as *sālārlıḳ*.

If an infidel opens his cask and sells his wine, one *medre* in 50 is to be taken, [measured] by the *medre* of Edirne.

From wine coming from outside to be sold, for each cask 15 *aḳçe* are to be taken.

(iii) Tithe on hives: one in ten is to be taken, good [from good] and bad [from bad].

(iv) From pigs which roam in the open and are tended with cows, 1 *aḳçe* is to be taken for every 2; from those that are fattened up in sties in the house for slaughter, 1 *aḳçe* per pig.

(v) The sheep-tax which is taken from infidels is 1 *aḳçe* for 3 sheep, as for Muslims.

(vi) Bride-chamber-tax: from a very rich Muslim, 60 *aḳçe* are to be taken, but from the poll-tax payers of the *ḫudāvend-i a'ẓam*,[39] the half: from a very rich one, since the time of his father and grandfather[40] (may their dust be fragrant!), it has been 30 *aḳçe*, and below this 20, and below this – that is, very poor – 10 *aḳçe*.

(vii) In cases of striking and cutting open the head and wounding with a sword or a knife and causing injury,[41] and other quarrels which are proven before the *ḳāḍī*, on the matter of what counts as 'rich' and what as 'poor', attention is to be paid to the rates of fines on Muslims, and the sentence [for infidels] is to be half of that, so that the poll-tax[42] payers may not vanish.

(viii) After the *ispençe* of 25 *aḳçe* has been taken from tailors and weavers and furriers and shoemakers and carters and other infidels practising a trade, nothing else is to be taken from them on the ground that they are tradespeople: they are not to be made to work, unless they consent at the rate of the local tariff; then they may work.

[Chapter VIII.] On the matter of tolls.

(i) If a Muslim or an infidel . . . [the text repeats Chapter 5 (i-iii) above, with slight modifications in wording, but inserts the following between (ii) and (iii)]:

---

[37] *Monapolye* (from Greek: *μονοπωλία)*: a period during which the *tīmār*-holder enjoyed the sole right to sell wine produced on his *tīmār*.

[38] 'Broach': reading *aç-* ('open'), this could also be read as *iç-* ('drink').

[39] *Ḫudāvend-i a'ẓam* ('almighty sovereign'): the reigning sultan.

[40] Emending *vālidesi* ('his mother') to read *dedesi* ('his grandfather'). This appears to refer to the father and grandfather of the sultan [VLM].

[41] Fines for these offences are dealt with in Chapter II. In compiling the text, the editor has combined material from different sources without editing to remove discrepancies or to achieve uniformity.

[42] The *jizya*, the tax payable by non-Muslim adult males.

Whatever comes from Wallachia and Islāmbol,[43] 2 *akçe* in the hundred is to be taken.[44]

(ii) From a load of pitch-pine (*çıra*) which is sold at 15 *akçe* one [*ṣūreti*][45] or one piece of pitch-pine is to be taken.

(iii) From a donkey-load of firewood,[46] the gatekeeper is to take one log for the *ḳul*s of the *beg* who come and go from the outer town (*şehr*).[47]

(iv) From cows [which are sold], 2 *aḳçe* are to be taken from both [the seller and buyer].

(v) If a slave is sold, 4 *aḳçe* are to be taken from the two parties.

(vi) From goods weighed at the [public] balance, 2 *aḳçe* per *ḳanṭār* are to be taken, one from the seller and one from the buyer.

(vii) From a cartload of salt, 8 *aḳçe* are to be taken.

(viii) From a cartload of rice, 8 *aḳçe* are to be taken.

(xi) From a cartload of sheepskins, 5 *aḳçe* are to be taken, and from a horse-load 2.

(x) From a load of felt capes (*kepenek*), 2 *aḳçe* are to be taken.

(xi) On whatever comes from Wallachia and Islāmbol and the Franks,[48] 2 *akçe* in 100 are to be taken.

(xii) From whatever comes from the Franks via Dubrovnik, it was later confirmed as follows, that if it is thus contracted (*mu'āmele*) with the infidels of Dubrovnik, [then] in accordance with the practice (*'ādet*) of the *pādişāh*, from one load of cloth 2 *aḳçe* are to be taken.

(xiii) If sheep come from outside and are slaughtered, 1 *aḳçe* is to be taken for 2 sheep; if a local butcher brings them and slaughters them, then 1 *aḳçe* for 4 sheep.

(xiv) If a dealer (*rencber*)[49] brings sheep from outside and sells them,[50] with Islāmbol [as their ultimate] destination, 1 *aḳçe* is to be taken from 2 sheep as transit toll (*ayaḳ bācı*); if he sells them outside the boundaries [of the town] [but] comes and collects his money within the town, the toll on them is to be taken from the dealer who sold them.

(xv) If a cow is slaughtered, 1 *aḳçe* is to be taken.

(xvi) If private property (*mülk*) is sold – that is, vineyards, mills, and orchards (*bāġçe*), or houses and shops[51] – there is no toll [to be paid].

(xvii) Whatever is sold in villages [as opposed to towns], there is no toll [to be paid].

---

[43] Istanbul.

[44] Cf. clause (xi) below.

[45] The sense is unclear.

[46] A later recension of this clause adds 'entering the fortress'.

[47] The sense of this clause is uncertain. It perhaps refers to a levy of firewood, for the use of the Janissary garrison in the fortress.

[48] Franks (*Frenk*): a general term for Europeans. Here perhaps 'Italy'.

[49] Emending Kraelitz's reading (*incir*: 'fig') to *rencber* [VLM].

[50] Presumably, 'sells them in the town'.

[51] In Ottoman law, immoveable property which is above the ground – trees, vines or buildings – could be held as private property. The land itself could not be held as private property.

(xviii) If a person's horse or ox or mare enters a corn-field, he is to be fined 5 *aḳçe* and receive 5 strokes; if a cow enters, he is to receive 4 strokes and be fined 4 *aḳçe*; if a calf or a sheep, 1 *aḳçe* and 1 stroke; if a pig,[52] 2 *aḳçe* and 2 strokes. But first [the authorities] are to issue a warning (?) (*ḥüccet*), and if hereafter people pay no heed and do not look after their animals, so that they are found in the crops and the crop is damaged, they are to be fined and beaten in this way and are to pay compensation and be warned to look after the animals, so that the grain and the crops of the Muslims and the infidels are not destroyed.[53]

Anyone, whoever he may be, who infringes this *ḳānūn* will deserve punishment and becomes culpable. Written in the last decade of Jumādā'l-ukhrā of the year 893 (2–10 June 1488).

2 The *kānūnnāme* of Ḫüdāvendgār, 1487

REGISTER giving the particulars of the names[54] of the *re'āyā* of the *livā*[55] of Ḫüdāvendgār[56] . . ., set out by the noble sultanic command . . . of . . . Sultan Bāyezīd . . . and under the superintendence of . . . Meḥmed . . . The inscribing and checking of it was completed in the second decade of Ṣafar 892 (6–15 February 1487).

EXPOSITION of the particulars of the current *şer'ī ḳānūn*s[57] and the rules for the recognised *'örfī* taxes which are the bases for the Ottoman registers and the sources for the sultanic commands; written to the following effect:

(i) The *çift*-tax [taken] from a *ra'īyet* who is enregistered '*çift*'[58] as holding a full *çiftlik* is 33 *aḳçe*; the tax from a half-*çift* is the half of that; the tax from a *bennāk* holding less than a half-*çift*, who is enregistered as 'with land' (*ekinlü*), is 12 *aḳçe*, and from a *caba bennāk*[59] it is [only] 9 *akçe*, [for] it is a laudable practice that the weakest among the *re'āyā* should be protected.

From bachelors (*mücerred*) of *re'āyā* descent who are not earning their own living (*ehl-i kisb*), nothing is to be taken, and in the registers no tax has been noted against their names; but it has been commanded that, from bachelors who do earn their own living, taxes are to be taken to the amount appropriate for each.

If a person entered in the register as 'bachelor' marries, then the *bennāk*-tax is taken from him; if a *caba bennāk* becomes *ekinlü*, then the *ekinlü*-tax is taken; [if a person] not registered as '*çift*' comes to possess a *çift* and *çiftlik*, then the *çift*-tax is taken. The criterion in this matter is the amount of *çiftlik*: a person holding more land than the amount of a *çiftlik* pays taxes on the scale of an 'outsider'[60] *ra'īyet* in proportion to the excess [over a single *çiftlik*].

---

[52] *Ḳara canavar* ('common creature'): a euphemism for pig, a canonically forbidden animal.

[53] This clause repeats Chapter V (v) above with small variations. Again, the compiler has made no attempt to achieve uniformity.

[54] The *ḳānūnnāme* is appended to the detailed land-and-tax register of the *sancaḳ* of Ḫüdāvendgār, which recorded the names of all the taxpayers in the *sancaḳ*.

[55] *Livā* (Arabic: 'flag, banner'): a *sancaḳ* (Turkish: 'flag, banner').

[56] Ḫüdāvendgār ('monarch'): the *sancaḳ* of Bursa. The epithet Ḫudāvendgār was applied to Murād I, who held this *sancaḳ* as a personal appanage.

[57] That is, a *ḳānūn* that is in conformity with the *sharī'a*.

[58] That is, if his name appears in the register to which this *ḳānūnnāme* is appended, as holding a whole *çift*.

[59] A *bennāk* is a peasant holding less than half a *çift*. A *caba bennāk* is a landless peasant.

[60] *Ḫāric* ('outside'): a *ra'īyet* whose name does not appear in the register but is awarded land on a *tīmār*. See clause (v).

(ii) It is a patent injustice (*ḥayf*) to take *çift*-tax from a man who, through becoming old or being afflicted by poverty, has given up his land, especially if the land he has given up is being worked [by someone else], so that there is no deficiency in the taxes entered in the register.

(iii) After the *çift*-tax has been taken according to the *ḳānūn*, from a *ra ʿīyet* registered as '*çift*' on the *tīmār* of a fortress-soldier (*ḥiṣār eri*) a further 6 *aḳçe* is to be taken under the name 'straw and wood tax', and from a half-*çift* a further 3 *aḳçe*; this *ḳānūn* is confirmed and entered in the registers.

(iv) The 'ground-tax' (*resm-i zemīn*) taken from an 'outsider' (*ḫāric*) *ra ʿīyet* who [comes and] receives land from a *sipāhī* is, for a complete *çiftlik*, the full *çift*-tax, and for a half-*çiftlik*, the half. As to areas less than a half, it is in conformity with the [general] *ḳānūn* for [this] tax that 1 *aḳçe* is taken for every 2 *dönüm*, if it is irrigated land or high quality land which is worked and harvested every year; 1 *aḳçe* for 3 *dönüm*, if it is medium land; and 1 *aḳçe* for 4 or 5 *dönüm*, if it is poor land. The criterion for a complete *çiftlik* is 70–80 *dönüm* of high quality land, 100 *dönüm* of medium land, and 130–50 *dönüm* of poor land.

(v) A *dönüm* is an area of forty standard paces in length and breadth.

(vi) *Çift*-taxes and *bennāk*-taxes, together with their supplements, used to be taken after the threshing, but it has now become the established *ḳānūn* that they be taken in March.[61] Mill-taxes also are taken then.

(vii) A second tithe is taken from any *ra ʿīyet* who abandons his land on the *tīmār* of his own *sipāhī* and goes off and raises crops elsewhere. But if a person has no cultivable land on the *tīmār* of his own *sipāhī* and [for that reason] raises crops elsewhere, then it is an unacceptable injustice (*ḥayf-i nā-ma ʿrūf*) to take a second tithe from him.

(viii) If a *ra ʿīyet* who is settled (*yerlü*) goes off elsewhere, it is the ancient *ḳānūn* that he should be fetched back to his place. But it has been forbidden to fetch back anyone who has been settled in a place for fifteen years. Especially if he is a *bennāk*, it is forbidden to move him, wherever he may be, after he has paid his taxes. If a person who is of *ra ʿīyet* descent lives for fifteen years in a town but is not specifically listed in the register of *re ʿāyā*, it has been commanded and has become the *ḳānūn* that such a person is not *ra ʿīyet* but is to be added to the 'townsmen' (*şehirlü*).

(ix) The sheep-tax, both for *yürük*s and for the settled, is 1 *aḳçe* for 2 sheep. It has become the *ḳānūn* that sheep and lambs are counted together.

The *resm-i ḳara* due from a *yürük* who has no sheep is 12 *aḳçe*. If a *yürük*'s sheep are killed, so that he has none left or so that the sheep-tax [due from him] does not exceed the *resm-i ḳara*, from him 12 *aḳçe* are taken, under the name *resm-i ḳara*.

(x) If a *yürük* obtains some land from a *sipāhī* and cultivates it, [then], after paying the tithe and the *sālārlıḳ*, he pays 12 *aḳçe* as 'yoke-tax', but no further tax beyond that: for if he paid a further tax, a second tax [on a single obligation] would be taken, and [hence] an injustice (*ḥayf*) contrary to the ancient *ḳānūn* would occur; this matter has been considered (*teftīş*) time

[61] Based on the Julian calendar. The Ottoman treasury used the solar Julian calendar rather than the lunar Islamic calendar, as the months of the latter did not correspond to the seasons of the year when taxes fell due.

and again, and [the rule] has been confirmed, by a command of the *pādişāh*, in the terms set out above.

(xi) Taxes from the *yürük*s used to be taken when the lambs are sheared; it is the practice now, according to the *ḳānūn*, that they are taken in April.

Sheepfold-tax has been customarily taken at [the rate of] 3 *aḳçe* per flock.

(xii) On crops of wheat, barley, oats and millet, [both] tithe and *sālārlıḳ* are taken, at a total rate of 1 *müdd* per 8 *müdd* of grain, [that is,] 2½ *kīle* per *müdd*. But on other crops, like chick-peas and lentils and beans, or like cotton and flax, only tithe is taken, and not *sālārlıḳ*.[62]

(xiii) To transport the *sipāhī*'s [share of the] crops to his barn or that of the fortress-soldier to the fortress [where he is stationed] is an accepted uncanonical imposition (*bid'at-i ma'rūfe*) upon the *re'āyā*; but it has been commanded that, if the distance is more than one day's journey, it is not to be imposed (*teklīf*), in order to save [the *re'āyā* from] the expense.

(xiv) If tithe-land capable of cultivation is left uncultivated for no good reason,[63] and consequently the *tīmār* suffers loss [of revenue], the *sipāhī* is permitted by custom (*'örfen*), in order to prevent this loss, to take the land from the holder (*ṣāḥib*) and to grant it for *ṭapu* to someone else. But it is forbidden to take it and give it to another, if it is left uncultivated because it is mountainous or barren; or because it is subject to flooding and so cannot be cultivated every year; for in those cases the cultivator has not been persistently remiss. It is not forbidden for a *ra'īyet* to leave a few *dönüm* uncultivated as pasture to meet the needs of his plough-oxen, or as threshing-ground. A decree of the *pādişāh* has once again been issued on these matters.

(xv) To plough up or to enclose or to grant for *ṭapu* the pasture which has from of old existed as the grazing-ground of the animals of townsfolk or villagers has been stopped and forbidden, because it causes injury to the community.

(xvi) To demand *ṭapu* from an orphan is an unacceptable and forbidden *bid'at*:[64] his father's lands have been regarded as equivalent to his inherited property (*mülk*). In the event that land coming to an orphan from his father is granted to another because [otherwise] it cannot be cultivated, if the orphan, on reaching maturity, claims it, it has been commanded that it be returned to him.

(xvii) If a woman[65] does not leave uncultivated the land which she holds and if she pays the tithe and the taxes on it, then it is contrary to the *ḳānūn* to take it from her.

(xviii) If a *ra'īyet* dies leaving sons, one or more of whom is registered as '*çift*' and others as '*bennāk*', it has been commanded, out of regard for equity, that they may hold their father's land jointly and pay the *çift*-tax and the *bennāk*-tax jointly among all of them.

(xix) At one time it had been commanded that land held by an 'outsider' *ra'īyet* in return for the payment of *ṭapu*-tax should be taken from him and given to a [local] *ra'īyet*; later

---

[62] *Sālārlıḳ* was originally a levy of barley for the lord's horse, and so was not always levied on non-cereal crops. See above 1 (xxi).

[63] Later *ḳānūnnāmes* were to specify three years as the period beyond which a *ra'īyet* could not leave his land uncultivated.

[64] *Bid'at*: in Islamic jurisprudence, an innovation that contravenes the *sharī'a* and is therefore, in most cases, ruled to be illegal. Here the term is used to denote a practice which contravenes custom and *ḳānūn*.

[65] Normally a widow. In this period, land could not legally be granted to women *ab initio*.

[however] the *ṭapu*-tax was confirmed [as guaranteeing possession], and it was forbidden to discriminate between 'outsider' and *ra ʿīyet*.

(xx) To take a tithe on the produce of vineyards and gardens is in conformity with the prescription of the *sharīʿa* (*ḳānūn-i şerʿ*); but since it causes hardship for the *ra ʿīyet* to put aside (*taḫlīs*) the tithe, to prevent this hardship, a cash-equivalent (*bedel*) has been estimated for the amount of the tithe and is regarded as *ḫarāc*[66] [on produce]. In the various districts in accordance with the productivity, from each *dönüm* (measuring by vineyard *dönüm*) in some regions (*vilāyet*) 10 *aḳçe* have customarily been taken, in some regions 5 *aḳçe*, and in some regions 3 *aḳçe*. From gardens and house-precincts (*ḥarīm*), too, a fixed sum (*kesim*) is taken in respect of the tithe [due from them]. [The matter] has been noted again in the registers to this effect; and now in the new register the [due from the] crop has been determined in this way.

(xxi) Tithe on honey [due] from the *ra ʿīyet* has been entered [in the register] as accruing in this *sancaḳ* to the *ṣāḥib-i ra ʿīyet*.[67] But as cash-equivalent for the tithe on honey, [varying] according to productivity, in some regions 2 *aḳçe* have customarily been taken for each hive and in some regions 1 *aḳçe*. It has been entered again to this effect.

(xxii) Bride-tax (*resm-i ʿarūsāne*) is 60 *aḳçe* from a virgin and 40 *aḳçe* from a woman; from a poor one, it is half the tax on a rich one; and from one in medium circumstances it is the sum in between.

As regards settled people, the criterion for assigning a woman's marriage-tax (*resm-i nikāḥ*) and bride-tax is the soil;[68] as regards *yürük*s, who have no fixed habitation, the virgin and the non-virgin (*s̱eyyibe*), treated alike, follow the liability of the father.

The marriage-tax (*resm-i nikāḥ*) is one *dīnār*[69] at the highest rate and 12 *aḳçe* at the lowest; for those between, it is taken according to the circumstances of the man and the woman who are marrying.

From a man who divorces his wife and marries [her] again, the marriage-tax is taken, but it is the accepted custom (*ʿörf-i ma ʿrūf*) not to take the bride-chamber-tax (*resm-i gerdek*) [again].[70]

(xxiii) Tax on [legal] documents (*mekātīb*) used to be taken according to the various rulings of the authoritative jurists (*eʾimme-i müctehidīn*); later it was fixed at 17 *aḳçe*. It has been confirmed also that the tax on the division of inheritances[71] (*resm-i ḳısmet-i mevārīs̱*) shall be at the rate of 20 *aḳçe* per thousand[72].

---

[66] The term *ḫarāc* here refers to the canonical *ḫarāc-i muḳāseme*, a tax on crops of up to 50 percent, according to the productivity of the land.

[67] The term *ṣāḥib-i ra ʿīyet* ('holder of the *ra ʿīyet*') refers to the *sipāhī* on whose land the *ra ʿīyet* is registered. The problem with beehives was that they were often moved and that the honey was produced on a *tīmār* belonging to another *sipāhī*. The question was to determine whether the *sipāhī* on whose *tīmār* the *ra ʿīyet* was registered, or the *sipāhī* on whose *tīmār* the honey was produced should receive the tax.

[68] That is, the place of residence.

[69] *Dīnār* was not the name of a coin in circulation, but refers here to an Ottoman gold coin, based on the Venetian ducat, with a value of 60 *aḳçe*.

[70] The difference between the marriage (*nikāḥ*) tax and the bride-chamber (*gerdek*) tax is that that the first goes to the *ḳāḍī* and the second to the *sipāhī*.

[71] The division of inheritances followed the rules of Islamic law and was carried out under the supervision of the local *ḳāḍī*.

[72] These taxes were a lucrative source of income for *ḳāḍī*s and *ḳāḍī ʿasker*s.

(xxiv) In places in this *sancaḳ* noted as [subject to] grazing-tax (*resm-i otlaḳ*), grazing-tax is taken for each flock of sheep; but no tax is to be taken where it is not noted.

For each flock of sheep which moves from one region and has a wintering-ground (*ḳışlaḳ*) elsewhere, wintering-tax (*resm-i ḳışlaḳ*) is taken in proportion to the number [of the flock].

(xxv) Skins of lynxes and leopards (*ḳaplan*) caught in this territory belong to the *sancaḳbegi*, unless they are caught by a *yaya* or a *müsellem*, in which case they belong to the [*yaya*'s or *müsellem*'s] *sancakbegi*.

(xxvi) On 'free' (*serbest*)[73] *tīmār*s, the rewards (*cuʿl*) on stray animals and runaway slaves and slave-girls caught by *reʿāyā*, and not by *yaya*s and *müsellem*s or the ruler's nomads (*yürükān-i ḫudāvendgār*), fall to the holder of the *tīmār* (*ṣāḥib-i tīmār*). After the customary period for them has elapsed, they are auctioned in the markets with the cognizance (*maʿrifet*) of the *ḳāḍī*, and the money raised by the sale of the male or female slave or of the animal is held by a trustee (*emīn*), until the owner is identified. (The customary period for a slave, male or female, is three months; for animals, it is one month, but for a valuable [animal] it is half that for a runaway slave.) When *reʿāyā* make the capture, the criterion [for the *tīmār*-holder's benefitting] is whether the *tīmār* is 'free'.

On *tīmār*s which are not free, it makes no difference whether [the *tīmār*-holder's] own *reʿāyā* or the *reʿāyā* of another made the capture; if no procedure is laid down in the register, [the matter] is arranged in favour of the *sancaḳbegi*, or of the *subaşı*s, or according to established practice. The strongest criterion is the entries in the register and, after that, established practice.

Captures made by *yaya*s and *müsellem*s and *yürük*s are also dealt with in this way, except that when reference is made to 'the *sancaḳbegi*' it means [each group's] own *sancaḳbegi*.

(xxvii) On free *tīmār*s, all fines taken from the *reʿāyā* belong to the *ṣāḥib-i tīmār* ('holder of the *tīmār*').

On non-free *tīmār*s, half goes to the *ṣāḥib-i raʿīyet*, and the other half goes to the *sancaḳbegi* or the *subaşı*s who have the right to intervene (*daḫl*); if both have the right, they take a quarter each (but in this *sancaḳ* the case of their both having the right does not occur).[74] In places where sheep-tax and bride-tax are so noted, they intervene[75] in this manner.

(xxviii) The punishment (*siyāset*) of bandits and thieves and homicides and other criminals according to the degree [of their offences] is the duty of the *sancaḳbegi* of the cavalry (*atlu sancakbegi*), who is the pivot for the good order of the territory (*memleket*) and the mainstay (*menāṭ*) for the security of the region (*vilāyet*). But if for any reason [the offender] is pardoned in accordance with *şerʿ* and *ʿörf*, it is contrary to the ancient *ḳānūn* to exact money from him as 'cash-equivalent of *siyāset*[76]-punishment' (*bedel-i siyāset*). No fine is to be taken from a man who suffers *siyāset*-punishment; but if he is pardoned, it is the *ṣāḥib-i raʿīyet* who fines him.

The amounts of fines are: for unjustifiable homicide, from a man in good circumstances,

---

[73] A free (*serbest*) *tīmār* is one where all the proceeds of fines and other incidental income go to the *sipāhī*. On 'unfree' *tīmār*s, the *sipāhī* shares the proceeds with the *sancaḳbegi*. See clause (xxviii).

[74] Here the compilers clearly copied the clause from the earlier regulations for the *sancaḳ* of Kütahya, where the exclusion noted here did not apply.

[75] That is, they share.

[76] *Siyāset* has the general sense of an extra-canonical punishment inflicted for the maintenance of good order. In Ottoman usage it usually means the death penalty.

300 *akçe*, from one in medium circumstances, 200 *akçe*, from one in poor circumstances, 100 *akçe*; for knocking out an eye, 150 *akçe*; for wounding the head so as to expose the bone, and for causing the loss of a tooth, and for wounding with a knife so that [the victim] takes to his bed, 100 *akçe*; for causing the loss of a hand, half the fine for taking life. It is the accepted usage (*ʿörf-i maʿrūf*) to take 30 *akçe* for offences less serious than these, which entail beating and correction (*taʿzīr ve teʾdīb*), and 12 *akçe* as the fine for inflicting a black bruise.[77]

(xxix) It is forbidden for the *sancakbegi* or the *subaşı* or their men to take something and release an offender (*mücrim*) before he has been examined (*teftīş*), or before the misdeeds patently committed by him have been dealt with according to the *şerʿ*[78] and the *ʿörf*,[79] [for then] they themselves are open to accusation and their men are offenders meriting punishment. It is a violation (*taʿaddī*) contrary to *şerʿ* and *ʿörf* to seize and punish (*siyāset*) a suspect offender before his crime has been proven and made patent before the local *kāḍī* or in the presence of a commissioner (*müfettiş*) and he has been handed over [in due form] to the executive officers (*ehl-i ʿörf*). However, if an offender or a suspect is refractory and obstinate and refuses to come to the court when summoned, then it is not forbidden to bring him to the court for punishment (*taʿzīr*) by using force, but without beating him up (*bilā teʿzīb*).

In short, every matter among the *ʿörfī* matters (*każāyā-yi ʿörfīye*) which occurs is to be [dealt with] with the cognizance of the *kāḍī*s of the region (*vilāyet*) and according to the commands (*yasak*) of the great *emīr*s and of the agents (?) (*aʿvine*) and of the servants of the ruler (*ḫüdāvendgār*), [for] it is the mainstay for the execution of the decisions of judges (*ḥükkām*) and the condition for the observance of good order among men that obedience be shown to what is entailed by the *sharīʿa* and submission to what is demanded by *ʿörf*.

(xxx) If on any *tīmār* where there are no beehives or sheep or vineyards or gardens or mills, and these are introduced later, the tithes and taxes on them go to the holder of the *tīmār*.

3 Extracts from the 'general' *kānūnnāme*, c1500

Book of the Ottoman *ʿörfī kānūn*s

Praise be to the True Ruler, Who commands justice and equity and forbids lewdness and iniquity, and has made sultans to be the means (*sabab*) for the good order of the world and has made their decrees to be effective over all dwellers in tents and houses (*ahlu ʾl-wabar waʾl-madar*); and prayers and salutations upon the establisher (*wāḍiʿ*) of the *sunna*, our lord Muḥammad al-Muṣṭafā, the best of mankind: and upon his Family and his Companions, who are characterised by excellence of character and goodness of life.

Thereafter:
Inasmuch as a command ... came forth to the effect that the prescription of the world-protecting regulations (*kavāʿid*) and the Ottoman *ʿörfī kānūn*s – which are the pivot for the

---

[77] This *kānūnnāme* was compiled before the promulgation of Bāyezīd II's 'general' *kānūnnāme* of c1500, which contained a penal code. After 1500, compilers of *sancak kānūnnāme*s, such as this one, would not normally include penal statutes, but instead refer users to the 'general' *kānūnnāme*. See below 5 (xii).

[78] *Şerʿ*; the *sharīʿa*.

[79] *ʿÖrf*: custom; customary law, *kānūn*.

reformation of the world and the point from which all peoples depend – should all be written down and inscribed in the form of a bound register, they have, in obedience to the exalted command, been collected together so as to comprise three chapters (*bāb*), each chapter being divided into several sections (*faṣl*), in the following fashion:

Chapter I is in four sections setting out the fines and punishments due for offences, which are of common application to the *sipāhī* and *ra'īyet*, high and low, so that whoever is guilty of one of these offences is to be punished with the punishment laid down . . .

Chapter II is in seven sections, setting out . . .

1. The position (*aḥvāl*) of the *tīmār*-holder (*ṣāḥib-i tīmār*).
2. What matters are at the disposition (*taṣarruf*) of the *sipāhī* on his *tīmār* and how he exercises this disposition.
3. On tolls (*bāc*) and *beytü'l-māl.*[80]
4. On *çift*-tax and *bennāk*-tax and sheep-tax and mill-tax.
5. On tithes (*a'ṣār*).
6. On *bād-i havā.*[81]
7. Matters relating to the *yaya*s and the *müsellem*s.

Chapter III is also in seven sections, setting out matters relating particularly to the *re'āyā.*

1. The duties entailed by the status of *ra'īyet.*
2. Matters relating to infidels only.
3. The *ḳānūn* concerning *'azab*s.[82]
4. Matters relating to nomads (*yürük ve ḫaymāne*).
5. Concerning the Vlachs.
6. Innovations (*bida'*)[83] abolished [in Ḳaramān].
7. The *ḳānūn* for [palace] firewood.

[from II.1]

(i) The holder of a *tīmār* of 1000 *aḳçe* [is to appear] himself *cebelü*;[84] of 2000, himself *cebelü* with 1 *ġulām*;[85] of 3000, himself *bürüme*[86] with 1 *ġulām*; of 4000, 4,500, 5000, himself *bürüme*, with 1 *cebelü*, 1 *ġulām* and 1 *tenktür*[87] . . .

(v) If a *tīmār*-holder who has been ordered to campaign with the victorious troops does not come and render the full service due, the income of the *tīmār* is 'stopped' (*mevḳūf*); the *tīmār*

[80] *Beytü'l-māl* ('treasury'): unclaimed inheritances. These would accrue to the treasury if no heir appeared to claim them.

[81] *Bād-i havā* ('wind of the air'): income from incidental taxes, fines and fees. The term is evidently a calque of Byzantine ἀερικόν or αερ ('fine, supplementary tax').

[82] *'Azab*: an infantryman recruited through a levy on urban youth. *'Azab*s often served as garrison troops.

[83] *Bida'*: plural of *bid'at.* See n. 47.

[84] *Cebelü* ('armoured'): equipped with sufficient armour to cover the torso, sword, shield, lance and mace; a retainer so equipped.

[85] *Ġulām* ('youth, servant'): a retainer, armed or unarmed.

[86] *Bürüme* ('covering the whole body'): full body armour.

[87] *Tenktür*: a small tent.

is given to another, and the income arising until the date that the new *berāt* comes into effect falls to the *mevḳūfcı*[88] . . .

(x) If a timar-holder takes part in a battle but is wounded and so not present at the roll-call (*yoḳlama*); or if he is absent through illness; or if, having been wounded in one campaign, he is still incapacitated for the next but sends his *cebelü*(s) under his officer (*yarar adam*) and so performs his service [by proxy] – this being attested by the *sancaḳbegi* or confirmed by the testimony of witnesses – this is acceptable, and there is to be no intervention [by the *mevḳūfcı*].

(xi) The *mevḳūfcı* is not to meddle over the *sipāhī*'s *cebelü*s and the *oġlan*s listed in the register, raising contention about whether he has brought a *cebelü* instead of an *oġlan* or an *oġlan*[89] instead of a *cebelü*; the *mevḳūfcı* is not to check the *cebelü*s.

[from II.2]

(ix) If a *su eri* takes from a *ra'īyet* his dues (such as the sheep-tax and the *dönüm*-tax) before the [proper] time and is dismissed (*ma'zūl*) before that proper time comes and his *tīmār* is given to someone else, the incoming *su eri* is to collect [what is due] from the dismissed *su eri*, not demanding anything from the *ra'īyet*. But the the *ra'īyet* should get a *ḥüccet*[90] from the *ḳāḍī* establishing what the outgoing *su eri* took, so that [the newcomer] may go and demand [his due] on the strength of the *ḥüccet*.

(x) *Beglerbegi*s, it is reported, sometimes give a *sipāhī* a letter and send him to the *ḳāḍī*, saying: 'Let this man collect such-and-such from his *ra'īyet*s before the due time'. *Beglerbegi*s are not to give such letters. If they pay no attention and do [issue letters], the *ḳāḍī*s are not to act on them and are not to be reprimanded for refusing to act.

(xv) The command (*ḥükm*) regarding the *sipāhī*'s *ḫāṣṣa çiftlik*[91] and *ḫāṣṣa* land is that it cannot be made the *mülk*[92] of any [*ra'īyet*] by the granting of *ṭapu*; *ṭapu* on it is not permissible.

(xviii) If the holder of *ra'īyet*-land dies or flees so that the land is vacant, the *tīmār*-holder may occupy it himself as if it were *ḫāṣṣa* land . . . Yet the fact that the *sipāhī* is occupying it does not make it *ḫāṣṣa*: it is essentially *ra'īyet* land, so that if *'avārıż*[93] does occur and are imposed on each *çift* . . . the *sipāhī* must bear the *'avārıż* burden in respect of that land, unless, with the passage of time, it has been entered in a subsequent register as belonging to this *sipāhī*: for thus it has passed from the totality of *ḫavāṣṣ*[94] and should be treated as *ḫāṣṣa*.

(xxii) Every time *'avārıż* occur, the *subaşı*s and the *tīmār*-holders are to present their *ra'īyet*s before the *ḳāḍī*, and the *ḳāḍī* is to list them and carry out the *pādişāh*'s command; the *ḳul* who is sent [with the command] is to reduce to obedience any who object.

---

[88] *Mevḳūfcı*: the official charged with collecting for the treasury revenues from *tīmār*s and other fiefs which are temporarily in abeyance.

[89] *Oġlan* ('youth, boy, servant'): synonym of *ġulām*. See n. 85.

[90] *Ḥüccet*: a confirmatory document issued by a *ḳāḍī*. See Chapter VI.

[91] *Ḫāṣṣa çiftlik*: the area of land on a *tīmār* set aside for the use of the *sipāhī*.

[92] *Mülk* ('property'): private property; land, the revenues from which are held as private property.

[93] *'Avārıż*: extra-ordinary taxes.

[94] *Ḫavāṣṣ*: plural of *ḫāṣṣa*.

[from II.6]

(i) The taxes listed in the register as *bād-i havā* are bride tax, fines, *ṭapu* on a *çiftlik*, *ṭapu* on a house-site and the smoke-tax (*tütün resmi*) on people coming from outside [the *tīmār*] to winter [on it].

[From II.7]

(i) A *sipāhī* who takes part in the sultan's campaigns is *ʿaskerī*,[95] while campaigning and also after retiring, provided that in retirement he is not registered as somebody's *raʿīyet*.

(ii) So too the *ḳul*s of the *ḫüdāvendgār*[96] and his female slaves (*cāriye*) (provided they are married to *ʿaskerī*s). After manumission (*iʿtāḳ*) they, too, are *ʿaskerī*.

(iii) Holders of the posts of *ḳāḍī*, *müderris*,[97] *şeyḫ*,[98] *mütevellī*,[99] *nāẓir*[100] and the like, which have been granted as a result of application (*mülāzemet*) to the Porte, are also *ʿaskerī*.

(iv) These too count as *ʿaskerī*: the child of an *ʿaskerī* who is [*derece* ?] and is not registered as *raʿīyet* to anyone; his wife, if actually married to him; his slave (*ḳul*) who, after manumission, serves an *ʿaskerī* and is supported by him and is not registered as *raʿīyet* to anyone; the daughter of a *raʿīyet* married to an *ʿaskerī*, so long as she is actually married.

(v) *Resm-i ḳısmet*[101] for these belongs to the *ḳāḍīʿasker*: his *ḳassām*[102] divides the estate and collects the *resm-i ḳısmet* for the *ḳāḍīʿasker*. This was the *ḳānūn*, but now marriages and manumissions made by the *ʿaskerī*s have been allocated to the *ḳāḍīʿasker* . . .

(vi) However, with regard to marriages, deeds of manumission (*iʿtāḳ-nāme*) and *ḥüccet*s, the *sipāhī* is free to choose; he may apply to whichever authority [*ḳāḍīʿasker* or *ḳāḍī*] he wishes, paying the tax to that authority.

(vii) A falconer (*doġancı*) with a *berāt* who actually serves as a falconer and is not anyone's registered *raʿīyet*, a campaigning *yaya*, *müsellem*, *cānbāz*, *yürük*, *tatar* and *voynuk*[103] – these too are *ʿaskerī*. But with regard to those who are rich, their *resm-i ḳısmet* being a hundred [*aḳçe*] or more, it goes to the *ḳāḍīʿasker*; if it is less, to the *ḳāḍī* of the district . . .

(x) If a *sipāhī*'s slave is freed and leaves his service and opts for a settled life (*ḥużūr*) and becomes gainfully employed (*kāsib*); and if one of my *cāriye*s or the daughter of a *sipāhī* marries a *raʿīyet* [such a person is not *ʿaskerī*] . . .

---

95 *ʿAskerī* ('military'): a member of the military class. This section defines the membership of the tax-exempt military class, the rules for the division of their inheritances and the fees payable for the issue of their diplomas of appointment and other official and legal documents.

96 *Ḫudāvendgār* (Persian: 'ruler'): the sultan.

97 *Müderris*: a teacher in a *medrese*.

98 Here, probably the head of a dervish lodge.

99 *Mütevellī*: an administrator of a *waqf*.

100 *Nāẓir*: the supervisor of a *waqf*.

101 *Resm-i ḳismet*: the fee payable for dividing inheritances.

102 *Ḳassām*: the official responsible for dividing inheritances of the *ʿaskerī* class.

103 These are all groups of military auxiliaries.

(xi) Holders of posts granted only by the report (*iʿlām*) of the *ḳāḍī* . . . such as Qurʾān- and *tesbīḥ*[104]-[reciters], are like the *yamaḳs*[105] of *yayas* and *müsellems* . . .; their taxes for *ḳismet* and marriage and *ḥüccets* belong to the *ḳāḍī* of the district (*vilāyet*).

(xii) If the wife of an *ʿaskerī* dies as a widow after the *ʿaskerī*'s death, then if her father was *ʿaskerī*, so is she; if he was *şehirlü*[106] or *raʿīyet*, then so is she . . .

(xvi) The *ḳāḍīs* of Ḳaramān,[107] it is reported, on being moved from a post, do not hand over the *sicill*[108]-registers to their successors, but take them away with them. They must be urged to hand them over, so that the affairs of the Muslims are not disorganised.

[from III.1]

(i) If a *raʿīyet* dies leaving a *çiftlik* and a young son unable to perform the obligations of the *çiftlik*, the *sipāhī* is not to demand *çift*-tax from him because it is his father's *çiftlik*, but to give it to someone else, getting him to cultivate it and bear the services (*ḳulluḳ*) on it until the son is able to manage it himself . . .

(ii) The daughter of a *sürgün*[109] is to be married to a *sürgün*, and to nobody else . . . When a noble command is due to be written concerning *sürgüns*, the text is to be submitted to the *pādişāh*.[110]

[from III.2]

(iv) If an infidel from the *dārüʾl-ḥarb* dies in my well-protected territories and if after the payment of debts there remains over an estate, it is to be listed with the cognizance of the *ḳāḍī* and held . . . If there is no dispute over who inherits or over the will, the estate is to be held in a safe and secure place, and the *beytüʾl-mālcı*[111] is not to intervene; when a man from the dead man's country comes with a letter regarding the estate [all the papers are to be sent to the Porte and a *firman* will be issued.]

4 The *ḳānūnnāme* of Siverek, 1518

Exposition of the *ḳānūnnāme* of the *livā*[112] of Siverek, according to the *ḳānūn* of Ḥasan Pādişāh[113]

(i) Firstly, from the *reʿāyā* class (*cins*) dwelling in villages, both Muslim and infidel: from him who had a *çift* and was able to cultivate land to the extent of a *çiftlik* , they used to take, under

---

[104] *Tesbīḥ*: reciting praise to God with the help of prayer beads.
[105] *Yamaḳ*: a member of a military-auxiliary group who is not on active service but contributes to the upkeep of the campaigner.
[106] *Şehirlü*: townsman.
[107] *Ḳaramān*: the province in south-central Anatolia, with its capital at Konya.
[108] *Sicill*: a *ḳāḍī*'s register; an entry in a *ḳāḍī*'s register.
[109] *Sürgün* ('deportee'): member of a population that has been forcibly relocated.
[110] This clause indicates that the sultan did not see all the commands written in his name.
[111] *Beytüʾl-mālcı*: the official responsible for managing unclaimed inheritances.
[112] *Livā*: a *sancaḳ*.
[113] Uzun Ḥasan (d. 1478): ruler of the Aḳḳoyunlu Empire. Siverek was part of the province of Diyārbekir, which the Ottomans conquered in 1516. The *ḳānūnnāme* records the taxes levied under the Aḳḳoyunlus, which were in force in the area at the time of the conquest.

the name *resm-i çift*, one *eşrefī*,[114] which is worth 40 Ottoman *aḳçe*. It has been confirmed thus. The time for taking it is spring, at *nevrūz*.[115]

(ii) From their crops, [a share] used to be collected, at the rate of one-fifth. Confirmed.

(iii) From every household (*ḫāne*): three days of labour (*ırġadīye*) used to be taken which, at 3 *aḳçe* a day, is 9 *aḳçe*: the time for taking it is half in spring, at the sowing, and half at reaping time.

(iv) Mill-tax: they used to take 1 *şāhrukī*[116] per month for every month the mill turned, which is 6 Ottoman *aḳçe*. Confirmed.

(v) Sheep-due: there used to be taken, from 100 sheep, one sheep plus 4 *tenge*,[117] which is equivalent to 1 *aḳçe* for 2 sheep. The time for taking it is spring, at *nevrūz*: it is to be taken then.

(vi) From their vineyards at the rate of one-tenth. Confirmed.

(vii) But from the people in the villages of this *livā*, they used to take 300 gold pieces (*sikke-i ḥasene*) as a lump sum (*maḳṭūʿ*), 150 of it called *ḳara ṣalġun* and the other 150 called *ḫarc-i timūr*. This sum of 300 gold pieces has been abolished, and nothing [under this head] has been noted in the new register.

(viii) Under the name *şıḫnaġī*, from every threshing one *ġarbīl* used to be taken, which is approximately one Istanbul *kīle*:[118] and from every village as festival-tax (*resm-i ʿīdīye*), one sheep, and the same as New Year tax (*resm-i nevrūzīye*): and from each of their looms, one *tenge* per year. These have been abolished and have not been entered as revenue.

(xix) Bride-tax: for every wedding (*ʿarūsīye*) one animal used to be taken. This is confirmed.

(x) On the matter of tolls (*tamġa*): on every load of silk passing through, half an *eşrefī* was taken, which is 25 Ottoman *aḳçe*;[119] from loads of whatever else passes through, 4 *tenge* were taken per load, which is 8 Ottoman *aḳçe* . . .; also 1 *tenge* per load, called *noḳṭa başı*, was taken, which amounts to 2 Ottoman *aḳçe*. A lump sum was also taken from each butcher; and if fresh fruit comes in and is sold, 2 *ḳaraca aḳçe*[120] was taken per load. Other items, too, which have not been noted in the register, are confirmed according to the old code (*düstūr*).

5 The *kānūnnāme* of Sīs, 1518

Exposition of the *ḳānūnnāme* of Sultan Ḳāyitbāy[121] in the *livā* of Sīs[122]

---

[114] A Mamlūk gold coin, named after the Mamlūk sultan al-Malik al-Ashraf Barsbay (r. 1422–38).

[115] *Nevrūz* ('New Year's Day'): the vernal equinox, 22 March.

[116] A large silver coin weighing 4.7 g in circulation during the Aḳḳoyunlu period, named after Timur's grandson Shāhrukh.

[117] A silver coin in circulation in the Aḳḳoyunlu period.

[118] About 35 litres.

[119] *Sic*. In clause 1, the *eşrefī* is valued at 40 *aḳçe*.

[120] A silver coin of the Aḳḳoyunlu period, valued at one-third of an Ottoman *aḳçe*.

[121] Ḳāyitbāy: Mamlūk sultan (r. 1468–96). The area was conquered in 1516. The *ḳānūnnāme* records the taxes which the Mamlūks had previously levied in the area.

[122] Present-day Kozan.

(i) On wheat, barley, oats, rye, millet, sesame, vetch, cotton, onions, garlic, melons, water-melons – in short, on every type of crop and cereal and fruit, there is to be a tithing (*taʿşīr*).

(ii) From a rice-field, tithe of one in ten is to be taken from the *ṣāḥib-i arż* on whose land it is sown.

(iii) From Turkish *reʿāyā* (*reʿāyā-yi etrāk*): from a married man, household tax (*resm-i ḫāne*) of 70 *ḥalebī aḳçe*[123] a year is to be taken at the vernal equinox (*nevrūz-i sulṭānī*), and from a bachelor capable of earning his living, 10 *ḥalebī aḳçe*.

(iv) From *ẕimmī reʿāyā*: from a married man, household tax of 132 *Ḥalebī aḳçe* is to be taken, 66 at *nevrūz* and 66 on the first day of the first month of autumn: from every married man and every bachelor, *jizya*[124] of 50 *ḥalebī aḳce* at *nevrūz*. From every married man and bachelor among the infidels of the fortress of Pārsībeyt (?), *jizya* of 50 *aḳçe* are to be taken.

(v) For every mill that works throughout the year, 120 *ḥalebī aḳçe* are to be taken each year, and for one that works for six months, 60.

(vi) Sheep tax: 1 *ḥalebī aḳçe* per sheep is to be taken; and from sheep coming from outside, from a good flock, 1 sheep, as lairage tax (*resm-i yataḳ*).

(vii) Bride tax: 120 *ḥalebī aḳçe* are to be taken for a virgin (*ḳız*) and 60 for a widow (*bīve*), and no more.

(viii) For a head-wound, 60 *ḥalebī aḳçe* are to be taken and for a knife wound not causing death, 100.

(ix) From some agricultural lands (*mezraʿa*) which are *mülk*,[125] there is a tithing of one in ten: the *sipāhī* takes one-fifth as *begvāne*, and the owner of the *mülk* takes one-fifth as *mülūkāne*.

(x) From of old, *reʿāyā*, though belonging to the *sancaḳ* of Sīs, have lived in the *sancaḳ* of Adana, [but] pay their *ʿörfī* taxes to the *sancaḳbegi* of Sīs. This practice has been confirmed, and no action contrary to the *ḳānūn* is to be taken.

(xi) On each load of honey and oil and cheese, 2 *ḥalebī aḳçe* are to be taken as toll (*bāc*).

(xii) When matters involving fines (*cerāʾim*) occur, the ancient Ottoman *ḳānūn*[126] is to be consulted, and [its provision] is not to be exceeded.

6 The *ḳānūnnāme* of Nikopol, reign of Süleymān I

6a Instructions on dealing with the tīmārs *of the district*

At present the noble command of the *pādişāh* has been issued to the following effect:

(i) The *tīmār*s listed in the register of the district (*vilāyet*) are to remain as they are: no *tīmār* is to be added to another *tīmār*, nor is any village to be transferred from one *tīmār* to another:

---

[123] *Ḥalebī aḳçe* ('Aleppo *aḳçe*'): a Mamlūk silver coin. 1 Ottoman *aḳçe* was valued at 2.5 Aleppo *aḳçe*.

[124] *Jizya*: the poll-tax levied on adult, non-Muslim males.

[125] This clause refers to lands where half the revenue went to a *sipāhī* and half to a private owner.

[126] The reference is to the penal code which forms the first section of the 'general' *ḳānūnnāme* of c1500.

no *tezkerelü tīmār*[127] is to be cancelled and made *tezkeresiz*, nor is any *tezkeresiz tīmār*[128] to be made *tezkerelü*.

(ii) If any *tīmār* falls vacant, [the local authorities] are to look for an unbeneficed candidate (*ma'zūl*) from within that *sancaḳ*. If no substitute candidate can be found from that *sancaḳ*, it may be given to a substitute candidate from another *sancaḳ*, but on condition that so long as he occupies the *tīmār* he does not reside in another *sancaḳ*, but comes and resides in his [new] *sancaḳ*. If he resides in another *sancaḳ*, this is to be a reason for his dismissal.

If a *tīmār* or *ze'āmet* falls vacant and there is no candidate deserving so extensive a *tīmār* or *ze'āmet*, it is to be given to two persons [jointly].

(iii) This command is not to be infringed. If it is, the [provincial] *defterdār* is to warn the *beglerbegi*. If the *beglerbegi* insists and tells the *defterdār*: 'Register it. I will take the responsibility', the *defterdār* is not to do so. If he registers a transaction contrary to what has been commanded, this will be a reason for his dismissal.

(iv) *Tīmār*s of *subaşı*s and *sipāhī*s are not to be taken from them on trivial pretexts, but only if [the holder] fails to partake in an imperial campaign, or if he commits homicide. [The facts] are to be stated (*ma'lūm*) by certificates (*mektūb*) of the *sancaḳbegi* and the *ḳāḍī*. The certificates are to be kept, and the *tīmār* is to be given to someone else. If later the [dispossessed] *subaşı* or *sipāhī* comes and complains: 'It was not I who committed the crime', he is to be answered by the production of the certificates. If the certificates have been issued upon the misrepresentation of the facts, this will be a reason for the dismissal of the *sancaḳbegi* and of the *ḳāḍī*, too.

(v) If a *sipāhī* commits a crime other [than homicide], he is to be punished by the *sancaḳbegi* and his agents, with the cognizance of the *ḳāḍī*, in the way that is required by *şer'* and *ḳānūn*. If it is necessary to refer the question to the Porte, the report is to be submitted with precise details (*vuḳū'ı üzre*).

(vi) All the *subaşı*s and *sipāhī*s of the *sancaḳ* are to be [resident] within the *sancaḳ*, and not elsewhere. If anyone is [resident] in another *sancaḳ*, this will be a reason for dismissal.

(vii) If a *ra'īyet* of one *tīmār* leaves one village and goes to the *tīmār* of another *sipāhī*, the *sipāhī* to whose *tīmār* he has come is to investigate what village he has come from, and send word to the [first] *sipāhī* and to the people of that village, who are to come and take him back: or if it is near, [the second *sipāhī*] may send him back under the escort of one of his men. If [the second *sipāhī*] ignores this, being simply greedy for the smoke-taxes[129] or for the tithe from the land which [the incomer] cultivates, this will entail dismissal.

(viii) If Muslim or infidel [peasants] not listed in the register (*ḫāric ez defter*) come to the *tīmār*s of *subaşı*s or *sipāhī*s or fortress-soldiers, the *sancaḳbegi* and other [provincial officers] are not to object to [the presence of] these newcomers. They are to permit the *tīmār*-holder concerned to collect the *şer'ī* dues and *'örfī* taxes[130] of each newcomer in the same way as they are collected from other [registered] *re'āyā*. Until a new survey is made, they are not to intervene

[127] *Tezkerelü tīmār*: a *tīmār* granted with a certificate from the Porte.
[128] *Tezkeresiz tīmār*: a *tīmār* granted by a *beglerbegi*, without a certificate from the Porte.
[129] *Resm-i tütün* ('smoke-tax'): a charge payable for temporary residence.
[130] This means no more than all taxes levied according to the *sharī'a* and *ḳānūn*; in other words, all taxes.

with the allegation: 'He is a vagrant (*ḫaymana*). He is not a *raʿīyet* registered as belonging to you', for the newcomers are not registered as providing income for the *sancaḳbegi* or other [officers] [and so they will have no valid cause to object]. It has been commanded that each [newcomer], wherever he may be, belongs to the [relevant] *tīmār*-holder.

(ix) In this *sancaḳ*, half of the *niyābet*[131] arising from the *tīmār*s of the *sipāhī*s and fortress-soldiers (but not that from *zeʿāmet*s or from the *tīmār*s of *çeribaşıs*[132]) has from of old been regularly registered as income for the *sancaḳbegi*s, to provide for the protection (*muḥāfaẓat*) of the district. When a fine is to be paid, no sum in excess of what is prescribed in the *ḳānūnnāme*[133] is to be exacted. The *sancaḳbegi* is to receive half of the fines prescribed by the *ḳānūn* and the *tīmār*-holder the other half. If the *sancaḳbegi*'s agents or a *tīmār*-holder exacts a fine in excess of [the prescription of] the *ḳānūn*, the *ḳāḍī* is to prevent them from taking it. If they do not refrain, the *ḳāḍī* will make a submission to the Porte.

(x) The *sancaḳbegi*s are not to intervene on the *tīmār*s of *subaşı*s, *çeribaşı*s and fortress commanders which are free (*serbest*), unless a person has incurred capital punishment (*ṣalb*), or the punishment of the loss of a limb: in that case, the *sancaḳbegi*, with the cognizance of the *ḳāḍī*, is to order his men to carry out the punishment. When [such] punishment (*siyāset*) is to be inflicted, it is to be carried out at the scene [of the crime]: [the criminal] is not to be taken to another *ḳāḍīlıḳ* or elsewhere. And no money is to be taken[134] from a person with the words: 'We will punish (*siyāset*) you'.

If on such a free *tīmār*, there occurs a crime not incurring capital punishment or the loss of a limb, the punishment is to be carried out by the *subaşı*s: the *sancaḳbegi*'s officer is not to intervene, saying: 'I will carry out the punishment'; if he does, he will be prevented by the *ḳāḍī*s of the district, and if he refuses to refrain, the *ḳāḍī* is to make a submission to the Porte, so that he can be duly punished.

(xi) Because, when this *sancaḳ* was originally surveyed, there were many empty and deserted areas and the villages did not have clearly defined boundaries, hive-taxes were divided into three, with one-third assigned as income to the *sancaḳbegi*, another third to the *subaşı* (if there was a *zeʿāmet*[135] nearby), and the other third to the *tīmār*-holder; or, if there was no *zeʿāmet* nearby, the two-thirds were assigned to the *tīmār*-holder. Then, as time went on, that custom (*ʿādet*) was abandoned, and the custom was adopted that the *sancaḳbegi* and the *tīmār*-holder should each collect 1 *aḳçe* per hive. [Hence], if a man had hives, the *sancaḳbegi*'s agent and the *tīmār*-holder would collect their taxes: but the *subaşı* would also intervene in districts where one-third was registered as belonging to the *zeʿāmet*, so that excessive taxes were collected from hives, which might be good or poor. So people gave up keeping hives, there was an enormous (*fāḥiş*) fall in the revenues from hive-tax, and the populace was very discontented (*müteşekkī*). Therefore, it has been commanded that[136] it should all be assigned to the *tīmār*-holder, at the rate of one hive in ten: from good hives, one good one, from poor hives, one poor one, and without any demand for cash, [except that] if there are fewer than ten hives, their

[131] *Niyābet*: income arising from fines.
[132] *Çeribaşı*: an officer in the provincial *sipāhī* army.
[133] The *ḳānūnnāme* referred to is the criminal code forming the first section of Bāyezīd II's 'general' *ḳānūnnāme*, or a later recension.
[134] That is, extorted.
[135] *Zaʿīm* (holder of a *zeʿāmet*) is a synonym for *subaşı*.
[136] This phrase is an indication that this clause originated as a decree.

value is to be estimated in the presence of a number of people, and 1 *aḳçe* taken per 10 *aḳçe* [of the estimate]. No income from hives has been registered for the *sancaḳbegi*: he has been excluded from [any share] in beehives, so that henceforth the *sancaḳbegi* is not to participate (*daḫl*) in the hive-taxes of the *sipāhī*s. If he attempts to, the *ḳāḍī* is to make a submission to the Porte.

(xii) The time for collecting *ispence* is the beginning of March, so that *ispence* is to belong to the *sipāhī* into whose period of tenure (*taḥvīl*) the first of March falls.

(xiii) The time for collecting sheep-due is April, [so that] the sheep-due is to belong to [the *sipāhī*] into whose period of tenure the first of April falls: but the due is to be collected after the lambing. Sheep and lambs are to be counted together and 1 *aḳçe* tax is to be taken for 2 sheep, and no more. If anyone attempts to take more, the *ḳāḍī* is to prevent him: if the *ḳāḍī* does not, he himself becomes culpable.

(xiv) In this district, the infidels have a day which they call by the Greek term (*Yunanlılar ıṣṭılāḥınca*) St Elias' Day,[137] in which they believe very strongly. It is said that, when that day comes round, it drives out all the swarms and brings to completion the honey, and that the hive-due belongs to the *sipāhī* in whose period of tenure that day falls. This [practice] has been [confirmed], so that the hive-due is not to be collected until that day is reached. The hive-due falls to the *sipāhī* in whose period of tenure it falls.

(xv) The time for collecting hay-tax is to be when the sickle is to be taken to the hayfields (*çayır*): at whatever time the sickle is taken to the hayfields of each district (*nāḥiye*), the hay-tax of that district is to be collected then. The *ḳāḍī*s are to assign the hay-tax to the *sipāhī*s in whose period of tenure that day falls in each district.

(xvi) In this district, the mill-tax is to be collected after the threshing-floor has been cleared: it is not to be collected while the crops are still on the [threshing] ground. The mill-tax is to be assigned to the *sipāhī* in whose period of tenure the time of clearing the threshing floor falls.

(xvii) [As to] the tithe on gardens (*bāġçe*), the tithe on vegetables and fruits is to be assigned to the *sipāhī* in whose period of tenure the time for stripping the trees and clearing the vegetable gardens (*bostān*) falls.

(xviii) [Further on] the tithe on *bostān*s: if a person does some planting in front of his house or in his courtyard, or grows vegetables for his own use, 2 *aḳçe* are to be collected as 'tithe on *bostān*', because [so small a quantity] cannot be tithed. But nothing is to be taken from a person who sows nothing.

(xix) According to the ancient *ḳānūn* of this district, at threshing time one hen and one pastry-cake (*buġaça*) are to be taken for the *sipāhī* from every married man, or 1 *aḳçe* from a man with no hens. No hens or cakes are to be taken at any other time.

If a *sipāhī* or *subaşı* or *voyvoda*[138] of the *sancaḳ* comes to a village, he is not to demand by force fodder and hay for his horse, or a sheep or chickens, or to impose a house-to-house levy (*ṣalġun*). If the things he wants are to be found in the village, he is to buy them with his own money, and with the consent [of the sellers]: if they are not, he is not to insist that [the

---

[137] 20 July.

[138] *Voyvoda*: an official charged with collecting revenue; a synonym for *subaşı*.

villagers] go and find them. [If they act] otherwise, the *ḳāḍī*s are to prevent them; and if they are not restrained by [the *ḳāḍī*s'] prohibition, the *ḳāḍī*s are to make a submission to the Porte.

(xx) If a *ḳāḍī* knows that injustice (*ẓulm*) is being perpetrated and does not stop it, or if, being unable to stop it, he does not make a submission to the Porte, this will be a reason for his dismissal.

(xxi) The prices of cereals being publicly known in the various areas, the *sancaḳbegi*s and *subaşı*s are not to make villagers accept lower prices and so carry out a forced levy (*ṣalġun*) of barley;[139] when they are short of barley, they are to buy it, paying for it at the current tariff (*narḫ-i rūzī*).

(xxii) The imposition on the district of emergency levies (*'avārıż*) is permitted only to a person who carries my noble command [ordering it] for the defence of the land (*ḥimāyet-i memleket*).

(xxiii) The pig-tax is to be collected at the same time as hive-due is collected, for 2 pigs 1 *aḳçe*, but for one fattened pig 1 *aḳçe*.

(xxiv) On cereals, both tithe and *sālāriye* are to be taken. Together they amount to 2½ *kīle* per *müdd*, [that is] the rate of one *kīle* in eight. 2 *kīle* per *müdd* is tithe, and the half *kīle* is *sālāriye*. If, before carrying the harvest to the threshing-floor, the *rā'īyet* gives the *sipāhī* his tithe in sheaves, then [ten sheaves in] the hundred is tithe and three is *sālāriye*.

(xxv) Tithe is to be taken on chickpeas, lentils, beans, kidney beans, silk cocoons, Judas tree [flowers], fruits and vegetables.

(xxvi) On the vineyards of Muslims, 4 *aḳçe* per *dönüm* is to be taken, but there is to be no tithing [of the produce.]. On the grape-juice (*şıra*), both tithe and *sālāriye* are to be taken; it has been commanded that they give 10 *medre* in the hundred as tithe and 3 as *sālāriye*.[140]

(xxvii) When the *subaşı*s are to hold the *monapolye*, they may hold it for two months and ten days at any time of the year they wish: during that time, the jars and casks of the infidels are to be sealed, and they are not to sell wine (*şarāb*) to anyone, [but] at that time the *subaşı*'s grape-juice (*şıra*) [only] is to be sold. If it is not sold within that time, [the *subaşı*] is not to hold *monapolye* in extra time and force the *re'āyā* to buy it [then] in the same way as he sold it during the days of *monapolye*, unless they willingly accept it at the current tariff.

(xxviii) If somebody's *ra'īyet* gives up agriculture and goes off to engage in a trade (*ṣan'at*), or becomes a carter or a fisherman or a day-labourer, he is, if he is a Muslim, to pay his *sipāhī* 50 *aḳçe* as tithe-equivalent (*bedel-i 'öşr*) and, if he is an infidel, 62 *aḳçe*: in addition, if he is a Muslim, he is to pay 22 *aḳçe* as *çift*-tax and, if he is an infidel, 25 *aḳçe* as *ispence*.

(xxix) If a *ra'īyet*, although he has cultivable land within his *sipāhī*'s boundaries, leaves that place and sows his crops on the land of another *sipāhī*, he is to pay one tithe to his own *sipāhī* and another [to the other *sipāhī*] in respect of the land he has cultivated; if he refuses, he is to return and grow crops on his own *sipāhī*'s land. But if he has no cultivable land under his own *sipāhī*, he is to pay tithe only on the land he cultivates.

---

139 Barley for horses.

140 The fact that *sālāriye* is levied on grape-juice is an indication that its original purpose as a levy of fodder for the *sipāhī*'s horse had long been forgotten.

(xxx) The *re ʿāyā* of *subaşı*s and *tīmār*-holders are to carry their tithes and *sālāriye* to the nearest market, and the *re ʿāyā* of fortress-soldiers are to carry them to the fortress. They are not to make excuses or advance pretexts [for not doing so]; if they do, the authorities of the district (*ḥükkām-i vilāyet*) are to order them to transport them.

(xxxi) Furthermore, [the taxes] noted in the register as *bād-i havā* – fines (*cürm ü cināyet*), *ṭapu*-tax, and smoke-tax at 6 *aḳçe* from people who have come from outside – are to be taken.

(xxxii) *Ze ʿāmet*s and the *tīmār*s of *çeribaşı*s and of fortress-commanders are free, and the *sancaḳbegi* is not to participate in their *bād-i havā*. [The position regarding] the *tīmār*s of *tīmār*-holders and of fortress-soldiers has been explained previously: of their *bād-i havā*, the bride-chamber-tax (*resm-i gerdek*) of the girls [on their *tīmār*s] belongs to the *sancaḳbegi*. No one else is to participate.

(xxxiii) [As to] the bride-tax (*resm-i ʿarūs*), 60 *aḳçe* is to be taken for a virgin and 30 for a non-virgin. [As to] *resm-i gerdek*, if the daughter of a *ra ʿīyet* comes out,[141] the criterion is the soil:[142] the *resm-i gerdek* has been assigned to the lord of the *ra ʿīyet*.[143]

6b Exposition of the ḳānūnnāme *of the* voynuḳs[144]

(i) A *voynuḳ* is exempt from paying *ḫarāc* and *ispence* and tithe on what he produces on his *baştina*,[145] and the tithe on hives and the pig-tax and the sheep-tax, if he has no more than 100 sheep. But if he has more than 100 sheep, 1 *aḳçe* of tax for every two sheep is to be taken on the excesses, and if he engages in cultivation outside his *baştina* (either elsewhere or on the *tīmār* of his *sipāhī*), and if he plants a vineyard, he pays the tithe and the *sālāriye* on this [extra land] according to the *ḳānūn*. [*Voynuḳ*s] are exempt from *ʿavārıż-i dīvāniye*.

(ii) Each year, the one whose turn it is serves on the imperial campaign; but beyond this, the *sancaḳbegi* and the *subaşı* of the district (*vilāyet*) are forbidden to levy barley from them, or make them reap meadows, or make them perform other services. But if any man does not present himself for an imperial campaign and fails to render the service due to the imperial stables, he is, after being corrected (*te ʾdīb*), to pay 300 *aḳçe* to the imperial treasury (*ḫāṣṣa-i hümāyūn*).

(iii) If a *voynuḳ* commits an offence, after he has been corrected in the presence of the *ḳāḍī*, the *çeribaşı* is to punish him and exact the due fine according to the *ḳānūn*; the *sancaḳbegi* is not to intervene, unless the culprit deserves capital punishment or the loss of a limb.

(iv) These *voynuḳ*s are grouped together in [groups of] three *yamaḳ*s. It is the *ḳānūn* that each group of three pays 16 *aḳçe* a year as 'lance-tax' (*gönder aḳçesi*), the one campaigning that year paying 6, and the others 5 each. Since the 'lance-taxes' have from of old belonged to the *sancaḳbegi*, they have now again been assigned as income to the *sancaḳbegi*. The time [for collecting them] is the *ispence* time: they are collected when *ispence* is collected.

---

[141] That is, gets married.
[142] That is, the place of residence.
[143] *Ra ʿīyet ṣāḥibi*: the holder of the *tīmār* on which her father is a registered *ra ʿīyet*.
[144] *Voynuḳ*: a Christian military auxiliary in the Balkans. *Voynuḳ*s had special responsibility for the sultan's horses, mules and camels.
[145] *Baştina*: a peasant tenement in the Balkans.

(v) In the old register, the *voynuḳ*s were registered scattered [throughout the register], and when their sons, too, were collected together according to where they were, a total income of 45,000 *aḳçe* [arising] in about 150 villages was grouped together and granted to the *subaşı* Maḥmūd, but because they were scattered, he was unable to collect (*żabṭ*) it, and he renounced it. Thereafter, [this consolidated income] was divided up and distributed among the *sipāhī*s concerned, by way of shares (*ḥiṣṣe*). Now [when this survey was made] because these people are registered scattered, *tīmār* income (?) of 5,000 *aḳçe* was traced (?), but the rest was lost. When, on this occasion, a submission was made [to the Porte] about these people, by the noble command of the *pādişāh*, those *voynuḳ* villages which consist solely of *voynuḳ*s, and those villages in which the *voynuḳ*s exceed the *ra ʿīyet* – 47 villages – were separated off, and the villages where *voynuḳ*s' sons and incoming vagrants (*ḥaymana*) were settled were grouped together and made *ḫāṣṣ*, with the intention that if one of these *voynuḳ*s becomes sick or disabled and hence unable to serve, his place is to be filled by one of these fit [reservists], who is [then] to be registered as *voynuḳ* and exempted from *ḫarāc* and taxes: thus no *sipāhī*'s *tīmār*-income will suffer loss through these [reservists] supplying the deficiency, and the *voynuḳ*s will always be at full strength.

As for those *voynuḳ*s who live scattered in twos and threes in each village, they have more or less mixed in with the *re ʿāyā* [of the village] and become settled. Their sons have been registered as *ra ʿīyet* in the villages where they are settled, and henceforth there is to be no registration of [new] *voynuḳ*s from among them – unless [the serving *voynuḳ*s] have sons or relations (*ta ʿalluḳāt*) who are 'outside the register'; these may be registered [as new *voynuḳ*s], for thus the income of the *sipāhī*'s *tīmār* suffers no loss. If [the 'scattered' *voynuḳ*s] have no sons or relations [outside the register], so that their places (*gedik*) are going to be left vacant, then the number may be made up from [those] sons of *voynuḳ*s, mentioned above, who have been set aside for the *ḫāṣṣa-i hümāyūn*.[146]

(vi) If a son of one of these *voynuḳ*s is living with his father, he is to pay, besides the *ḫarāc*, only 25 *aḳçe* as *ispence*. If he is married and living with his father, he is to pay 25 *aḳçe ispençe* and 12 *aḳçe* as 'hay and firewood' and 30 *aḳçe* as 'bread-tax' (*resm-i nān*). If he is married and has a separate area of cultivation, he is to pay 50 *aḳçe* as 'bread-tax'; if he has hives, he is to pay tithe on them; and if he has animals,[147] he is to pay tax on them at the rate of 1 *aḳçe* for two; if he has a vineyard beyond the *baştina* assigned to his father, he is to pay tithe on it according to the *ḳānūn*.

If a man is a *voynuḳ* or a reserve *voynuḳ* (?) (*zevā'id-i voynuḳ*) and he brings in wine in casks and sells it then; if he is a [serving] *voynuḳ*, he is to pay 15 *aḳçe* cask-tax to his *çeribaşı*: if he is a son of a *voynuḳ*, being one of those set aside for the *ḫāṣṣ*, then the cask-tax is to be taken for the *ḫāṣṣ*: if he is a son assigned [as *ra ʿīyet*] to a *tīmār*, then the *tīmār*-holder is to take it.

(vii) So, too, fines: the fines paid by a *voynuḳ* belong to the *çeribaşı*; the fines of a son set aside for the *ḫāṣṣa-i hümāyūn* are to be taken for the *ḫāṣṣ* and those of a son assigned to a *tīmār* for the *tīmār*.

[146] *Ḫāṣṣa-i hümāyūn* ('imperial *ḫāṣṣ*'): revenues set aside for the sultan.

[147] *Canavar* (Persian: 'animal'): here the word is a euphemism for pigs.

7 Extracts from the *kānūnnāme* of Egypt, after 1525[148]

(i) The corps of *göñüllü*s

The *firman* currently in force is as follows: each member of the aforesaid group should maintain a good horse and be able both to wield a lance and to fire arrows to the right and left from horseback. Their *aġa*s[149] should constantly test them, and teach those who do not know how to use a lance and bow and make them practise . . .

(ii) The corps of mounted arquebusiers

This group also has an independent *aġa, ketḫüdā*[150] and secretary (*kātib*). They, too, should each maintain a good horse and be skilled in firing an arquebus (*tüfenk*) from on hoseback. Their *aġa*s should teach those who do not know how [to do this] and make them practise. Each month, with the cognizance of the chief armourer (*cebeci başı*), they should draw a sufficient quantity of powder from the treasury and distribute it for teaching [the use of the arquebus]. They should give warning that the powder should not be used for anything other than instruction . . .

(iii) The garrison in the Cairo citadel

The *aġa* of this corps, called the warden (*dizdār*), the garrison troops (*ḥiṣār eri*), armourers (*cebeci*) and maintenance men (*meremmetçi*) occupy their positions by virtue of a *berāt*, like other garrisons in the Well-Protected Realms. Garrison troops receive 6 *aḳçe* per day and their divisional officers (*bölük başı*) 7 *aḳçe* per day; they defend the citadel. They, too, should have a perfect mastery of the arquebus and, to ensure the continuous instruction of those who lack the knowledge, [the officers] should each month draw a sufficient quantity of powder from the government stock (*beglik*) and make them practise. They should not waste the powder they receive, but use it for instruction . . .

(iv) The *ʿazab*[151] corps stationed at the Silsila Gate

These form an independent corps, with separate *aġa*s. They have captains (*reʾīs*) and *oda başı*s.[152] The captains have 8 *aḳçe* each [per day], the *oda başı*s 6 and the *ʿazab*s 5. They serve the sultan in the fortress . . .

(v) The Circassian corps[153]

The *aġa, ketḫüdā* and secretary of the corps of Circassians should be Ottomans (*Rūmlu ṭāʾifesi*).[154] In the matter of their employment in services for the sultan, they are like the corps of *göñüllü*s . . .

---

[148] Following two rebellions in 1523 and 1524, Süleymān I sent the grand vizier Ibrāhīm Paşa to Egypt to pacify the recently conquered Ottoman province and to reorganise its administration. The *ḳānūnnāme* of Egypt was compiled after Ibrāhīm's return to Istanbul in 1525, on the basis of his work in Cairo.

[149] *Aġa*: a commanding officer.

[150] *Ketḫüdā*: a deputy; a second-in command.

[151] *ʿAzab*: an infantryman recruited through a levy on urban youth.

[152] *Oda başı*: a commander of a detachment of 10 Janissaries or *ʿazab*s.

[153] Circassians: these were the *mamlūk*s, troops brought to Egypt as slaves from north of the Black Sea. The Ottomans retained the practice of importing *mamlūk*s after the conquest of Egypt in 1517.

[154] 'People from Rūm': Rūm was the term for the Ottoman lands in Anatolia and the Balkan peninsula. Turkish speakers from these regions were deemed more reliable than Circassians or native Egyptians.

(vi) Concerning the *kāşif*s[155] in the districts of Egypt

The services owed by the *kāşif*s are as follows: first, each one must fully maintain and repair the dykes and canals in their administrative area (*küşūfīyet*) at the [proper] time and [proper] season and not leave any dyke or canal in a state of disrepair.

They should also order the villagers and local sheikhs to maintain and repair the dykes in the area of their governorship.

They should make every effort to prevent any land remaining unirrigated as a result of the dykes and canals being in a state of disrepair.

When the blessed Nile floods, as soon as it reaches its maximum height and everywhere is covered, they should make the peasants prepare and sow all inundated places and not leave a single *z̲irā'*[156] of land uncultivated.

If there is any deserted village in the area of their governorship, they should make every effort to bring it into cultivation by whatever means possible. They should be extremely careful not to take any action that might result in cultivated villages becoming uncultivated.

The practice current at the time of Qā'itbāy was as follows: it was the duty and obligation of each *kāşif* that the instalments [of tax] due from places in the area of his governorship be raised in full in accordance with the *irtifā'* registers[157] and that it reach the imperial treasury. This *ḳānūn* is confirmed as it was.

(vii) Concerning *'āmil*s

The *'āmil*s and tax-commissioners (*mübāşir*) should be brought before the inspector of finances (*nāẓir-i emvāl*) and the *emīn* of the city. [These] should inspect the arrears for the year 922 (20 November 1522–9 November 1523) and income for the year 930 (10 November 1523–29 October 1524), [ascertaining] how much [revenue] they have raised, how much of this has been delivered and how much is in arrears. When their accounts have been inspected, they should levy in full whatever they are revealed to be owing, without omitting a single *aḳçe*. If any of them makes excuses or is shown to be incapable, their goods and property will be sold. If this is insufficient and they have a guarantor, it will be raised from their guarantor. If this is not enough, the *'āmil* will suffer severe torture and be made to confess if he has anything hidden away. [If he has], this will be seized and delivered to the treasury . . .

(viii) Concerning unirrigated lands

The rules for unirrigated lands are as follows: when the surveyors first surveyed the land [they found] elevated places which the [flood] water had been unable to reach for some time and which had not been surveyed and are not counted as unirrigated lands (*şerāḳī*). However, because some of these places are very grassy, they are able to serve as pasture and, because the local villagers graze their cattle and sheep [on them], they should each pay some tax which should be collected for the treasury.

Places which have long been flooded and are good for cultivation, but which the water [no longer] reaches and which are left uncultivated should be inspected. If this happened because the dykes and canals have not been properly maintained, the peasants should [first] be made to make good the loss, and [then] they and the sheikhs of the region should be executed

[155] *Kāşif*: a provincial governor in Egypt.

[156] *Z̲irā'*: a variable measure of length, usually between 60 and 70 cm.

[157] *Irtifā'*: a fiscal register of the Mamlūk era.

(*siyāset*).[158] If the dykes and canals were sultanic,[159] the *ḳāḍī* and the surveyor should submit a report and then, after the *kāşif* and the Arab sheikh have been made to pay an indemnity, they should be executed in accordance with the decree. In short, they should make the peasants prepare all places which the floodwater is able to reach. If these are not prepared and remain as waste, the Arab sheikh, the *kāşif* and the *ʿāmil*[160] should make good [the loss of] tax, and then they should be executed.

(ix) The *ḳānūn* of the mint

Concerning *aḳçe* coins which are struck in the Cairo mint, whether they are cut from ingots, from Ottoman *aḳçe* coins or from silver vessels, for every 100 *dirhem* melted, 84 *dirhem* should be pure silver and 16 *dirhem* alloy, and 250 *para*[161] should be struck from 100 *dirhem*. As for gold *sulṭānīyes*, if the gold is coming from Takrūr, when the caravan arrives [in Cairo], it should be bought by the treasury at the market-price (*si'r-i müslimīn*) and coined unalloyed in the mint. If every *sulṭānīye* is minted at 18½ *ḳırāṭ*[162] in accordance with the *ḳānūn* of the Istanbul mint, whether from gold ingots or gold vessels, 10 gold coins in every 100 *mis̱ḳāl*[163] should be taken as tax.

[. . .]

It has been reported that, when the juice from the sugar [cane] being processed for my imperial household (*ḫāṣṣa-i hümāyūnum*) is produced, [the purchase of it] is forced on the workers, accounting poor-quality juice as middling and middling quality as high. In this matter, the copious seas of my compassion and benevolence have surged, and I have abolished this injustice. In the future, not a drop of the juice that is produced in the sugar refinery should be loaded onto anybody. After the sugar which has been boiled for my imperial household has been set aside, the resulting juice should be sold at the current market-price to anyone who comes to the sugar-refinery of their own free will and asks for it, and it should be sold at whatever is the [proper] price for high, middling and low quality. Absolutely nothing should be forced on anyone whomsoever against their will.

SOURCES

1 Friedrich Kraelitz-Greifenhorst, 'Ḳānūnnāme Sultan Meḥmed des Erobererers: Die ältesten osmanischen Straf- und Finanzgesetze', *Mitteilungen zur Osmanischen Geschichte* (1921–2), 13–48, repr. Osnabrück (1972); Ömer Lütfi Barkan, *XV ve XVI Asırlarda Osmanlı İmperatorluğunda Ziraî Ekonominin Hukukî ve Malî Esasları*, Istanbul (1943), 387–95; Ahmet Akgündüz, *Osmanlı Kanûnnâmeleri*, 1, Ankara (1990), 347–57.

2 Barkan, *XV ve XVI Asırlarda*, 1–6; Akgündüz, *Osmanlı Kanûnnâmeleri*, 2: 180–5.

---

[158] The term *siyāset* in *sharīʿa* law has the sense of extra-canonical punishment imposed for the good order of society. In Ottoman usage it generally refers to the death penalty. Here, however, it may mean severe corporal punishment.

[159] Irrigation works in Egypt were classified either as 'sultanic' (*sulṭānī*) or 'local' (*baladī*). It was the duty of the local authorities to maintain the dykes and canals classified as *sulṭānī* and the duty of the local villagers to maintain those classified as *baladī*.

[160] *ʿĀmil*: an agent, tax-collector.

[161] *Para*: a silver coin in circulation in Egypt, also known as *niṣf fiḍḍa*.

[162] *Ḳırāṭ*: a measure of weight for precious metals and jewels, originally the weight of 4–5 grains of barley.

[163] *Mis̱ḳāl*: a weight of 4-5 g.

3 M. ʿĀrif, ʻḲānūnnāme-i Āl-i ʿO<u>s</u>mān', *Taʾrīẖ-i ʿO<u>s</u>mānī Encümeni Mecmʿası*, supplement (1329/1911), vi, vii, 11–13, 15–18, 38, 39–42, 50, 56, 57.

4 Barkan, *XV ve XVI Asırlarda*, 170–1; Akgündüz, *Osmanlı Kanûnnâmeleri*, 3: 283–4.

5 Barkan, *XV ve XVI Asırlarda*, 200–1; Akgündüz, *Osmanlı Kanûnnâmeleri*, 3: 487–8.

6 Barkan, *XV ve XVI Asırlarda*, 265–6; Akgündüz, *Osmanlı Kanûnnâmeleri*, 3: 414–18.

7 Barkan, *XV ve XVI Asırlarda*, 355, 356, 357, 358, 360, 365, 375, 386–7; Akgündüz, *Osmanlı Kanûnnâmeleri*, 6: 101, 102, 104–5, 106, 107, 109–10, 115–16, 127, 139, 140.

CHAPTER VIII

Taxation and Finance

Much of the revenue raised in Anatolia, Syria and the Balkans never entered the treasury but was instead collected directly by the holders of *tīmār*s and other fiefs (see Chapter V) or went to support *waqf*s (see Chapter IX). *Tīmār*-income was overwhelmingly, although not exclusively, agricultural and raised directly from peasant households: the revenues of *waqf*s and of *ḫāṣṣ*es supporting the imperial family, viziers and governors were drawn from a broader tax-base. Passages **1** and **2** indicate that revenues of all kinds not diverted to fiefs or *waqf*s went directly to the treasury.

The treasury could appoint a salaried official (*emīn*) to collect a specified bundle of revenues (*muḳāṭa'a*) or to oversee revenue-producing enterprises such as salt pans (see passage **1**) or mines (see passages **1, 3**), but this was unusual. As passages **1** and **2** show, from the earliest times, the sultans preferred to contract out revenue-collection and the administration of taxable resources to tax-farmers, usually for a period of three years. While tax-farming provided opportunities for personal enrichment, and unlike political office, was open to non-Muslims, as evident from passages **2a, 2b, 2e** and **2f**, a farmer who failed to raise the sum contracted would be subject to penalties. They would either have to make up the shortfall from their own resources (see passage **2e**), or, if they were unable to do this, would be liable to imprisonment or even execution. In these circumstances, it is not surprising to find sources such as passage **2b** which mention tax-farmers absconding when they could not meet their obligations.

Finding mention in passage **4**, one of the most productive sources of treasury income was the tax usually known in Ottoman administrative terminology as *ḫarāc*, levied on the sultan's non-Muslim subjects. Passages **4b** and **4c** demonstrate that this tax was equated with *jizya*, the poll-tax which Islamic law imposes on adult, non-Muslim males in return for legal protection. Ottoman *ḫarāc*, however, differs from *jizya* in that it was levied on households rather than on individuals, as shown in passage **4**, and might in a few instances be levied on Muslims, as was the case with the Muslim gypsies mentioned in passage **1a**.

The most important coin in daily use (and unit of account) was the silver *aḳçe*, valued in terms of the number of *aḳce* to the gold ducat, the latter being based on the Venetian standard, as can be seen in passage **1a**. The same passage demonstrates that, if the treasury was in deficit, one remedy was to debase the *aḳçe*, recalling old *aḳçe* coins and minting more coins from the same weight of silver. Passage **5a** gives testimony that

Meḥmed II had recourse to debasement several times during his reign (r. 1451–81). Although this did not provoke an immediate violent reaction, it was undoubtedly a factor in his unpopularity which became evident after his death. From the reign of his successor, Bāyezīd II (r. 1481–1512) until the late sixteenth century, the value of the *aḳçe* remained steady at about 1:50. There was a small debasement in 1572, but in 1585, in the face of an enormous deficit, the silver content of the *aḳçe* was halved; passage **5b** describes how these measures led to a major riot by the troops returning to Istanbul from the front.

1 Annual income and expenditure of the Imperial Treasury

1a An estimate of treasury income and expenditure, c1475–80[1]

Ordinary income of the Grand Turk from all Grecia[2]

Firstly, he has in Grecia and all the aforesaid provinces belonging to it . . . *ḫarāc*[3] payers, that is, payers of the hearth-tax (*focagii*), all Christians, to the number of 550,000, from whom he has for each hearth or household 70 *aḳçe*, which is a little more than 1½ ducats. The sultan chooses twenty agents (*procuratori*) as collectors of the said *ḫarāc*, who, each with twenty men on horseback, distributed over the various provinces, go to collect the *ḫarāc* from the month of June, and they have to return with the said *ḫarāc* in August. They travel at their own expense . . . And besides the 70 *aḳçe* for the sultan, every household is obliged to give his agent 2 *akçe* . . . It amounts in all to ducats: 850,000

Ordinary income of Gallipoli and Constantinople

He has as ordinary income from taxes (*gabelle*) sold for the sultan, just from the heads of male and female slaves who pass into Turkey as booty, which make 5 to 7 ducats per head; and similarly for men crossing with horses, 5 *aḳçe* and for pedestrians, 2 *aḳçe* . . . sold for 3 years at 150,000 ducats, that is, per annum:[4] 50,000

Customs (*comerchio*) of Constantinople on all sorts of merchandise, both entering and leaving, 5 percent for foreigners and 4 percent for his subjects; customs on fish called *leparchio*; tax on wine; tax on all sorts of wood; tax of rents (*pensione*) for shops of the sultan, bathhouses and *bedestans*;[5] sold all together, and bring in for three years 210,000 ducats . . .: 70,000

Customs of Gallipoli, paid in full by everyone except the Turks, who pay only on things sold by weight, at 1 *aḳçe* per *ḳanṭār*;[6] for three years, 27,000 ducats, that is, per annum: 9,000

[1] This estimate is the work of Iacopo de Promontorio de Campis, the scion of a Genoese ducal family and resident at the court of Meḥmed II. The inclusion of the income from the Crimea indicates that the work was completed after 1475, the year of the Ottoman conquest of the peninsula.

[2] *Grecia* ('Greece'): Ottoman lands in Europe; the province of Rūmeli.

[3] In Ottoman usage, the term *ḫarāc* refers to the *jizya*, the poll-tax levied on Christians and Jews. In Islamic law, the *jizya* should be levied on adult male non-Muslims. In Ottoman practice, the *ḫarāc* was levied on non-Muslim households, not on individuals, hence Iacopo's definition of *ḫarāc* as 'hearth-tax'.

[4] For tolls on slaves, see Chapter III.

[5] *Bedestan*: a covered market.

[6] *Ḳanṭār*: a measure of weight, probably 56.45 kg.

Salt pans of all Grecia . . . are sold for 276,000 ducats, that is, per annum: 92,000

The mint in which are made the silver *aḳçe*s, for three years 360,000 ducats, per annum: 120,000

The mint for gold ducats on the Venetian model (*in stampa Venetiana*), per annum 3,000 ducats: 3,000

Silver mines in Serbia, Novo Brdo; in Bosnia, Srebrenica; Kratovo, Priština, Serres, Salonica, Sofia are sold by various sales for three years, bringing in altogether 360,000 ducats: the tenth of the silver extracted is levied from the buyer [?], per year: 120,000

. . .

Customs of Enez, including the *ḫarāc* on the hearths of the Greeks there not included in the number of Christians previously given, together with other rights to salt pans, are sold per annum for: 11,000

Customs of Salonica, with other rights to salt pans: 2,500

Customs of the island of Negroponte, including all tolls, *gabelle* and *ḫarāc*, 12,500 ducats per annum: 12,500

Customs of Morea, tolls and rights, for 3 years 31,500 ducats, [per annum]: [10,500]

Valona,[7] for 3 years, including fisheries 4,500, [per annum]: 1,500

The fifth part of all the cereals of all Grecia and parts of certain provinces thereto belonging, sown on his [the sultan's] holdings in respect of the share belonging to him, for three years 60,000 ducats, per annum: 20,000

Customs of Sofia, for three years 3,000, per annum: 1,000

Customs of Edirne, transit toll (*pedagio*) on male and female slaves, the public balance, for three years 36,000, per annum: 12,000

Comerchio of gypsies; *ḫarāc* for the gypsies[8] of all of Grecia, for three years 27,000, per annum: 9,000

Baths of the sultan throughout Grecia, for three years 24,000, per annum: 8,000

[7] *Valona*: Vlorë.
[8] The sense of *comerchio* in this context is unclear. It is noteworthy that not all gypsies were non-Muslims and that to charge Muslim gypsies *ḫarāc*/*jizya* was, strictly speaking, illegal.

Rice fields, that is *gabelle* of rice for Filibe,[9] Zagora, Serres and other places in Greece and adjoining provinces, for three years 45,000, per annum: 15,000

Comerchio on pasturage for animals in his country, for three years, 30,000, per annum: 10,000

Tribute of Greater Wallachia, towards Nicopolis, on the Danube, per annum: 10,000

Tribute of the Venetians, per annum: 10,000

Tribute of Chios, per annum: 12,000

Ragusa[10] was paying tribute of 20,000 ducats, per annum: 20,000

[Total: 1,479,000]

Ordinary income of Turchia[11]

Customs of Chios, with the *comerchio* of four provinces and certain salt pans therein, that is, Saruhan, Menteşe, Aydın and Balat near Rhodes. They are sold for three years for 96,000 ducats per year, [per annum]: 32,000

Customs of Alanya, with certain tithes and tolls belonging to the sultan himself, for three years 36,000, [per annum]: 12,000

Old and New Phocaea.[12] The customs are sold, with the *ḫarāc* on the Christians there, [together] with [the revenues from] alum, for three years, altogether 60,000 ducats, of which half is from the sale of alum, [per annum]: 20,000

From Greater Bursa, with tolls, together with the balance for silk, and customs from foreigners. [These] are sold for three years 150,000, [per annum]: 50,000

Customs of Kastamonu, which belonged to the Isfendiyār[13] lords. [The sultan] extracts an infinite amount of copper from the pits and mines existing here, which he causes to be worked at his own expense; and he sells them as tax-farms to only two persons, to one who exports [the copper] by sea, and the other by land (?); he always maintains a tower[14] – a site of a treasury – full of this copper. Together with other taxes, he normally raises 150,000 ducats each year: 150,000

---

[9] *Filibe*: Plovdiv.

[10] *Ragusa*: Dubrovnik.

[11] *Turchia*: 'Turkey', the sultan's possessions in Anatolia, comprising the provinces of Anaṭolı, Rūm and Ḳaramān.

[12] *Old and New Phocaea*: Foça.

[13] *Isfendiyār*: This was the name of the dynasty formerly ruling in Kastamonu and Sinop, conquered in 1424 and 1460, respectively.

[14] This is probably a reference to the Castle of the Seven Towers in Istanbul.

Trabzon province, Amasra and Samsun, all told, 10,000 ducats of revenue per year, sometimes collected by *factori*, sometimes sold [per annum]: 10,000

Caffa,[15] that is, customs, salt pans etc., with all [its] surroundings, Balaklava, Tana etc., including part of Gothia,[16] 10,000 ducats per year, after paying the soldiers and *'ulūfecis*,[17] per annum: 10,000

Most of Ḳaramān; almost all the province has been conquered. Various [revenues], that is, *gabelle* on rice and cereals which he has sown, tolls etc., from which he raises, per annum: 35,000

Salt pans belonging to the sultan, per annum: 12,000

[Total: 331,000]

Note that besides the aforesaid 550,000 *ḫarāc*-payers, there are in Grecia and Turchia 60,000 households of Christians free of *ḫarāc*, because they maintain many breeds of horses and buffaloes at their own expense, and similarly they till and tend the vineyards of the Great Turk: but they have the privilege to sow and plant vineyards and harvest wine on his holdings without paying tithe . . .

Ordinary expenses of the Great Turk

Expenditure on the stables: 500 warhorses, 2,700 horses, 2,500 camels, 600 mules and 600 she-mules for his person and the aforesaid wagoner, which number 6,300 and more, and to which he gives new saddles, harnesses, coverings and pack-saddles. The packsaddles are adorned with various cowry-shells (*porzelette*), each saddle costing 25 ducats, apart from 50 saddles of solid silver, covered and gilded, which he sometimes gives with warhorses to his [lords] each year. Apart from the *porzelette*, which he changes infrequently (?), they amount to the sum of 100,000 ducats: 100,000

Pay of troops of his person

Expenditure on the pay of *sipāhī*s, *çaşnigīr*s, *çavuş*es, all gentlemen, *garīboġlan*s, Tatar horsemen, the four gatekeepers of the main (*primo*) palace, including their households (*famiglia*), *solaḳ*s, and similarly the aforesaid *siliḥdār*s, which number 6,400 men and, beyond these, 6,000 Janissaries, in all 12,400 men, paid at most (*a longo numero*) 550,000 ducats: 550,000

The ladies' court

Expenditure on the ladies' court, 400 [persons], including the provision of eunuchs, their clothing brocaded with gold and silver, and other jewels and clothes which the sultan gives them. 100,000 ducats 100,000

15 *Caffa*: Feodosiya (Crimea).
16 *Gothia*: the southern tip of the Crimean Peninsula, named after the Goths settled in the area.
17 In this context *'ulūfeci* must mean anyone receiving a salary from the treasury.

Various gifts

Expenditure on various gifts made to his 400 favoured youths in the palace, including their pay; similarly, to other lords; and similarly, to ladies when they leave the palace to be married. 200,000 ducats, including jewels etc. 200,000

Extraordinary

Annual expenditure on arming galleys: for having them built and repaired, and for other things, for which he attracts experts (*maestri*) from abroad (*a longi*) by money. Altogether 300,000 ducats, including *fusta*s[18] and similar 300,000

Also including *palandaria*s[19] and the like

[Total: 1,375,000]

Summary of income from all Grecia

The Grand Turk has an ordinary income from all Grecia of 1,469,000 ducats of revenues: 1,469,000

Summary of income from all Turchia

He also has a total income from all Turchia, and all attached provinces of 331,000 ducats of revenue: 331,000

Summary of income from all his lands

From the revenues of all his lands, not counting the maintenance of 40,000 troops whom he supports from other revenues, perquisites and benefices, without any stipend; and not counting the profit from the 60,000 households of Christians in regard to his animals (*raze*) etc., the Grand Turk has an ordinary annual income of 1,800,000 ducats: 1,800,000

Summary of ordinary expenses

The Grand Turk has an annual ordinary expenditure of 1,375,000 ducats: 1,375,000

Yet it sometimes happens that the extraordinary expenses reach such a sum that, when everything is counted, the expenses considerably exceed the income, so that it is necessary to lay hands on his treasury.[20]

Normal strength of the army

When the Grand Turk campaigns in person, he brings with him men of the court, named above, numbering: 12,800

[18] *Fusta*: a light galley.

[19] *Palandaria*: a ship for transporting cavalry.

[20] That is, the inner treasury, usually reserved for the sultan's personal expenditure.

The *beglerbegi* of Grecia with all his 17 captains, plus 6,000 *aḳıncıs*[21] and 6,000 ʿ*azab*s,[22] amounting in all to 32,800 men 32,800

The *beglerbegi* of Turchia with all his captains and warriors, plus 6,000 *aḳıncıs* and 6,000 ʿ*azab*s, amounting in all to 30,400 men 30,400

[Total: 76,000]

1b An estimate of treasury income and expenditure for the years 1527–8

Summary accounts of revenues and expenditure, together with *tīmārs*[23]

Summary accounts of the estimated revenues and expenditure of the provinces of Rūmeli, Anaṭolı, Ḳaramān, Rūm, Ẕū'l-ḳadriyye,[24] Egypt, Damascus, Aleppo and Diyārbekir, together with the revenues of the *ḫāṣṣes*[25] of viziers, *beglerbegi*s, *defterdārs*[26] of the Imperial Treasury, and of *tīmār*-holders and *tīmār*s of the garrisons of fortresses in the said provinces.

Total income in a complete year	**477,431,168**
From the provinces of Rūmeli, Anaṭolı, Ḳaramān, Rūm, Ẕū'l-ḳadriyye:	294,858,899
From the provinces of Egypt, Damascus, Aleppo and Diyārbekir:	182,572,269
From Rūmeli, per annum:	**187,319,348**
Revenues from the *jizya*, *muḳāṭaʿa*s, quays etc.:	94,784,238
Revenues from the *ḫāṣṣes* of viziers, governors, *defterdār*s of the Imperial Treasury etc, and of *tīmār*s of *sipāhī*s, and *tīmār*s of the garrisons of fortresses in the said provinces:	92,535,110
From Anaṭolı, Ḳaramān, Rūm, Ẕū'l-ḳadriyye, per annum:	**107,539,551**
Revenues from the *jizya* [etc], per annum:	34,018,288
Revenues from the *ḫāṣṣes* [etc.], per annum:	73,521,264
From Egypt, Damascus, Aleppo and Diyārbekir, per annum:	**21,460,862**
Revenues from the *jizya* [etc], per annum:	7,169,190
Revenues from the *ḫāṣṣes* [etc.], per annum:	14,291,670
From this [deduct] expenses for a complete year	**403,388,321**
From Rūmeli, Anaṭolı, Ḳaramān, Rūm, Ẕū'l-ḳadriyye, per annum:	**322,134,755**
Instalments [paid to] the *pādişāh*, excluding the revenues of Egypt:	3,476,452

[21] *Aḳıncı*: a raider, receiving land and tax-exemptions on the frontier in return for carrying out raids on enemy territory.

[22] ʿ*Azab*: an infantry levy, serving in the army and in garrisons.

[23] The income from *ḫāṣṣes*, *tīmār*s and other fiefs did not come directly to the treasury but was collected directly by the fief-holder. It is here accounted as treasury-revenue.

[24] *Ẕū'l-ḳadriyye*: the province in south-east Anatolia, comprising the lands of the former emirate of Dūlḳadir, annexed in 1522. Ẕū'l-ḳadriyye is an Arabized form of Dūlḳadir.

[25] *Ḫāṣṣ*; a fief valued at more than 100,000 *akçe* per year.

[26] *Defterdār*: a director of finances in the central or provincial treasuries.

Salaries of those in attendance on the Sublime Porte, 27,049 persons: Per diem 186,110	65,887,940
For the *ḫāṣṣ*es of viziers, *beglerbegi*s, governors, *defterdār*s of the Imperial Treasury, *tīmār keth̲üdā*s and *defterdār*s, *za'īm*s and *tīmār*s of *sipāhī*s in the said provinces, 24,625 persons:	152,164,838
From Rūmeli [etc], 10,668 persons:	62,552,427
From Anaṭolı [etc], 7,536 persons:	35,735,733
From Ḳaramān, Rūm, Ẕū'l-ḳadriyye [etc], 6,318 persons:	33,976,678
For the salaries of garrisons, captains, *'azab*s, mounted *'ulūfeci*s, *martolos*es[27] in the fortresses etc., 122 [fortresses], 23,017 persons:	40,134,662
From Rūmeli, 75 [fortresses], 6,620 persons:	30,302,358
From Anaṭolı [etc.], 47 [fortresses], 5,530 persons:	9,832,304
For the *tīmār*s of garrison-troops in the said provinces:	13,891,353
From Rūmeli, 125 [*tīmār*s], 6,620 persons:	10,082,683
From Anaṭolı [etc], 45 [*tīmār*s], 2,614 persons	3,308,852
For *ḫāṣṣa*[28] expenditure in Istanbul, Galata, Edirne, Salonica, Gallipoli, Vlorë, Bursa, Caffa, Trabzon, Konya, Rhodes, including expenditure on newly constructed buildings:	19,236,292
For gifts, alms, honours, favours to governors, etc.:	3,005,544
For purchase of various types of cloth:	4,934,127
For costs of the imperial kitchen:	2,379,505
For costs of the imperial stables:	5,640,000
For cost of cloth for the Janissaries [for uniforms]:	2,955,348
For payments for Janissaries' bows and quivers, falconers' gold braids and payments to new Muslims:	855,120
For expenditure on robes of honour:	70,909
For costs of the imperial armoury and gun-foundry:	339,833
For cost of bread rations:	517,421
For costs of the *ḫāṣṣa* chambers:	124,456
For costs of salaried staff of congregational mosques and mosques in fortresses, fees for [collecting] the *jizya*, together with other expenditures:	390,828
For the salaries of superintendents and *emīn*s,[29] the pay of the pious, *şeyḫ*s, keepers of the *zāviye*s[30] of various mosques and *an'ām*-chanters;[31] costs of İkizceler sheep, feed for hunting-birds; [pensions] of some retired persons etc.:	1,094,849
For the annual salaries of some *sancaḳbegi*s and [. . . ?]; and the annual salaries of keepers of *zāviye*s, falconers etc.:	650,434
For costs of various buildings, repairing fortresses, building new ships on the Danube etc., together with other expenses:	3,057,725

[27] *Martolos*: a Christian military auxiliary in the Balkans.

[28] *Ḫāṣṣa*: belonging to the sultan, or the state in the person of the sultan. Here expenditure falling to the sultan's treasury.

[29] *Emīn*: a salaried agent of the government.

[30] *Zāviye*: a dervish convent.

[31] *An'ām*: the sixth *sūra* of the Qur'ān (*al-An'ām*). Here, the section of the Qur'ān containing this *sūra*.

For expenditure on Küre the Prosperous:[32]	1,326,930
[Total]	**322,134,755**
From the provinces of Egypt, Damascus and Aleppo in a complete year:	**61,143,784**
For the annual salaries of the *beglerbegi* of Egypt, the superintendent of finances (*nāẓir-i emvāl*) etc.:	5,105,000
For the recipients of tri-monthly salaries, including *çavuş*es:	783,928
For the corps of *göñüllü*s of Egypt, arquebusiers, mounted Circassians[33] and retired Circassians, 3,761 persons:	10,211,192
For the garrison-troops, captains and *ʿazab*s in the said province, 2,742 persons:	8,088,177
For the *tīmār*s of garrison troops in the Arab province, 14 fortresses, 419 persons:	669,054
For the *ḫāṣṣ*es of the *beglerbegi* of Damascus and governors of the province; and [for] the *ketḫüdā*, *defterdār*, *zaʿīm*s[34] and other *tīmār*-holders, 2,275 persons:	19,169,296
For expenditure on the Noble Kaʿba of God:	4,286,475
For expenditure on the *ḫāṣṣa* sugar:	500,000
For expenditure on the *ḫāṣṣa* gunpowder and armoury:	1,200,000
For expenditure on robes of honour:	154,360
For expenditure on *cassia fistula*:[35]	300,000
For some rents in Aleppo:	56,826
For salaries and *ḫāṣṣa* expenditures in Jeddah and cost of *ḫāṣṣa* ships:	619,476
For land which is flooded, waste, fallow or out of reach of the Nile flood:	10,000,000
From the province of Diyārbekir:	**20,109,782**
For the recipients of tri-monthly salaries, 15 persons:	176,644
For the salaries of *ġulām*s[36] in the said province, 446 persons:	1,816,020
For the salaries of garrison-troops, captains and *ʿazab*s in the fortresses in the said province, 1,858 persons:	3,801,948
For expenditure on robes of honour and tent-dues for the Arabs in the said province:	23,500
For the *ḫāṣṣ*es of the *beglerbegi*s, *sancaḳbegi*s, *zaʿīm*s and *sipāhī*s' *tīmār*s in the said province, 1,071 persons:	14,291,670
Surplus to the Treasury:	**74,042,847**

[32] This appears to refer to the copper-producing district of Kastamonu.

[33] Names of four military divisions stationed in Egypt, excluding the garrison in the Cairo Citadel. See Chapter VII.

[34] *Zaʿīm*: the holder of a fief worth between 20,000 and 100,000 *aḳçe* per year.

[35] A tree with medicinal properties, imported from India.

[36] *Ġulām*: a *ġulām* is a slave in the service of a monarch. The identity of these *ġulām*s is not clear.

2 Customs and *muḳāṭaʿas*

2a Entry from a register of muḳāṭaʿa*s*

Ab initio: *muḳāṭaʿa* of the village of Ḫrişne in the district *(nāḥiye)* of Yeñice Ḳaraṣu,[37] which was in the possession of Yaʿḳūb the physician.[38] Contracted to Şīrmerd b. ʿAbduʾllāh, *ʿāmil*[39] of the mine at Ḳavala, from 25 Ṣafar 882 (8 June 1477).

On 23 Rabīʿuʾl-ākhir in the same year (4 August 1477). [Contracted] together with the monopoly on the grape-juice from the said village in Ḳavala.

For three years: 60,000 [*aḳçe*] Fee for *berāt*[40] etc: 870

2b Entry from a register of muḳāṭaʿa*s*

Ab initio: *muḳāṭaʿa* of the fish-traps in the *zeʿāmet* of Ostrova, a dependency of Timür Ḥiṣār. Contracted to Ilya b. Çokarik and Astrati b. Astanice (they have absconded).

From 14 Rabīʿuʾl-ākhir 884 (15 July 1479). On 17 Shaʿbān 884 (3 November 1479).

For three years: 96,000 [*aḳçe*] Fee for *berāt* etc: 1,584

2c A decree granting a muḳāṭaʿa

The reason for the writing of the *miṡāl*[41] . . . is this, that:

To the bearers, [X] and [Y], I have 'given for the *muḳāṭaʿa*' the quays (*iskele*) of Gallipoli and Üsküdar for three years from 1 Ramaḍān falling in this *taḥvīl*[42] of 884 (16 November 1479) for 8,000,000 *aḳçe* (the half of which *ḳısṭ*[43] is 4,000,000). They are to take and possess (*taṣarruf*), according to the old regulation and rule, the *pencik*[44] on every slave; 5 *aḳçe* per horse; [?] per camel; [?] per sheep; and [?] for every load and every pedestrian.

None of my *beg*s or *sipāhī*s or anyone else is to hinder them or interfere, or to hide his slaves, or to refuse to pay *pencik*. No ship is to pass to the other side until my *ʿāmil*s have searched it and granted permission. . . .

The *ʿāmil*s are to pay instalments (*ḳısṭa cevāb vereler*) once every six months, without making any excuses. When their years are completed, they are to take a *ḥüccet*[45] from my Porte . . . Second decade of Ramaḍān, 884 [26 November–5 December 1479]

---

[37] Yeñice Ḳaraṣu: Genisea.

[38] This refers to Iacopo of Gaëta who, as Yaʿḳūb Pasha, served as Meḥmed II's personal physican. See Bernard Lewis, 'The privilege granted by Meḥmed II to his physician', *Bulletin of the School of Oriental and African Studies*, 14/3 (1952), 560–3.

[39] *ʿĀmil*: a factor; an agent of the sultan, usually acting as tax-collector.

[40] A *berāt* is a diploma of appointment. Fees levied for issuing *berāt*s were a major source of treasury income.

[41] *Miṡāl*: here a decree.

[42] *Taḥvīl*: the sum to be transferred from the tax-farm to the treasury by the end of the stipulated period, usually three years.

[43] *Ḳısṭ*: the sum payable to the treasury from a tax-farm, as an instalment due for a specified portion of the contract.

[44] *Pencik*: here the toll payable for transporting a slave across the Bosphorus from Istanbul to Üsküdar.

[45] *Ḥüccet*: here a document issued by the treasury to confirm the completion of a tax-farmer's term and the delivery of the sum contracted.

2d The problems of a tax-farmer

Order to the *ḳāḍī*s of Anaṭolı, Ḳastamonı and Kanġrı:[46]

Heretofore I had granted as a farm to [X] the stopped revenues (*mevḳūfāt*)[47] of the *sancaḳ*s and *subaşılıḳ*s of Anaṭolı, Ḳastamonı and Kanġrı. Now he has come to my Porte and stated: 'Since I have no felicitous decree, [the moneys] cannot be taken and many persons rebuff me'. Therefore, my order is this: his agents shall travel round and enquire, and if they find after this date a *sancaḳ* or a *subaşılıḳ* which is 'stopped' (*mevḳūf*), you are to adjudicate its revenues to my *ḳul* so that he can take them in full; if a *sancaḳbegi* or a *subaşı* dies, or if his *sancaḳ* or his *subaşılıḳ* is taken from him and given to someone else, you are to adjudicate all the revenue [arising] until the date of the *berāt* of his successor to my *ḳul* for him to take it: if a *subaşı* does not go on his due service, or leaves the army before his service is complete, his *tīmār* is *mevḳūf* and you are to adjudicate its revenue to my *ḳul*. On the matter of my moneys, you are to render all assistance.

2e Demand for the delivery of payment due from a tax-farm

[To] . . . the *ḳāḍī* . . . the inspector of the *muḳāṭaʿa*s of Niġbolı:[48]

When the exalted imperial sign[49] arrives, it should be known that, in accordance with the register of the *sancaḳbegi* of Semendire,[50] Meḥmed . . . the tri-monthly pay of the 22 *ʿazab*s in the fortress of Borağı varoşı[51] in the said *sancaḳ* from 1 Muḥarram 997 to the end of Jumādāʾ l-ūlā [997] (20 November 1588–15 May 1589) is 8,892 *aḳçe*, at a daily rate of 104 *aḳçe*, and their six-monthly pay is 17,784 *aḳçe*. This being so, [I have ordered] the transfer of the said sum [to be paid] from the *taḥvīl* of the *muḳāṭaʿa* of the quay of Niġbolı and its dependencies, held jointly by Salomūn, Abrāhām and Yāġūb, from the portion due from [9] November, falling on 3 Ṣafar [1001] and reserved for the fortress. I have commanded that, when the *ḥavāle*,[52] Muṣṭafā b. Ḥüseyn Ketḫüdā, arrives with my noble command, you should not pay the said 17,784 *aḳçe* from the *aḳçe*s destined for my Imperial Treasury, but collect it in full from the *aḳçe*s reserved for fortresses and deliver it in full to the said *ḥavāle*. After delivering it, you should write a *ḥüccet* on the reverse of my imperial command and give it to the said tax-farmers (*mültezimūn*), so that they may have documentation when the accounts are drawn up.

[On reverse]

. . . Ḥusām b. Meḥmed, *ḳāḍī* in the *ḳażā* of Fetḥ-i Islām[53] recorded the matter as it occurred. The reason for writing this legal document . . . is as follows:
In accordance with the noble command, the *ḥavāle* called Muṣṭafā, [named] in [this] noble

46 Kanġrı: Çankırı.

47 *Mevḳūfāt*: income coming to the treasury from vacant *tīmār*s and other revenue sources which are temporarily unassigned.

48 *Niġbolı*: Nikopol.

49 The 'sign' is the *ṭuġra* at the head of the document, authenticating it as coming from the sultan.

50 *Semendire*: Smederovo.

51 *Borağa varoşı*: Porača, Porečje. 'Varoş' means 'suburb'. The *ʿazab*s were probably stationed in the town outside the fortress.

52 *Ḥavāle*: here the official charged with transferring the sum due from the tax-farm to the treasury.

53 *Fetḥ-i Islām*: Kladovo.

command appeared in the court of the noble *sharīʿa*. In accordance with the noble command, the 17,782 *aḳçe* for the pay of the *ʿazab*s in Boraġı varoşı in the *sancaḳ* of Semendire have been transferred from the Jews called Salomūn, Yāġūb and Abrāhām who had contracted for the *taḥvīl* of the quays of Vidin and Niġbolı for the year 1001 (1592/3). There is no surplus from the quay at Vidin. [Now] the *muḳāṭaʿa*s of Vidin and Niġbolı are joined, and it is a condition that the surplus of one should be accounted with the deficit of the other. Therefore, because there is also a deficit in the sum contracted for the quays of Niġbolı and Rahova,[54] the said Jews paid the full amount from their own resources. When they acknowledged and confirmed this under oath, the facts as they occurred were written on the reverse of the noble command.

12 Rabīʿu'l-awwal 1003 (25 November 1594).

Witnesses to the proceedings: Yūsuf ʿAbdu'llāh; Ḥasan Beg el-Cündī; Yaʿḳūb Beg el-Cündī; and others who were present.

2f Tax avoidance

Mevlānā Muṣliḥü'd-Dīn, *ḳāḍī* of Edirne . . . and the *subaşı* . . .:

When the sublime imperial sign arrives, you are to know this:

At the present time, Miḫāl Mavrūdī, who holds the *muḳāṭaʿa* of the customs of Edirne, has come to my Exalted Port and made this submission: 'Various people interfere in my affairs, which are being carried out according to custom and regulation (*ʿādet ve ḳānūn*), and obstruct them'.

This being so, the regulation and rule (*ḳāʿide*) on this matter is as follows: On lynx-skins, sables . . . [etc.], I have commanded that if Frankish merchants bring them, customs of 4 *aḳçe* per hundred is to be taken, but from Muslim merchants 1 *aḳçe* per hundred, and no more. If people attempt to take more, you are to prevent them.

Certain merchants bring their goods (*ḳumaş*) and leave them somewhere near the city and then, to evade customs duty, sell them to merchants within the city. Now I have commanded that this *ʿāmil* is to investigate such [dealings] and is to put [alleged offenders] strictly to the oath. If, in places under your jurisdiction, he finds such goods hidden away in order to evade the payment of customs, I have commanded that besides the [normal] customs-due, twice the due is to be taken. In this matter you are to give every assistance, for the moneys involved are mine, and not the *ʿāmil*'s. This you are to know.

When the customs duty is paid, no one is to declare his goods at less [than they really are]. No [Muslim] is to come to an agreement [with an infidel] and enable the infidel's goods to evade [full] customs-duty by claiming that they are his. If such [evasions] occur, you are to forbid it strictly, and these [offenders] also are, as stated above, to pay twice the customs-duty over and above the [basic] duty. You are to be duly attentive in this matter and to restrain those who interfere in the affairs of this *ʿāmil* or unjustifiably resist him and to prevent them from interfering. Those who are refractory you are to list and report to my felicitous Porte: you should not act otherwise.

In matters relating to my moneys, you are to demonstrate perfect endeavours and zeal. This you are to know . . . Second decade of Jumādā'l-ukhrā 898 (30 March–9 April 1493)

---

[54] Rahova: Oryahovo

2g Tax arrangements in newly conquered fortified towns

Ḳānūnnāme for the customs (*gümrük*) and other taxes (*rüsūm*) of Aḳkerman;[55] it was written to the *sancaḳbegi* and the *ḳāḍī* [of the fortress] and its commander:

A tithe is reportedly taken from all fish and for what is produced from vineyards; 12 Ottoman *aḳçe* are taken from each cask of grape-juice.

On cloth (*ḳumaş*), if the people of the fortress (*ḳal'a*) bring it from outside or send it out, they pay 2 percent customs. If an outsider brings in cloth and sells it, both the buyer and the seller pay 5½ percent. Merchants who, whether they are Rūs[56] or others, come from 'below' and take away their goods by sea, or who come in by sea and depart for Rūs taking their goods, pay customs of 10 percent on 300. If cereals are loaded onto ships . . . [etc.]

If cloth coming from Rūs is sold, the seller pays, besides customs, 4 *aḳçe* per 100 *arşun*[57] as toll (*bāc*), and the buyer, too, pays 2½ *aḳçe* per 100 *arşun* as toll.

. . .

If besides these taxes [listed] there is any other not mentioned here, it is to be collected according to the ancient custom (*'ādet-i ḳadīme*); and the *emīn* who collects all the taxes, those listed and those not, is to hold (*żabṭ*) them for the *beglik*,[58] omitting nothing. If, in the past, the fortress-commanders used to collect anything beyond these, from fish or anything else, or if there were taxes taken for the service of clerks or of gate-keepers, they are to belong to the *beglik* and be held for the *beglik*.

All the shops are *beglik*: they are to be rented to the occupiers and the proceeds held for the *beglik*. The bath (*ḥammām*) in the city (*şehr*) is also *beglik*: you are to lease it out (*muḳāṭa'aya ṣat-*) and hold the proceeds for the *beglik*. The houses of the deported infidels are also *beglik*: as tenants are found, you are to rent them out and hold the money arising. With the cognizance of the *ḳāḍī* and the fortress-commander, some houses of the deportees are to be allocated to the fortress troops according to their rank, so that they are accommodated.

You who are the *ḳāḍī* of the fortress (*ḳal'a*) are to adjudicate whenever a matter relating to the *sharī'a* arises among the fortress-troops who are *ḳul*s;[59] other matters the fortress commander is to adjudicate, and no one else. The *sharī'a* business of the *'azab*s and the *re'īs*es,[60] you, the *ḳāḍī* are to attend to; all other matters are to be under the jurisdiction of the *ḳapudan*,[61] and nobody else is to intervene. The *dīvānī* matters[62] of the fortress troops [who are not *ḳul*s], of the *'azab*s and of the infidels of the city, which are the concern of *sancaḳbegi*, those *'örfī* matters[63] the *sancaḳbegi* will decide: the fortress-commander and the *ḳapudan* are not to intervene in matters which the *sancaḳbegi* is to attend to – particularly such affairs of the infidels

[55] *Aḳkerman:* Bilhorod-Dnistrovskyi. This *ḳānūnnāme* regulating the customs and other fiscal and administrative matters was drawn up immediately after the Ottoman conquest of Aḳkerman in 1484.

[56] *Rūs*: 'Russia', the Grand Duchy of Moscow.

[57] *Arşun*: a measure of length, probably about 68 cm.

[58] *Beglik*: the property of the sultan; belonging to the treasury.

[59] *Ḳul*s ('slaves'): here presumably Janissaries.

[60] *Re'īs* ('captain'): probably here the captain of a vessel allocated to the defence of the port and fortress.

[61] *Ḳapudān*: captain, usually of a fleet or squadron of ships. Here probably the commander of the ships defending the port and castle of Aḳkerman.

[62] *Dīvānī* matters: cases that are heard in the *sancaḳbegi*'s *dīvān* rather than in the *ḳāḍī*'s court.

[63] *'Örfī* matters: like '*dīvānī* matters', cases decided by customary (*'örfī*) law before the *sancaḳbegi*.

as are the concern of the *sancaḳbegi* are to be decided only by the *sancaḳbegi*. No other procedure than this is to be followed.

Written on the last day of Rajab 889 (23 August 1484).

2h A command written to the ḳāḍī *and the fortress-commander [and the* emīn*] of Kili*[64]

A command was written to the *ḳāḍī* and the fortress-commander [and the *emīn*] of Kili to this effect:

I have made all the shops in the fortress of Kili *beglik*. You, the *emīn*, are to make a list of all the shops and submit it: you are to rent them out and to collect and hold the proceeds. I have made the *iḥtisāb*[65] of Kili *beglik* also. You, the *emīn*, are to hold for the *beglik* the proceeds of the *iḥtisāb* [as they arise] according to the traditional custom and record them in your register. The *ḥammām* also is *beglik*: you are to hold the proceeds from that, too, for the *beglik*.

The fortress-commander, it is reported, has carried out some repairs and has held the income arising over a short period [to cover the expenses]. You [the *emīn*] are to discover what his expenses have been and how much he has retained from the income: if, to meet the expenses, he needs more than the income he has retained, you are to pay him [what is necessary].

. . .

You, the *emīn*, are to appoint your men at the quay (*iskele*) and at the customs and for the collection of the tithe from fish and to see that the revenue is levied, so that nothing is lost.

The priests in the fortress have, it is reported, asked permission to depart. You are to grant them permission and let them go wherever they wish, with nobody obstructing them.

When any of the fortress-troops or the *ʿazab*s wish to marry a woman or girl from among the infidels of the city, you are to permit him to marry according to the *sharīʿa*, provided that the infidels agree and there has been no compulsion.

It is reported that the horse herd (*hergeleci*) who formerly looked after the infidels' horses in the city, having fled to Moldavia and taking the horses with him, has returned with some of the horses; you are to return any such horses to the owners whose ownership is [attested] according to the *sharīʿa*, and those whose owners are not known, you are to make *beglik*.

The fortress-commander and the *ḳapudan* are to demand nothing from fishermen who bring fish for sale.

. . .

In matters relating to *beglik* funds of all kinds, the *emīn* is to exercise supervision; financial affairs are the concern of the *emīn*, and no one else is to intervene in them.

Last day of Rajab 889 (23 August 1484).

3 Silver mines

3a Instructions to a farmer of silver mines

The order of the felicitous *nişān*[66] is this, that:

Into the hand of [. . .], the bearer of this noble *misāl*, who has taken the farm of my mines

[64] Kili: Kiliya. This command was issued immediately after the conquest of Kiliya in 1484.

[65] *Iḥtisāb*: market regulations; the money accruing from fines for breaches of market regulations.

[66] *Nişān* ('sign'): the sultan's cypher at the head of the document, guaranteeing its authenticity.

in Srebrenica, Sase and Rudnik and of the land of Laz[67] and of their villages of associates (*yamaḳ*), I have given this decree, and I have commanded that he is to go and is most strictly to set the infidels of these mines and their associates to work in the pits and at the refineries according to the rules and regulations (*ḳānūn ve ḳāʿide*) which have come down from of old[68] and is to punish those who refuse to work, but just roam about.

The priests and the elders (*knez*) and the foremen of the miners of these mines and of the associates' villages and all people, high and low, are to render complete obedience to this *ʿāmil* and his men and always apply themselves to their work: if anyone is refractory and refuses to obey, the *ʿāmil* is to set him to work. No one but the *ʿāmil* and his men is to concern himself with my *ḫāṣṣa* mines and their villages of associates. The *sancaḳbegi*s and the *ḳāḍī*s and *subaşı*s of those regions and their representatives are to give every assistance with regard to my moneys (*māl*) and my agents, and not proffer excuses: let them know that otherwise they will incur punishment from me and that I will bring a heavy calamity (*belā*) on them.

Furthermore, many *reʿāyā* from my *ḫāṣṣa* mines and their villages of associates have, it is said, dispersed and gone off. This being so, I have commanded that wherever the bearer finds *reʿāyā* listed in the register, authenticated by the *nişān* (*nişānlu*) which he has, the *ḳāḍī*s and *subaşı*s of those places are to give orders and fetch them back to their homes. No one is to hinder him: if anyone does, he is to report it to my Porte for me to punish [the offender].

3b Extract from a register for Bosnia, 1489

This place [Kreševo] is a silver mine. Since the district was conquered, the *ḳānūn* has been to this effect that: When they dig out the earth and bring it to the head of the pit, from this earth called *ruda*,[69] the tithe is taken: and when the miners have 'burned' the earth left to them and made of it refined silver, again the tithe of that silver is taken. When the farmer (*ʿameldār*) puts the earth which he has taken into the oven to heat it, all the expenses fall upon him: the *reʿāyā* render him nothing. They do not have to assist him in melting it and extracting the pure silver.

Those who are miners do not pay *ḫarāc* and *ispence*: they pay 1 *filori*[70] per house (*ev*). They pay tithes on all kinds of cereals according to the custom (*ʿādet*). They pay hive and vegetable garden and pig taxes. They are exempt (*muʿāf ve müsellem*) from all *ʿavārıż* and *tekālīf-i ʿörfiyye*.[71] They hold the felicitous decree to this effect, and the provisions have accordingly been entered in [this] register.

4 *Jizya*

4a Instructions to a jizya*-collector*

The reason for the writing . . . of the felicitous decree is this:

I have sent the bearer, the scribe (*kātib*) . . . to collect the *ḫarāc* of the regions of Grebena[72]

---

[67] *Laz*: the despotate of Serbia.

[68] That is, from before the Ottoman occupation. Meḥmed II conquered the silver-mining districts in Serbia in the campaigns of 1454 and 1455.

[69] *Ruda*: (Slavonic) 'ore'.

[70] *Filori*: a gold coin; florin.

[71] *ʿAvārıż, tekālīf-i ʿörfiyye*: extra-ordinary taxes, normally levied in times of war.

[72] Grevená (in northern Greece).

and Premeti[73] for the year 880 (1475/6), and I have ordered that he is to go and collect the *ḫarāc* of those regions, acting with complete uprightness, and to bring it to my Porte in accordance with [the date of] the register.

He is to inspect the *berāt*s[74] of all persons in those regions who have received *berāt*s in respect of abandoned *mezraʿa*s[75] in order to see whose terms have expired, and on the infidels congregated on such lands he is to impose *ḫarāc*.

Wherever *ḫarāc*-paying *reʿāyā* have fled from a *tīmār*, he is to take half the *ḫarāc* in question from the *tīmār*-holder and the other half from the infidels remaining there: he is to list and report the names of the infidels who have fled so that I may send a *ḳul*[76] to search them out and deport them to Anatolia and take their sons for Janissary service.

It has been reported that, when an infidel dies, they take the *ḫarāc* only from his relatives and not from his fellow villagers. My command is as follows: if such a deceased infidel has left an inheritance (*tereke*), then in the first place the *ḫarāc* is to be taken from that; if he has left no inheritance, it is to be taken from the person who is now holding his *baştina*:[77] if he left no *baştina* but an inheritance that has passed to his relatives, then the *ḫarāc* is to be taken from that, so far as it is sufficient, but, if it is not sufficient, then from [the deceased's fellow-] villagers. The collector is to remove [the dead man's] name from the register, but he is not to take the *ḫarāc* only from his relations.

The *sancaḳ begi*s and *ḳāḍī*s and *subaşı*s and their representatives and the *nāʾib*s[78] and *ketḫüdā*s and *tīmār*-holders of that region are to collect together the infidels under their jurisdiction and to present them before my *ḫarāc*-collector and to exert themselves to see that their *ḫarāc* is paid quickly, for I have instructed my collector that his going and collecting and returning is not to take longer than four months from 1 Shaʿbān 881 (19 November 1476) and, if possible, less. Thus, if anyone shows slackness or negligence in the matter of the collection of my money, then by the soul of the Ḫüdāvendgār, I will not stop short of taking back his *tīmār*, but will punish him severely.

The collector, having taken the money that is really mine, is to take from every house 2 *aḳçe* as 'secretarial tax' (*resm-i kitābet*), but not a farthing more.

I have sent this collector with all the registers of those regions, which have my felicitous *nişān* written at the beginning and the date at the end, and I have commanded that the criers (*dellāl*) and magistrates (*ḥükkām*) of the region are to supervise the *ḫarāc*-collector: he is not to take one *aḳçe* without their cognizance, and they are to weigh, in one another's presence, the *ḫarāc* collected each day.

You who are *ḳāḍī* are to make a separate register. My *ḫarāc*-collector is to take charge of the money and, after the collection is finished, you are to write out a copy of the register you have drawn up, village by village, and give it to my collector and send it to my Porte with a letter making a report. If there is any doubt about the name of an infidel, my register is to be consulted, and it is to be accepted in the form in which it is written there. If like previous [officials], [the *ḳāḍī*s] are negligent and ignore this order and do not take a full part in the collection of the *ḫarāc*, then, by the soul of the Ḫüdāvendgār, I will not stop short of taking away

[73] Permeti (in southern Albania).
[74] *Berāt*: a diploma of appointment by the sultan.
[75] *Mezraʿa*: an area of cultivated land without a settlement.
[76] *Ḳul*: a servant of the sultan.
[77] *Baştina*: a peasant tenement in the Balkans.
[78] *Nāʾib*: a deputy *ḳāḍī*.

their appointments (*manṣıb*), but will visit them with heavy afflictions: let them not pretend that they have not been warned.

When the collector arrives at a place, he is to send an agent to the villages around to issue a warning: but his agent is not to take one farthing from anybody. The *tīmār*-holder of each village is in person to bring his infidels before my collector and to render assistance in completing the collection of the *ḫarāc*.

However many [widowed] women and dead infidels there may be, [the collector] is to collect their *ḫarāc* in a separate [account] and bring it to my Porte. When he is taking the *ḫarāc*, he is not to say 'Your *ḫarāc* is so much', but just demand the *ḫarāc*: if they give more than is written in the register, he is to enter it separately with their names and to bring the list to my Porte.

The one *aḳçe* per house (*ev*) which the *il ketḫüdā*s have hitherto brought in, he is to collect according to the register, without any deficiency, and bring to my Porte in (?) advance (*karşu*) by his subordinate (*adam*). He is not to show any negligence. He is not to enquire after new payers (*nev-yāfte*) in these regions, but if he finds that any entered as 'dead' are, in fact, alive, he is to enter the fact.

Thus they are to know . . .

4b Two extracts from a jizya *register*

ACCOUNTS for the *jizya* of the infidels of the *vilāyet*s of Arġiroḳasri[79] and Zaġorya[80] in the *sancaḳ* of Albania, due for the year 893 (1487/8), written on 5 Ṣafar 895 (29 December 1489), with the cognizance of the secretary Luṭfī.

<u>*Vilāyet* of Arġiroḳasri</u>

<u>*ḫānes*</u>,[81] including widows	<u>*jizya*</u>
original 5,760	160,918
(checked by Dervīş ʿAlī)	
Subtract	
18	476

lost over the year, being those who fled from the village of Vişani, according to the *ḥüccet* of the *ḳāḍī* of Arġiroḳasri, Aḥmed b. Maḥmūd.

add [to the year's figure of]:

5,742	160,442

new payers (*nev-yāfte*) over the year, without widows, 472 [persons] at 5 *aḳçe*:

	2,360

new payers in respect of *baştina*s and *iltizām-i sipāhīyān*,[82] 13 of them being *baştina*s:

38	789

---

[79] *Arġiroḳasri*: Gjirokastër

[80] *Zaġorya*: Zagori

[81] *Ḫāne*: a house; a household as a taxable unit, 'hearth'.

[82] This term perhaps refers to tax-farms granted to *tīmār*-holding *sipāhī*s to supplement the inadequate income from their *tīmār*s.

<u>*Vilāyet* of Zağorya</u>

	1,935	51,712
supplement for the *jizya* of new payers, over the year, without widows, 158 at 5 *aḳçe*:	790	
total:	1,935	52,502

<u>Together</u>

original: 7,695		212,630
subtract, lost over the year, as above:	18	476
add (to the year's figure of):	7,677	
new payers (as above):	38	
supplement for new payers, without widows, 630 at 5 *aḳçe*:		3,150

<u>Total including taxes</u> (*rüsūm*)

ḫānes 7,715	*jizya*: 216,073
secretarial- and accounting-tax at 1 *aḳçe* per 10 *ḫānes*:	771
accounting-tax at 2 per 1,000 [*aḳçe*]:	432
'one-*aḳçe* tax' [*per ḫāne*]:	7,715
'hand-kissing' tax (*'ādet*) 200 [*akçe*] per 1,000 *ḫānes*:	1,543
From this:	
paid into the Imperial Treasury, [?] Ṣafar, 895	222,575
pay for the staff of the Arġiroḳasri mosque, 17 Shaʿbān 894 (16 June 1489) to 17 Shaʿbān 895 (6 July 1490) at 6 [*aḳçe*] per day:	2,160
porterage and cost of sacks:	[no figure]
Balance:	3,959

Received at the Treasury in full, 6 Ṣafar 895 (30 December 1489)

4c Accounts for the jizya *of the infidels of the* vilāyet *of Menlik*[83]

tīmār of His Excellency Ibrāhīm Paşa[84]

due for the year 894 (1488/9): written on 2 Muḥarram 896 (15 November 1490) with the cognizance of the secretary Kemāl, agent of His Excellency the Paşa.

original:	*ḫānes*	*jizya*
	2,741	245,230
	widows	
	189	3,697
total:		248,927

[83] Melnik.

[84] Çandarlı İbrāhīm Paşa (1429–99), grand vizier 1498–9.

from this:

Annual stipend of His Excellency Ibrāhīm Paşa, added to his *tīmār*, per annum:	180,000
Pay of the *imām* and the *müʾezzin* of the mosque of Menlik at 2 *akçe* per day:	720
Porterage and cost of sacks:	270
porterage, 1 load:	250
sacks and rope, 2 bags:	20
Balance:	67,937

Received in full, 2 Muḥarram, 897 (5 November 1491).

5 Debasement of the coinage

5a Debasement under Meḥmed II

The order of the felicitous *nişan* . . . is this that:

I have sent the bearer, my *ḳul* [. . .], to the *sancaḳ*s of Ayasuluġ,[85] Aydın, Saruḫān and Menteşe, and to the district of Ṭoñuzlu[86] to carry out the injunction (*yasaḳ*) concerning silver and old *aḳçe*s, and I have commanded that he is to go and search the shops and the *bedestan*s,[87] the caravanserais, the ships and the merchants in the harbours and the baggage of travellers: if anyone is found in possession of [ingot-]silver not bearing my *ḳul*'s stamp or of old *aḳçe* coins, it is to be taken to my mint and [the owner] is to be given [only] 2 *aḳçe* per *dirhem*[88] for it. He is to forbid any dealing or trading in the old *aḳçe*: and if anyone does trade with them, my *ḳul* is to arrest and punish him. To people working in towns in precious metals, like jewellers and drawers of silver wire, silver may be sold up to 200 *dirhem*s, but no more. If anyone is found in possession of counterfeit coins, [my *ḳul*] is to bring him before the *sancaḳbegi* and the *ḳāḍī*, and they are to examine him; if it is proven according to the *sharīʿa* that the person is a counterfeiter, they are to give my *ḳul* a *ḥüccet* for him to hang the offender and to confiscate his possessions for the *beglik* . . .

5b A debasement heralds a mutiny[89]

On 4 Jumādāʾl-ukhrā 997 (20 April 1589), while the army under Ferhād Paşa was in winter quarters in Erzurum, Süleymān Çavuş arrived from the capital with imperial orders and other letters. He also brought news of quite inconceivable events.

When the majority of the household cavalry returned from the Gänjä campaign, they went to the palace [to receive their pay]. However, five coins are [now] being cut from one old [withdrawn] one, no one is being punished for this, and there is no value left in the currency. While it used to be sultanic law that 500 *aḳçe* coins be cut from 100 *dirhem*[90] of silver, the

[85] Ayasuluġ: Selçuk, Ephesus.

[86] Ṭoñuzlu: Denizli.

[87] *Bedestan*: a covered market; the central commercial building in a town.

[88] *Dirhem*: a measure of weight, about 3.2 g.

[89] My thanks to Dr Christine Woodhead for permitting me to use her translation of this linguistically puzzling extract.

[90] *Dirhem*: in 1585, the weight of the *aḳçe* had been reduced from 0.682 gm to 0.384 g.

same weight of silver is now being turned into 2,000 worthless *akçe* coins which are no good for anything. By degrees, a *dirhem* of silver came to be traded for 12 *akçe* coins, and a *kuruş*,[91] which used to be worth 40 *akçe*, is now traded for 80; the exchange rate for a gold coin has risen from 60 to 120 *akçe*. As a result, merchants have doubled their prices, and the costs of food and clothing have risen accordingly. [But] anyone whose salary is valued at [the old rate for] ten gold coins now receives, in effect, the equivalent of only five. The cavalry therefore went in a body to Şeyhi Efendi,[92] the chief *muftī*, taking their debased *akçe* coins, and posed the following question: 'Our salary has been paid in these so-called *akçe* coins, but no one will accept them, and we are obliged to use force to pay with these for food and clothing. Is what we buy in this way licit?' Şeyhi Efendi ruled that it was illicit.

SOURCES

1a Franz Babinger (ed.), *Die Aufzeichnungen des Genuesen Iacopo de Promontorio de Campis über den Osmanenstaat um 1475*, Munich (1957), 62–72.

1b Ö. L. Barkan, '933–934 (M. 1527–1528) malî yılına ait bir bütçe orneği', *İstanbul Üniversitesi İktisat Fakültesi Mecmuası*, 15 (1953), 280–5.

2a M. Tayyib Gökbilgin, *Edirne ve Paşa Livası*, Istanbul (1952), 149.

2b Gökbilgin, *Edirne ve Paşa Livası*, 149.

2c Nicoară Beldiceanu, *Recherche sur la Ville Ottomane au XVe Siècle*, Paris (1973), no. 4.

2d Nicoară Beldiceanu, *Les Actes des Premiers Sultans*, Paris, The Hague (1964), I, no. 17; Anhegger and İnalcık, *Ḳānūnnāme*, no. 17; Ahmet Akgündüz, *Osmanlı Kanûnnâmeleri*, 1: 581.

2e Klaus Schwarz (ed. Claudia Römer), *Osmanische Sultansurkunden: Untersuchungen zur Einstellung und Besoldung Osmanischer Militärs in der Zeit Murāds III*, Stuttgart (1997).

2f Beldiceanu, *Recherche sur la Ville Ottomane*, no. 14.

2g Beldiceanu, *Recherche sur la Ville Ottomane*, no. 13.

2h Beldiceanu, *Recherche sur la Ville Ottomane*, no. 12.

3a Beldiceanu, *Actes*, I, no. 7; Robert Anhegger and Halil İnalcık, *Ḳānūnnāme-i Sulṭānī ber Mūceb-i 'Örf-i 'Osmānī*, Ankara (1956), no. 7, Akgündüz, *Osmanlı Kanûnnâmeleri*, 1: 499.

3b Beldiceanu, *Actes*, II, no. 31.

4a Beldiceanu, *Actes*, no. 55; Anhegger and İnalcık, *Ḳānūnnāme-i Sulṭānī*, no. 54; Akgündüz, *Osmanlı Kanûnnâmeleri*, 1: 509–10.

4b Halil İnalcık, 'XV. asır Osmanlı maliyesine dair vesikaları', *Tarih Vesikaları*, 1/16 (1955), 130–2.

4c Ö. L. Barkan, '894 (1488–89) yılı cizyesinin teşkilâtına ait muhasebe bilançoları', *Belgeler*, 1/i, (1964), 45.

5a Beldiceanu, *Actes*. I, no. 2; Anhegger and İnalcık, *Ḳānūnnāme-i Sultānī*, no. 2; Akgündüz, *Osmanlı Kanûnnâmeleri*, 1, 573.

5b Mustafa Selânikî, ed. Mehmed İpşirli, *Tarih-i Selânikî*, I, Istanbul (1989), 209–10.

[91] *Ḳuruş* ('Groschen'): a large silver coin, in this period imported from Europe.

[92] Mü'eyyedzāde 'Abdü'l-ḳādir Şeyhī Efendi: chief mufti from 1587 to 1589.

CHAPTER IX

*Waqf*s

SECTION 1 FOUNDATION AND FUNCTION

A *waqf* (Turkish: *vakf*) is a trust where the founder (Arabic: *wāqif*; Turkish: *vāḳıf*) makes an endowment of property to be dedicated in perpetuity to the charitable cause named in the deed of trust (Arabic: *waqfīya*; Turkish: *vakfiye*). For a *waqf* to be valid in law, the founder had to be the owner of the property to be converted. He or she had then to go before the *ḳāḍī*, as representative of the sultan, and declare his or her intention to convert it to *waqf*. Once the *ḳāḍī* had ruled that the *waqf* was valid, the property passed from his or her ownership. The problem in Ḥanafī law was how to make a *waqf* in perpetuity. An opinion attributed to Abū Ḥanīfa gives the founder the right to retract his or her donation; another opinion, attributed to Abū Ḥanīfa's two disciples Abū Yūsuf and al-Shaybānī, deny this right. It was therefore essential that the *ḳāḍī* make clear in his ruling that the founder was following the opinion of the 'two disciples' and that the *waqf* was to be non-retractable, hence the procedure adopted in Ottoman courts as shown in passage **1**.

Typically, *waqf*s supported religious institutions, providing finance for the construction and maintenance of mosques and dervish convents (*zāviye*s) and paying the salaries of their staffs. Passages **2** and **3** demonstrate that *waqf*s also supported Islamic education, from primary schools to the higher *medrese*s attached to sultanic and vizieral mosques. In the countryside in particular, part of the *waqf*-income of *zāviye*s was often dedicated to lodging travellers; passages **3, 4b, 4c, 5b** and **7b** give testimony to that effect. In the cities, the soup-kitchens (*ʿimāret*s) attached to large mosques provided sustenance for the poor and the transient, as indicated in passage **2**.

While the townscapes of Ottoman cities were dominated by mosques, bath-houses and other public buildings endowed as *waqf* by sultans, viziers and the wealthy, the hundreds of smaller *waqf*s established by persons of modest means were equally important in maintaining the social fabric of Ottoman society. A second type of *waqf* was the family trust. In Islamic law a testator may bequeath only one-third of his or her property to nominated heirs. The remaining two-thirds goes in fixed proportions to members of his or her family. This has the effect of dividing up property on the owner's death. As evident from passages **4a, 4b, 4c, 6, 8**, as well as **SECTION 2, passage 1** below, many people chose to convert their private property to *waqf*, nominating their chosen relatives and heirs as beneficiaries. According to **SECTION 2, passage 1** below, they could also nominate themselves and their heirs as administrators (*mütevellī*) of the *waqf*. In this way, the property remained intact, in principle in perpetuity, and would descend to the founder's chosen heirs.

In the period of Ottoman expansion in the fourteenth and fifteenth centuries *waqf*s also served as instruments of colonisation. The sultans would grant possession of land in newly conquered areas to dervishes who – sometimes after expelling its original inhabitants, as seen in passages **4a** and **4b** – would convert it to *waqf* and use the income to establish *zāviye*s which might then form the nucleus of a new settlement. In cases at the one described in passages **5a** and **5b**, the same family could occupy a *waqf*-property acquired in this way for centuries.

1 Founding a *waqf*

Question: When a man wishes to make part of his property *waqf*, what action should he take to make the *waqf* binding?

Answer: After he has made the *waqf* and determined the expenses to be paid out in perpetuity, he should go to the *ḳāḍī* and state that he has made the *waqf*, determined the expenses, and handed over [the property] to the *mütevellī*: after the *mütevellī* has confirmed this, [the endower] should say, 'By the ruling of Abū Ḥanīfa, this is not a *waqf*; I retract and take back the property', and demand the property from the *mütevellī*. The latter should refuse to give the property up, saying, 'It is binding by the ruling of the two imāms'.[1] The *ḳāḍī* must say, 'I give judgement that the *waqf* is valid and binding', after which there can be no retraction. (Ebū'ṣ-su'ūd).

2 A vizieral *waqf*

Waqf of the late Maḥmūd Paşa[2]

For the noble congregational mosque (*cāmi'-i şerīf*), *'imāret*, *medrese*, school and mosques in Istanbul, and the congregational mosques and mosques[3] in Rūmeli and Anaṭolı. Transacted on 11 Ṣafar 878 (8 July 1473), signed by the *ḳāḍī'asker* Mevlānā 'Alī b. Yūsuf el-Fenārī.

Capital endowments in the city of Istanbul etc.

In Istanbul

	Per annum
Shops by the *medrese* of the said founder: 11	3,384
Shops by the rooms for bachelors: 4	720
Dyers' shops by the poultry-market: 14	7,068
Shops opposite the dyers' shops: 14	2,688
2 shops opposite the school (*mu'allimḫāne*) of the founder	324
Shop and depot by the *'imāret* of the said founder	300

[1] 'The two imāms' are Abū Yūsuf and al-Shaybānī.
[2] Grand vizier to Meḥmed II, executed 1474.
[3] A congregational mosque (*cāmi'*) is a large urban mosque where the congregational prayer is held on Friday. A smaller mosque is a *mescid*.

3 shops by the garden of the noble congregational mosque (*cāmiʿ-i şerīf*)	1,020
Numerous houses (*ḫānehā*) and rooms (*ḥücerāt*) opposite the *medrese* of the said founder: 35	8,784
9 houses near the *ʿimāret* of the founder	2,556
16 ground-floor rooms by the garden of the noble congregational mosque	3,840
13 ground- and upper-floor rooms near the *ʿimāret* of the said founder	4,740
13 rooms near Ḫayrü'd-Dīn Paşa's house	2,880
5 rooms in front of the stable for travellers	840
Garden by the noble congregational mosque	2,000
Caravanserai and shops near the bath-house	10,700
Plot leased (*zemīn-i maḳṭūʿ*) to the *waqf*s of 'Abdü's-Selām Beg	4,948
Plot leased to the *waqf*s of Aya Sofya	3,360
Plot leased to various [lessees]	2,160

Waqf of the said deceased which he made for the benefit of his descendants

His descendants have now died out. In accordance with the conditions [stipulated by] the founder, it has been retained for expenses of the *ʿimāret* of the said founder.

Double bath-house by the *ʿimāret* of the said founder	63,000
Houses of the said founder in the Ḳāsim Paşa el-Cezerī quarter	5,040
Share in the *başḫāne*[4]	660
3 houses by the bath-house of the said founder	1,860
Rooms by the houses of Maḥmūd Çelebi the *defterdār*	144
50 shops near the said bath-house	16,700
36 shops opposite the said shops	10,044
12 upper and ground-floor rooms opposite the said bath-house	2,424
11 rooms by the storeroom of the founder's *ʿimāret*	2,040
Plot leased out near the Şengül bath-house	812
Plot leased to various [lessees]	598
Market-garden by the houses of the said founder	---

In Rūmeli

In the city of Edirne

Double bath-house in the tanners' quarter	20,000
Upper and ground-floor rooms known as the Armoury, in the ʿĪsā Beg quarter	2,500
House in the Saruca Paşa quarter	360
Plot near Taşlık, leased to various [lessees]	1,670

[4] This seems to be a shop for selling sheep's heads and trotters.

In various villages

Village of Çatalca and the villages of Bosna, Hurb and Martenek, with their dependencies, in the *ḳażā*[5] of Silivri	120,000
Village of Ḫāṣṣ, and the villages of Os̱manlu, Kulaġuzlu and Musuca, in the *ḳażā* of Kırkkilise	42,600
Village of Veled-i Süle, with its dependencies, in the said *ḳażā*	5,774
Bath-house and shops in the village of Ḫāṣṣ	13,179
Village of Çene, with its dependencies, in the *ḳażā* of Hayrabolu	26,000
Villages of Mehler, Ulubeglu and Sofiler in the *ḳażā* of Akçakızanlu	61,587
Village of Vigoşta, in the *ḳażā* of Drama	35,797
Bath-house and shops in the town of Gügercinlik[6]	800

In Anaṭolı

In the city of Bursa

Khan in the said city	49,000
Shops by the said khan in the said city	1,000

In the city of Ankara

Covered market: 102 [shops]	35,000
Numerous shops in the said city	14,596
Caravanserai in the said city	4,667
Başḫāne in the said city	2,640
Market-garden in the town of Midillü[7]	---

Books allotted to the *medrese* in Istanbul

Tafsīr, 23 volumes; *ḥadīth*, 31; *uṣūl al-ḥadīth*, 11; *uṣūl al-fiqh*, 13; *furū'*, 49; books on Arabic, 35; books on logic, 9; books on *ḥikma*; books of prayers (*da'avāt*), 11[8]

Books allocated to the *medrese* in the village of Ḫāṣṣ

Tafsīr, 8 volumes; *ḥadīth*, 11; *uṣūl al-ḥadīth*, 6; *uṣūl al-fiqh*, 10; *furū'*,17; books on Arabic, 17; books on logic, 8; books on *ḥikma*, 3; books on astronomy, 4; the book of the *Mathnawī*,[9] [-]; books of prayers, [-].

---

[5] *Ḳażā*: the judicial and administrative district of a *ḳāḍī*.

[6] Golubac in Serbia.

[7] Midillü is the Turkish name for Mitylene on Lesbos. This probably refers to a different Midillü.

[8] *Tafsīr*: Qur'ānic exegesis; *ḥadīth*: traditions of the Prophet; *uṣūl al-ḥadīth*: methodology for the study of *ḥadīth*; *uṣūl al-fiqh*: methodology for the study of jurisprudence; *furū'* [*al-fiqh*]: substantive law; *ḥikma*: literally 'wisdom'. Its sense here is not clear.

[9] *Mathnawī*: presumably the *Mathnawī* of Jalāl al-Dīn Rūmī.

EXPENSES

For Medina the Enlightened. In gold.		Coins: 1,000

Pay of the staff of the *medrese* in the city of Istanbul

	per day	per year
Pay of the *müderris*[10]	50	
Pay of the *mu'īd*[11]	5	
Pay of the students	30	
Pay of the doorkeeper	2	
Pay of the librarian	5	
Total	92	33,120

Pay of the staff of the noble congregational mosque in the said city

Pay of the imam	15	per year
Pay of the muezzins, 2 at 5	10	
Pay of the *ḳayyūm*s, 2 at 3	6	
Pay of the lamplighter	3	
Pay of the *mu'arrif*[12]	4	
Pay of the *devirḫvān*s,[13] 9 at 3	27	
Pay of the teacher of orphans	5	
Pay of the reciters of *eczā'*,[14] 5 at 2	10	
Total	101	56,360

Pay of the staff of the *'imāret* in Istanbul

Pay of the director of the *'imāret*	10	
Cellar-keeper	5	
Major-domo	5	
Head-servants, 2 at 3	6	
Cooks, 3 at 3	9	
Tevlīyet,[15] 2 at 2½	5	
Dish-washer	2½	
Bakers, 2 @ 3	6	
Meat-porter	2½	
Stableman	2½	
Corn-grinder	1	
Sweeper of the *medrese*	2	
Total	56½	20,340

[10] *Müderris*: a professor at a *medrese*.
[11] *Mu'īd*: a teaching assistant.
[12] *Mu'arrif*: an usher at the Friday Prayer.
[13] *Devirḫ*v*ān*: a member of a group that recited the Qur'ān in relays.
[14] *Eczā'*: plural of *cüz'*, one-thirtieth part of the Qur'ān.
[15] *Tevlīyet* would normally mean the office or functions of a *mütevellī*, here perhaps assistants of the *mütevellī*.

Pay of the staff of the *medrese* and noble congregational mosque in the village of Ḫāṣṣ

Pay of the *müderris*	20	
Pay of students	20	
Pay of the doorkeeper	2	
Pay of preacher and imam	10	
Pay of teacher of orphans	5	
Pay of *müʾeẕẕin*s, 2 at 2½	5	
Pay of reciters of *eczāʾ*, 5 at 2	10	
Pay of *ḳayyūm*	2	
Pay of servant in the caravanserai	1	
Pay of handymen, 2 at 1	2	
Pay of revenue-collectors, 2 at 5	10	
(Collection from the said village, per day:	5)	
(Collection from Edirne, per day:	5)	
For the annual subsistence of the staff of the said mosque, wheat 350 *keyl*[16]	–	
Cost of oil, candles and matting	2	
Total	94	33,840

Pay of the staff of the noble congregational mosque in the city of Sofia

Pay of preacher	10	
Pay of imam	6	
Pay of *müʾeẕẕin*	3	
Pay of *sermaḥfil*	2	
Pay of Qurʾān reciters and *muʿarrif*, 6 at 1	6	
Pay of *ḳayyūm*	3	
Cost of oil, candles and matting	2	
Total	32	11,520

Salaries of the staff in the city of Bursa

Pay of imam of the mosque at the khan	4	
Pay of *müʾeẕẕin* of the said mosque	2	
Pay of revenue-collector of the *waqf*s	5	
Pay of handyman	1	
Pay of water carrier	2	
Pay of rubbish-collector	2	
Cost of oil, candles and matting	2	
Total	17	6,120

[16] *Keyl*, *kile*: a measure of weight, here probably about 25.6 kg.

Salaries of the staff in the city of Ankara

Pay of *ḥāfiẓ*es[17] in the noble congregational mosque of Şeyḫ Ḥāccī Bayram,[18] 10 at 1	10	
Pay of imam of the mosque in the covered market	2	
Pay of the *mü'ezzin* of the said mosque	1	
Pay of imam in the mosque at the khan	2	
Pay of the *mü'ezzin* at the said mosque	1	
Pay of handyman	3	
Pay of watchmen	5	
Pay of water carrier	1	
Cost of revenue-collection	10	
Cost of food for the servants of Şeyḫ Ḥāccī Bayram	5	
Total	40	14,400

Pay of various staff

Pay of Mevlānā the *ḳāḍī'asker*	5	
Pay of *mütevellī*	50	
Pay of *nāẓir*[19]	30	
Pay of secretary of the *'imāret*	7	
Pay of revenue-collector for Istanbul	5	
Pay of handyman	3	
Pay of water carrier (*rahābī*)	4	
Pay of sweeper	3	
Pay of miller	3	
Pay of imam of Serv mosque	2	
Pay of *mü'ezzin* of the said mosque	1	
Pay of imam of the Şeref Aġa mosque	3	
Pay of *mü'ezzin* of the said mosque	2	
Cost of oil, candles and matting for the said two mosques	2	
Pay of revenue-collector for the village of Çatalca	8	
– for the village of Çöke	5	
– for the village of Veled-i Süle	5	
– for the village of Vidagoşta	5	
– for the village of Mehler	4	
Pay of secretary for the said village[s]	4	
Total	151	54,360

[17] *Ḥāfiẓ*: a person who has memorised the Qur'ān

[18] Ḥāccī Bayram of Ankara (d.1430) was the founder of the Bayrami order of dervishes.

[19] *Nāẓir*: the general overseer of a *waqf*.

Expenses for the kitchen of the *ʿimāret* of the late Maḥmūd Paşa, in accordance with the *waqfīya*.

Rice	Kile
For cooking *dāne*, *zerde*[20] and *zīrebāc*[21]	
on the nights in Ramaḍān and every Friday night	6
For cooking *dāne* and *zerde* on the day of the Two Festivals	6
For cooking soup, every day	2
Wheat for soup, every day	½
Flour	
For bread, every day	8
For soup, every 6 days	1
Salt	
For bread, every 10 days	1
For soup, every 6 days	1
Chickpeas, every 10 days	1

Almonds, every night: ½ *vuḳiyye*[22]; starch, every night: 1 *vuḳiyye*; red *meviz*: 12 *vuḳiyye*; black plums: 3 *vuḳiyye*; apricots: 3 *vuḳiyye*; saffron: 30 *dirhems*[23]

	Per day	Per year
Cost of meat	100	
Feeding guests		5,000
Preserves and pickles		2,000
Cost of firewood		7,000
Cost of dishes	2	
Cost of matting	1	
Oil and candles	2	
Cost of vegetables and minor expenses	2	

Endowment income from the *waqf*s of the said late Maḥmūd Paşa in a complete year: 606,513

Subtract expenses 396,313

For the poor of Medina the Enlightened (may God ennoble it), [paid in] gold. 1,000 coins at 59 59,000

Salaries		210,060
Kitchen expenses etc		127,144½
Balance		210,200

---

[20] *Zerde*: sweetened saffron rice.

[21] *Zīrebāc*: stew flavoured with cumin.

[22] *Vuḳiyye*: an *okka*, measure of weight: c1.3 kg.

[23] *Dirhem*: a measure of weight, 1/400th of an okka, probably about 3.3 gr.

Stipulations of the late endower: the post of *mütevellī* to go to his sons and his sons' sons and, after extinction, to the most pious of the sons of his freedmen and, after extinction, to the most upright of the sons of the sons of his freedmen, generation after generation and, after extinction, the matter to be referred to the *pādişāh* the Refuge of the World that a suitable pious person be appointed. Income to be expended firstly on repairs, then to the stipulated expenses and pay of the staff; 1,000 *filori*[24] to the poor of Medina; if the *mütevellī* is a freedman or an outsider, he is not to receive more than 50 *akçe* a day.

The endower also stipulated: if the surplus accumulated to the extent that it could pay for the building of a congregational mosque, then a congregational mosque is to be built in Edirne. If there was still a surplus, then 100,000 *akçe* is to be kept permanently in reserve, and the *mütevellī* is authorised to expend any surplus beyond this in payments to deserving freedmen and descendants of freedmen of the endower and to pious *'ulemā*.

The endower also stipulated: so long as one of his freedmen is fit to occupy any post laid down in the *waqfīya*, that post is not to be given to anyone else. Written in the second decade of Ṣafar 878 (8–20 August 1473).

Now [953/1546] the revenue of the *waqf*s has permitted the building of a congregational mosque in Edirne and, after 100,000 *akçe* [are kept in reserve according to the stipulations of the endower, some 100,000 *akçe*] per year remain for equitable allocation to the *'ulemā* and the poor according to the stipulation of the endower.

The present *mütevellī* is 'Alī Beg.

3 A new *waqf*

Waqf of Ḥāccī Memi son of Yaḥyā Faḳīh. At Yer Kesigi in the *ḳażā* of Muġla he built a *zāviye*; near the *zāviye* he made a water-point; by the village, he dug a well and built a caravanserai, making it a *waqf* for those who should lodge there; and he also built a school.

For the expenses of the *zāviye*, 2000 *akçe* in cash, producing:	400 per year
Two shops in the market of Yer Kesigi, producing:	50 per year
For the expenses of the water point and the well:	500 *akçe* in cash
One shop in the market, producing:	120 per year
For the caravanserai, 200, producing at interest:	40 per year
For the expenses of the school:	2,500 *akçe* in cash
A *ḫarāc*-paying vineyard of three *dönüm*, from the vineyards at Yaḳa.	

His half-share of the summer-pasture called Ḳaymaḳçıoġlu Yurdu, for the teacher to live there in the summer.

He made *waqf* eight shop-sites, let at 24 *akçe* per year, producing: 650 per year (*sic*)

He stipulated that the teacher, besides teaching the children, should recite one *cüz'* for the soul of the Prophet every day except Friday.

For the stipend of the *mütevellī*, 1,800 *akçe* cash, producing at interest: 360 per year.

The post of *mütevellī* to himself, then to his son Ṭayyib, and then to the most suitable of his descendants.

[24] *Filori*: 'florin', a gold coin.

4 *Waqfs* established by conquerors and colonisers

4a The waqf *of Murād I*

Ṭuġra of Murād I

The command of this document is this: The land possessed by Şeyẖ Ulaş, the bearer of this document, was made into a *waqf* and given to him by Rüstem Beg. It was the private property (*mülk*) [of Rüstem Beg] from which he had expelled and scattered its infidel [inhabitants]. Maintaining it as tax-exempt (*müsellem*), I, for my part, have made it *waqf* for the sons' sons and daughters' daughters [of Şeyẖ Ulaş]. He is to be exempt from courier[-service],[25] corvée labout and all *ʿavārıż*. No one is to harass him. If hereafter anyone contests its validity, may he be accursed . . . In the second decade of [. . . ?] 785 (1383/4).

4b The waqf *of the Ṣaru Şeyẖ*

Çiftlik[26] of Ṣaru Şeyẖ in the village [of Ḳarı Yolu]: Of old, Ṣaru Şeyẖ expelled the infidels of this place and was given a command and a *ḥüccet* from the Ṣaruẖānoğlı[27] for a family *waqf* (*vaḳfīyet-i evlād*). Later, in the time of the late Sultan Meḥmed [II], a timariot named Karagöz claimed the service of the *reʿāyā*,[28] but judgement was given before the *ḳāḍī ʿasker* Cemālü'd-dīn in favour of the *waqfīya* dated 849 (1445/6), which they held. They also have the *ḥüccet*[29], and [hold] documents in confirmation, dated 858 (1454/5), from Sultan Meḥmed [II]; confirmation by the late Sultan Bāyezīd, dated 887 (1482/3) and a *berāt* from Sultan Selīm (may the dust of both of them be sweet), dated 924 (1518/9). The *çiftlik* is now in the possession of Ṣaru Şeyẖ's descendants, Dervis ʿAlāʾü'd-Dīn, Ḥamza and Dervish [. . .], by the *berāt*[30] of our Pādişāh.

They are *şeyẖ*s of the *zāviye* of Ṣaru Şeyẖ and serve travellers. Date of *berāt* 917 (1511/2).

4c A note protecting the dervishes who descend from the district's conqueror

. . . Since the *aʿyān*[31] of the district reported: 'These dervishes (*zāviyedār*) are descendants of the conqueror of the district;[32] they are poor men (*fuḳarā*), fully deserving of protection, who do everything in their power to serve travellers on the road. It is wrong that the *mīrlivā*'s[33] *subaşıs* should intervene', a note has been made in the new register that there is to be no intervention by the *mīrlivā*, unless capital punishment (*ṣalb ü siyāset*)[34] is required.

---

[25] This refers to the obligation to provide lodging and horses for couriers carrying messages and commands from and to the sultan.

[26] *Çiftlik*: a farm, tenement.

[27] The Ṣaruẖānoğlı: a ruling member of the Ṣaruẖān dynasty, whose lands Meḥmed I (r. 1413–21) had annexed in 1415. After annexing the principality, the sultan recognised the validity of the *waqf*.

[28] That is to say, the *waqf* was converted to a *tīmār* in the reign of Meḥmed II (r. 1451–81). It was re-converted to *waqf* during the reign of his successor, Bāyezīd II.

[29] *Hüccet*: 'proof', a confirmatory document issued by a *ḳāḍī*.

[30] *Berāt*: a diploma of appointment by the sultan.

[31] *Aʿyān*: the local notables in a district.

[32] 'The district' here is Şebin Karahisar.

[33] *Mīrlivā*: a *sancaḳbegi*.

[34] VLM translates *ṣalb ü siyāset* as 'capital punishment or *siyāset*-punishment'.

5 The *Waqf* of Mūsā

5a A note on the village of Ḳızıl Delü, 1412

Ṭuġra of Mūsā[35]

The command of this document is this: The earlier *begs* made the village of Ḳızıl Delü, the bearer of this writing (*mektūb*), into a *waqf* and made it exempt. Therefore, I too have given into his hand an imperial *nişān*, to this effect: henceforth it is to be immune and exempt; no one – *nā'ib*,[36] *ḥācib*[37] or *subaşı*, slave of the Ḫüdāvendgār[38] travelling on his affairs, falconer, keeper of the hounds, traveller – is to go and disturb him. He is to be secure against forced labour or courier [service] . . . Whoever contravenes this command will be held guilty in the eyes of the Ḫüdāvendgār[39] and in my eyes . . . Written in the first decade of Muḥarram 815 (13–22 April 1412).

5b A register entry on the waqf *of Ḳızıl Delü, sixteenth century*

Waqf: *mezra'a* of Taru Bükü, village of Büyük Vīrān, and the village of Turfillü Vīrānı,[40] possessed from of old as *waqf*. They hold confirmations from past sultans. Later, in the time of the late Sultan Meḥmed [II], it was abrogated and made a *tīmār*. Sultan Bāyezīd [II] reconfirmed it as *waqf* and gave a command which said: 'Gülşehri, İlyās, Bilāl, İsḥāḳ and Sinān, descendants of Ḳızıl Delü, possess it jointly as a family *waqf* (*vaḳf-ı evlād*), rendering service to travellers who lodge at their *zāviye* . . .'

5c A renewed berāt *for Ḳızıl Delü Sultan's* waqf, *1641/2*

The *ḳuṭbü'l-'ārifīn*[41] Ḳızıl Delü Sultan was granted by the sultans of old the *mezra'as* of Taru Bükü, Büyük Vīrānı and Turfillü Vīrānı as private property (*mülk*), and he made it a *waqf* for his descendants jointly. Since his descendants, the bearers of this *nişān*, Seyyid 'Abdü'r-raḥmān, Seyyid 'Ivaż and Seyyid Zeynel . . . have brought their *berāt* and requested its renewal, I have given them in renewal this my *berāt*, and I have commanded that they are to go and are henceforth to possess jointly these *mezra'as* and, after performing the necessary service, are to occupy themselves in prayer for the soul of the founder and for the continuation of my rule . . .

---

[35] Prince Mūsā ruled the Ottoman Balkans from 1411 to 1413. He was defeated and killed by his brother, Meḥmed [I].

[36] *Nā'ib* ('deputy'): this term came to have the sense of 'deputy-*ḳāḍī*', which may be its meaning here.

[37] *Ḥācib* ('chamberlain'): the sense here is uncertain; perhaps simply a 'courtier'.

[38] *Ḫüdāvendgār* ('lord'): the sultan.

[39] *Ḫüdāvendgār* ('lord'): God.

[40] 'Vīrān' means 'ruined, deserted' indicating that these are *mezra'as*, cultivated lands without habitations.

[41] *Ḳuṭbü'l-'ārifīn* ('The pole of gnostics'): an honorific title bestowed on revered heads of Sufi orders.

5d An undated register entry on the waqf *of Ḳızıl Delü*

Waqf of the descendants of Ḳızıl Delü: When the lands of Rūmeli were honoured with the honour of Islam, Ḳızıl Delü also crossed over, and Sultan Yıldırım Ḫān[42] granted him as *mülk* the villages of Taru Bükü, Büyük Vīrānı and Turfillü Vīrānı, with their bounds and limits, bestowing on him a *mülknāme*[43] dated 804 (1401/2), which said: 'I have given Taru Bükü, Büyük Vīrānı and Turfillü Vīrānı on Tañrı-dağı, with their bounds and limits, and no one is to interfere'. Ḳızıl Delü made them a *vaḳf-ı evlād*, and each one of the Ottoman sultans in succession has recognised the validity of that [original] command . . . and earlier *emīn*s,[44] too, in obedience to these commands, have noted it in the register of the region . . .

5e Note appended to an undated register entry on the waqf *of Ḳızıl Delü*

[Note appended to (d), dated Ramaḍān 1305 (May–June 1888)]: When, according to the command of the late Sultan Maḥmūd [II], all properties and lands attached to Bektaşi convents were seized,[45] the tithes of the villages and *mezra'a*s allocated (*meşrūṭ*) to the benefit of the descendants of Seyyid 'Alī, also called Ḳızıl Sultan, buried in the *ḳażā* of Dimetoka,[46] were also seized'.

6 The *Waqf* of Orḫān

Ṭuġra of Orḫān

My command is this that: I have made the *çiftlik* of Aḳpınar at Taşköprü into a *waqf* and have given it to the bearer of this document, Ḥamza Faḳīh. He is to possess it and pray for the continuation of my rule (*devlet*). Whoever sees this document is to recognise it as valid. Written in Ṣafar of the year 754 (March 1353).

Mezra'a[47] of Aḳpınar. *Waqf.* Possessed by Ḥamza Faḳīh,[48] who held the *nişān*s[49] from Orḫān Beg and Murād Beg and our present [sultan] and the *ḳāḍī'asker*s. Now, Ḥamza Beg having died, our *pādişāh* . . . has given and consigned this waqf-*mezra'a* to Mevlānā Ḫayrü'd-Dīn, the son of the son of Ḥamza Faḳīh; he is to possess it, as did his grandfather.[50]

---

[42] Bāyezīd I (r. 1389–1402), known as Yıldırım ('the Thunderbolt').

[43] *Mülknāme*: a document confirming ownership of private property.

[44] *Emīn*: a salaried official of the sultan; here an official charged with compiling a land-and-tax register.

[45] After the massacre of the Janissaries in 1826, Maḥmūd II (r. 1808–39) ordered the suppression of the Bektaşi order of dervishes, with which the Janissaries were closely associated, and the seizure of their properties.

[46] Didymoteicho in western Thrace, Greece.

[47] *Mezra'a*: a piece of cultivated land without habitations.

[48] The title *faḳīh* (Arabic: 'jurist') indicates that Ḥamza was a man of learning.

[49] *Nişān* ('sign'): letters patent. *Nişān* refers to the sultan's *ṭuġra* at the top of the document, guaranteeing its authenticity.

[50] This document appears to be an early form of a *waqfiya*. Taşköprü is in Kocaeli, the district immediately to the east of Istanbul.

7 *Waqfs* in decline

7a The Waqf *of Dervīş Bāyezīd in Seydī Kavağı*

His slave named Ṭoğan was the *mütevellī*; when he died, it was given to his son Maḥmūd. Allowance of the *mütevellī*: one-tenth of the income after repairs; the remainder expended on travellers.

Caravanserai in Gallipoli	375 [*akçe*] per year
Bath-house in Bolayır	845 per year
Bath-house in Ḳavaḳ	645 per year
Mill	155 per year
Orchard in Ḳavaḳ	(abandoned)
Milch-cows	14 (lost)
There is a farm	(now lost)
Part of a salt pan	1415
Caravanserai in Bolayır	(ruined)
Caravanserai in Ḳavaḳ	(sold and lost)
Total	2525 (*sic*)

A slave named Şīrmerd is a servant in the *zāviye*.[51]

7b The Waqf *of Sağrı Ḫatun*[52]

She built a *zāviye* in the village of Kızılca and made a vineyard of hers *waqf* for it seventy or eighty years ago. It used to serve travellers. Later, the *zāviye* fell into ruin, and the *waqf* was too small to pay for its repair. Since Memdūḥ undertook to repair it and to serve travellers, the post of *şeyḫ* was granted to him by the late Sultan Selīm [I] and he was given a *berāt*. Now renewed by our *pādişāh*.[53] Date of *berāt* 926 (1520).[54]

7c Waqf *of the* zāviye *of Ḳāḍī Ṣalāḥu'd-Dīn*

Now held by Seyyid Meḥmed at the command of the *pādişāh*; he possesses it according to the *waqfīya*.

Vineyard: 7 *dönüm*[55] (abandoned)

Shops: 2 [producing] 15 per month. 1,700 *akçe* (*sic*) in cash.

With this cash they bought a slave to look after the vineyard, but he died, and the money was lost.

Revenue: 185 (*sic*)[56]

---

[51] The document dates from the reign of Meḥmed II (r. 1451–81).

[52] Ḫatun: 'lady'.

[53] Süleymān I (r. 1520–66).

[54] This *waqf* was in Saruḫān, near Manisa.

[55] A square measure of 40 paces by 40 paces.

[56] The *waqf* was sited near Malkara. The *waqfīya* dates from the reign of Meḥmed II.

8 The *waqfīya* of Selçük bint ʿAbduʾllāh, freedwoman of Meḥmed[57]

Waqf of Selçük bint ʿAbduʾllāh, freedwoman of Meḥmed . . .

Copy of the *waqfīya* signed by Mevlānā[58] Meḥmed b. Ḥasan taken from the *sicill*[59] recorded on Shawwāl 931 (22 July–20 August 1525). Gist as follows:

Capital endowment: 3 ground-floor rooms, a basement (?) room, anteroom, veranda, a bakehouse, a well, a latrine, a garden and a surrounding wall in the Dāye Ḫatun quarter, near Ṭaraḳlu Gate, bounded by the new bath-house, the private property of Iskender, the private property of Fāṭima and the public road.

Stipulations: the big house on the Fāṭima side to her son Yaḥyā; the room on the Iskender side to Yaḥyā's son Meḥmed; the big room on the bath-house side to Yaḥyā's daughter Ümmī; the room inside the gate on the bath-house side to Yaḥyā's daughter Fāṭima. The bakehouse, the well and the latrine to be shared. Thereafter to their descendants: if one line dies out, its share to be enjoyed by the others; after final extinction to the *imām*, who is to recite one *cüz*ʾ[60] daily. Repairs to be carried out by the occupants. Now held by their descendants.

SECTION 2 PROBLEMS

A serious legal obstacle to the creation of *waqfs* was the stipulation that the endowment should consist of immoveable property. In cases such as books donated to *medrese* libraries (**SECTION 1, passage 2 above**) this rule could perhaps be overlooked. In the Ottoman realms, however, innumerable *waqfs* were based on cash lent out at interest (**1; 2a–d**). Not only is cash moveable property but, in Islamic law, interest-taking is forbidden. There were various legal devices (*ḥīle*) for circumventing the prohibition on interest (**3a**), some of which clearly troubled the pious (**3b, 3c**), and the question of the legality of cash *waqfs* became the source of a major controversy in the mid-sixteenth century.

Cash *waqfs* were, however, essential to the economic and spiritual well-being of the people. They were, in the first place, the only source of credit available to the general population, and the income they generated supported local mosques (**2a, 2b, 2d**), *zāviyes* (**2d**) and other causes (**2c**). In converting a house to *waqf*, for example, a person might also donate a sum of money to be lent at interest to pay for its upkeep (**1**). It was clearly in recognition of their importance to the well-being of society that the *muftīs* Kemālpaşazāde and Ebūʾs-suʿūd in the sixteenth century defended cash-*waqfs* so vigorously against attempts to abolish them (**3**).

One significant problem for Ottoman governments was that *waqfs* diverted revenues, especially rents and revenues from land that might otherwise have been available to the treasury. It was to prevent the illegal proliferation of *waqfs* that, whenever a new land-and-tax survey was made, the surveyor would inspect the foundation documents of every *waqf* in the district in order to establish its legality and enter the details in the register (**SECTION 1, passages 4b, 4c, 5 above**). As a large city, Istanbul in the sixteenth

[57] This is not the original *waqfīya*, but a summary in the Istanbul *waqf*-register of 1546.
[58] *Mevlānā*: literally, 'our lord', a title given to *ḳāḍīs*.
[59] *Sicill*: a *ḳāḍī*'s register, or a single entry in such a register.
[60] *Cüz*ʾ: one-thirtieth part of the Qurʾān.

century had its own dedicated register of *waqfs* **(SECTION 1, passages 2 and 8 above; below 1, 2a, 2b, 2d)**. Sultans might also be tempted to seize *waqf* revenue for the treasury. Notoriously, Meḥmed II (r. 1451–81), late in his reign, ordered the conversion of a large number of *waqfs* to *tīmārs*. The popular outrage forced his successor, Bāyezīd II (r. 1481–1512) to revoke his father's command **(SECTION 1, passage 5b above)**.

1 A cash and family *waqf*

Waqf of Muṣṭafā b ʿAbduʾllāh

The said donor (*vāḳıf*) has a *waqfīya* dated first decade of Muḥarram 952 (15–24 March 1545), with the signature of Mevlānā Ḥasan b. Meḥmed. Gist as follows.

Capital endowment:

Cash: 3000 [*aḳçe*] annually: 300 [*aḳçe*]

3 ground-floor rooms, stable, upper room, bakehouse, latrine and courtyard in the Zeyrek mosque quarter; bounded by the freehold of ʿAlī Beg and Meḥmed Çelebi.

Ground rent annually: 60 [*aḳçe*]

Stipulations: From the interest, 100 *aḳçe* per year to be the stipend of the *mütevellī*: 60 *aḳçe* to be kept in reserve for repairs. The [whole] residence to be for himself; then for his children and his children's children. When they die out, the house by the door to his wife Hümā, provided she has not married again; then to his brother Ḥasan and then Ḥasan's descendants; the other two houses and the stable [etc.] to Ḥasan's descendants. After extinction: a pious and poor man of learning is to live there and recite the *sūras* of *Iḫlāṣ*[61] and *Fātiḥa*[62] three times a day. *Tevlīyet*[63] and change and modification to himself; *tevlīyet* thereafter to a suitable person. At present held by the founder (*vāḳıf*).

2 Cash and charitable *waqfs*

2a The Waqf *of charitable donors (*erbāb-i ḫayrāt*) in the quarter*

The congregation of the quarter made into *waqf* 7,800 *aḳçe*, stipulating that from the interest 100 *aḳçe* be expended on lighting for the mosque, 200 to the *müʾezzin* to recite the *Iḫlāṣ* a hundred times a day, the rest to go to the *imām*. The *mütevellī* is now Muḥarrem Çelebi.

Annual income: 780.

2b Waqf *of charitable donors*

The congregation collected some money to roof the mosque with lead. Put out to interest, it now amounts to 9,297 *aḳçe*. The brocade-dealer (*kemḫācı*) Sinān is the *mütevellī*, and he is holding it.

[61] *Sūra* 112.

[62] The opening *sūra* of the Qurʾān.

[63] *Tevlīyet*: the office of *mütevellī*; the administratorship of a *waqf*.

2c Waqf *of Ḥāccī Meḥmed in the village of Şeynelü*[64]

He set aside 5,000 *aḳçe* of his own money to gain interest at 12 for 10[65] for the *ʿavārıż* of that village, with himself as *mütevellī* until his death, and thereafter whomever the people of the village should choose: 1,000 per year.

Since in some years there are no *ʿavārıż*, an extra 5,000 has accumulated, bringing in: 1,000 per year.

2d The Waqf *of Ḥāccī Ḥasan b. Ūrūc the Felter*

The aforenamed founder (*vāḳıf*) has a *waqfīya* with the signature of the current inspector of *waqf*s, Mevlānā ʿAbdüʾr-raḥmān, transacted in the middle decade of Dhūʾl-ḥijja 952 (12–21 February 1546). Gist as follows:

Capital endowment	Per annum
Qurʾāns: 3	
Candlesticks: 2	
Cash: 14,000	1,400 [*aḳçe*]

From the interest of this sum, three of the dervishes of Maḥmūd Çelebi outside the Edirne Gate are to be given one *aḳçe* a day and to recite one *cüzʾ* a day from the Qurʾāns which the endower deposited in the mosque of the *zāviye*; and 50 *aḳçe* a year should be spent on candles for the candlesticks which he deposited there; and 30 *aḳçe* per year should be given to the *ḳayyūm*[66] for lighting them. [A sum of] 70 *aḳçe* should be spent once a year on food when they recite the whole Qurʾān. Once a year, one ewer should be bought for the said *zāviye* for 20 *aḳçe*. [A sum of] 100 *aḳçe* should be spent on administration. Administration belongs to the *mütevellī* of the said *zāviye*. The dismissal and appointment of the Qurʾān reciters (*cüzʾḫᵛān*) is in the hands of the *mütevellī*. The *mütevellī* should retain 50 *aḳçe* per year for maintenance (*raḳaba*) and, whenever necessary, spend it on the needs of the *waqf*. If it is not necessary, when the sum reaches 300 [*aḳçe*], the *mütevellī* should spend it on whatever charitable causes (*ḫayrāt*) he wishes. Currently it is retained for the said *waqf*.

3 Cash *waqf*s: Questions of legality

3a A question on donating profit from interest

Question: If Zeyd asks ʿAmr[67] for 1,000 *aḳçe* and receives 1,000 *aḳçe* at 11 for 10,[68] and ʿAmr takes off his *ḳaftan*, saying: 'I sell this to Zeyd for 100 *aḳçe*, and Zeyd takes it and donates it to Bekr, who then donates it to ʿAmr, is such a transaction (*muʿāmele*) legal (*şerʿīye*)?

Answer: It is. (Ebūʾs-Suʿūd.)

---

[64] In the *sancaḳ* of Menteşe, southwest Anatolia.

[65] That is, 20 percent.

[66] *Ḳayyūm*: a caretaker of a mosque.

[67] Ottoman *fatwās* such as these do not name the protagonists in a case, but instead use the fictitious names Zeyd, ʿAmr and Bekr for men, and Hind, Zeyneb and Ḫadīce for women. See Chapter VI.

[68] That is, 10 percent, the rate of interest which, in Ottoman practice, was accepted as legal.

3b A question on interest

Question: If someone says: 'Interest (*ribḥ*) arising in this fashion is *ḥarām*', is any action against him necessary?

Answer: If it is a valid transaction, it should not be called *ḥarām*. (Ebū's-Suʿūd.)

3c A question on using legal devices

Question: If Zeyd says in regard to various legal devices (*ḥīle*): 'To use a legal device is to deceive Allāh', what is necessary?

Answer: An eloquent chastisement and a renewal of Faith. (Aḥmed.)[69]

3d A question on making restitution for not lending out waqf *moneys*

Question: If Zeyd, the *mütevellī* of a cash *waqf* whose product is stipulated to be spent on the *ʿavārıż*[70] of a [city] quarter, does not put this cash out at interest, but pays so much from the capital to those ordered to exact the *ʿavārıż*, must Zeyd make restitution of this sum?

Answer: Yes. (Ebū's-Suʿūd.)

SOURCES

Section 1

1 M. E. Düzdağ, *Şeyhülislam Ebussuud Efendi Fetvaları*, no. 299.
2 Ömer Lütfi Barkan and İbrahim Hakkı Ayverdi, *İstanbul Vakıfları Tahrir Defteri: 953 (1546) Tarîhli*, Istanbul (1970), no. 269.
3 Ömer Lütfi Barkan, 'Kolonizatör Türk Dervişleri', *Vakıflar Dergisi* II (1942), 321, no. 64.
4a Paul Wittek, 'Zu einigen frühosmanischen Urkunden (I)', *Wiener Zeitschrift für die Kunde des Morgenlandes*, 53 (1957), 309; Irène Beldiceanu-Steinherr, *Recherches sur les Actes des Règnes des Sultans Osman, Orkhan et Murad I*, Munich (1967), no. 36.
4b Barkan, 'Kolonizatör', no. 82.
4c Barkan, 'Kolonizatör', no. 158.
5a Wittek, 'Zu einigen frühosmanischen Urkunden (II)', *Wiener Zeitschrift für die Kunde des Morgenlandes*, 54, (1957), 240–1; M. Tayyib Gökbilgin, *XV.–XVI. Asırlarda Edirne ve Paşa Livası Vakıflar Mülkler Mukataalar*, Istanbul (1952), 183.
5b Register entry, undated. Reign of Süleymān I (r. 1520–66).
5c Renewal of *berāt*, 1051 (1641/2).
5d Undated register entry.
5e Barkan, 'Kolonizatör', nos 172–3; Gökbilgin, *Edirne*, 183–7.
6 Wittek, 'Zu einigen (I)', 302, 305; Beldiceanu, *Recherches*, no. 11.
7a Barkan, 'Kolonizatör', no. 190.
7b Barkan, 'Kolonizatör', no. 85.
7c Barkan, 'Kolonizatör', no. 191.
8 Barkan and Ayverdi, *İstanbul Vakıfları Tahrir Defteri*, no. 210.

[69] Aḥmed is the *şeyḫü'l-islām* Kemālpaşazāde (in office 1525–34).
[70] *ʿAvārıż*: an extra-ordinary tax, levied usually in times of war.

Section 2

1 Barkan and Ayverdi, *İstanbul Vakıfları Tahrir Defteri*, no. 1450.
2a Barkan and Ayverdi, *İstanbul Vakıfları Tahrir Defteri*, no. 848.
2b Barkan and Ayverdi, *İstanbul Vakıfları Tahrir Defteri*, no. 214.
2c Barkan, 'Kolonizatör', 321, no. 68.
2d Barkan and Ayverdi, *İstanbul Vakıfları Tahrir Defteri*, no. 2433.
3 Barkan and Ayverdi, *İstanbul Vakıfları Tahrir Defteri*, xxxv, no. 49.

CHAPTER X

Treaties and Foreign Relations

The earliest reference to an agreement concluded between an Ottoman ruler and a foreign power is to a treaty made in 1351/2 between Orḫān (r. 1324?–62) and the Genoese. The text of the treaty itself does not survive, but its terms were evidently re-enacted in several later pacts which Orḫān and his son Murād I (r. 1362–89) concluded with the Genoese. Of these, the treaty of 1387 reproduced in passage **1**, is the earliest to survive. The Ottoman–Genoese alliance was to last, to the mutual benefit of both parties, until the accession of Meḥmed II in 1451. The text of the treaty presents the negotiating parties as enjoying equal status, which is not the case in the Byzantine–Turkish treaty of 1403, as seen in passage **2**.This agreement was a consequence of the defeat and captivity of the Ottoman sultan Bāyezīd I (r. 1389–1402) at the Battle of Ankara in 1402, and it was negotiated when his conqueror Timur was still in Anatolia. After the battle, Bāyezīd's eldest son Süleymān returned as ruler to his father's territories in Europe and, in order to survive, needed to make peace with the local powers. To this end, he opened discussions with the acting Byzantine Emperor John VII, who negotiated the treaty on his own behalf and on behalf of a league of Latin powers in the Aegean. The weakness of Süleymān's position is evident in the territorial and other concessions made to the emperor and the league and in his acceptance of Byzantine protocol in his reference to the emperor as 'my father' in passage **2**.

In the mid-fifteenth century, Murād II (r. 1421–51) also faced a perilous situation. In 1443, after overcoming an attack from Karaman in the east, he narrowly defeated a Hungarian invasion from the west. In order to establish peace on both frontiers and to prepare for his planned abdication and the accession of his son Meḥmed (later to become Mehmed II), he imposed a settlement on the defeated Emir of Karaman, effectively reducing him to vassalage, as shown in passage **3a**, and negotiated a peace with the King of Hungary at Edirne, as demonstrated in passage **3b**. The treaty of Edirne and particularly the generous terms offered to the Despot of Serbia, George Branković, an ally of the king during the campaign of 1443, reflect the delicacy of Murād's situation in 1444. In August 1444, the king solemnly swore to accept the treaty, but subsequently broke his oath. In the autumn, he led an army against the sultan, only to meet defeat and death at Varna on 10 November.

Passages **1** and **2** show the Ottoman sultan negotiating as an equal partner or as supplicant. From the accession of Meḥmed II in 1451 onwards, the format of treaty-texts altered to reflect growing Ottoman power; as passages **4**, **6** and **7** exemplify, they now typically presented the terms agreed in the form of a decree bestowing the sultan's favour and protection, rather than as the outcome of negotiation. During the expansionary period of the fourteenth and fifteenth centuries, the Ottomans had often, as guarantee of their protection and non-aggression, imposed terms of vassalage on neighbouring rulers: according to passages **2**, **3b**, **5** and **6**, the Ottomans required the latter to pay an annual tribute; according to passage **3a**, the neighbouring rulers had to provide troops; and according to passages **3a** and **3b**, they were forced to send a son or other hostage to the sultan's court.

By the mid-sixteenth century, and especially when confronted with the power of the Habsburg monarchy in central Europe and the Mediterranean, this system had become outdated. Nonetheless, the mindset persisted. In addressing the Habsburg Charles V – Holy Roman Emperor and king of Spain – Süleymān I (r. 1520–66) denies Charles the title Emperor, addressing him only as 'King of Spain', as evident in passage **6**. Moreover, passage **5** indicates that, in demanding the tribute due for the parts of the old kingdom of Hungary in Habsburg hands, he continues to regard him as a tributary monarch. By the early seventeenth century, this view had become unsustainable. Reproduced here in passage **9**, the peace terms agreed upon in 1606 at Zsitva-Torok between the representatives of Emperor Rudolf II and Sultan Aḥmed I (r. 1603–17) brought to an end a thirteen-year war in which it had become clear that the Ottomans were no longer the superior military power. Negotiations were conducted as between equals, although subsequent wrangling over the terms, including the use of the title 'emperor' and the Ottoman claim that the emperor should resume the annual payment of tribute, rather than making a single and final payment indicate that the Ottoman side for a while continued to think unrealistically in terms of an agreement with a tributary power.

An increasingly important category of agreements with foreign powers were the capitulations, as seen in passage **7**, the term coming from the Italian *capitolo* ('heading'), referring to the headings under which the clauses were arranged. These governed the status of foreign communities settled in the Ottoman Empire for purposes of trade, their immunity from the *jizya* and other legal privileges setting them apart from local non-Muslims. The Turkish texts of the capitulations take the form of commands, presenting the sultan as graciously bestowing a favour on a petitioner.

1 The Genoese treaty with Murād I, 1387[1]

[1] In the name of the Lord, amen. The magnificent and powerful lord Murād Beg, great Emīr and lord of the Emīrs of Turchia on the one side and the noble, prudent lords Gentile de Grimaldi and Janono de Boscho, ambassadors, syndics and procurators of the renowned Comune of Genoa, on the other side, the latter having been granted their mandate by a public instrument written by Petro de Bargiallo, notary and *cancellarius* of the Comune of Genoa, on the second of March, 1387, ratified by all possible means, right and form by which they best could, approved and confirmed all pacts, conventions and agreements made between the magnificent lord Murād and with the lord, lord Orḫān Beg, his father on one side and the illustrious Comune of Genoa on the other. The said parties renounced in the said names the right to plead

[1] I am grateful to Dr Kate Fleet for allowing me to use her translation of his document.

[against the fulfilment of the terms of the treaty] on the grounds of the agreement, pacts and promise not having been made, and the matter not having been conducted as above and below, and renounced the right to make a plea of trickery, or an action for recovery or any unjust reason for a lawsuit, and all other rights. The said parties promised in the said names mutually with solemn stipulations here inserted to observe without fail those pacts, conventions and promises and not to act against them, or any one of them on any pretext, or for any reason or cause which can be stated or contrived in law or in deed.

[2] The ambassadors promised in the name of and on behalf of the Comune of Genoa to do and ensure that the *comerchiarii* of Pera[2] and the collectors of the tax of *censaria*[3] shall restore to the aforesaid lord Murād Beg all quantities of money taken and received from Giovanni Demelode, *burgensis* of Pera, for the goods and merchandise of lord Murād Beg bought and sold in Pera at the time when Giovanni was acting for lord Murād Beg, with the exception of eight *karati* per 100 *hyperpera*[4] paid to the *censarii* or to the collectors of the said tax of the *censaria.*

[3] The ambassadors promised that the Turkish subjects of the magnificent lord Murād Beg among other things shall not pay in Pera any *commercium*[5] to the Genoese for any goods and merchandise brought into Pera or taken out by the said Turks or any one of them.

[4] The aforesaid ambassadors promised that the Turkish subjects of the aforesaid lord Murād Beg shall not pay in Pera to the *censarii* or the collectors of the tax of *censaria* for their goods and merchandise brought or sold other than eight *karati* per each *hyperpyra.*

[5] In return the magnificent lord Murād Beg, accepting all the above, promised to the said ambassadors, who received his promise in the name of and on behalf of the aforesaid Comune of Genoa, to do and ensure that the Genoese, among other things, shall stay, remain in and traverse the whole of his territory safe and secure, and that they can trade there, buying and selling all the merchandise they wish of their own free will, without anyone being impeded, attacked or molested, paying the *commercium* of the said magnificent lord Murād Beg, as it is customarily paid according to the form of the old conventions. Moreover, the aforesaid lord Emīr promised to do and ensure that all ships of the Genoese and those being handled for and considered as Genoese, can load victuals in the whole of his territory, paying to the aforesaid magnificent lord Murād Beg or his factors for each *modio*[6] of Romania of grain, barley, millet and other pulses, that which the Arabs, Greeks, Venetians and others who pay at a lesser rate, pay.

[6] Both parties promised each and every one of the above things in the above names mutually and to each other, and for the greater surety of the things promised, they swore by the Holy Gospels of God, touching the Scriptures, that is, the said ambassadors in the said names and the magnificent Murād Beg, according to the manner and customs of the Muslims, to abide by, fulfil and observe, and not act against them or any one of them on any pretext or for any reason or cause which can be stated or contrived in law or in deed, under penalty of a fine of double the value, as well as the loss of the total goods for which there will have been a contravention

[2] Pera was the Genoese town on the eastern side of the Golden Horn opposite Constantinople, corresponding roughly to modern Beyoğlu.

[3] *Censaria*: a brokerage tax on goods traded in Pera.

[4] A *hyperperon* was a Byzantine gold coin, weighing 24 *keratia*. By 1387 it was probably a unit of account, divided into 24 *keratia*, rather than a coin.

[5] *Commercium*: customs.

[6] *Modio*: a measurement of weight for grain.

or, as was observed above, all and each of the above firmly enduring, and under pledge and obligation in the said names of all their goods which they had and have, being however those things which are not prohibited from being pledged under the sections and the regulations of the said Comune. Enacted in the present agreement and each part of it that the ambassadors in the said names are held to ensure that the lord Podestà of Pera and his Council swear to abide by and observe all of the above.

[7] It was enacted in the present agreement between the contracting parties in the said names that, whenever any slave of the aforesaid lord or his subjects shall flee to Pera, each inhabitant of Pera and its suburbs, into whose hands such a slave shall come, is held to present such a slave to the lord Podestà of Pera who is now, or in the past shall have been, under pain of paying the slave's price to his master, as well as 100 *hyperpyra* at the weight of Pera to the Comune of Genoa in Pera or to the *massarii*, acting in the name of and on behalf of the said Comune, and that a proclamation and order about these aforesaid things must be made in the land of Pera. In return the aforesaid lord Murād Beg solemnly agreed and promised to the said ambassadors in the said names, acting and receiving the promise in the name of and on behalf of the Genoese Comune, to ensure that all slaves of the Genoese fleeing from their masters to Turchia or Greece should be restored freely to their aforesaid master without reservation, unless those fleeing should be Muslims, in which case the aforesaid lord shall not be held to anything other than the settlement of a fair and just price for such a slave, recognised as a Muslim.

[8] They ordered me, Quilico de' Tadei, the notary whose name appears below, to draw up the present public instrument concerning the aforesaid clauses, as witness of the promises made.

[9] Enacted in Turchia in a certain small settlement called Mallaina,[7] in the courtyard of the house presently inhabited by the aforesaid lord, in the year of the lord 1387, ninth indiction according to the Genoese reckoning, the eighth day of June, a little after Vespers, in the presence of witnesses summoned and specially requested: Bartolomeo de Lamgascho, *burgensis* of Pera, translator from Greek into Latin of the present instrument, Giovanni de Draperis, Dario Spinola, Anthonio de Mentono, *burgenses* of Pera and Amgelino de Saulo, citizen of Genoa, as well as Csassanus Bassa[8] and Tomortassius,[9] Muslim barons of the said lord.

I, Quilico de' Thadei, notary by Imperial authority, was present at all the aforesaid things and was asked to write, but being occupied with my various affairs, permission was granted that I should have it copied by another.

2 The Byzantine–Turkish Treaty of 1403

Copy of the agreements made with the lord Süleymān Çelebi, written in the Turkish language and signed with his and his barons' signatures. Translated by Sir Pietro Zeno.[10]

[1] In the name of the true God. I, who am Süleymān Çelebi, son of the great Sultan Bāyezīd: after the great Emperor Caloiani,[11] emperor of the Greeks, my father, emperor Palaeologus,

[7] Malagina, in the Sakarya valley, to the east of Constantinople.

[8] Ḥasan Paşa.

[9] Timurtaş

[10] The original text of the treaty would almost certainly have been written in Greek. Zeno's text is therefore a translation of a translation.

[11] John VII Palaiologos.

[of] the empire of Constantinople were satisfied with the command of our Lord God, together with the great comunes of Rhodes with its hospital, Venice, Genoa together with the island of Chios, and the Duke of Naxos, with all the settlements and islands belonging to their lands and possessions in the Aegean and Black Seas, and among the emperor's city and places belonging to it and to the league,[12] which is in his following: we have sworn and we have made a true peace, with good will. Now, with the will of the Lord God, I swear by He who created heaven and earth, by my Muḥammad Muṣṭafā and by my seven Mustafi (*sic*) and by my most high and great Prophet in whom we believe. By the soul of my grandfather and by the head of my father, the sultan, and by my soul, I have made peace with all of these. Together with all my barons, subjects and men, and also with all the land which God shall give me, if other lords become my subjects, I have made this peace with my father the emperor and with the empire of the Greeks and the company of the comunes, the emperor's castles and towns and their neighbours, and with the lands, islands and villages in the Aegean and Mediterranean and on land. We have made peace for so long as we shall live; may the sons of our sons be with them in good peace.

[2] To my father, the emperor of the Greeks, I have freely given Salonica and Calamarea with all their dependencies, as we have agreed, and Galicho[13] up to the Paravardaro[14] [river] and up to the shore. I have given Salonica and its tower, and that which he gave to my father: I give it to him. I have given him [the shore] from Panidos[15] to Mesembria[16] and Palateoria, together with their castles, salt pans and all dependencies. I have given them without any [demand for] tribute to my father, the emperor and to the empire of the Greeks. I concede it to him to drive out those Turks who are in possession; and anyone, whether Greek or Turk, who has bought anything with their own money, it should be theirs. I have given Constantinople, with all its free confines, from Parapolia up to Panidos, without any [demand for] tribute. In these places I have conceded to the emperor that he may build castles as he wishes, wherever he wishes.

[3] I have returned those castles which the emperor held in Turkey.

[4] If there is any news of Tamerlane,[17] I shall, at my own expense, provide as many galleys and sailors as I have, to come to Constantinople, if needed.

[5] I have given him [the islands of] Skopelos, Skiathos and Skyros, opposite Salonica, and I have given him the tribute for the said places from the tenth of November until now.

[6] All citizens of Constantinople who are living [in my territory] may return home unimpeded.

[7] All lawsuits and litigation surviving from the time of my grandfather and father until now should be dissolved and not be pursued, except that, if an individual debtor has to pay [what he owes] to another person, [the debt] should be honoured.

[8] [Stephen] Lazarević[18] should retain his lands which he held in the time of my father. He should pay the tribute which he previously paid to my father and send his men to the army as he used to. If he wishes to come in person, he may come securely; when he does not wish, he

[12] John VII was a signatory to the treaty on his own behalf and on behalf of a league of the Latin powers in the Aegean enumerated in clause [1] and the Despot of Serbia, Stephen Lazarević (clause [8]).

[13] Galicho: the Gallikos river.

[14] Paravardaro: The Vardar river. The area described here comprises Chalkidike and the Thermaic Gulf,

[15] A town on the Sea of Marmara to the west of Constantinople.

[16] Mesembria: Nesebŭr.

[17] Timur. The form 'Tamerlane' and its variants derive from Timur-i Leng ('Timur the Lame').

[18] Despot of Serbia. Stephen Lazarević (d. 1427) accepted Ottoman over-lordship after the death of his father Lazar at the Battle of Kosovo in 1389.

should send his men. When he comes with his army, neither he nor any member of his army shall be harmed. I shall send him and his men [home] without suffering any harm from me.

[9] All Frankish, Venetian, Genoese, Rhodian and Greek merchants may come to my lands, and if God gives me other lands, by sea or by land, no one shall suffer harm. They shall pay whatever it used to be customary to pay, with no further impost.

[10] If any merchant commits a crime, no other merchant should suffer a penalty, only the one who committed the crime.

[11] If any ship is wrecked in my lands and territories, any goods or persons who survive should be saved and restored.

[12] All ports which I have shall be open, and however much grain [merchants] may want, they may take. My merchants shall not trouble them. They may buy wherever they wish. For customs, they shall pay 1 *hyperperon* for each *modius* of Constantinople.

[13] None of my oared ships may leave the Dardanelles, whether above or below, without permission of the emperor and all of the League. If, by any chance, one should do so and is found and damaged, the damage shall not be compensated, and the peace [in] Romania[19] [shall remain] intact.

[14] I will release all the captives from Constantinople who are in my prisons, or in the hands of my barons, or those with me who are in chains or have chains around their necks.

[15] The Genoese prisoners who are found with me, in my prisons or with my barons shall be freed. Wherever a Genoese prisoner is found, I shall release him.

[16] If any slave should escape from the Genoese and turn out to be Muslim, I will return him; with this condition all of my [slaves who came into] their hands after the victory of Tamerlane shall be released.

[17] Twenty-five prisoners shall be returned from the prison on Chios.

[18] The Genoese shall not be required to pay tribute for the castles which they hold on the Black Sea [coast].

[19] The Chiots no longer have to pay anything of the 500 ducats which they paid to the lord[20] of Alto Luogo.[21]

[20] I will return any lands, castles and settlements, or anything else taken from Venetian territories, and also give them Athens.

[21] I will give them five miles inland on the mainland opposite Negroponte, but if there are any salt pans or ports there, they are to be mine. If grain is removed from my lands without customs-duty being paid, those who removed it are to be punished.

[22] The Marquis of Bodonitsa[22] shall not be held liable for anything beyond that for which he was held liable by my father.

[23] If any slave or servant [of mine] escapes to their territory, they shall return them to me. Similarly, if any slave or servant of theirs should escape to my territory, there is an obligation to return them.

[24] Naxos, Alto Luogo and Palatia[23] shall no longer pay what they used to, that is, 200 ducats.

---

[19] Romania: the Latin term for the Byzantine and former Byzantine territories in Greece and the Balkan peninsula; Ottoman Rūmeli.

[20] The Emir of Aydın.

[21] Alto Luogo: Theologos, Selçuk.

[22] The Latin lord of Bodonitsa, a fortress near Thermopylae.

[23] Palatia: Balat.

[25] I shall return 500 Venetian prisoners, so long as, by this treaty, they return all the Turks whom they hold.

[26] I have relinquished 500 ducats of the tribute of Phocaea.[24]

[27] If any dispute should arise between us, whether over blood, words or anything else, all such disagreements should be settled amicably through mediators.

[28] I have freely given Salona[25] and its territories which the Countess seized to the Hospital of Rhodes.

3 The peace settlement of 1444

3a The sworn statement of Ibrāhīm Beg of Ḳaramān, 1444

I bear witness by God and 'God is sufficient witness'.[26] 'And fulfil your covenant and do not break oaths when you have confirmed them. You have made God your surety'.[27]

I who am Ibrāhīm Beg son of the late Meḥmed of Ḳaramān, place my hand on the Word of God (*Teñri*) and in honesty and sincerity, without evasion or exception, I swear:

By God, through God and for the sake of God, who seeks and overwhelms, who perceives and destroys, the ever self-existent, who never sleeps and never dies in all eternity, who took no consort and has no son; and out of veneration for the word of God which descended through Gabriel to Muḥammad Muṣṭafā (may God bless him and give him peace). I will not in any way, outwardly or inwardly, show enmity to the noble persons, lives or honour of Murād Beg son of the late Meḥmed Ḫān, nor to his son Meḥmed, nor to their friends, lands and territories; nor to the towns, castles, villages and borders of their lands; nor to their settled peasants and nomads; nor to their governors, cavalrymen and servants; nor to their followers, possessions and all dependents. Nor will I incite anyone to show enmity or become the helper or accomplice of anybody who wishes to do so. If anyone wishes to show enmity, I will hinder and prevent them as far as lies within my power.

I will not fall short. I have become the friend to their friends and the enemy to their enemies. I will be nowhere that might harm their high estate. I will send neither agent, nor word, nor letter, in secret or in public, to the enemies of Murād Beg, whether Muslim or infidel, who do not wish for his prosperity and high estate. I will inform Murād Beg and his son Meḥmed Beg, word for word, of the letters and information that come to me from their enemies and from those who wish them evil.

If any subject of theirs betrays them and gives any of their castles or towns to me, I will not accept. And if any slave belonging to the said Murād Beg or to his son Meḥmed Beg, or any slave belonging to any of their followers, or any male or female slave, or animal belonging to anyone in the territories dependent on them should flee or be stolen and enter my territory, I will find and return [the fugitive].

I will not make excuses but, in short, I will be friend to their friend and enemy to their enemies. Every year I will send one of my sons with my troops to serve Murād Beg.

By God, in respect of these matters, I will not break my oath and, if I break it, I will neither expiate it nor have it expiated. By God, whenever I break the oath, may the oath be upon me.

---

[24] Phocaea: Foça.

[25] Salona: Amfissa.

[26] Qur'ān 4:79.

[27] Qur'ān 16:91.

By God I have sworn truthfully, without evasion or exception. I will not act contrary to nor transgress this oath. If I do, by God, may this Word of God seek restitution from me and my descendants.

God is the agent for what we say. He is sufficient for men and excellent is the agent.

3b The Treaty of Edirne, 1444

To the great and excellent lord, the great Emperor Ladislaus,[28] Emperor of Hungary and King of Poland etc., and also our most esteemed brother and friend: Amurath Beg,[29] great lord, great *emīr* [and] sultan: greetings and a fortunate increase in brotherhood and friendship.

Your Excellency will be aware that the noble and distinguished man, your faithful envoy Stojka [Gisdanić] has brought a letter from Your Excellency which is highly esteemed and pleasing to me. Through this letter Your Excellency has made it known that whatever your faithful envoy Stojka negotiates on your behalf, we should believe it exactly as if it were from your own person.

[1] We make known to Your Majesty what your esteemed Stojka said to us first concerning the despot George [Branković],[30] namely that I should give up his sons[31] and his places and that George himself should be bound in all our services, just as he was in the past. I have agreed to this for the sake of brotherhood with Your Excellency.

[2] He also told us that it would be agreeable for me to keep the peace with Blado,[32] the voivode of the Vlachs, on the following conditions: that the said Blado should pay me tribute as was previously the custom, and that he should again be bound to us in all our services, just as he was before, except that he should not come in person to our court. We agree to this out of love for Your Excellency: namely that the voivode Vlado should pay tribute; that he should once again do everything that he was obliged to do in our service; and that he should not come to our court personally but instead send us a hostage; and also that, if our subjects flee to his territories, he should send them back; and also that we should do the same if his subjects flee here from those places.

[3] This should be understood as follows: namely, that Your Excellency should at the same time enjoy peace, fraternity and good friendship with us. For this reason, we swore in the presence of Your Excellency's envoy, namely Stojka, that we should maintain a good and firm peace, without artifice or deceit for ten years. To this end we are sending our faithful, noble and distinguished [Baltaoğlu] Süleymān Beg, namely that it should please Your Excellency to swear properly and faithfully, without artifice of any kind, that you will maintain a good and firm peace with us for ten years.

---

[28] Władysław III of Poland (r. 1424 44) and I of Hungary (r. 1440 44).

[29] Murād II.

[30] George Branković was Despot of Serbia.

[31] In 1441 Murād II had blinded and imprisoned George Branković's sons, Gregory and Stephen.

[32] Vlad Dracul, voivode of Wallachia (r. 1436 42, 1443 7).

4 A grant of peace and of free passage for merchants

The order of the felicitous *nişān*[33] is this that:

At present I have made peace with the distinguished *emīr* the voivode Petor, *beg* of the land of Bogdan[34] and removed hostility from between [us], and I have commanded that the merchants in Akkerman[35] in his territories may come with their ships and deal and traffic and trade with the people in Edirne, Bursa and Istanbul. In their coming and going, no one of my *beg*s or *subaşı*s or *sipāhī*s or *ḳul*s[36] is to cause injury or loss to their lives or their goods. If they disobey my command and harm [them] in any way, I will send a *ḳul* and visit them a heavy calamity . . . 5 Rajab 860 (9 June 1456).

In the camp at the town of Rudnik.[37]

5 An offer to pay tribute

The *sancaḳbegi* of Bosnia to the Porte:

Since it is throughout the world as clear as the sun that the felicitous *pādişāh* is in every matter sustained [by God] and victorious, a renowned and outstanding *ban*[38] of Croatia, named Ivan son of Karli, fearful of the majesty of the bloody *ḫāḳān*ic sword, has sent me a messenger with a letter and, after humble submission, has said: 'Let me too be a *ḳul* of the *pādişāh* and live in tranquillity in his felicitous shadow', undertaking to pay each year 1,200 *filori*[39]of *ḫarāc*[40] after the fashion of Moldavia and Wallachia. He sent his messenger and the money and said, making me his intermediary and intercessor: 'Do you exert yourself that my money and submission (*ḳulluḳ*) may be accepted at the Exalted Court of the *pādişāh*'. Therefore, his money and his messenger, together with the very letter that came to me, have been sent to the gate of felicity with my officer, your slave Ferhād. Now, be it not concealed from the world-adorning intelligence that, if this man's money and submission are accepted, it is hoped that instructions will be given that no one is to attack the fortresses and territory which he has held (*taṣarruf*) from the time of his father and his grandfather, and that a felicitous *'ahdnāme*[41] in Serbian, after the style of Moldavia and Wallachia, may be graciously granted to his messenger, so that he may prosper in the days of the felicitous *pādişāh* and be counted among his other servants. If the *pādişāh*'s grace is shown to him and his *ḫarāc* and his submission are accepted, all the *ban*s about his territory, on seeing this, will most certainly seek eagerly to offer service and *ḫarāc* to the *pādişāh*.

So be it known. The circumstances have been reported accurately to the Gate of Felicity. It is for the *pādişāh* to command.

---

33 *Nişān* ('sign'): the sultan's cypher (*ṭuġra*) at the head of the decree, indicating that the order comes from the sultan.

34 Moldavia.

35 Akkerman: Bilhorod Dnistrovskyi

36 The phrase covers provincial governors, fief-holders in the provinces and salaried servants of the sultan – that is, everyone on whom the sultan has bestowed executive powers.

37 A mining district in central Serbia. Meḥmed II issued this decree during his Belgrade campaign of 1456.

38 A governor in the Kingdom of Hungary.

39 A gold coin, florin.

40 *Ḫarāc*: tribute.

41 A treaty; a letter of agreement bestowing a privilege.

6 The peace terms offered by Süleymān I to Charles V, 1547

Through the exalted grace of God Most High – may He be praised – and with the blessings of the miracles of His Excellency the Bearer of Prophecy – may God bless him and bring him peace – I, who am the sultan of sultans, proof of the *ḫāḳān*s,[42] shadow of God on the lands, *pādişāh* and sultan of the Mediterranean and Black Sea, Rūmeli, Anaṭolı, Rūm, Ḳaramān, Erzurum, Diyārbekir, Kurdistan, Lūristān, Persia, Ẕū'l-ḳadriyye, Egypt, Syria, Aleppo, Jerusalem and all the Arabian lands, Baghdad, Basra and the realms of Yemen and Aden, the regions of the Tatars and the Qipchaq steppes, the throne of Buda and its dependencies, and many realms conquered by my sword, Sultan Süleymān-şāh son of Sultan Selīm-şāh Ḫān: you, who are Carlos, king of the land of Spain:

[You] should know that your brother, King[43] Ferdinand, has sent a letter through his ambassador Yerārdo[44] to our threshold, the refuge of the world and our court, the workplace of felicity. Your own letter has also arrived. You have sought our imperial favour from the foot of our throne, the refuge of the world, concerning a peace and an accord. Your said ambassador has submitted that he is acting on behalf of both you and your brother and has in many ways asked for grace and compassion in the matter of [my] granting my imperial peace.

This being so, through the perfection of my royal clemency, my imperial peace has been granted to you and your brother for five years. [1] The land of Hungary which, by the exalted grace of God Most High – may He be praised – was conquered by my victorious sword, is our realm. For the parts of that land which are not under the rule of the Muslims, a fixed sum of 30,000 gold coins is to be paid into my imperial treasury each year for five years. [2] It has been made a condition that my protected realms, the province of Algiers in the west, and other Muslim realms in the occident[45] shall not be attacked or suffer harm from either land or sea, and peace shall be observed by both sides. [3] The *pādişāh* of France[46] who nurtures friendship towards my threshold of felicity and also the doge of Venice should be included in my noble treaty, and their lands should not be attacked and harmed by you or your brother, either from the land or from the sea.

It has been decreed that my imperial treaty should be observed by both sides.

My detailed imperial command has been sent to your said brother [setting out] whatever conditions have been stipulated for my imperial peace. Your ambassador also has accepted my imperial treaty in this form on behalf of both of you. A term of three months has been granted, and he has been sent back [to you] with my gracious regal permission.

My Porte, the refuge of felicity, is always open. No one is prevented from coming and going. If God the most glorious is willing, when you have learned on what conditions my imperial command has been bestowed, an ambassador should again be sent to my threshold, the refuge of the world, so that my detailed imperial treaty may be granted.

Written in the first decade of the month of Jumādā'l-ūlā in the year 954 (19–28 June 1547). In Constantinople.

---

[42] *Ḫāḳān*: a *khan*, a title of rulership.

[43] Charles V's brother Ferdinand had been elected 'King of the Romans' – designated heir to the crown of the Holy Roman Empire – in 1531. The sultan recognises his title as 'king'.

[44] Gerhard Veltwyck.

[45] Charles V had conquered Tunis in 1535 and reinstated the Ḥafṣid ruler Mulāy Ḥasan. In 1541 he had led an unsuccessful expedition against Algiers.

[46] Francis I (r. 1515 47).

7 The English capitulations, 1580

This is the command of the noble, exalted, lofty, sultanic *nişān* and the illustrious, world-conquering *ḫāḳān*ic *ṭuġra*[47] (may it be effective through Divine aid and eternal protection!)

At this present time, Elizabeth, Queen of the domains of England and France and Ireland, the model of ladies honoured in the Messiah's religion (may her last moments be concluded with good) has sent letters to our court, the abode of justice and place of audience, the seat of glory, which is the refuge and shelter of the sultans of the world and the sanctuary and haven of the *ḫāḳān*s of the age, by means of her agent named William Harborne, one of her lords who are entrusted with affairs of state, her agent having come formerly to our threshold, which is the nest of felicity, displaying obedience and sincerity and communicating subservience and devotion, [and] seeking permission for her men to come and go from that part of the world to our protected dominions for trade, whereupon our imperial permission was joined in that matter and our noble commands were issued as follows: 'Let no one annoy and molest them by land and sea, in the halting places and stages and in the passages and ports', and because it has been submitted and deposed at the foot of our royal felicitous throne how she presented respectful service to our court, the abode of justice, with sincerity of heart and purity of faith, and how friendship has been established with the aforementioned queen also, just like the mutual friendship and amity concluded between us and France and Venice and Poland and the other kings who display sincere friendship towards our exalted threshold, and how her agent and other merchants have come to our well-protected dominions with their wares, in peace and security and have traded, minding their own business and occupied with their ordinary duties, and how certain of her subjects were captured in the place named [. . .], and how also she has requested favour in the matter of her subjects named [. . .], who are now actually imprisoned, being released and according to our imperial treaty-letter associated with glory, and our noble commands which are given to the aforementioned kings according to the requirements of friendship, [similar privileges] being granted on behalf of the aforementioned queen also.

Therefore, the aforementioned queen's request has fallen into the area of acceptance within the glory of our effulgent presence, and we graciously granted this our imperial treaty-letter. With justice and, our noble commands having been sent out to our servants, the *beglerbegi*s and *beg*s who hold office in our well-protected dominions and to the *ḳāḍī*s and in general to the intendants in the seaports, our incontrovertible *firman* has issued forth in the following manner: as long as the conditions of the treaty and league shall be respected on the part of the aforementioned queen and the rules of peace and protection are respected as is fitting, then on this side also

[1] let no one at all ever trouble and molest her subjects who come with their own property and other goods and wares: whether it be her galleons and other ships, coming by sea and her subjects who are aboard and their goods and wares and their property, or her subjects and their riding beasts and goods and property and wares, travelling overland: let them mind their own business and be occupied with their ordinary duties.

[2] If, whilst going from and coming to our well-protected dominions or else to other domains, they should by any means be taken captive while they are about their proper business, those kind of people shall be set free again.

---

[47] *Nişān* and *ṭuġra* are synonyms, referring to the sultan's cipher at the head of the document, guaranteeing its authenticity.

[3] And their galleons and other ships shall at all times come to and go from the ports and harbours and the rest of our well-protected dominions in peace and security.

[4] Let those who happen to be present, be it the crew of imperial ships or of others, give assistance when storms at sea distress people such as these and in their other moments of need, and let no one prevent and inconvenience them in the obtaining of their supplies and provisions [in exchange for] *aḳçe*s.

[5] And if the sea should fling their ships onto the land, let the *beg*s[48] and *ḳāḍī*s and others give assistance; the goods and properties which are rescued shall be given back to them; let no harm be done.

[6] Let no one hinder the English who are travelling either by sea or land, minding their own business: they shall not trouble and molest them.

[7] And the merchants of that country and their interpreters and other people shall come to our well-protected dominions, by sea and by land, and engage in selling and buying and trade, so that, after they have paid their ordinary taxes according to the established custom and *ḳānūn*,[49] let no person from among the admirals and seafaring captains and others, and from among the military people hinder them in coming and going, and let them not trouble and molest them and their men and their goods and their riding beasts.

[8] If one of the English should fall into debt, let the debt be claimed and taken from the debtor; no other person, as long as he is not standing bail, shall be arrested and sued.

[9] And if one of them should die, let his goods and properties be given to whomsoever he has bequeathed them; should he die intestate, let [the effects] be given to that person's compatriot, with the cognizance of their consul: let no one interfere.

[10] And whenever merchants and interpreters and consuls of England and the lands which are dependent on it are engaged in the affairs of selling and buying and trade and guarantee and other matters administered by the Holy Law in our well-protected dominions, they shall go to the *ḳāḍī*[50] and have him register [the matter] in his *sicill*,[51] or else they shall take a *ḥüccet*.[52] Afterwards, should a dispute occur, let the *ḥüccet* and the *ḳāḍī*'s *sicill* be inspected and action taken according to it. Should neither one of these two [proofs] exist and [people] bring an allegation, contrary to the upright Holy Law, solely by making false witnesses stand, as long as they have no *ḥüccet* from the *ḳāḍī*s or else [the matter] shall not be found registered in the *ḳāḍī*'s *sicill*, let not such men as these be allowed to deceive, and let not their allegation which is contrary to the Holy Law be heard.

[11] And when certain people calumniate, saying 'You have insulted us', [and] make false witnesses stand, wishing to afflict and affright, contrary the upright Holy Law, solely for the sake of extortion, let them be prevented.

[12] And should one of these people fall into debt or else come under suspicion in some way and abscond, let no other person, who is not standing bail, be arrested on his behalf.

[13] And if slaves belonging to the English, whom their consul has been seeking, should be found, if it be clear that they are not English and there is no possibility of doubt, they shall be taken and let them hand them over to the English.

[14] Those people from England and the lands which are dependent on it who have settled

---

[48] *Beg*: here a *beglerbegi* of *sancaḳbegi*.

[49] *Ḳānūn*: sultanic law.

[50] *Ḳāḍī*: a judge in an Islamic court, acting also as a notary.

[51] *Sicill*: a *ḳāḍī*'s register, or an entry in his register.

[52] *Ḥüccet*: a document issued by a *ḳāḍī*, recording the proceedings in court and the *ḳāḍī*'s decision.

down in our well-protected dominions, whether they be married or bachelors, shall pursue their professions: let not the *ḫarāc* be demanded from them.

[15] When they change the consuls whom they had appointed to the ports of Alexandria and Tripoli-in-Syria and Algiers and Tunis and Tripoli of the West and Cairo and elsewhere, let no one hinder them when they appoint and send in their place men fitting for the responsibility of that post.

[16] If their interpreter be engaged on important business [legal proceedings] shall be delayed until he arrives; on the other hand, they, for their part shall not seek idle pretexts, but shall hold their interpreter in readiness.

[17] And if the English should have disputes one with the other, let their aforesaid ambassador and consul decide it according to their usages; let no one hinder them.

[18] Should irregular (*levend*) boats travel by sea and take Englishmen captive after the date when the treaty letter has been granted and bring and sell them in Rumelia and Anatolia, when such people as these are found let investigation be made with proper attention and care and, in whosoever's possession he shall be found, they shall discover from whom he bought him; if that captive should become Muslim, let the person who has bought him obtain the price [of the slave] from him and, being free, he shall let him go.

[19] When ships and galleys and fleets which put to sea in our well-protected dominions shall meet with the ships of England at sea, let them show friendship to one another and not commit harm or damage.

[20] Let the articles written and enregistered in our imperial treaty-letters which have been granted to the Venetians and France and the other kings who are on terms of friendship [with us] be confirmed on behalf of the English also: let no one hinder and molest them contrary to the upright Holy Law and our imperial treaty-letter.

[21] And when their galleons and other ships come to our well-protected dominions, let them be guarded and protected and depart safe and sound.

[22] And if it should happen that their goods and properties are plundered, let there be effort and diligence in the matter of discovering the crew of their ship and the goods and properties which have been pillaged: the evil-doers, whosoever they may be, shall be brought to their proper punishment.

[23] Let my slaves the *beglerbegi*s and admirals and *sancaḳbegi*s and my slaves the seafaring admirals and the *ḳāḍī*s and the intendants and the imperial captains and the volunteer captains act in accordance with the tenor, made happy by justice, of our imperial treaty-letter aforementioned: let them not permit what is contrary to it.

As long as they shall be steadfast and enduring in sincerity and candour, according to the treaty which has been mentioned, from this side also the conditions of the treaty and pact shall be respected and observed as before, and never in any way shall what is contrary to it be permitted.

Written in the first decade of Rabīʿu'l-ākhir 988 (16–25 May 1580).

In the residence of Constantinople, the well-protected.

[Note by copyist:] Copy transcribed from the original without addition or omission. The poor Meḥmed b. Aḥmed, deputising for the chief *ḳāḍī* of Galata (may the sins of both of them be forgiven) wrote it.

8 The troubles of an ambassador

A command to the *ḳāḍī* of Galata:

You have sent a letter to my exalted court by the hand of Mevlānā ʿOs̱mān, the former *ḳāḍī* of Mecca, and made this submission (*ʿarż*): A numerous body of people of Ṭopḫāne[53] have come to the *sharīʿa* court and made this statement: 'The ambassador of England is dwelling with his people (*tevābiʿ*) in the house of ʿArab Aḥmed Paşa in Ṭopḫāne, but he does not behave unobtrusively. He is always engaging in lewdness and debauchery, and numerous other ungodly people come in from outside and bring in prostitutes and never cease from depravity and wickedness. Because this house is on the seashore, they hide fugitive slaves and smuggle them out. At prayer times, they beat drums and blow trumpets. They throw filth over the graves of the Muslims and commit numerous such acts of depravity'. Therefore, the Muslims delivered a letter (*kāğıd*) [? to the law-court] saying: 'Either you get rid of the ambassador or we will burn the quarter down'. Their depravity and insolence are beyond all measure. It is better for the Muslims in every way that these people should live in the house they have always lived in in Galata.'

By my *ḫaṭṭ-i hümāyūn*[54] 'He is to reside in the houses where he formerly resided', my exalted command has been issued: I have commanded that, when [. . .] arrives, you are to charge and direct this ambassador that he is, in accordance with the tenor of this glorious order of mine, to leave that house and to go and reside in the houses where he formerly resided in Galata, so that the Muslims are rid of this kind of insolence.

On this matter you are not to allow the ambassador to present any protest or excuse, but you are to expel him from this house straightaway.

9 Latin text of the agreement at Zsitva-Torok, 1606

[1] When ambassadors appear before each other's emperors, the one should deport himself as father and the other as son; let it be thus for this embassy.

[2] In all writings, letters and audiences, courtesy should be observed; the one should call the other Caesar and not king.

[3] The Tatars and other nations should be included in the peace; and during the peace they should not cause any harm to the kingdom and provinces of the Christians.

[4] There should be peace between the two emperors in all places and provinces, particularly in Hungary, belonging to them from of old, both on sea and land; all dominions belonging to the noble House of Austria, or dependent upon it, are included; and if the Spanish king should wish to be included in the peace, we shall not be opposed.

[5] All raiding should be completely stopped; if, by chance, any robbers should come raiding and cause damage to any place, it should be permitted to imprison this kind of plunderer and to inform the other party of their captivity. Afterwards they should be tried before that captain in whose captaincy such acts of violence occurred, and the stolen goods should be restored.

[6] It shall not be lawful to enter and occupy fortresses, secretly or openly, or by any means; nor to attempt to occupy them under any pretext; or to give refuge or help to evil men and

[53] Topḫāne ('gun-foundry'), a suburb on the Bosphorus, outside the city wall of Galata where most embassies were situated. It was the site of the main Ottoman gun-foundry.

[54] *Ḫaṭṭ-i hümāyūn*: A written command in the sultan's own hand.

enemies of either Caesar. What has been granted to the most illustrious lord Bocskai[55] shall remain [in place] according to the agreement concluded in Vienna.[56]

[7] Captives should be returned from either side, with equal numbers being exchanged. (Thus, on both sides they should be released as consequence of the negotiations of their lord. Anyone who agreed on redemption with his own [fellows] should be freed; anyone captured during the truce should be released.)

[8] Every effort should be made by the captain-general of Győr, the Pasha of Buda and others dependent on him, the *ban* in Slavonia and the other supreme captains on either side of the Danube to avoid any disputes or problems. If any matter of great importance arises which cannot be settled by them, for such matters, recourse should be had to either emperor.

[9] It is permissible to rebuild and fortify fortresses in their old places, but it is not permitted to build new fortresses or castles.

[10] An ambassador shall be sent with gifts by us to the emperor of the Turks. The magnificent commander Murād Pasha shall also send with gifts his ambassador to our Most Serene Archduke Mathias, our most benign lord. When our legates arrive in Constantinople to ratify the peace, the emperor of the Turks shall also send an ambassador to our emperor in Prague, with more gifts than was previously the custom.

[11] The ambassador of His Imperial Majesty shall bring to Constantinople a gift in the value of 200,000 florins, as promised, once and for all time.

[12] The peace shall last for twenty years from 1 January next year [1607]. After three years each emperor should in turn send an ambassador with gifts, with no obligation as to the number of gifts, but as he wishes, so far as is fitting between persons [of] equal [status]. All legitimate heirs of His Imperial Majesty and successor kings of Hungary are understood under these twenty years; similarly, brothers, nephews and their legitimate heirs are included and should remain [thus].

[13] Vác may be built and extended, remaining in our hands.

[14] When the embassy of His Holy Imperial Majesty arrives at the Porte, they should be free to demand whatever they wish from the Turkish Emperor.

[15] Concerning the estates which have been unconditionally surrendered [to the Turks][57] (*deditiliis*), it has been agreed that those which have been liberated from subjection to the Turkish yoke, together with the fortresses of Fülek, Somoskő, Hainaczko, Divény, Kékkő, Zechen, Gyarmach, Palanka, Nógrád and Vác, shall not in future be subject or tributary to them. In the future, those fortresses will be in our hands, and no Turk or *sipāhī* (*ispaja* ?), wherever they might live, shall have any jurisdiction over them, or compel them to surrender. [This is] with the exception of those districts which have continuously and always been tributary to the captain of Eger, which must remain in subjection. Apart from these [districts] of Eger, the Turks should not subjugate any estate to themselves.

[16] As to the region of Esztergom, when the Christians recaptured [Esztergom] from the Turks, just as at that time the Turks subjected and held the estates themselves, these should

[55] Stephen Bocskai, Prince of Transylvania. In 1605, he transferred his allegiance from the Habsburg Emperor Rudolph to the Ottomans.

[56] By the Treaty of Vienna (23 June 1606), the Emperor Rudolph recognized Stephen Bocskai's hereditary rights as ruler of Transylvania.

[57] Latin: *deditiliis*. This probably has it classical Roman sense of people collectively subjugated through unconditional surrender, and therefore of legally inferior status.

now and henceforth be subject to [Esztergom], but others apart from these are not compelled to surrender to the Turks.

[17] Concerning the estates around Kanisza, it has been agreed that the Pasha of Buda and, in like manner, Francis Batthyány should send their distinguished men to record and survey the estates and set them right. Among the subject estates, if some nobles live there or have residences there, they should pay neither tribute nor tithes to the Turks; nor should they be tributaries in any way, but be free both in their goods and in their persons. Anyone who pays nothing to the legitimate king, should pay nothing to the Turks. The Turks should not go out to the estates, but demand through the judges of the estates that their people come [to them]. If the judges are truly unable to do this, they should write to their captains and territorial lords, so that these can compel them. If nothing can be achieved in this way, the Turks may go out to compel them. The procedure should be acted upon and understood by the Hungarians.

SOURCES

1 Kate Fleet, 'The treaty of 1387 between Murād I and the Genoese', *Bulletin of the School or Oriental and African Studies*, 56/1 (1993), 16–18.

2 George T. Dennis, 'The Byzantine-Turkish treaty of 1403', *Orientalia Christiana Periodica*, 33 (1967), 77–82.

3a Yaḥyā b. Meḥmed el-Kātib (ed. Şinasi Tekin), *Menāhicü'l-inşā*, Cambridge, MA (1979), 23–4; İ. H. Uzunçarşılı, 'İbrahim Bey'in Karaman imareti vakfiyesi', *Belleten*, 1 (1937), 120–1.

3b Ciriaco of Ancona (ed. and trans. Edward W. Bodnar), *Ciriac of Ancona: Later Travels*, Cambridge, Mass. (2003), 38–41; Dariusz Kołodziejcyk, *Ottoman-Polish Diplomatic Relations, 15th-18th century*, Leiden (2000), 100–9.

4 Friedrich Kraelitz, *Osmanische Urkunden in türkischer Sprache aus der zweiten Hälfte des 15. Jahrhunderts*, Vienna (1922), no. 1.

5 British Library, Or. 1194, late fifteenth to early sixteenth century.

6 Anton C. Schaendlinger, *Die Schreiben Süleymāns des Prächtigen an Karl V., Ferdinand I. und Maximilian II*, Vienna (1983), document 6.

7 Bodleian Library, MS. Laud Or. 67, ff. 81v–85r. Translation by S. A. Skilliter.

8 Başbakanlık Archives, Istanbul, *Mühimme Defteri* vol. 72, no. 329, dated 19 Ramaḍān 1002 (8 June 1594).

9 Gabriel Noradounghian, *Recueil d'Actes Internationaux de l'Empire Ottoman*, I, Paris (1897), 103–8.

Glossary

ʿ**Acemī oğlan**: a boy levied through the *pencik* (*q. v.*) or the *devşirme* (*q. v.*), in training before his admission to the Janissary corps.
Aġa: a senior officer in a military or other organisation serving the sultan.
ʿ**Ahdnāme**: a treaty; letter of agreement bestowing a privilege.
Aḳçe: a silver coin, the basic unit of account in the Ottoman treasury.
Aḳın: a raid on enemy territory.
Aḳıncı: a raider; a soldier holding land on the frontier in return for conducting raids into enemy territory.
Alaybegi: literally 'rank commander'; the holder of a *zeʿāmet* (*q. v.*), serving as an officer of the *tīmār* (q. *v.*)-holding cavalry.
Amān: mercy, quarter; safe-conduct.
ʿ**Āmil**: a factor; agent, especially an agent of the sultan, usually acting as a tax-collector.
Amīruʾl-muʾminīn: literally 'Commander of the Faithful'; a Caliphal title.
Anaṭolı: Anatolia; as an administrative unit, the province situated in the western part of Anatolia.
Anatolia: a general term for the area covering approximately the area of modern Turkey to the east of the Bosphorus.
Arşun: a measure of length, probably about 68 cm.
ʿ**Arż**: a submission, petition.
Arż-i mīrī: land at the disposal of the sultan, the revenues of which are not assigned to private individuals or *waqf*s (*q. v.*).
ʿ**Askerī**: literally 'military'; a member of the military class, comprising everyone in receipt of a fief or a salary from the sultan and exempt from taxation.
ʿ**Avārıż**: an extra-ordinary tax, originally levied in times of war or emergency. By the seventeenth century *ʿavārıż* had become a regular levy.
Aʿyān: local notables; the prominent persons in a district.
ʿ**Azab**: literally 'bachelor'; an infantryman recruited through a levy on urban youth.
Bāb-i saʿādet: literally 'the gate of felicity'; the gate leading from the second to the third court of the palace, where the sultan held audiences; by extension, the palace, the sultan's government.
Bād-i havā: literally 'wind of the air'; incidental taxes.
Baştina: a tenement held by a Christian peasant on the Balkans, the equivalent of a *çift* (*q. v.*).

Bayʿa: the oath of allegiance offered by the 'men of loosing and binding' to a new Caliph.
Bayram: a festival; one of the two festivals, *ʿīdü'l-fiṭr*, celebrating the breaking of the fast at the end of Ramaḍān, or *ʿīdü'l-aḍḥā* celebrated on 10–13 Dhū'l-ḥijja.
Bedestān: a covered market; the central commercial building in a town.
Beg: lord; commander, governor.
Beglerbegi: literally 'lord of lords'; the governor of a province.
Beglerbegilik: a province.
Beglik: see **mīrī**.
Benlāk: see **bennāk**.
Bennāk: a peasant possessing less than half a *çift* (*q. v.*) of land.
Berāt: a diploma of appointment by the sultan.
Beşlü: literally 'fiver'; an auxiliary fortress guard.
Beşlü-başı: a commander of the *beşlü*s (*q. v.*).
Beytü'l-māl: literally 'house of property'; the treasury; unclaimed inheritances coming into the treasury.
Beytü'l-mālcı: the official responsible for managing unclaimed inheritances.
Bölük: literally 'division'; a unit of the Janissaries or other military corps; the term often refers to one of the six divisions (*altı bölük*) of the sultan's household cavalry.
Bölük-başı: literally 'head of a division'; the Janissary officer commanding a *bölük* (*q. v.*).
Bostancı: literally 'gardener'; a member of the corps working in the palace gardens. They might also act as armed guards.
Bostancı-başı: head of the corps of *bostancı*s, acting also as helmsman of the sultan's barge, and a close attendant of the sultan.
Caba bennāk: a landless peasant.
Çaḳırcı-başı: head falconer.
Caliph (Arabic, *ḫalīfa*): the successor to the Prophet and supreme head of the Islamic community.
Cānbāz: one of a body of military auxiliaries in Rūmeli (*q. v.*), organised in groups of ten, with one man serving in the army and the remainder paying a fixed sum for his maintenance.
Cāriye: a female slave; the lowest rank among the women of the imperial harem.
Çāşnigīr: taster; an officer of the inner palace, serving the sultan's meals.
Çāşnigīr-başı: the head taster.
Çavuş: a herald; member of a corps of officers at the sultan's court, acting as messengers, escorts and executioners, as well as in ceremonial and other functions.
Çavuş-başı: the head *çavuş* (*q. v.*) in the palace.
Cebelü: literally 'armoured'; an armed retainer in the suite of a *sipāhī* (*q. v.*).
Celālī: the term applied to rebels in Anatolia in the late sixteenth and early seventeenth centuries.
Cereḫor: labour service in support of the army.
Çeri-başı: literally 'troop-commander'; an officer commanding a division of *tīmār* (*q. v.*)-holding cavalry in a *sancaḳ* (*q. v.*).
Çift: literally 'pair, yoke'; a peasant tenement, nominally the amount of land a family could cultivate in a year with one yoke of oxen.
Çiftlik: see **çift**.
Çift-tax: the annual rent paid by the holder of a *çift* (*q. v.*) to the holder of the *tīmār* (*q. v.*) where the *çift* was located.

Çıḳma: literally 'going out'; the graduation ceremony when pages left the palace schools or the inner palace for service outside.
Çoḳadār: literally 'keeper of the linen'; a page of the sultan's privy chamber, responsible for the sultan's outer garments.
Cüzʾ: literally 'fraction'; one thirtieth part of the Qur'ān.
Dānişmend: a senior student in a *medrese* (*q. v.*).
Dārüʾl-ḥarb: literally 'the abode of war'; the lands that are not under a Muslim sovereign.
Defterdār: a treasurer, accountant; one of the chief *defterdār*s with a seat on the imperial council (*q. v.*) and responsible for the financial affairs of the empire.
Defter emīni: literally 'superintendent of the register'; head of the office responsible for the registers recording assignments of *tīmār*s, *zeʿāmet*s and *ḫāṣṣ*, and therefore of military obligations.
Deli: literally 'madcap'; a lightly armed volunteer soldier on the frontier in Europe. The suicidal attacks of the *deli*s sowed confusion in enemy ranks. Also called *serdengeçti*.
Devşirme: the levy of non-Muslim boys for service in the palace and the Janissary corps.
Dhimmī: a non-Muslim subject of a Muslim polity.
Dil: literally 'tongue'; an enemy prisoner retained as an informant.
Dirhem: a measure of weight, probably about 3.3 gram; a drachma, a notional unit of currency used in Islamic legal texts.
Dirlik: literally 'living'; a fief; a revenue source providing a living.
Dīvān: a council; the sultan's imperial council meeting under the presidency of the grand vizier (*q. v.*); the council of a princely governor.
Dolama: a jacket of fine wool or silk, worn beneath an over-garment.
Dönüm: a measure of land, 40 paces by 40 paces.
Eczāʾ: plural of *cüzʾ* (*q. v.*).
Ellici: one of a group of Christian peasants in the service of the military. The role of *ellici*s is unclear.
Emānet: the management of a tax-farm or other undertaking by a salaried agent.
Emīn: a salaried official administering an enterprise.
Emīr: prince; ruler; governor.
Emīrüʾl-ümerā: Arabic term for **beglerbegi** (*q. v.*).
Enderūn: literally 'interior'; the inner palace; the sultan's private quarters.
Eşkinci: an auxiliary soldier.
Eşrefī: an Egyptian gold coin of the Mamlūk era.
Faḳīh: a Muslim jurist.
Fatwā: an authoritative legal opinion issued by a *muftī* (*q. v.*) in answer to a question.
Fesād: intrigue, mischief, corruption. See also **fitna**.
Filori: a gold coin, florin.
Firman: a *fermān*; a decree of the sultan.
Fitna: chaos, disorder; dissent, rebellion. The term is frequently paired with *fesād* (*q. v.*).
Friday prayer (Arabic: *jumʿa*): the congregational prayer performed on Friday in a congregational mosque (Arabic: *jāmiʿ*). During the sermon, a prayer is offered for the sovereign.
Fusta: a light galley.
Ġarīb: literally 'stranger'; a member of the corps of *ġarīb-oğlan*s, one of the six divisions (*altı bölük*) of the sultan's household cavalry.
Ġazā: a raid; military campaign; a campaign in the service of holy war.
Ġāzī: one who wages *ġazā*.

Göñüllü: a volunteer; a member of the corps of *göñüllüs*, a military corps stationed in Cairo.

Grand vizier (Ottoman: *Ṣadr-i aʿẓam, vezīr-i aʿẓam*): the sultan's chief vizier, presiding over the imperial *dīvān* (*q. v.*).

Ġulām: a servant; a retainer, armed or unarmed.

Ġusl: total ablution of the body to remove a major ritual impurity.

Ḫāḳān: see Ḫān.

Ḥalāl: permissible according to the *sharīʿa* (*q. v.*).

Ḥalebī aḳçe: a Mamlūk silver coin in circulation in Syria, valued at 2.5 to 1 Ottoman *aḳçe* (*q. v.*).

Ḫalīfa: Caliph; a local leader of the *ḳızılbaş* (*q. v.*), representing the Safavid shah in his community.

Ḫān (contracted form of *ḳāġān, ḫāḳān*): a ruler; a title of the Ottoman sultans.

Ḫāne: a house; household, especially a household as taxable unit.

Ḫarāc: in the *sharīʿa*, a tax on land; in Ottoman usage, the *jizya* (*q. v.*), sometimes referred to as *baş ḫarācı* ('head *ḫarāc*').

Ḫarāc-i muḳāseme: in the *sharīʿa*, a levy of up to 50 percent on crops growing on land, which remained in the possession of the infidels at the time of the Muslim conquest.

Ḥarām: forbidden by the *sharīʿa*.

Ḥarbī: a non-Muslim resident of the *dārü'l-ḥarb* (*q. v.*).

Ḥarem: women's quarters in a Muslim household; the sultan's private apartments.

Ḥarem-i ḫāṣṣ: the sultan's private apartments.

Ḫāṣṣ: a fief worth more than 100,000 *aḳçe* per year, assigned to the sultan, a provincial governor or the treasury.

Ḫāṣṣa: private; belonging to the sultan, or to the sultan's treasury or government.

Ḫāṣṣa çiftlik: an area of land on a *tīmār* (*q. v.*) set aside for the use of the *sipāhī* (*q. v.*).

Ḫaṭīb: a preacher.

Ḫaṭṭ-i hümāyūn: literally 'imperial rescript'; a command written in the sultan's own hand.

Ḫoca: a teacher of religion.

Ḥüccet: literally 'proof'; a document issued by a *ḳāḍī* (*q. v.*), recording the proceedings in court and the *ḳāḍī*'s decision.

Ḫüdāvendgār: (1) God; (2) a monarch; (3) the Ottoman sultan; (4) Sultan Murād I; (5) the *sancaḳ* (*q. v.*) of Bursa.

Ḫünkār (contracted form of **Ḫüdāvendgār**): the sultan.

Ḫuṭbe: the sermon during the Friday prayer, which includes a prayer for the ruler.

ʿIdda: the period following divorce or the death of her husband, during which a woman may not legally re-marry.

İḥtisāb: market regulations; the money accruing from fines for breaches of market regulations.

İlḥād: heresy.

İltizām: the management of revenue collecting by a tax-farmer.

Imām: (1) a leader or ruler; (2) a prayer leader in a mosque; (3) the Caliph, as leader of the entire Muslim community; (4) title accorded to the founder and leading jurists of a legal School.

ʿİmāret: a soup-kitchen attached to a mosque and supported by a *waqf* (*q. v.*).

İspence: a poll-tax levied on non-Muslims in place of the *çift*-tax (*q. v.*).

Janissary (Turkish: *yeñiçeri*, before *c*1500 sometimes *yenisar*): the sultan's standing infantry corps, levied through the *devşirme* (*q. v.*) and the *pencik* (*q. v.*).

Jihād: holy war; *jihād* refers to holy war in general, while the term *ġazā* refers to a specific raid, campaign or battle during a *jihād.*

Jizya: in Islamic law, a poll-tax payable by adult non-Muslim males in exchange for legal protection of life, limb and property. In Ottoman usage it is often referred to as *ḫarāc* (*q. v.*).

Ḳāḍī: a judge in a Muslim court, acting as both judge and notary. Ottoman *ḳāḍī*s were also the chief administrators in their judicial districts.

Ḳāḍī'asker: literally 'military judge'; one of the two chief *ḳāḍī*s (*q. v.*) – that is, the *ḳāḍī'asker* of Rumelia and the *ḳāḍī'asker* of Anatolia – both having a seat in the imperial *dīvān* (*q. v.*).

Ḳāḍīlik: see **ḳażā.**

Ḳā'immaḳām: a deputy; a vizier appointed to deputise for the grand vizier (*q. v.*).

Ḳanṭār: a measure of weight, about 56.5 kg.

Ḳānūn: a law or regulation issued by or ratified by the sultan; sultanic law in general.

Ḳānūnnāme: a code of sultanic laws.

Ḳapu aġası: literally '*aġa* of the gate'; also *bāb-i sa'ādet aġası.* The officer guarding the gate between the inner and outer palace and responsible for conveying messages between the two.

Ḳapucı-başı: literally 'head-gatekeeper'; head-gatekeeper in the sultan's palace.

Ḳassām: the official responsible for dividing the inheritances of the *'askerī* (*q. v.*) class.

Kāşif: a provincial governor in Egypt.

Kātib: a scribe; secretary.

Ḳayı: the senior grandson of the mythical Oġuz Ḫān (*q. v.*), from whom the Ottoman sultans claimed descent.

Ḳayyūm: a caretaker at a mosque.

Ḳażā: the judicial and administrative district of a *ḳāḍī* (*q. v.*). Also **ḳāḍīlik**.

Ketḫüdā: a deputy, representative; a representative authorised to act as commander.

Kīle: a measure of weight for grain, perhaps about 25 kg., but with many regional variations.

Ḳılıç: literally 'sword'; the core of a *tīmār* (*q. v.*) which could not be sub-divided.

Ḳısṭ: the sum payable to the treasury from a tax-farm, as the instalment due for a specified portion of the contract.

Ḳızılbaş: literally 'redhead'; an adherent of the Safavid religious order, of which the Safavid shahs of Iran were the leaders.

Küfr: unbelief.

Ḳul: a slave; a servant of the sultan, paid through the treasury. The term is often used to refer to members of the Janissary (*q. v.*) corps or of one of the household cavalry divisions.

Ḳulaç: a measure of depth, probably about 1.83m.

Ḳuruş: 'Groschen'; a large silver coin, before the late seventeenth century imported from Europe.

Lālā: tutor; the tutor of a prince.

Lidra: a measure of capacity.

Livā: flag, banner; a *sancaḳ* (*q. v.*).

Maḏhhab (Ottoman: *meẕheb*): literally 'pathway'; doctrine; one of the four Sunnī Schools of Islamic law: Ḥanafī, Shāfi'ī, Mālikī and Ḥanbalī.

Martolos: a Christian military auxiliary in the Balkans.

Medre: a liquid measure.

Medrese: a higher college of Islamic learning.

Melik (plural, *mülūk*): king; in Islamic usage, sometimes in a pejorative sense.

Metropolitan: a bishop in the Greek Orthodox Church.
Mevḳūf: a source of revenue that is temporarily unassigned.
Mevḳūfāt: income coming to the treasury from vacant *tīmār*s and other revenue sources that are temporarily unassigned.
Mevḳūfcı: the official charged with collecting for the treasury revenues from *tīmār*s and other fiefs which are temporarily in abeyance.
Mevlānā: literally 'our lord'; the title given to a *ḳāḍī* (*q. v.*).
Mezraʿa: an area of arable land without habitations.
Miʿmār aġası: the sultan's chief architect.
Mīr-āḫur: master of the sultan's stables.
Mīr-ʿalem: literally 'lord of the standard'; keeper of the sultan's standard and other standards and banners in the palace for ceremonial or battlefield use.
Mīrī: literally 'pertaining to the ruler'; synonym of *beglik*, assets reserved for the use of the sultan; the treasury.
Mīrzā: a prince.
Mis̱āl: the *ṭuġra* (*q. v.*); by extension, a sultanic decree.
Mollā: a title of respect for members of the *ʿulemā* (*q. v.*).
Monapolye: the period during which the sale of wine produced on a *tīmār* (*q. v.*) is reserved for the *tīmār*-holder.
Muʿarrif: an usher at the Friday Prayer.
Müd: a measure of capacity. The *müd* of Bursa was *c*112 litres.
Müderris: a teacher in a *medrese* (*q. v.*).
Muftī: a recognised authority on Islamic law, authorised to issue *fatwas*. The *muftī* of Istanbul (*müftīʾl-enām*, *şeyḫüʾl-islām*) was the senior *muftī* in the Ottoman Empire and, from about the mid-sixteenth century on, head of the Ottoman *ʿulemā* (*q. v.*).
Muḥtesib: an inspector of markets.
Muʿīd: a teaching assistant in a *medrese* (*q. v.*).
Mujāhid: a warrior; a fighter of *jihād*.
Mujtahid: a qualified authority on the interpretation of Islamic law.
Muḳābele: literally 'collating'; the office checking payments and grants against centrally held registers.
Muḳāṭaʿa: a specified bundle of revenues; a tax-farm.
Mülk: private property; land whose revenues are privately owned.
Mülknāme: a document confirming ownership of private property.
Müsellem: member of a group exempted from certain taxes in exchange for auxiliary service in the army.
Müteferriḳa: a miscellaneous group of elite palace servants who were entitled to accompany the sultan when he was on horseback.
Mütevellī: the administrator of a *waqf* (*q. v.*).
Nāḥiye: an administrative sub-division of a *sancaḳ* (*q. v.*).
Nāʾib: deputy; a deputy *ḳāḍī* (*q. v.*).
Naḳībüʾs-sādāt: literally 'chief of the *seyyid*s'; the senior *seyyid* (*q. v.*) in the Ottoman Empire.
Nāẓir: an overseer, supervisor.
Nedīm: a companion of the sultan, providing companionship and entertainment, but having no recognised political role.
Nevrūz: literally 'New Year's Day'; the vernal equinox; between 20 and 22 March.
Nişān: literally 'sign'; the *ṭuġra* (*q. v.*); by extension, a sultanic decree.

Nişāncı: chancellor; head of the sultan's scribal service, with a seat on the imperial *dīvān* (*q. v.*).
Niyābet: the income arising from fines.
Oğlan: youth, boy, servant; synonym of *ġulām* (*q. v.*).
Oğuz: the western Turks.
Oğuz Ḫān: the legendary ancestor of the western Turks, from whom the Ottoman sultan claimed descent in the senior line. See also *Ḳayı*.
ʿÖrf: custom; law sanctified by custom; *ḳānūn* (*q. v.*).
ʿÖrfī: customary.
ʿÖşr: literally 'tithe'; in Ottoman law, the tithe levied on crops; in the *sharīʿa*, the tithe levied on crops growing on land that passed to a Muslim at the time of the Muslim conquest.
Pādişāh: a sovereign; the Ottoman sultan.
Palandaria (Turkish: *at gemisi*): a ship for transporting horses.
Paşa: a title of respect. In the fourteenth century it could designate a ruler or a prince; in the Ottoman Empire from the mid-fifteenth century owards, it was the title given *beglerbegi*s (*q. v.*) or viziers (*q. v.*). In European sources it usually refers to viziers.
Pencik: the levy of (nominally) one-fifth of prisoners-of-war for the sultan's service; the toll levied on slaves being ferried across the Bosphorus or the Dardanelles.
Pencikçi-başı: the officer in charge of the *pencik*.
Porte: the sultan's palace; by extension, the sultan's government.
Raʿīyet: a member of the tax-paying peasantry in the countryside.
Reʿāyā: plural form of *raʿīyet* (q. v.); the tax-paying peasantry. The term may also refer to taxpayers in general.
Resm-i ḳismet: the fee collected for dividing inheritances.
Resm-i tütün: literally 'smoke tax'; a charge payable for temporary residence on a *tīmār* (*q. v.*).
Rikābī: an officer of the palace entitled to accompany the sultan when he was on horseback.
Rūmeli: Rumelia; the Ottoman province comprising the major part of Ottoman territories in Europe.
Rumelia: a general term for the Ottoman territories in Europe.
Rūznāme: literally 'day-book'; a ledger; the office maintaining a daily account of the income and expenditure of the treasury.
Rūznāmeci: the official responsible for maintaining the *rūznāme* (*q. v.)*.
Şaġāvul: an escort, accompanying official visitors.
Şāhī: a large silver coin worth 6–8 *aḳçe*s (*q. v.*), minted in the eastern provinces of the Ottoman Empire.
Şāḥib-i raʿīyet: literally 'holder of the *raʿīyet*'; the *sipāhī* (*q. v.*) on whose *tīmār* (*q. v.*) a *raʿīyet* (*q. v.*) is registered.
Şāḥib-i tīmār: the holder of a *tīmār* (*q. v.*).
Şāhrukī: a large silver coin weighing 4.7 gram, in circulation in the Akkoyunlu Empire, named after Timur's grandson Shāhrukh.
Sālārlıḳ: A tax on grain at 2.5 percent, paid in addition to the tithe, originally to provide fodder for the *sipāhī*/*su eri*'s horse.
Sālāriye: see **sālārlıḳ**
Sancaḳ: the most important military-administrative division of the Empire, a sub-division of a *beglerbegilik* (*q. v.*).
Sancaḳbegi: a governor of a *sancaḳ* (*q. v.*).

Şecere-i ṭayyibe; literally 'the pure genealogy'; the accredited record of the descendants of the Prophet in the Ottoman Empire.
Segbān: keeper of the sultan's hounds. The sultan's *segbān*s also served as a military force. From the mid-fifteenth century onwards, they were incorporated as a unit in the Janissary corps.
Şehinşah: literally 'king of kings'; monarch.
Şehirlü: a townsman; a tax-paying subject of the sultan, resident in a town.
Şerʿ: Islamic law; the *sharīʿa*.
Serdār: an army commander.
Şeyḫ: an old man; a title of respect for a venerable figure; the head of a *zāviye* (*q. v.*).
Şeyḫüʾl-islām: the *muftī* (*q. v.*) of Istanbul, from the mid-sixteenth century the head of the hierarchy of Ottoman *ʿulemā* (*q. v.*), known also as *muftīʾl-enām* (literally 'the *mufti* of mankind').
Seyyid: a descendant of the Prophet.
Sicill: a *ḳāḍī*'s (*q. v.*) register; an entry in a *ḳāḍī*'s register.
Sicillāt: plural form of *sicill* (*q. v.*).
Sign: see **nişān**.
Siliḥdār: literally 'weapons bearer'; a member of the corps of *siliḥdār*s, one of the six divisions (*altı bölük*) of the sultan's household cavalry.
Sipāhī: a cavalryman; a member of the corps of *sipāhī*s, one of the six divisions (*altı bölük*) of the sultan's household cavalry; a cavalryman holding a *tīmār* (*q. v.*) in return for military service.
Siyāset: in the *sharīʿa*, an extra-canonical punishment imposed for the maintenance of good order; in Ottoman usage, the death-penalty or severe corporal punishment.
Şolaḳ: Janissary (*q. v.*) permanently assigned to the sultan's retinue.
Subaşı: literally 'army head'; an officer in a *sancaḳ* in possession of a *zeʿāmet* (*q. v.*), responsible for law and order in his district and, on campaigns, acting as an officer of the *tīmār* (*q. v.*)-holding cavalrymen.
Su eri: 'army man'; a *tīmār*-holding *sipāhī* (*q. v.*). The term went out of use after *c*1500, or it came to be read as *süvārī* (Persian: 'cavalryman').
Sürgün: member of a population that has been forcibly relocated.
Taḥvīl: the sum to be transferred from a tax-farm to the treasury by the end of the stipulated period, usually three years.
Ṭapu: title to land or property; the entry-fee payable to gain title to a *tīmār* (*q. v.*) or other property.
Taʿzīr: a punishment imposed at the discretion of a *ḳāḍī* (*q. v.*) or other authority, usually understood as strokes of the lash.
Tekālif-i ʿörfiye: literally 'customary obligations'; extra-ordinary taxes.
Tenge: a small silver coin, in circulation in the Timurid and Akkoyunlu Empires.
Tenktür: a small tent.
Tevḳīʿ: the *ṭuġra* (*q. v.*).
Teẕkerelü tīmār: a *tīmār* (*q. v.*) granted by a certificate from the Porte (*q. v.*).
Teẕkeresiz tīmār: a *tīmār* (*q. v.*) of lower value, granted by a *beglerbegi* (*q. v.*) without a certificate from the Porte (*q. v.*).
Tīmār: a military fief valued at less than 20,000 *aḳçe* a year, supporting a cavalryman.
Töre: custom; customary law.
Ṭovıca: an officer of the *aḳıncı*s (*q. v.*).

Tuġ: literally 'horsetail'; a 'horsetail' attached to a standard or an item of headgear, their number indicating rank.

Ṭuġra: the sultan's cipher affixed to sultanic decrees to guarantee their authenticity.

Ulaḳ: a courier; the obligation to provide horses for the sultan's courier service.

ʿUlemā: literally 'those who know'; members of the religious learned class.

ʿUlūfeci: literally 'salaryman'; a member of the corps of *ʿulūfeci*s, one of the six divisions (*altı bölük*) of the sultan's household cavalry.

Umm walad: literally 'mother of a child'; a female slave who has borne her master's child, which he has recognised as his own.

Üsküf: a type of headgear, usually conical.

Vizier: a minister of the sultan, attending the imperial *dīvān* (*q. v.*) and having both a governmental and a military role.

Voynuḳ: a Serbian auxiliary soldier.

Voyvoda: a military commander; a governor in the kingdom of Hungary; a ruler of Wallachia or Moldavia; an official in charge of collecting revenue; a *subaşı* (*q. v.*).

Vuḳiyye: an *oḳḳa*, about 1.3 kg.

Wāqif (Turkish: *vāḳıf*): the founder of a *waqf* (*q. v.*).

Waqf (Turkish: *vaḳıf*): a trust supporting a religious or charitable cause.

Waqfīya (Turkish: *vaḳfiye*): a deed of trust, establishing and laying out the conditions of a *waqf* (*q. v.*).

Yamaḳ: a member of a military-auxiliary group who is not on active service but contributes to the upkeep of the campaigner.

Yaya: literally 'footman'; member of a group exempted from certain taxes in exchange for auxiliary service in the army, probably originally as infantrymen.

Yaya-başı: literally 'head footman'; an officer of the Janissaries (*q. v.*).

Yük: literally 'load'; a sum of 100,000 *aḳçe* (*q. v.*).

Yürük: a semi-nomadic Turkish tribesman in the Balkans or Anatolia. The *yürük*s provided auxiliary military services.

Zakāt: alms-tax, a canonical tax, the proceeds of which are for the support of the poor.

Zāviye: a dervish lodge.

Zaʿīm: a *subaşı* (*q. v.*), a holder of a *zeʿāmet* (*q. v.*).

Zeʿāmet: a military fief valued at between 20,000 and 100,000 *aḳçe* per year. Also known as *subaşılıḳ*.

Ẕirāʿ: a variable measure of length, usually 60–70 cm.

Bibliography

Chapter I The Dynasty: Legitimation and Titulature

El Moudden, A., 'The idea of the Caliphate between Moroccans and Ottomans: political and symbolic stakes in the 16th and 17th century Maghrib', *Studia Islamica*, 82 (1995), 103–12.

Flemming, B., 'Political genealogies in the sixteenth century', *Journal of Ottoman Studies*, 7–8 (1987), 123–37.

Fodor, Pál, 'State and society, crisis and reform, in 15th–17th century Ottoman mirrors for princes', *Acta Orientalia* (Budapest), 40/2–3 (1986), 217–40.

Imber, Colin, 'The Ottoman dynastic myth', *Turcica*, 19 (1987), 67–76.

Köhbach, Markus, '*Çasar* oder *Imperator*? Zur Titulatur der römischen Kaiser durch die Osmanen nach dem Vertrag von Zsitva-Torok', *Wiener Zeitschrift für die Kunde des Morgenlandes*, 82 (1992), 223–34.

Kurz, Marlene, 'Gracious sultan, grateful subjects: spreading Ottoman imperial "ideology" throughout the empire', *Studia Islamica*, 107/1 (2012), 96–121.

Markiewicz, Christopher, *The Crisis of Kingship in Late Medieval Islam: Persian Emigrés and the Making of Ottoman Sovereignty*, Cambridge: Cambridge University Press, 2019.

Menchinger, Ethan L., 'Dreams of destiny and omens of greatness: exceptionalism in Ottoman historical and political thought', *Journal of Islamic Studies*, 31/1 (2020), 1–30.

Mengüç, Murat, 'Histories of Bayezid I, historians of Bayezid II: rethinking late fifteenth-century Ottoman historiography', *Bulletin of the School of Oriental and African Studies*, 76/3 (2013), 373–89.

Moustakas, K., 'The myth of the Byzantine origins of the Osmanlis', *Byzantine and Modern Greek Studies*, 39/1 (2015), 85–97.

Necipoğlu, Gülru, 'Süleyman the Magnificent and the representation of power in the context of Ottoman-Habsburg-Papal rivalry', in Halil İnalcık and Cemal Kafadar (eds), *Süleyman II and his Time*, Istanbul: Isis Press, 1993, 161–94.

Necipoğlu, Gülru, 'The aesthetics of empire: arts, politics and commerce in the construction of Süleyman's magnificence', in Pál Fodor (ed.), *The Battle for Central Europe: The Siege of Szigetvár and the Death of Süleyman the Magnificent and Nicholas Zrínyi (1566)*, Leiden: Brill, 2019, 115–59.

Ogasawara, Hiroyuki, 'The search for biblical ancestors', *Turcica*, 48 (2017), 37–63.

Şahin, Kaya, *Empire and Power in the Reign of Süleyman: Narrating the Sixteenth Century Ottoman World*, New York: Cambridge University Press, 2013.

Woodhead, Christine, 'Murad III and the historians: representations of Ottoman imperial authority in late 16th century historiography' in Hakan Karateke and Markus Reinkowski, *Authority and Legitimacy in the Ottoman Empire*, Leiden: Brill, 2005, 85–98.

Woodhead, Christine, 'Reading Ottoman "Şehnames": official historiography in the late sixteenth century', *Studia Islamica*, 104/105 (2007), 67–80.

Chapter II The Dynasty: Princes

Babinger, Franz, 'Mehmed's II. Heirat mit Sitt-Chatun,' *Der Islam*, 29/2 (1950), 217–34.
Bouquet, Olivier, 'The sultan's sons-in-law: analysing Ottoman imperial *damads*', *Journal of the Social and Economic History of the Orient*, 58/3 (2015), 327–61.
Çıpa, Hakan Erdem, *The Making of Selim: Succession, Legitimacy and Memory in the Early Modern Ottoman World*, Bloomington: Indiana University Press, 2017.
Fisher, Alan, 'Süleyman and his sons', in Gilles Veinstein (ed.), *Soliman le Magnifique et son Temps*, Paris: Documentation Française, 1992, 117–26.
Kappert, Petra, *Die Osmanischen Prinzen und ihre Fürstenresidenz Amasya im 15. und 16. Jahrhundert*, Leiden: Nederlands Historisch Archaeologisch Instituut te Istanbul, 1976.
Kastritsis, Dimitri, *The Sons of Bayezid: Empire Building and Representation in the Ottoman Civil War*, Leiden: Brill, 2007.
Kunt, I. Metin, 'A prince goes forth (perchance to return)', *International Journal of Turkish Studies*, 13 (2007), 63–71.
Peirce, Leslie P., 'The family as faction: dynastic politics in the reign of Süleyman', in Gilles Veinstein (ed.), *Soliman le Magnifique et son Temps*, Paris: Documentation Française, 1992, 105–16.
Peirce, Leslie P., *The Imperial Harem: Women and Sovereignty in the Ottoman Empire*, Oxford and New York: Oxford University Press, 1993.
Peirce, Leslie P., *Empress of the East: How a European Slave Girl became Queen of the Ottoman Empire*, New York: Basic Books, 2017.
Vatin, Nicholas, *Sultan Djem*, Ankara: Türk Tarih Kurumu, 1997.
Vatin, Nicholas and Veinstein, Gilles, *Le Sérail Ébranlé: Essais sur les Morts et Avènements des Sultans Ottomans*, Paris: Fayard, 2003.

Chapter III Recruitment into the Sultan's Service

Beldiceanu-Steinherr, Irène, 'En marge d'un acte concernant le *penğyek* et les *aqınğı*', *Revue des Études Islamiques*, 37 (1969), 21–47.
Demetriades, V., 'Some thoughts on the origins of the Janissaries', in Elizabeth A. Zachariadou (ed.), *The Ottoman Emirate, 1300–1389*, Rethymnon: Crete University Press, 1993, 23–34.
Graf, T. P., *The Sultan's Renegades: Christian-European Converts to Islam and the Making of the Ottoman Elite*, Oxford: Oxford University Press, 2017.
Imber, Colin, 'The origin of the Janissaries', *Journal of Turkish Studies*, 26/2 (2002), 15–19.
Ménage, V. L., 'Sidelights on the *devshirme* from Idrīs and Saʿduddīn', *Bulletin of the School of Oriental and African Studies*, 18/1 (1956), 181–3.
Ménage, V. L., 'Dewshirme', *Encyclopaedia of Islam* (2nd edition), Leiden: Brill, 1965.
Ménage, V. L. 'Some notes on the *devshirme*', *Bulletin of the School of Oriental and African Studies*, 29/1 (1966), 64–78.
Repp, R. C., 'A further note on the *devshirme*', *Bulletin of the School of Oriental and African Studies*, 31/1 (1968), 137–9.
Veinstein, Gilles (ed. Elisabetta Borromeo), *Les Esclaves du Sultan chez les Ottomans: des Mameloukes aux Janissaires*, Paris: Les Belles Lettres, 2020.
Vryonis, Speros, 'Isidore Glabas and the Turkish *devshirme*', *Speculum*, 31 (1956), 433–43.
Vryonis, Speros, 'Seljuk *gulams* and Ottoman *devshirmes*', *Der Islam*, 41 (1965), 224–51.
Zachariadou, Elizabeth A., 'Les "janissaires" de l'Empereur byzantin', in A. Gallota (ed.), *Studia Turcologica Memoriae Alexii Bombacci Dicata*, Naples: Istituto Universitario Orientale, 1982, 591–7.

Chapter IV The Vizierate and the *Dīvān*

Faroqhi, Suraiya, 'Das Gross-wesir-*telhis*: eine aktenkundliche Studie', *Der Islam*, 45 (1969), 96–110.
Fodor, Pál, 'Sultan, imperial council, grand vizier: changes in the Ottoman ruling élite and the formation of the grand vizieral "*telḫīṣ*"', *Acta Orientalia* (Budapest), 47/1–2 (1994), 67–85.

Fodor, Pál, 'The grand vizieral *telhis*: a study in the Ottoman central administration, 1566–1656', *Archivum Ottomanicum*, 15 (1997), 137–88.

Kissling, Hans Joachim, 'Quelques problèmes concernant Iskender Paša, vizir de Bâyezîd II', *Turcica*, 2 (1970), 130–7.

Kunt, İ. Metin, 'Derviş Mehmed Paşa, *vezir* and entrepreneur: a study in Ottoman political-economic theory and practice', *Turcica*, 9/1 (1977), 197–214.

Kunt, Metin, 'Royal and other households', in Christine Woodhead (ed.), *The Ottoman World*, London: Routledge, 2012, 103–15.

Lowry, Heath W., *Hersekzade Ahmed Pasha: An Ottoman Statesman's Career and Pious Endowments*, Istanbul: Bahçeşehir University Press, 2011.

Markiewicz, Christopher, 'Books on the secretarial arts and literary prose', in Gülru Necipoğlu, Cemal Kafadar and Cornell Fleischer (eds), *Treasures of Knowledge: An Inventory of the Ottoman Palace Library (1502/3–1503/4)*, *Muqarnas* Supplements, Leiden: Brill, 2019, 657–72.

Reindl, Hedda, *Männer um Bāyezīd: Eine prosoprographische Studie über die Epoche Sultan Bāyezīds II.*, Berlin: Klaus Schwarz, 1983.

Reindl-Kiel, Hedda, 'The tragedy of power: the fate of grand *vezir*s according to the *Menakıbname-i Mahmud Paşa-i Veli*', *Turcica*, 35 (2003), 247–56.

Reindl-Kiel, Hedda, 'Some notes on Hersekzade Ahmed Pasha, his family, and his books', *Journal of Turkish Studies*, 40 (2013) 315–26.

Stavrides, Theoharis, *The Sultan of Vezirs: The Life and Times of the Ottoman Grand Vezir Mahmud Pasha Angelović (1453–1474)*, Leiden: Brill, 2001.

Taeschner, Franz and Wittek, Paul, 'Die Vezirfamilie der Ǧandarlyzade und ihre Denkmäler', *Der Islam*, 18 (1929), 60–115.

Turan, Ebru, 'The marriage of Ibrahim Pasha (ca. 1495–1536): the rise of Sultan Süleyman's favourite to the grand vizierate and the politics of the elites in the early sixteenth-century Ottoman Empire', *Turcica*, 41 (2009), 3–36.

Chapter V The Provincial Administration and the *Tīmār* System

Acun, Fatma, 'Ottoman administrative priorities: two case-studies of Karahisar-i Şarki (Şebinkarahisar) and Giresun', *Archivum Ottomanicum*, 17 (1999), 213–31.

Ágoston, Gábor, 'A flexible empire: authority and its limits on the Ottoman frontiers', *International Journal of Turkish Studies*, 9 (2003), 15–31.

Amedoski, Dragana et al., 'The Koznik district (*nâhiye*) in central Serbia in the sixteenth century: settlements and population dynamics', *International Journal of Turkish Studies*, 17 (2011), 1–19.

Bacqué-Grammont, J.-L., 'Sur deux timariotes agressés dans la région de Florina en 1546', *Journal of Turkish Studies*, 10 (1986), 1–6.

Bakhit, M. A., *The Ottoman Province of Damascus in the Sixteenth Century*, Beirut: Librairie du Liban, 1982.

Beldiceanu, Nicoară and Beldiceanu-Steinherr, Irène, 'Recherches sur la province de Qaraman au XVIe siècle', *Journal of the Economic and Social History of the Orient*, 11/1 (1968), 1–97.

Blackburn, J. R., 'The documents on the division of Yemen into two *beglerbegilik*s (973/1565)', *Turcica*, 27 (1995), 223–36.

Costantini, Vera, *Studies on Ottoman Nicosia from the Ottoman Conquest to the Early British Period*, Istanbul: Isis Press, 2019.

Cvetkova, Bistra, 'Sur certaines reformes du régime foncier au temps de Mehmet II', *Journal of the Social and Economic History of the Orient*, 6/1 (1963), 104–20.

Dávid, Géza, 'The age of unmarried children in the *tahrīr-defter*s: notes on the co-efficient', *Acta Orientalia* (Budapest), 31/3 (1977), 347–57.

Dávid, Géza, 'Data on the continuity and migration of the population in 16th century Ottoman Hungary', *Acta Orientalia* (Budapest), 45/2-3 (1991), 219–52.

Dávid, Géza, '*Timar-Defter* oder *Dschizye-Defter*? Bemerkungen zu einer Quellenausgabe für den Sandschak Stuhlweissenburg', *Wiener Zeitschrift für die Kunde des Morgenlandes*, 81 (1991), 147–53.

Dávid, Géza, 'The *sancaq* of Veszprem', *Acta Orientalia* (Budapest), 47/1–2 (1994), 57–65.

Dávid, Géza, 'Ottoman administrative strategies in western Hungary', in Colin Heywood and Colin Imber (eds), *Studies in Ottoman History in Honour of Professor V. L. Ménage*, Istanbul: Isis Press, 1995, 31–43.

Dávid Géza and Fodor, Pál, 'Changes in the structure and strength of the timariot army from the early sixteenth to the end of the seventeenth century', *Eurasian Studies*, 4/2 (2005), 157–88.

Dehqan, Mustafa and Genç, Vural, 'Kurdish emirs in the 16th century *ruus* registers', *Der Islam*, 96/1 (2019), 87–120.

Delilbaşı, M., 'Christian *sipahi*s in the Tirhala taxation registers (fifteenth and sixteenth centuries)', in A. Anastasapoulos (ed.), *Provincial Élites in the Ottoman Empire*, Rethymnon: Crete University Press, 2005, 87–114.

Filipović, Nedim, '*Ocaklık* timars in Bosnia and Herzegovina', *Prilozi za Orijentalna Fililogia*, 36 (1986), 149–80.

Fodor, Pál, 'Ottoman policy towards Hungary', *Acta Orientalia* (Budapest), 45/2–3 (1991), 271–345.

Gözler, Kemal, *Les villages pomak de Lofça au XVe et XVe siècles d'après les* tahrir defter*s ottomans*, Ankara: Turkish Historical Society, 2001.

Gradeva, Rossitsa, 'Administrative system and provincial government in the central Balkan territories of the Ottoman Empire', in Rossitsa Gradeva (ed.), *Rumeli under the Ottomans*, Istanbul: Isis Press, 2004, 23–51.

Howard, Douglas A., 'The BBA *Ruznamçe Tasnifi*: a new resource for the study of the Ottoman *timar* system', *The Turkish Studies Association Bulletin*, 10/1(1986), 1–19.

İlhan, M. M., 'Some notes on the settlement and population of the *sancak* of Amid according to the 1518 Ottoman cadastral survey', *Tarih Araştırmaları Dergisi*, 14 (1981–2), 415–36.

İlhan, M. M., 'The Katif district (*livā*) during the first few years of Ottoman rule', *Belleten*, 51 (1987), 781–800.

İlhan, M. M., 'Tripoli (Trablusşam) in the sixteenth century: a demographic and ethnological study based on two Ottoman cadastral registers', *Mediterrâneo*, 3 (1993), 167–93.

Káldy-Nagy, Gy., 'Two sultanic *ḫāṣṣ* estates in Hungary during the XVIth and XVIIth centuries', *Acta Orientalia* (Budapest), 13/1–2 (1961), 31–62.

Káldy-Nagy, Gy., 'The administration of the *ṣanjāq* registrations in Hungary', *Acta Orientalia* (Budapest), 21/2 (1968), 181–223.

Káldy-Nagy, Gy., 'The first centuries of the Ottoman military organisation', *Acta Orientalia* (Budapest), 31/2 (1977), 147–83.

Kayapınar, Ayşe, *Le Sancak Ottoman de Vidin du XVe Siècle à la Fin du XVIe siècle*, Istanbul: Isis Press, 2011.

Kermeli, Eugenia, 'Central administration versus provincial arbitration: Patmos and Mount Athos monasteries in the 16th century', *Byzantine and Modern Greek Studies*, 32/2 (2008), 189–202.

Kiel, Machiel, 'Central Greece in the Suleymanic age', in Gilles Veinstein (ed.), *Soliman le Magnifique et son Temps*, Paris: Documentation Française, 1992, 399–422.

Kiel, Machiel, 'Tatar Pazarcık: the development of an Ottoman town in central Bulgaria', in Kreiser, K. and Neumann, C. K. (eds), *Das Osmanische Reich in seinen Archivalien und Chroniken*, Istanbul: Franz Steiner Verlag in Kommission, 1997, 31–67.

Kiel, Machiel, 'Ottoman sources for the demographic history and the process of Islamisation of Bosnia-Hercegovina and Bulgaria in the fifteenth-seventeenth centuries', *International Journal of Turkish Studies*, 10 (2004), 93–119.

Kiprovska, Mariya, 'Ferocious invasion or smooth incorporation?' in J. O. Schmitt (ed.), *The Ottoman Conquest of the Balkans*, Vienna: Verlag der Österreichischen Akademie der Wissenschaften, 2016, 79–102.

Kupusović, Amina, '*Tâpû tahrir defteri*s relating to Bosnia', *International Journal of Turkish Studies*, 10 (2004), 179–88.

Lellouch, B. and Michel, N. (eds), *Conquête Ottomane de l'Égypte (1517)*, Leiden: Brill, 2013.

Lopasic, Alexander, 'Islamization of the Balkans, with special reference to Bosnia', *Journal of Islamic Studies*, 5/2 (1994), 163–86.

Lowry, Heath W., *The Evrenos dynasty of Yenice-i Vardar: Notes and Documents*, Istanbul: Bahçeşehir University Press, 2010.

Mandaville, Jon E., 'The Ottoman province of al-Hasā in the sixteenth and seventeenth centuries', *Journal of the American Oriental Society*, 98, (1970), 486–513.

Ménage, V. L., 'An Ottoman manual of provincial correspondence', *Wiener Zeitschrift für die Kunde des Morgenlandes*, 68 (1976), 31–45.

Michel, N., 'Disparition et persistence de l'*iqtā*ʿ en Égypte après la conquête ottomane', *Turcica*, 41 (2003), 247–90.

Mutafčieva, Vera P., 'Sur le caractère du *tīmār* ottoman', *Acta Orientalia* (Budapest), 9/1 (1959), 55–61.

Oruç, H., 'Christian *sipahi*s in the Bosnian *sanjak*', *Archivum Ottomanicum*, 26 (2009), 5–16.

Oruç, H., '*Tahrîr defter*s on the Bosnian *sanjak*', *Archivum Ottomanicum*, 25 (2008), 255–82.

Öz, Mehmed, 'Ottoman provincial administration in eastern and south-eastern Anatolia: the case of Bidlis in the sixteenth century', *International Journal of Turkish Studies*, 9 (2003), 144–56.

Özbaran, Salih, 'A note on the Ottoman administration of Arabia in the sixteenth century', *International Journal of Turkish Studies*, 3 (1983–4), 93–9.

Özel, Oktay, 'The limits of the Almighty: Mehmed II's "land reforms" revisited', *Journal of the Economic and Social History of the Orient*, 42/2 (1999), 226–46.

Özel, Oktay, *The Collapse of Rural Order in Ottoman Anatolia: Amasya, 1576–1643*, Leiden: Brill, 2016.

Pamuk, Şevket, 'The Ottoman monetary system and frontier territories in Europe, 1500–1700', *International Journal of Turkish Studies*, 9 (2003), 175–82.

Reindl-Kiel, Hedda, 'A woman *timar* holder in Ankara during the second half of the 16th century', *Journal of the Economic and Social History of the Orient*, 40/2 (1997), 207–38.

Römer, Claudia, 'Einige Urkunden zur Militärverwaltung Ungarns zur Zeit Süleymāns des Prächtigen', *Acta Orientalia* (Budapest), 43/1 (1989), 23–80.

Roberts, H., *Berber Government: The Kabyle Polity in Pre-Colonial Algeria*, London: I. B. Tauris, 2017.

Röhrborn, Klaus, *Untersuchungen zur Osmanischen Verwaltunggeschichte*, Berlin: De Gruyter, 1973.

Römer, Claudia, 'Drei Urkunden Murāds III. zu Tīmārangelegenheiten', *The Journal of Ottoman Studies*, 12 (1992), 289–306.

Sinclair, Tom, 'The Ottoman arrangements for the tribal principalities of the Lake Van region of the sixteenth century', *International Journal of Turkish Studies*, 9 (2003), 119–43.

Toledano, Ehud, 'The *sanjaq* of Jerusalem in the sixteenth century: aspects of topography and population', *Archivum Ottomanicum*, 9 (1984), 279–319.

Vatin, Nicholas, 'Notes sur l'entrée d'Alger sous la souverainté ottoman (1519–1521)', *Turcica*, 44 (2012–13), 131–66.

Venzke, Margaret, 'Aleppo's *mālikāne-dīvānī* system', *Journal of the American Oriental Society*, 106 (1986), 451–69.

Venzke, Margaret, 'The case of a Dulgadir-Mamluk *iqtā*ʿ: a re-assessment of the Dulgadir principality and its position within the Ottoman-Mamluk rivalry', *Journal of the Economic and Social History of the Orient*, 43/3 (2000), 399–474.

Williams, Sherry L., 'Ottoman land-policy and social change: the Syrian provinces', *Acta Orientalia* (Budapest), 35/1 (1981), 89–120.

Winter, Michael, *Egyptian Society under Ottoman Rule*, London: Routledge, 1992.

Zachariadou, Elizabeth A., 'Lauro Quirini and the Ottoman *sanjak*s (c.1430)', *Journal of Turkish Studies*, 11 (1987), 239–47.

Chapter VI The Religio-legal Institution

Atçıl, Abdurrahman, 'The route to the top in the Ottoman *ilmiye* hierarchy of the sixteenth century', *Bulletin of the School of Oriental and African Studies*, 72/3 (2009), 489–512.

Aykan, Yavuz, 'A legal concept in motion: the 'spreader of corruption' (*sāʿī biʾl-fesād*) from Qarakhanid to Ottoman jurisprudence', *Islamic Law and Society*, 26/3 (2019), 252–71.

Baldwin, James E., 'Prostitution, Islamic law and Ottoman societies', *Journal of the Social and Economic History of the Orient*, 55/1 (2012), 117–52.

Baldwin, James E., *Islamic Law and Empire in Ottoman Cairo*, Edinburgh: Edinburgh University Press, 2016.

Baltacıoğlu-Brammer, Ayşe, 'The formation of *kızılbaş* communities in Anatolia and Ottoman responses, 1450s–1630s', *International Journal of Turkish Studies*, 20 (2014), 21–47.

Baltacıoğlu-Brammer, Ayşe, '"These heretics gathering secretly . . .": Qizilbash rituals and practices in the Ottoman Empire according to early modern sources', *Journal of the Ottoman and Turkish Studies Association*, 6/1 (2019), 39–60.

Beldiceanu-Steinherr, Irène, 'Fiscalité et formes de possession de la terre arable dans l'Anatolie pré-ottomane', *Journal of the Social and Economic History of the Orient*, 19/1 (1976), 233–312.

Bulunur, İ. K., 'An honor killing in Aintab: the issue of killing fornicators in the Ottoman Empire', *Acta Orientalia* (Budapest), 69/3 (2016), 231–48.

Burak, Guy, 'Dynasty, law and the imperial provincial *madrasa*: the case of al-Madrasa al-ʿUthmāniyya in Ottoman Jerusalem', *International Journal of Middle East Studies*, 45/1 (2013), 111–25.

Burak, Guy, *The Second Formation of Islamic Law: The Hanafi School in the Early Modern Ottoman Empire*, New York: Cambridge University Press, 2015.

Burak, Guy, 'Evidentiary truth claims, imperial registers, and the Ottoman archive: contending legal views of archival and record-keeping practice in Ottoman Greater Syria', *Bulletin of the School of Oriental and African Studies*, 79/2 (2016), 233–54.

Çağatay, Neşʾet, '*Ribā* and interest concept and banking in the Ottoman Empire', *Studia Islamica*, 32 (1970), 53–68.

Cohen, Ammon, 'Communal legal entities in a legal setting: the Jewish community in sixteenth-century Jerusalem', *Islamic Law and Society*, 3 (1996), 75–90.

Çoşgel, Metin and Ergene, Boğaç, *The Economics of Ottoman Justice: Settlement and Trial in the Shariah Courts*, Cambridge: Cambridge University Press, 2016.

Faroqhi, Suraiya, 'Social mobility among the Ottoman *ʿulemâ* in the late sixteenth century', *International Journal of Middle East Studies*, 4/2 (1973), 204–18.

Gara, Eleni, 'Lending and borrowing money in an Ottoman province town', in Markus Köhbach, Gisela Procházka-Eisl and Claudia Römer (eds), *Acta Viennensia Ottomanica*, Vienna: Institut für Orientalistik, 1999, 113–19.

Gerber, Haim, 'The Muslim law of partnerships in Ottoman court records', *Studia Islamica*, 53 (1981), 109–19.

Gradeva, Rossitsa, 'On *kadi*s of Sofia', *Journal of Turkish Studies*, 26/1 (2002), 265–92.

Gradeva, Rossitsa, 'Orthodox Christians in the *kadi* courts', *Islamic Law and Society*, 4/1 (1997), 37–69.

Hacker, J., 'Jewish autonomy in the Ottoman Empire, its scope and limits: Jewish courts from the sixteenth to the eighteenth centuries', in A. Levy (ed.), *The Jews of the Ottoman Empire*, Princeton: Darwin Press, 1994, 153–202.

Heyd, Uriel, 'Some aspects of the Ottoman *fetvā*', *Bulletin of the School of Oriental and African Studies*, 32/1 (1969), 35–56.

Heyd, Uriel (ed. V. L. Ménage), *Studies in Old Ottoman Criminal Law*, Oxford: Clarendon Press, 1973.

Imber, Colin, 'Involuntary annulment of marriage and its solutions in Ottoman law', *Turcica*, 25 (1993), 40–73.

Imber, Colin, *Ebuʾs-suʿud: The Islamic Legal Tradition*, Edinburgh: Edinburgh University Press, 1997.

Imber, Colin, 'The cultivation of wasteland in *Hanafī* and Ottoman law', *Acta Orientalia* (Budapest), 61/1–2 (2008), 101–12.

Imber, Colin, 'Warrant for genocide? Ottoman propaganda against the Qizilbas', in Robert Gleave and István Kristó-Nagy (eds), *Legitimate and Illegitimate Violence in Islamic Thought*, Edinburgh: Edinburgh University Press, 2018.

İnalcık, Halil, 'The *rūznamče* registers of the *kadiasker* of Rumelia', *Turcica*, 20 (1988), 257–69.

Jennings, R. C., 'Loans and credit in early 17th century Ottoman judicial records: the *shariah* court of Anatolian Kayseri', *Journal of the Social and Economic History of the Orient*, 16/1 (1973), 168–216.

Jennings, R. C., 'The office of *vekil* (*wakil*) in 17th century Ottoman *sharia* courts', *Studia Islamica*, 42 (1975), 147–69.

Jennings, R. C., '*Kadi*, court and legal procedure in 17th c. Ottoman Kayseri', *Studia Islamica*, 48 (1978), 133–87.
Jennings, R. C., 'Limitations on the judicial powers of the *kadi*', *Studia Islamica*, 50 (1979), 151–84.
Jennings, R. C., 'Divorce in the Ottoman *sharia* court of Cyprus, 1580–1640', *Studia Islamica*, 78 (1993), 155–67.
Jennings, R. C., 'The use of oaths of denial at an Ottoman *sharia* court: Lefkoşa (Nicosia), 1580–1640', *Journal of Turkish Studies*, 20/1 (1996), 13–23.
Kermeli, Eugenia, 'The right to choice: Ottoman justice vis-à-vis ecclesiastical and communal justice in the Balkans', in A. Christmann and R. Gleave (eds), *Studies in Islamic Law*, Oxford: Oxford University Press, *Journal of Semitic Studies*, supplement 23 (2007), 165–210.
Kermeli, Eugenia, 'The right to choice: Ottoman, ecclesiastical and communal justice', in Christine Woodhead (ed.), *The Ottoman World*, London: Routledge, 2012, 347–61.
Mandaville, Jon E., 'Usurious piety: the cash *waqf* controversy in the Ottoman Empire', *International Journal of Middle East Studies*, 10/3 (1979), 289–308.
Meshal, Reem, 'Antagonistic *sharīʿa*s and the construction of orthodoxy in sixteenth-century Ottoman Cairo', *Journal of Islamic Studies*, 21/2 (2010), 183–212.
Meshal, Reem, *Sharia and the Making of the Modern Egyptian: Law and Custom in the Courts of Ottoman Cairo*, Cairo: American University of Cairo Press, 2014.
Mutaf, A. 'Amicable settlements in Ottoman law', *Turcica*, 36 (2004), 125–39.
Peters, Rudolf, *Crime and Punishment in Islamic Law*, Cambridge: Cambridge University Press, 2009.
Repp, R. C., *The Müfti of Istanbul*, Oxford: Ithaca Press, 1986.
Shaw, Stanford J., 'The land law of Ottoman Egypt 960 (1553): a contribution to the law of landholding in the early years of Ottoman rule in Egypt', *Der Islam*, 38 (1963), 106–36.
Veinstein, Gilles, 'Sur les *naʾibs* ottomans (XVème–XVIème siècles)', *Jerusalem Studies in Arabic and Islam*, 25 (2001), 247–67.
Yıldız, Sara Nur, 'A Hanafi law manual in the vernacular: Devletoğlu Yūsuf Balıḳesrī's Turkish verse adaptation of the *Hidāya al-Wiqāya* textual tradition for the Ottoman sultan Murad II (824/1424)', *Bulletin of the School of Oriental and African Studies*, 80/2 (2017), 283–304.
Yılmaz, Fikret, 'The line between fornication and prostitution: the prostitute versus the *subaşı*', *Acta Orientalia* (Budapest), 69/3 (2016), 249–64.
Zarinebaf-Shahr, Fariba, '"Heresy" and rebellion in Ottoman Anatolia', *Anatolia Moderna*, 7 (1977), 1–15.

Chapter VII *Ḳānūnnāmes*

Bayerle, G., 'The *kānūn-nāme* of the *sanjak* of Segedīn of 1570', *Archivum Ottomanicum*, 13 (1993–4), 55–84.
Beldiceanu, Nicoară, *Les Actes des Premiers Sultans*, Paris and The Hague: Mouton, 1960.
Cvetkova, B., 'L'influence exercée par certaines institutions de Byzance du moyen-âge sur le système féodal ottoman', *Byzantinobulgarica*, 1 (1952), 237–57.
Heywood, Colin J., 'The evolution of the Ottoman provincial law code (*sancak kanunname*): the *kanunname-i liva-i Semendire*', *Turkish Studies Association Bulletin*, 15 (1991), 223–51.
Howard, Douglas A., 'Historical scholarship and the classical Ottoman *ḳānūnnāme*s', *Archivum Ottomanicum*, 14 (1995–6), 79–109.
Howard, Douglas A., 'Ottoman administration and the *tîmâr* system: *sûret-i kânûnnâme-i ʿOsmânî berây-i tîmâr dâden*', *Journal of Turkish Studies*, 20/1 (1996), 46–125.
Imber, Colin, '"An illiberal descent": Kemalism and Ottoman law', *Eurasian Studies*, 4/2 (2005 [2007]), 215–43.
Imber, Colin, 'Women as outsiders: the inheritance of agricultural land in the Ottoman Empire', in Jutta Sperling and Shona Wray (eds), *Across the Religious Divide: Women, Property and Law in the Wider Mediterranean (ca.1300–ca.1800)*, New York: Routledge, 2011, 256–70.
Imber, Colin, 'The law of the land', in Christine Woodhead (ed.), *The Ottoman World*, London: Routledge, 2012, 41–56.
Imber, Colin, 'Law and legislation under Süleyman', in Pál Fodor (ed.), *The Battle for Central Europe: The*

Siege of Szigetvár and the Death of Süleyman the Magnificent and Nicholas Zrínyi (1566), Leiden: Brill, 2019, 98–114.
Lowry, Heath W., 'The Ottoman *liva kanunname*s contained in the *defter-i hakani*', *The Journal of Ottoman Studies*, 2 (1981), 43–74.
Stanley, T. C., 'Men-at-arms, hauberks and bards: military obligations in the *Book of the Ottoman Custom*', in Çiğdem Balım-Harding and Colin Imber (eds), *The Balance of Truth: Essays in Honour of Professor G. L. Lewis*, Istanbul: Isis Press, 2000, 331–63.

Chapter VIII Taxation and Finance

Ágoston, Gabor, 'The costs of the Ottoman fortress system in Hungary', in Géza Dávid and Pál Fodor (eds), *Ottomans, Hungarians and Habsburgs in Central Europe*, Leiden: Brill, 2000, 195–228.
Balla, Eliana and Johnson, N. D., 'Fiscal crisis and institutional change in the Ottoman Empire and France', *Journal of Economic History*, 69/3 (2009), 809–45.
Bojanić-Lukač, D., 'De la nature et l'origine de l'*ispendje*', *Wiener Zeitschrift für die Kunde des Morgenlandes*, 68 (1976), 575–610.
Buza, János, 'The exchange rates of the Hungarian and Turkish ducats in the mid-sixteenth century', *Acta Orientalia* (Budapest), 60/1 (2007), 33–54.
Çızakça, Murat, 'Tax-farming and financial decentralization in the Ottoman economy, 1520–1697', *Journal of European Economic History*, 22 (1993), 219–50.
Çoşgel, Metin M., 'Efficiency and continuity in public finance: the Ottoman system of taxation', *International Journal of Middle East Studies*, 37/4 (2005), 567–86.
Cvetkova, Bistra, 'Recherche sur le système d'affermage (*Iltizam*) dans l'Empire Ottoman au cours du XVIe-XVIIIe siècles par rapport aux contrées bulgares', *Rocznik Orientalistyczny*, 27 (1964), 111–32.
Fleet, Kate, '*Appalto* and *gabella*: farmed tax or monopoly?' *Eurasian Studies*, 2/1 (2003), 31–42.
Fleet, Kate, 'Tax-farming in the early Ottoman state', *The Medieval History Journal*, 6 (2003), 249–58.
Darling, Linda, *Revenue Raising and Legitimacy: Tax Collection and Finance Administration in the Ottoman Empire (1560–1660)*, Leiden: Brill, 1996.
Fodor, Pál, 'Some notes on Ottoman tax-farming in Hungary', *Acta Orientalia* (Budapest), 54/4 (2001), 427–35.
Fodor, Pál, *The Business of State: Ottoman Finance Administration and Ruling Elites in Transition (1580s–1615)*, Berlin: Klaus Schwarz Verlag, 2018.
Gerber, Haim, 'Jewish tax-farmers in the Ottoman Empire in the 16th and 17th centuries', *Journal of Turkish Studies*, 10 (1986), 143–54.
Hegyi, Klára, 'The financial position of the *vilayet*s in Hungary in the 16th-17th centuries', *Acta Orientalia* (Budapest), 61/1–2 (2008), 77–85.
Imber, Colin, 'The costs of naval warfare: the accounts of Hayreddin Barbarossa's Herceg Novi campaign in 1539', *Archivum Ottomanicum*, 4 (1972), 203–16.
Káldy-Nagy, Gy., 'The cash book of the Ottoman treasury in Buda in the years 1558–1560', *Acta Orientalia* (Budapest), 15 (1962), 173–82.
Kiel, Machiel, 'Remarks on the administration of the poll-tax (*cizye*) in the Ottoman Balkans', *Études Balkaniques*, 4 (1990), 70–104.
Majer, Hans-Georg, 'Ein osmanisches Budget aus der Zeit Meḥmeds des Eroberers', *Der Islam*, 59/1(1982), 40–63.
Mantran, Robert, 'Règlements fiscaux ottomans: la province de Bassora (2e moitié du 16e siècle)', *Journal of the Social and Economic History of the Orient*, 10/2 (1967), 224–77.
Matuz, Joseph, 'Contributions to the Ottoman institution of the *iltizam*', *The Journal of Ottoman Studies*, 11 (1991), 237–49.
Özbaran, Salih, 'Some notes on the *sālyāne* system in the Ottoman Empire as organized in Arabia in the sixteenth century', *The Journal of Ottoman Studies*, 6 (1986), 39–45.
Özvar, Erol, 'Transformation of the Ottoman Empire into a fiscal-military state', in Pál Fodor (ed.), *The Battle for Central Europe: The Siege of Szigetvár and the Death of Süleyman the Magnificent and Nicholas Zrínyi (1566)*, Leiden: Brill, 2019, 21–63.

Pamuk, Şevket, *A Monetary History of the Ottoman Empire*, Cambridge: Cambridge University Press, 2000.

Röhrborn, Klaus, 'Die Emanzipation der Finanzbürokratie im Osmanischen Reich (Ende 16. Jahrhundert)', *Zeitschrift der Deutschen Morgenländischen Gesellschaft*, 122 (1972), 118–39.

Römer, Claudia, 'Vier *Ḥüğğet*-Urkunden zur *Ğizye*-Einhebung in Slawonien', in Klaus Kreiser and Christoph K. Neumann (eds), *Das Osmanische Reich in seinen Archivalien und Chroniken*, Istanbul: Franz Steiner Verlag in Kommission, 1997, 191–210.

Römer, Claudia, 'Zu Verlassenschaft und ihrer fiskalischen Bearbeitung im osmanischen Reiches des 16. Jhs.', *Wiener Zeitschrift für die Kunde des Orients*, 88 (1998), 185–211.

Sahillioğlu, Halil, '*Sıvış* year crises in the Ottoman Empire', in Michael A. Cook (ed.), *Studies in the Economic History of the Middle East*, London: Oxford University Press, 1970, 230–54.

Schwarz, Klaus (ed. Claudia Römer), *Osmanische Sultansurkunden: Untersuchungen zur Einstellung und Besoldung Osmanischer Militärs in der Zeit Murads III.*, Wiesbaden: Franz Steiner Verlag, 1997.

Tekgül, Nil, 'Cash loans to Ottoman timariots during military campaigns (sixteenth-seventeenth centuries): a vulnerable fiscal system?' *Journal of the Social and Economic History of the Orient*, 59/4 (2016), 590–617.

Tezcan, Baki, 'The Ottoman monetary crisis of 1585 revisited', *Journal of the Social and Economic History of the Orient*, 53/3 (2009), 460–504.

Venzke, Margaret L., 'Special use of the tithe as a revenue raising measure in the sixteenth-century *sanjaq* of Aleppo', *Journal of the Social and Economic History of the Orient*, 29/3 (1986), 239–334.

Chapter IX *Waqf*s

Alleaume, Ghislaine, 'Heurs et malheurs du legs d'un grand officier imperial: le *waqf* de Sinân Pacha (v.1520–1596) à Alexandrie', *Turcica*, 43 (2011), 419–79.

Beldiceanu, Nicoară, Bacqué-Grammont, J.-L. and Cazacu, M., 'Recherches sur les Ottomans et la Moldavie ponto-Danubienne entre 1484 et 1520', *Bulletin of the School of Oriental and African Studies*, 45/1 (1982), 48–66.

Beldiceanu-Steinherr, Irène, 'Un legs pieux du chroniqueur Uruj', *Bulletin of the School of Oriental and African Studies*, 33/2 (1970), 359–63.

Bilici, Faruk, 'Support économique de l'Islam orthodoxe: le *wakf* de ʿAtâu-llâh Efendî (XVIe–XXe siècles)', *Anatolia Moderna*, X (2004), 1–51.

Boykov, Grigor, 'Karlızâde ʿAli Bey: an Ottoman dignitary's pious endowments and the emergence of the town of Karlova in central Bulgaria', *Journal of Turkish Studies*, 39 (2013), 247–68.

Çızakça, Murat, 'Cash *waqf*s of Bursa, 1555–1823', *Journal of the Social and Economic History of the Orient*, 38/3 (1995), 313–54.

Ergin, Nina, Neumann, Christoph K. and Singer, Amy (eds), *Feeding People, Feeding Power:* Imarets *in the Ottoman Empire*, Istanbul: Eren Yayınları, 2007.

Faroqhi, Suraiya, '*Vakıf* administration in sixteenth century Konya', *Journal of the Social and Economic History of the Orient*, 17/1 (1974), 145–72.

Fotić, Aleksandar, 'The official explanation for the confiscation and sale of monasteries (churches) and their estates at the time of Selim II', *Turcica*, 26 (1994), 33–54.

Fotić, Aleksandar, 'Yahyapaşa-oğlu's *evkaf* in Belgrade', *Acta Orientalia* (Budapest), 54/4 (2001), 437–52.

Griswold, W. G., 'A sixteenth century Ottoman pious foundation', *Journal of the Social and Economic History of the Orient*, 27/2 (1984), 175–98.

Haase, Claus-Peter, 'Eine kleinere *Waqf*-Urkunde Koca Sinan Psachas für Malkara, Thrakien', *The Journal of Ottoman Studies*, 11 (1991), 129–58.

Jennings, R. C., 'Pious foundations in society and economy of Ottoman Trabzon, 1565–1640', *Journal of the Social and Economic History of the Orient*, 33/3 (1990), 271–336.

Kiel, Machiel, 'The *vakıfnāme* of Raḳḳās Sinān Beg in Karnobat (Ḳarin-abad) and the Ottoman colonization of Bulgarian Thrace (14th-15th century)', *The Journal of Ottoman Studies*, 1 (1980), 15–32.

Meier, Astrid, 'The charities of a Grand Vizier: towards a comparative approach to Koca Sinan Pasha's endowment deeds (989–1004/1581–1596), *Turcica*, 43 (2011), 309–43.

Michel, N. 'Les *rizaq ihbāsiyya*, terres agricoles en mainmorte dans l'Égypte Mamelouke et Ottoman', *Annales Islamologiques*, 30 (1996), 105–98.
Michel, N., 'Les *waqf*-s d'un homme d'État ottoman dans la seconde moitié du XVIe siècle: essai de synthèse', *Turcica*, 43 (2011), 269–308.
Mutafchieva, Vera, *Le Vakıf, un Aspect de la Structure Socio-Économique de l'Empire Ottoman (XVe–XVIIe s.)*, Sofia: Jusautor, 1981.
Orbay, Kayhan, 'Detailed tax-farm registers and arrears registers as sources for the *waqf*'s financial analysis', *Acta Orientalia* (Budapest), 58/4 (2005), 331–47.
Orbay, Kayhan, 'On the *mukâta'a* revenues and the revenue collection of Bâyezîd II's *waqf* in Amasya', *Wiener Zeitschrift für die Kunde des Orients*, 95 (2005), 139–62.
Orbay, Kayhan, 'Structure and content of the *waqf* account books as sources for Ottoman economic and institutional history', *Turcica*, 39 (2007), 3–47.
Orbay, Kayhan, 'Filling the gap in demographic research on the Ottoman transformation history: *waqf* account books as sources for Ottoman demographic history (sixteenth and seventeenth centuries)', *Turcica*, 49 (2018), 85–118.
Orbay, Kayhan, 'The "*Celâlî* effect" on rural production and demography in central Anatolia: the *waqf* of Hatuniyye (1590s to 1638)', *Acta Orientalia* (Budapest), 71/1 (2018), 29–44.
Singer, Amy, *Constructing Ottoman Beneficence: An Imperial Soup Kitchen in Jerusalem*, Albany: SUNY Press, 2002.
Singer, Amy, '*Imarets*', in Christine Woodhead (ed.), *The Ottoman World*, London: Routledge, 2012, 72–86.
Yerasimos, Stéphane, 'Le *waqf* du *defterdar* Ebu'l Fazl Efendi et ses bénéficiaires', *Turcica* 33 (2001), 7–34
Zlatar, Behija, 'The importance of *vakf* registers in *defters* as historical sources', *International Journal of Turkish Studies*, 10 (2004), 175–8.

Chapter X Treaties and Foreign Relations

Bacqué-Grammont, J.-L., 'Autour d'une correspondence entre Charles-Quint et Ibrâhîm Paşa', *Turcica*, 15 (1983), 231–46.
Bacqué-Grammont, J.-L., 'Un compendium ottoman des dispositions du traité de Cambrai', *Wiener Zeitschrift für die Kunde des Orients*, 82 (1992), 37–50.
Bacqué-Grammont, J.-L., 'Sur deux lettres de Ferdinand Ier à Ibrâhîm Paşa', *Turcica*, 19 (1987), 175–93.
Bacqué-Grammont, J.-L., Kuneralp, S. and Hitzel, F., *Représentants Permanents de la France en Turquie, 1536–1991, et de la Turquie en France, 1797–1991*, Istanbul: Isis Press, 1991.
Bayerle, Gustav, 'The compromise at Zsitvatorok', *Archivum Ottomanicum*, 6 (1980), 5–53.
Berthier, Annie, 'Un document retrouvé: la première lettre de Soliman au roi François Ier', *Turcica*, 27 (1995), 263–5.
Blackburn, Richard, *Journey to the Sublime Porte – The Arabic Memoir of a Sharifian Agent's Diplomatic Mission to the Ottoman Imperial Court in the Era of Suleiman the Magnificent*, Beirut: Ergon Verlag in Kommission, 2005.
Brummett, Palmira, *Ottoman Seapower and Levantine Diplomacy in the Age of Discovery*, Albany: SUNY Press, 1994.
Burschel, Peter, 'A clock for the sultan: diplomatic gift-giving from an intercultural perspective', *The Medieval History Journal*, 16/2 (2013), 547–63.
Constantin, Gh. I., 'Le "traité" entre le sultan Bajazet Ier et la Valachie', *Der Islam*, 59/2 (1982), 254–83.
Casale, Giancarlo, 'The Ottoman administration of the spice trade in the sixteenth-century Red Sea and Persian Gulf', *Journal of the Social and Economic History of the Orient*, 49/2 (2006), 170–98.
Casale, Sinem, 'A peace for a prince: the reception of a Safavid child hostage at the Ottoman court', *Journal of Early Modern History*, 20/1 (2016), 39–62.
Cazacu, Mattei (edited, translated, and with an introduction by Stephen Reinert), *Dracula*, Leiden: Brill, 2017.
Charrière, Ernest, *Négociations de la France dans le Levant*, 4 vols, Paris: Imprimerie Nationale, 1848–60.
Dursteler, Eric, 'Commerce and co-existence: Veneto-Ottoman trade in the early modern era', *Turcica*, 34 (2002), 105–33.

Engel, Pál, 'János Hunyadi and the peace "of Szeged" (1444)', *Acta Orientalia* (Budapest), 47/3 (1994), 241–57.
Fenefşan, Cristina, 'Mihaloğlu Mehmet Beg et la Principauté de Valachie (1508–1532)', *The Journal of Ottoman Studies*, 15 (1995), 137–55.
Gürkan, Emrah Safa, 'Mediating boundaries: Mediterranean go-betweens and cross-confessional diplomacy in Constantinople', *Journal of Early Modern History*, 19/2–3 (2015), 107–28.
Gürkan, Emrah Safa, 'Dishonourable ambassadors: spies and secret diplomacy in Ottoman Istanbul', *Archivum Ottomanicum*, 35 (2018), 47–62.
Hattox, Ralph S., 'Mehmed the Conqueror, the Patriarch of Jerusalem and Mamluk authority', *Studia Islamica*, 90 (2000), 105–23.
İnalcık, Halil, 'A case study in Renaissance diplomacy: the agreement between Innocent VIII and Bāyezīd II on Djem Sultan', *Journal of Turkish Studies*, 3 (1979), 209–30.
Işıksel, Güneş, *La Diplomatie Ottomane sous le règne de Selîm II*, Paris, Leuven: Peeters, 2016.
Isom-Verhaaren, Christine, *Allies with the Infidel: The Ottoman and French Alliance in the Sixteenth Century*, London: I. B. Tauris, 2011.
Ivanics, Maria, 'Friedensangebot oder kriegerische Erpressung? Briefwechsel des Mehmed Pascha von Ofen mit Kaiser Rudolf II. im Jahre 1595', *Wiener Zeitschrift für die Kunde des Orients*, 82 (1992), 183–99.
Kołodzieczyk, Dariusz, 'Semiotics of behaviour in early modern diplomacy: Polish embassies in Istanbul and Bahçesaray', *Journal of Early Modern History*, 7/3 (2003), 245–56.
Kołodzieczyk, Dariusz, *Ottoman-Polish Diplomatic Relations (15th–18th Century): An Annotated Edition of* ʿAhdnames *and Other Documents*, Leiden: Brill, 2000.
Kołodzieczyk, Dariusz, *The Crimean Khanate and Poland-Lithuania: International Diplomacy on the European Periphery (15th–18th Century)*, Leiden: Brill, 2011.
Kornrumpf, H.-J., 'Eine Urkunde Süleymāns des Prächtigen aus dem Jahre 1535 in Bremen', *Wiener Zeitschrift für die Kunde des Orients*, 79 (1989), 139–54.
Leitsch, W., 'Sigismund von Herberstein bei Süleymān dem Prächtigen', *Wiener Zeitschrift für die Kunde des Orients*, 82 (1992), 269–87.
Lesure, Michel, 'Notes et documents sur les relations vénéto-ottomanes', *Turcica*, 8 (1976), 117–56.
Lesure, Michel, 'Michel Ćernović "explorator secretus" à Constantinople (1556–1563)', *Turcica*, 15 (1983), 127–54.
Ménage, V. L., 'The English capitulation of 1580: a review article', *International Journal of Middle East Studies*, 12/3 (1980), 373–83.
Ménage, V. L., 'On the constituent elements of certain sixteenth-century Ottoman documents', *Bulletin of the School of Oriental and African Studies*, 48/2 (1985), 283–304.
Mercan, F. Özden, 'A struggle for survival: Genoese diplomacy with the Sublime Port in the face of Spanish and French opposition', *Journal of Early Modern History*, 23/6 (2019), 542–65.
Muslu, Cihan Yüksel, *The Ottomans and the Mamluks: Imperial Diplomacy and Warfare in the Islamic World*, London: I. B. Tauris, 2014.
Noradounghian, Gabriel, *Recueil d'Actes Internationaux de l'Empire Ottoman*, vol. I, Paris: F. Pichon, 1897.
Panaite, Viorel, 'Power relationships in the Ottoman Empire: the sultans and the tribute-paying princes of Wallachia and Moldavia from the sixteenth to the eighteenth century', *International Journal of Turkish Studies*, 7 (2001), 26–53.
Panaite, Viorel, 'The *voivode*s of the Danubian principalities as *haracgüzarlar* of the Ottoman sultans', *International Journal of Turkish Studies*, 9 (2003), 59–78.
Panaite, Viorel, 'The *re'aya*s of the tributary protected principalities: the sixteenth through eighteenth centuries', *International Journal of Turkish Studies*, 9 (2003), 79–104.
Pedani, Pia Maria, 'Safiye's household and Venetian diplomacy', *Turcica*, 32 (2000), 9–32.
Radway, Robyn D., 'The captive self: the art of intrigue and the Holy Roman Emperor's resident ambassador at the Ottoman court in the sixteenth century', *Journal of Early Modern History*, 22/6 (2018), 475–99.
Reindl-Kiel, Hedda, 'Der Duft der Macht: Osmanen, muslimische Mächte und der Westen im Spiegel diplomatischer Geschenke', *Wiener Zeitschrift für die Kunde des Morgenlandes*, 95 (2005), 195–258.
Rothman, E. Natalie, 'Accounting for gifts: the poetics and pragmatics of material circulations in

Venetian-Ottoman diplomacy', in Georg Christ and Franz-Julius Morche (eds), *Cultures of Empire: Rethinking Venetian Rule, 1400–1700. Essays in Honour of Benjamin Arbel*, Leiden: Brill, 2020, 414–54.
Schaendlinger, A. C. and Römer, Claudia, *Die Schreiben Süleyman des Prächtigen an Karl V., Ferdinand I und Maximilian II*, Vienna: Verlag der Österreichischen Akademie der Wissenschaften, 1983.
Schaendlinger, A. C., 'Die osmanisch-habsburgische Diplomatie in der ersten Hälfte des 16. Jhdts.', *The Journal of Ottoman Studies*, 4 (1984), 181–96.
Servantie, Alain, 'Ambassadeurs de Charles Quint auprès de Soliman le Magnifique', *Anatolia Moderna*, 9 (2000), 1–45.
Skilliter, Susan A., 'The sultan's messenger, Gabriel Defrens: an Ottoman master-spy of the sixteenth century', *Wiener Zeitschrift für die Kunde des Morgenlandes*, 68 (1976), 47–59.
Skilliter, Susan A, *William Harborne and the Trade with Turkey, 1578–1582: A Documentary Study of the First Anglo-Ottoman Relations*, London: Oxford University Press, for the British Academy, 1977.
Stantchev, S. K., 'Inevitable conflict or opportunity to explore? The mechanics of Venice's embargo against Mehmed II and the problem of western-Ottoman trade', *Mediaevalia*, 32 (2011), 155–96.
Stefini, Tommaso, 'Ottoman merchants in dispute with the Republic of Venice at the end of the sixteenth century: some glances on the contested regime of the capitulations', *Turcica*, 46 (2015), 153–76.
Stein, J. M., 'A letter to Queen Elizabeth I from the grand vizier as a source for the study of Ottoman diplomacy', *Archivum Ottomanicum*, 11 (1986 [1988]), 231–48.
Theunissen, Hans, 'Ottoman-Venetian diplomatics: the *'Ahd-names*', *Electronic Journal of Oriental Studies* 1/2 (1998), 1–698.
Vatin, Nicholas, 'La traduction ottomane d'une letter de Charles VIII de France (1486)', *Turcica*, 15 (1983), 219–30.
Vatin, Nicholas, 'À propos du voyage en France de Huseyn, ambassadeur de Bajazet II auprès de Louis XI', *The Journal of Ottoman Studies*, 4 (1984), 35–44.
Vatin, Nicholas, *L'Ordre de St. Jean-de Jérusalem: L'Empire Ottoman et la Méditerrannée entre les Deux Sièges de Rhodes*, Louvain-Paris: Peeters, 1994.
Veinstein, Gilles, 'Une lettre de Selīm II au roi de Pologne Sigismond-Auguste sur la campagne d'Astrakhan de 1569', *Wiener Zeitschrift für die Kunde des Orients*, 82 (1992), 397–420.
Veinstein, Gilles, 'Les capitulations franco-ottomanes de 1536 sont elles encore controversables?' in Markus Koller and Vera Costantini (eds), *Living in the Ottoman Ecumenical Community*, Leiden: Brill, 2008, 71–88.
White, Joshua M., *Piracy and Law in the Ottoman Mediterranean*, Stanford, California: Stanford University Press, 2018.
Wright, Diana G., '"To temporize with dexterity – waiting for the benefit of time": four letters from Giovanni Dorio at the court of Beyazid II', *The Turkish Studies Association Bulletin*, 29/1–2 (2005–13), 1–31.
Yurdusev, A. Nuri et al., *Ottoman Diplomacy: Conventional or Unconventional?* London: Palgrave, 2004.

Index

Administrative and legal institutions and documents
account register, 33
ʿahdnāme, 84, 167
ʿarż-daşt, 68
berāt, 4, 34, 37n, 61, 68, 69, 85, 106, 107, 117, 130, 131, 136, 150, 151, 153
capitulations, 160, 169
court, sultan's, xviii, 5n, 6n, 15, 22, 29, 31, 32, 33, 35, 39, 49, 54, 57, 96, 122n, 125, 126, 160, 166, 167, 168, 169, 172
courts of law, 18, 39, 57n, 77, 78, 79, 81, 104, 132, 133n, 141, 170n, 171, 172
firman, xxiii, 42, 52, 64n, 96n, 108, 117, 169
harāc-register ***see*** *jizya*-register
hatt-i hümāyūn, 23, 51, 53, 172
hüccet, 73, 78, 106, 107, 108, 130, 131, 137, 139, 150, 170
irtifāʿ register, 118
jizya-register, 137–8
kānūnnāme, xviii, 29, 91–120
mukābele kalemi, 43
mülknāme, 152
nişān, 134, 135, 136, 139, 151, 152, 167, 169
rūznāme, 43
sicill; *sicillāt*, 29, 36, 73, 75, 76, 77, 79–82, 108, 154, 170
tevkiʿ, 64, 65, 66
tahrīr-register, 48, 56, 60–5
treaties, 159–66, 169–74; ***see also*** *ʿahdnāme*
tuğra, 26n, 28n, 36n, 65n, 131n, 150, 151, 152, 152n, 169
waqfīya, 84, 141, 142–54, 152n, 155–6

Administrative districts
kādīlik ***see*** *kazā*
kazā, 29, 30, 31, 36, 75, 76, 78, 85, 112, 131, 144, 149, 152
livā ***see*** *sancak*
nāhiye, 68, 113, 130
province, 31n, 34, 49n, 50n, 51, 57, 65, 91, 108n, 108n, 117n, 122n, 125, 127n, 129, 168
sancak, 14, 15, 27n, 31n, 44, 49n, 50, 56, 57n, 60n, 61n, 62, 65, 69, 75, 99, 102, 103, 104n, 108, 109, 110, 111, 112, 113, 131, 132, 137, 139, 156n
vilāyet, 115, 137, 138

Campaigns and battles
Algiers (1541), 168n
Ankara (1402), xv, 159
Çaldıran (1514), 45
Constantinople (1453), 61n
Cyprus (1570–3), 76n
Gänjä (1588), 139
Kosovo (1389), 163n
Lepanto (1571), 31n, 66n
Mohács (1526), 68n
Tunis (1535), 168n
Two Iraqs (1534–6), 69n

Chroniclers
Anonymous, 1, 2, 14, 19
ʿĀşıkpaşazāde, 1, 3–4
Celālzāde Mustafā, 10
Doukas, Michael, 21
Hasan Beyzade Ahmed, 23–4
Ibn Kemāl ***see*** Kemālpaşazāde

Kantakouzenos, John VI, 19
Kemālpaşazāde Ahmed, 21–2, 73
Neşrī Mehmed, 1, 4–5
Peçevī Ibrāhīm, 68–9
Şükrullāh, 6
Tuği, 11
Tursun Beg, 10
Uruj b. ʿĀdil, 22
Yazıcıoğlu ʿAlī, 1, 5–6

Currencies
Akçe, 3, 15, 16, 17, 18, 27, 28, 30, 36, 40, 41n, 42, 43n, 44, 45, 46, 47, 48, 51, 52n, 57, 58, 59, 61, 62, 63, 65, 69, 81, 82, 86, 87, 92, 94, 95, 96, 97, 98, 99, 100, 101, 102, 104, 107, 109, 110n, 111, 113, 114, 115, 116, 117, 121, 122–9, 130, 131, 132, 133, 136, 137, 138, 139, 140, 142–9, 153, 155, 156, 170
debasement, 122, 139, 140
dīnār, 69
ducat, 121, 122, 123, 124, 125, 126, 164, 165
eşrefī, 109
filori, 135, 149, 167
florin, 173
halebī akçe, 110
hyperperon, 161, 164
karaca akçe, 109
kuruş, 140
mints, 78n, 119, 123, 139
şāhī, 79
şāhrukī, 109
sultānīye, 119
tenge, 109

European reporters
Bassano, Luigi, 49–50
Iacopo de Promontorio, 56, 57–60, 122–7
Lello, Henry, 53–5

Garments and textiles
ağır çatma, 18
brocade, 155
dolama, 16
kaftan, 16, 17, 45, 156
sorguç, 22
tuğ, 15
üsküf, 15
Yazdī silk, 16
yūsufī turban, 24

Institutions of state
altı bölük, 16n, 18n, 32, 34n, 43, 45n, 69n, 87n, 93
aʿyān, 29, 150
baştina, 115, 116, 136, 137
bath-houses, 122, 123, 133, 141, 143, 144, 153, 154
bedestan, 122, 139
begvāne, 110
beytüʾl-māl, 42, 81, 82, 87, 105, 108
bribery, 42, 88
cerehor, 36
çıkma, 53
çift, *çiftlik*, 37n, 40, 62, 63, 86, 93, 94, 96n, 99, 100, 105, 106, 107, 108, 109, 114, 150, 152
churches, 7, 31, 36, 84
courier-corvée, 36, 37, 42, 95, 150, 151
devşirme, 26, 29–30, 31, 32
dīvān, 17, 45, 133n
dīvān[*-i hümāyūn*], 23, 30n, 39, 40, 41, 43, 45, 47, 49–50, 51, 76
ehl-i ʿörf, 104
executions, 19, 39, 43n, 47n, 51, 54n, 55, 75, 76, 85, 87, 88n, 118, 119, 121, 142n
fratricide, xv, 19–23
hammam ***see*** bathhouses
hāss, 41, 42, 45n, 56, 57n, 65, 67, 116, 121, 127, 128, 129
hāssa çiftlik, 106
hāssa-i hümāyūn, 18, 116, 119
hostages, 50, 160, 166
hutbe, 3, 4, 5, 35
ihtisāb, 134
iltizām, 47, 137
imamate ***see*** caliphate
ʿimāret, 142, 143, 145, 147, 148
kılıç, 41, 44
medrese, 7, 43 n 20, 71, 107 n 97, 141, 142, 143, 144, 145, 146, 154
metropolitanate, 34, 36, 37
mines, 67, 78n, 82, 121, 123, 124, 130, 132, 134, 135
mints, 78n, 119, 121, 123, 139
monasteries, 78
mosques, 3, 7, 32, 34, 35, 43n, 73, 74, 128, 129, 138, 139, 141, 142, 143, 145, 146, 147, 149, 154, 155, 156
mülūkāne, 110
mukataʿa, 17, 47, 65, 82, 127, 130, 131, 132
narh, 44
pencik, 26–9, 31n, 66, 81n, 85

Sahn-i semān, 43
salt pans, 121, 123, 124, 125, 153, 163, 164
schools, 32, 141, 142, 149
six divisions *see altı bölük*
slavery, slaves, 16, 17, 18, 20, 21, 26, 28–9, 30, 50, 58, 59, 59n, 64, 78, 79, 81, 82, 84, 85, 95n, 98, 103, 107, 117n, 122, 123, 129n, 130, 133, 151, 153, 162, 164, 165, 167, 170, 171, 172
sugar refinery, 119
tahvīl, 130, 131, 132
timar, 4, 6, 18, 21, 29n, 30, 41, 44n, 45, 48, 52, 56, 57n, 60–5, 66, 68, 69, 86n, 91, 92n, 93n, 94n, 96n, 97n, 99n, 100, 102n, 103, 104, 105, 106, 107, 110, 111, 112, 115, 116, 121, 127, 128, 131, 136, 137, 138, 139, 150, 151, 155
  free, 103, 112
  tezkerelü, 111
  tezkeresiz, 111
treasury, 36, 42, 45, 46–7, 52, 56, 88, 100n, 105n, 106n, 115, 117, 118, 119, 121, 122, 124, 127, 130n, 43, 45, 131n, 138, 168
ulak ***see*** courier-corvée
waqf, 7, 9, 35n, 63, 78, 84, 86n, 107n, 121, 141, 142–58
  cash, 155–7
  family, 154, 155
  of Mahmūd Paşa, 142–9
zāviye, 76, 128, 141, 142, 149, 150, 151, 153, 154, 156
ze'āmet, 41, 44, 45, 47, 57n, 68n, 69, 94n, 111, 112, 115, 130

Law, legal status, concepts and terminology

amān, 84
'askerī, 107–8
bāğī, 11n, 35
bail, 170
bay'a, 5, 11, 24
beglik, 96, 133, 134, 139
benlāk ***see*** *bennāk*
bennāk, 87, 93, 99, 100, 101, 105
bid'at, 101, 105n
blood-money, 86
burglary, 81
caba bennāk, 99
caliphate, 7, 8, 11, 76n; ***see also*** imāmate
crop-damage, 99
dānişmend, 48
dārü'l-harb, 68, 84n, 108
debt, 72, 79, 108, 163, 170
dhimmī, 31, 37, 73, 79, 84
divorce, 80, 83, 102
evidence, 78, 79, 81
fatwā, 8, 11, 71n, 72–6, 77, 78, 82–8, 156
fesād, 76, 87
fines, 74, 91, 94, 96, 97, 99, 103, 104, 105, 107, 110, 112, 115, 116, 134n, 161
fitne, 87
galleys, punishment by, 18, 76
gazā, 2, 3, 4, 5, 6, 27, 66, 68, 69
gāzī, 3, 4, 9, 10, 14, 15, 19, 22, 27, 35, 46, 67, 68, 69
halāl, 74, 86, 87
Hanafī, 36, 71, 73n, 74n, 75, 79n, 82n, 86n, 141
Hanbalī, 71
harām, 86, 157
harbī, 84
hayf, 29, 30, 100
heresy, 75, 76
hīle, 154, 157
homicide, 37n, 64, 86n, 92, 103, 111
ilhād, 75
imāmate, 10, 11
imprisonment, 26, 28, 31, 32, 54, 69, 85n, 164, 165
interest, 86, 149, 154, 155, 156, 157
inheritance, 8, 19, 20, 36, 81n, 82n, 101, 102, 105n, 107n, 108, 136
intention, 4, 83
jihād, 10, 27, 66
kānūn, 3, 4, 11, 28, 29, 33, 40, 44, 45, 82, 91–120, 132, 135, 170
kānūnnāme, 27, 28, 29, 91–120, 133
kufr, 75
land-tenure, 12, 62n, 73, 74, 79, 86, 87, 91, 92–3, 95, 98, 99, 100, 101, 106, 108, 111, 114, 142, 150, 151
loan, 73, 79, 86
madhhab, 21
Mālikī, 71
marriage, 2, 8, 21, 36, 72, 80, 82, 83, 85, 102, 107, 108
mezra'a, 63, 64, 65, 110, 136, 151, 152
mīrī, 83, 86; ***see also*** *beglik*
mujāhid, 10
mukhtasar, 71
mülk, 65, 106, 110, 152
mülknāme, 152
oath, 11n, 79, 81, 132, 159, 165, 166
'örf, *'örfī*, 5, 104, 111, 133

prayer, 1, 3, 4, 22, 23, 24, 35, 36, 39, 40, 42, 54, 55, 68, 74, 83n, 87, 104, 142n, 144, 151, 172
prison, prisoner ***see*** imprisonment
rāfizī, 76
ra'īyet, 29, 44, 48, 92, 93, 94, 95, 96, 99, 100, 101, 102, 103, 105, 106, 107, 108, 111, 112, 114, 115, 116
re'āyā, 29n, 35, 36, 44, 48, 67, 73, 86, 87, 88, 95n, 99, 100, 101, 103, 105, 108, 110, 111, 114, 115, 116, 135, 136, 150
sale, 72, 73, 74, 79, 81, 82, 103, 123, 124, 134
şehirlü, 108
şer', *şer'ī*, *şer'īye*, 5, 7, 36, 85, 102, 103, 104, 111, 156
Shāfi'ī, 71, 72, 73n
sharh, 71
sharī'a, 7, 10, 11, 17, 18, 31, 35n, 36, 71, 73, 74, 75, 76, 77, 78, 82n, 83, 84, 85, 86n, 87, 88, 91, 99n, 101n, 102, 104, 111n, 132, 133, 134, 139, 172; ***see also*** *şer'*
siyāset, 30, 35, 88n, 103, 119, 150
sürgün, 108
tapu, 74, 79, 86, 92, 101, 102, 106, 107, 115
ta'zīr, 74, 86, 88
tevlīyet, 145, 155
theft, 75, 88n, 92
töre, 5
torture, 17, 51, 86, 118
umm walad, 28
yoksul, 93n
zulm, 46, 88, 114

Military equipment and ships

arquebus, arquebusier, 117, 129
arrows, 54, 57, 59, 96, 117
bards, 58, 59, 60
bows, 57, 59, 96, 117, 128
bürüme, 105
coat of mail, 57
cuirass, 57, 59, 96
fusta, 126
galleon, 169, 170
galley, 18, 76, 126, 163, 171
gunpowder, 50, 51, 129
lance, 57, 96, 105n, 117
mace, 57, 59, 105n
palandaria, 126
shield, 57, 96, 105n
sword, 3, 4, 5, 8, 10, 11, 12, 21, 57, 59, 66, 96, 97, 105n, 167, 168
tenktür, 60, 105

Office-holders

'Abdu'r-rezzāk, ağa of the Porte, 23
'Alī b. Yūsuf el-Fenārī, kādī'asker, 142
'Ali Beg, son of Evrenos, 58
'Alī Ağa, ağa of the Janissaries, 51
'Alī Paşa, Muezzinzāde, grand admiral, 65n
'Alī Paşa, Uluç, grand admiral, 65n
Baltaoğlu Süleymān, ambassador, 166
Barbarossa, Hayrü'd-dīn, grand admiral, 49, 50
Bedreddīn, kādī of Buda, 36
Cemālü'd-Dīn, kādī'asker, 150
Ebū's-su'ūd, chief mufti, 7, 8, 71, 73–5, 77, 82–7, 154
Elvān Beg, *çaşnigīr başı*, 20
Es'ad Efendi, chief mufti, 87
Hāccī 'Abdü'r-Rahīm, chief mufti, 88
Hızr Ağa, *ağa* of the Janissaries, 21
Ilyās Beg, *sancakbegi* of Amasya, 75
'Īsā Beg, *beglerbegi* of Anatolı, 35
Iskender Çelebi, *defterdār*, 47
Kara Dāvūd Ağa, *silihdār*, great-grandfather of Peçevī Ibrāhīm, 69
Kara Malkoç Beg, *sancakbegi* of Bosnia, 69
Karaca Beg, *beglerbegi*, 35
Kemālpaşazāde, chief mufti, 46, 71, 73, 154, 157; ***see also*** Ibn Kemāl
Mahmūd, *defterdār*, 52
Mahmūd Çelebi, *defterdār*, 143, 156
Malkoç 'Alī Paşa, *beglerbegi* of Egypt, 51, 53
Mehmed Sādık, chief mufti, 88
Minnet-Begoğlı Mehmed Beg, *sancakbegi* of Bosnia, 68–9
Murād Paşa, *beglerbegi* of Buda, 173
Muhīyü'd-Dīn Mehmed, Çivizāde, chief mufti, 84n
Mustafā, Ebū'l-Meyāmin, chief mufti, 24, 54
Mustafā b. 'Īsā, *sancakbegi* of Zvornik, 66
Mü'eyyedzāde Şeyhī Efendi, chief mufti, 140
Pīrī, chief artilleryman 32
Sinān, chief architect, 32, 33
Yahyā-paşazāde Küçük Bālī Beg, *ze'āmet*-holder in Bosnia, 69
Yenişehirli Abdullah, chief mufti, 11
Yūnus Beg, chief dragoman, 49
Yūnus Paşa, governor of Bosnia, 66
Yūsuf, *pencikçi-başı*, 27

Offices

'acemī oğlan, 30, 31, 32, 33, 54
ağa of Anaṭolı, 31

ağa of the Janissaries, 21, 23, 30, 31, 32, 33, 42, 50, 51n
ağa of the Porte, 16, 17, 23
alay-begi, 68, 69
ʿāmil, 118, 119, 130, 132, 135
bayrakdār, 65
beglerbegi, 22, 31, 34, 35, 40, 42, 43, 44, 45, 47, 49, 50, 51, 53, 57, 59, 63, 65, 68n, 76, 106, 111, 127, 128, 169, 170n, 171
beytülmālcı, 82
bölük ağası, 45
bostāncı-başı, 22, 112
çakırcı-başı, 43
caliph, 3, 4, 7, 8, 10, 11, 76n
çaşnigīr, 34, 40, 43, 47, 125
çaşnigīr-başı, 20, 40, 47, 43
çavuş, 5, 6n
çavuş başı, 23, 24, 34, 43, 44, 76, 125, 129, 139
cebeci, 117
cebeci-başı, 117
çeri-başı, 61, 112, 115, 116
çokadār, 40
dadı, 16
dayı, 16
defter emīni, 45
defterdār, 39, 41, 43, 44, 45, 47, 49n, 52, 111, 127, 128, 143
*devirh*ᵛ*ān*, 145
dirlik, 66
doorkeeper, 16, 21, 23, 64, 145, 146
eczā-reciters, 145, 146
emānet, 47
emīn, 28, 29, 46, 78, 81, 82, 87, 118, 128, 134, 152
fakīh, 3, 5, 35, 75, 149, 152
falconers, 33, 34, 95, 107, 128, 151; ***see also*** *çakırcı-başı*
gardeners, 34; ***see also*** *bostancı başı*
grand admiral, 31n, 49n, 65n, 171
gulām, 28, 33, 64, 105, 106n, 129
hācib, 151
hatīb, 3, 5, 7, 35, 76
hoca, 16, 67, 78
imām, 3, 5, 7, 33, 36, 75, 76, 139, 142, 145, 146, 147, 154, 155
Imām ***see*** caliph
kādī, 3, 5, 18, 28, 29, 30, 31, 34, 35, 36, 43, 44, 47, 49, 57, 58, 59n, 65, 66, 71, 72, 73, 74, 75, 76, 77, 78, 79n, 82, 83, 84, 85, 97, 102n, 103, 104, 106, 107, 108, 111, 112, 113, 114, 115, 119, 131, 132, 133, 134, 135, 136, 137, 139, 141, 142, 144n, 150n, 153, 154n, 169, 170, 171, 172
kādīʿasker, 39, 45, 47, 49, 50, 76, 102n, 107, 142, 147, 150, 152
kāʾimmakām, 23
kapucı-başı, 40, 43, 51
kapudan, 133, 134
kapudan paşa ***see*** grand admiral
kāşif, 118, 119
kassām, 107
kātib, 34, 43, 44
kayyūm, 145, 146, 156
kedhüdā; *kethüdā*, 5, 23, 30, 34, 35, 43, 68, 81, 82, 117, 128, 129, 131, 136, 137
kira, 25n
kul, 7, 32, 51, 52, 53, 63, 95, 98, 106, 107, 131, 133, 136, 139, 167
lālā, 22
librarian, 145
metropolitan, 34, 36–7
mevkūfcı, 106
miʿmār ağa, 23
mīr-ahur, 43, 45, 64
mīr-ʿalem, 40, 43
mīrlivā ***see*** *sancakbegi*
muʿarrif, 146
mufti, 23, 24, 54, 71, 76, 77, 140, 154
muʿīd, 145
müderris, 43, 107, 145, 146
muezzin, 33, 139, 145, 146, 147, 155
muhtesib, 80
müteferrika, 33, 40, 43, 44
mütevellī, 35, 107, 142, 145n, 147, 149, 153, 155, 156, 157
nāʾib, 30, 35, 36, 62n, 67, 136, 151
nakībüʾs-sādāt, 48
nāzır, 15, 50, 107, 147
nāzır-i emvāl, 118, 129
nedīm, 34
nişāncı, 39, 41, 43, 45
nüzl emīni, 45
oda başı, 117
pencikçi-başı, 27, 28
podestà, 162
protoostiarios, 21
reʾīsüʾl-küttāb, 50n
rikābī, 33
rūznāmeci, 44
şagavul, 6
sancakbegi, 27, 35, 40, 43, 44, 45, 47, 53, 57, 58n, 67, 68, 75, 77, 81, 86, 88, 91, 103, 104,

106, 110, 111, 112, 113, 114, 115, 128, 129, 131, 133, 134, 135, 139, 150, 167
segbān, 95
ser'asker, 60
subaşı, 3, 14, 17, 30, 35, 57, 58, 59n, 66, 67, 77, 81, 91, 94, 97, 103, 104, 106, 111, 112, 113, 114, 115, 116, 132, 135, 136, 150, 151, 167
taster ***see*** *çaşnigīr*
tax-farmers, 121, 130, 131, 134, 135; ***see also*** *'āmil*
tesbīh-reciter, 108
tovıca, 27, 28
tutor ***see*** *hoca*
ucbegi, 27
vizier, 2, 4n, 5, 15n, 19, 20, 22, 23, 24, 39, 40, 41, 42, 43, 44, 45, 46, 47, 49, 50, 51, 52, 53, 56, 69, 87n, 117n, 121, 127, 128, 138n, 141, 142
voivode, 64, 166, 167
voyvoda, 113
yasavul, 62
yavacı, 82
yaya başı, 18, 29, 31
za'īm, 33, 44, 129; ***see also*** *subaşı*

Ottoman provinces

Anatolı, 12, 31, 34, 35, 39, 40, 50, 51, 124, 127, 128, 131, 142, 144, 168
Archipelago, 31, 49n, 65
Diyārbekir, 12, 45, 108, 127, 129, 168
Dulkadir ***see*** Zū'l-kadriyye
Egypt, 2, 3, 4, 9, 12, 33, 46n, 47, 51, 52, 53, 117, 118, 119n, 127, 129, 168
Erzurum, 12, 50n, 139, 168
Karamān, 12, 40, 50, 60, 105, 108, 124n, 125, 127, 128, 159, 165, 168
Rūm, 12, 20, 124n, 127, 128, 168
Rūmeli, 12, 20, 39, 49n, 57n, 63, 65, 68n, 73, 122n, 127, 128, 142, 143, 152, 164n, 168, 171
Zū'l-kadriyye, 12, 127, 128, 168

Ottoman sultans, Ottoman ancestors and the Ottoman family

'Abdu'l-'azīz, astrologer, supposed father-in-law of 'Osmān, 2, 3
Ahmed I (1603–17), 19, 23–4, 52, 54n, 160
Ahmed, son of Selīm I, 18, 19
'Ālemşāh, son of Bāyezīd II, 16–17
'Alī Paşa, mythical brother of Orhan, 14, 19, 22
Bāyezīd, son of Süleymān I, 87n
Bāyezīd I (1389–1402), xv, 10, 19, 20, 22n, 63n, 159
Bāyezīd II (1481–1512), 7, 10, 15, 20, 21n, 26, 39, 40, 41n, 69, 91, 92, 99, 104n, 112n, 122, 150n, 151, 152n, 155
Cem, brother of Bāyezīd II, 19, 20, 60n
Edebali, supposed father-in-law of 'Osmān, 2, 3, 14
Ertoğrul, 1, 2, 4, 6
Gök Alp, mythical ancestor of the dynasty, 3, 6
Gülrūh, mother of Prince 'Ālemşāh, 16
Kayı, senior grandson of Oğuz Hān, 1, 5, 6
Korkud, son of Bāyezīd II, 15, 16
Mahmūd II (1808–39), 152n
Mahmūd, son of Mehmed III, 53–4
Mehmed I (1413–21), 5, 7, 10, 19, 20, 63n, 150n, 151n, 165
Mehmed II (1451–81), 4n, 10, 15n, 19, 21, 43n, 56, 60n, 68, 84, 92, 122, 130n, 135n, 139, 142n, 150, 151, 153n, 155, 159, 165, 167n
Mehmed III (1595–1603), 18, 22, 23, 24, 25n, 52n, 53
Murād I (1362–89), 9, 10, 14, 15, 19, 34, 35, 99n, 150, 152, 159, 160, 161, 162
Murād II (1421–51), 1, 5, 6, 10, 20, 21, 92, 159, 165, 166
Murād III (1574–95), 22
Mūsā, son of Bāyezīd I, 19, 20, 151
Mustaf I (1617–18, 1622–3), 11
Mustafā, son of Mehmed II, 60n
Oğuz Hān, mythical ancestor of the Oğuz Turks, 1, 3n, 5, 6
Orhān (1324?-1362), 2, 3, 9, 10, 14, 15, 19, 22, 152, 159, 160
'Osmān I (d.1326?), 1, 2, 3, 4, 5, 6, 14
'Osmān II (1618–22), 88n
Rābi'a, supposed mother of 'Osman I, 3
Sāfīye Sultan, mother of Mehmed III, 25n, 53
Şāh Sultān, sister of Süleymān I, 40n
Selīm I (1512–20), 10, 12, 18, 19, 40, 41, 43, 45, 46, 48, 150, 153, 168
Selīm II (1566–74), 18, 82n
Süleymān I (1520–66), 8, 10, 11, 12, 19, 40, 42, 46, 50n, 52, 71, 73n, 87n, 110, 117n, 153n, 160, 168
Süleymān Paşa, son of Orhan, 14, 15
Süleymān, prince, son of Bāyezīd I, 10n, 19, 20, 63, 159, 162
Süleymānşāh, supposed ancestor of the dynasty, 3
Ya'kūb, brother of Bāyezīd I, 19, 20
Yıldırım ***see*** Bāyezīd I

Palace
arz odası, 23
bāb-i sa'ādet, 23, 35, 67, 68, 168, 169
courts, xxii, 23, 39, 49
enderūn, 33
eunuchs, 125
kitchen, 42, 47, 128
pantry, 33
privy chamber, 33, 40n
stables, 15, 43n, 47, 115, 125, 128
threshold [of felicity] ***see*** *bāb-i sa'ādet*
treasury, 2, 27, 33, 36, 42, 43n, 45, 46–7, 48, 52, 56, 81n, 83n, 88, 100n, 105n, 106n, 115, 118, 119, 121, 122, 124, 125n, 126, 127, 128, 129, 130n, 131, 133n, 138, 154, 155, 168
women's palace, 125

Peoples, clans and groups
Arabs, 5, 9, 10, 11, 63, 119, 129, 161
Arianit, 18
Armenians, 39, 63
Bayat, 5
celālīs, 50, 52n
Christians, 26, 31n, 36, 59, 63, 77, 84, 87n, 115n, 122, 123, 124, 125, 126, 128, 172, 173
'Franks', 46, 98
Greeks, 31, 34, 49, 57, 58, 123, 161, 162, 163, 164
Jews, 22, 25n, 31n, 77, 84, 86, 122n, 130, 132
Kurds, 42, 62, 63
Mongols, 6
Oğuz, 1, 3n, 5, 6
Persians, 5, 9, 10, 11
Quraish, 8
Tatars, 1, 5, 12, 48, 81n, 93, 94, 95, 107, 125, 168, 172
Turks, 1, 5, 6, 22, 31, 32, 33n, 49, 58, 59, 93, 95n, 110, 117n, 122, 161, 163, 165, 173, 174
Vlachs, 92, 105
yürüks, 33, 80, 92, 93, 95, 96, 100, 101, 102, 103, 107

Persons
Abū Hanīfa, jurist, 72, 75, 141, 142
Alp Gündüz, follower of 'Osmān I, 14
Batthyány, Francis, Hungarian magnate, 174
Duke of Naxos, 163, 164
Esparanza Malchi, *kira*, 25n
Gentile de Grimaldi, Genoese ambassador, 160
Gerhard Veltwyck, Habsburg ambassador, 168
Harborne, William, English ambassador, 169
Iacopo of Gaëta, physician to Mehmed II, 130
Ishāk, slave of Murād II, 21
Iskender, slave of Bāyezīd II, 20
Janono de Boscho, Genoese ambassador, 160
Korkut Ata, mythical sage of the Oğuz, 5
Mathias, Archduke, Habsburg archduke, later emperor, 173
Mihāl, companion of 'Osmān, 2
Muhammad al-Shaybānī, jurist, 72, 141, 142n
al-Mūsilī, jurist, 72
Prophet Muhammad, 2, 5, 7, 8, 10, 11n, 16, 17, 22, 39, 43, 48n, 51, 66, 73, 76n, 87n, 144n, 149, 104, 163, 165
Qādīkhān, jurist, 71n, 72
al-Qudūrī, jurist, 72
Skanderbeg, Albanian lord, 58
Stojka Gisdanić, Hungarian ambassador, 166
Turgut Alp, follower of 'Osmān I, 14
Tursun Fakīh, 3, 5
Ya'kūb Pasha, the physician ***see*** Iacopo of Gaëta
Zeno, Pietro, Venetian ambassador, 162

Place names
Adana, 31n, 110
Aden, 12, 168
Adrianople ***see*** Edirne
Akkerman, 66, 133, 167
Alanya, 60, 124
Albania, 30n, 58, 136n, 137
Aleppo, 12, 110n, 127, 129, 168
Alto Luogo ***see*** Ephesus
Amasya, 18, 59, 75
Anatolia, 4n, 7, 14, 15, 18n, 20, 26, 31, 33n, 34, 50, 51, 52n, 71, 73, 76n, 81n, 93n, 108n, 117n, 121, 124n, 127n, 136, 156n, 159, 171
Algiers, 12, 168, 171
Amfissa, 165
Ankara, xv, 2, 9, 60, 80, 81, 144, 147, 159
Antalya, 9, 60n
Arabia, 12, 168
Argirokasri ***see*** Gjirokastër
Armenia, 4
Arta, 58
Athens, 58, 164
'Avrethisarı, 63
Ayasulug ***see*** Ephesus
Aydın, 60, 124, 139
Aynegöl, 14
Baghdad, 12, 47, 168
Balaklava, 125

Balat, 124, 164
Basra, 7n, 12, 168
Belgrade, 37n, 63, 167n
Bergama, 32
Beşiktaş, 65
Bilecik, 4, 6, 14
Bitola, 58
Black Sea, 12, 58, 117n, 163, 164, 168
Bodonitsa, 164
Bogdan, 167; ***see also*** Moldavia
Bolayır, 153
Borağı varoşı ***see*** Poraça
Bosnia, 58, 66, 67, 68, 69, 123, 135, 167
Buda, 12, 36, 168, 173, 174
Budin ***see*** Buda
Bulgaria, 34, 37n
Bender, 33
Bilhorod Dnistrovskyi ***see*** Akkerman
Caffa, 125, 128
Çankırı, 75, 131
Chios, 124, 163, 164
Constantinople, 2, 22, 49, 50, 54, 58, 61n, 122, 161n, 162n, 163, 164, 168, 171, 173; ***see also*** Istanbul
Çorum, 75
Croatia, 167
Damascus, 12, 127, 129
Danube, river, 124, 128, 173
Dardanelles, 164
Demirkapu, 33
Denizli, 139
Dimetoka ***see*** Didymoteicho
Drama, 144
Dubrovnik, 98, 124
Didymoteicho, 152
Divény, 173
Edirne, 20, 21, 32, 35, 36, 40, 43n, 58, 61, 63, 64, 95, 97, 123, 128, 132, 143, 146, 149, 156, 159, 166, 167
Eger, 173
Egypt, 2, 3, 4, 9, 12, 33, 46n, 47, 51, 52, 53, 117–19, 127, 129, 168
Enez, 123
Ephesus, 139, 164
Erzurum, 12, 50n, 139, 168
Esztergom, 173
Evvoia, 123, 164
Filibe ***see*** Plovdiv
Fülek, 173
Galata, 47, 128, 171, 172
Gallikos, river, 163
Gallipoli, 9, 26, 58, 122, 128, 130, 153
Genisea, 130
Georgia, 12
Germany, 8
Germiyan, 3n
Gjirokastër, 137, 138
Golubac, 144
Gothia, 125
Greece, 31n, 49, 57, 124, 135n, 152n, 162, 164n
Grevená, 135n
Güğercinlik ***see*** Golubac
Gyarmach, 173
Győr, 173
Hainaczko, 173
Hijaz, 9, 46n
Hungary, 2, 12n, 51, 52n, 159, 160, 166, 167n, 168, 172, 173
India, 129n
Inönü, 14
Iran, 8, 52n, 71, 75n
Işkodra ***see*** Shkodër
Istanbul, 15, 23n, 26, 28, 30, 31, 32, 43n, 46, 51n, 61, 63, 64, 71, 76, 77, 84, 98, 109, 117n, 119, 122, 124n, 128, 130n, 142, 144, 145, 147, 152n, 154, 167; ***see also*** Constantinople
Iznik, 9
Jajce, 67
Jeddah, 129
Jerusalem, 12, 168
Kağıthane, 46
Kamengrad, 67
Kangrı ***see*** Çankırı
Kanisza, 174
Karahisar, 14
Karaca-hisar, 1, 3, 5
Kastamonu, 18, 40, 60, 64, 75, 76, 124, 129n, 131
Kékkő, 173
Kilkis, 51
Kluč, 67
Kocaeli, 65, 152n
Konya, 2, 5, 108n
Kostandin-ili ***see*** Kyustendil
Kozan, 31, 109
Kratovo, 123
Kreševo, 135
Kurdistan, 12, 168
Kyustendil, 37
Küre, 18, 76, 129
Lamia, 58
Laz, 135
Luristan, 12, 168

Malkara, 153n
Mecca, 11n, 12, 22, 40n, 46n, 55, 172
Medina, 11n, 12, 40n, 46n, 145, 148, 149
Menlik, 37, 138, 139
Menteşe, 60, 80, 124, 139, 156n
Mesembria *see* Nesebŭr
Mihaliç, 21
Modon, 49
Moldavia, 66, 134, 167
Monastir *see* Bitola
Morea, 58, 123
Mount Athos, 78
Muğla, 149
Naxos, 164
Negroponte *see* Evvoia
Nemçe *see* Germany
Nesebŭr, 163
Nicomedia, 15
Nicopolis *see* Nikopol
Nikopol, 58, 110–16, 124, 131
Niksar, 76
Nile, river, 118, 129
Nógrád, 173
Novo Brdo, 123
Oltu, 50
Osmancık, 60
Palanka, 173
Panidos, 58, 163
Phocaea, 124, 165
Ortapare, 18
Permeti, 136
Pirot, 61
Plovdiv, 61, 68, 124
Porača, 131, 132
Prague, 173
Prilep, 64
Priština, 123
Qipchak plain, 12, 168
Ragusa *see* Dubrovnik
Rhodes, 19, 31, 46n, 124, 128, 163, 165
Rudnik, 135
Rūm, 4, 5, 7, 73, 154
Rūs, 133
Salona *see* Amfissa
Salonica *see* Thessaloniki
Samsun, 125
San'a, 12
Saruhan, 60, 124, 139, 150, 153
Şebin Karahisar, 150n
Şehirköy *see* Pirot
Semendire *see* Smederovo
Serbia, 58, 123, 135, 144n, 159, 163n, 166n, 167n
Serres, 65, 123, 124
Shkodër, 66
Siderokaúsia, 78
Sidrekapsı *see* Siderokaúsia
Sığla, 18
Sinop, 21, 81n, 124n
Sīs *see* Kozan
Sivas, 4
Siverek, 108–9
Skopje, 58, 64
Slavonia, 173
Smederovo, 131, 132
Sofia, 37, 61, 63, 64, 123, 146
Söğüt, 2
Sokol, 67, 68
Somoskő, 173
Srebrenica, 66, 67, 123, 135
Štip, 64
Syria, 9, 121, 168, 171
Takrūr, 119
Tana, 125
Tepedelen *see* Tepelenë
Tepelenë, 30
Thessaloniki, 63, 65, 78, 123, 128, 163
Tokat, 59
Tophane, 172
Tonuzlu *see* Denizli
Trabzon, 125, 128
Transylvania, 173n
Tripoli (Lebanon), 171
Tripoli (Libya), 171
Turgut-eli, 14
Vác, 173
Valona *see* Vlorë
Vardar, river, 163
Varna, 58, 159
Venice, 163, 168, 169
Vienna, 173
Vlorë, 123, 128
Wallachia, 64n, 98, 124, 166n, 167
Yenice Karasu *see* Genisea
Yemen, 12, 168
Zagora, 58, 124
Zagori, 137
Zechen, 173
Zvornik, 66, 68

Religious groups

Bayramīs, 147
Bektaşīs, 152

dervishes, 1, 2, 7, 20, 22, 107n, 128n, 141, 142, 147n, 150, 152n, 156
halīfe, 75
kızılbaş, 71, 74n, 76
monks, 36, 49, 78, 84
ʿulemā, 1, 4, 7, 11, 20, 40, 43, 76, 77, 149
sunnīs, 8, 11n, 71

Rulers and dynasties
Abaka Khān, 4
ʿAbbāsids, 4
Ahmed Jalāyir, 33
Akkoyunlus, 59, 62n, 108n, 109n
ʿAlāʾed-dīn, fictitious Seljuk sultan, 2, 3, 5
ʿAlāʾed-dīn III, last Seljuk sultan, 1, 4, 5
Al-Hākim bi-amriʾllāh, 4
Ashraf, Ghalzay, 11
Aydın, 9, 164
Barqūq, 9
Bocskai, 173
Branković, George, 58n, 159, 166
Branković, Lazar, 58n
Byzantine emperors, 2, 64, 84; ***see also*** Kantakouzenos, John VI
Cihānşāh, 1, 6
Danoğlu ***see*** Vladislav II
Elizabeth I, 169
Ferdinand I, 8, 12, 168
François I, 50
Germiyanoğlu, 3
Ghaznavids, 6
Habsburgs, 8, 11n, 160
Ibrāhīm Beg of Karaman, 165–6
Ilkhāns, 4
Isfendiyār, 21, 124
Jenghizids, 5
John VII, 159, 162–4
Kantakouzenos, John VI, 19
Kara Yūsuf, 6
Karakoyunlu, 1, 6n
Kayhosrev II, 9
Kāyıtbāy, 109
Khwārazmshāhs, 6
Mamlūks, 9n, 46n, 60, 110n, 109n, 110n, 118n
Masʿūd, 4
Nāder Shāh, 8
Orthodox Caliphs, 7, 8, 76
Rudolph II, 160, 173n
Safavids, 45n, 47n, 52n, 71, 75n
Saruhān, 150
Seljuks, 1, 2n, 3, 4, 5, 6, 7
Shāh Ismaʿīl, 45
Shāhrukh, 109n
Stephen Lazarević, 163
Tamerlane ***see*** Tīmūr
Tīmūr, 6, 20, 59n, 109n, 159, 163
Uğurlu Muhammad, 59n
Uzun Hasan, 59n, 108
Vlad Dracul, 166
Vladislav II of Wallachia, 64
Władisław III and I, 166

States, communes and leagues
Byzantine Empire, 2, 7, 159, 162–5
England, 169, 170, 171, 172
France, 50, 168, 169, 171
Genoa, 160–2, 164
Hungary, 2, 12n, 159, 160, 166, 167n, 168, 173
Karaman, 159, 165–6
Latin league, 159, 163, 164
Poland, 166, 169
Rhodes, hospitallers of, 163, 165
Serbia, despotate of, 67, 159, 163n
Spain, 160, 168
Venice, 102n, 121, 123, 124, 161, 163, 164, 165, 168, 169, 171

Taxes, imposts, fines and fees
ʿavāriz[-*i dīvānīye*/*ʿörfīye*], 36, 48, 63, 73, 96, 106, 114, 115, 135, 150, 156, 157
bāc, 3; ***see also*** toll
bachelors, tax on, 86, 99, 110, 171
bennak-tax, 87, 99, 100, 101, 105
bevvābī, 62, 63
bride-chamber tax, 92, 94, 97, 102, 115
bride-tax, 86, 87, 102, 103, 107, 109, 110, 115
carters, tax on, 93, 97, 114
cattle-tax, 62, 63
çift-tax, 37n, 63, 73, 86, 87n, 93, 94, 96n, 99, 100, 101, 105, 108, 109, 114
customs, 83, 122, 123, 124, 125, 130, 132, 133, 134, 161, 164
dehnīm, 62, 63
festival-tax, 109
fodder-tax, 37, 62, 94n, 96, 113
gardens and vineyards, taxes on, 93, 96, 97, 102, 104, 109, 113, 114, 115, 116, 133, 149, 135
harāc (in the sense of *jizya*), 37, 96, 115, 116, 121, 122, 123, 124, 125, 135, 136, 137, 171
harāc (on produce), 102, 149
harāc (as tribute), 167
harāc-i mukāseme, 74

harc-i timūr, 109
hay-tax, 113
'hearth-tax', 59, 122, 123
hive-tax, 86, 94, 97, 102, 112–13, 115, 116, 135
ırgadiye, 109
ispence, 37, 87, 96, 97, 113, 114, 115, 116, 135
jizya, 7, 30n, 73, 97, 110, 121, 122n, 127, 128, 135, 137, 138, 160; ***see also*** harāc
kara salgun, 109
lance-tax, 115
marriage-tax, 102, 108
mill-tax, 95, 100, 105, 109, 110, 113
monapolye, 97, 114
nā'ibcik and *vālīcik*, 62, 63
New Year tax, 109
niyābet, 112
nokta başı, 109
'öşr, 74, 94, 114
pig-tax, 87, 97, 99, 114, 115, 116
resm-i hāne, 110
resm-i kara, 100
resm-i kışlak, 103
resm-i kismet[*-i mevārīs*], 102, 107
resm-i kitābet, 136
resm-i nān, 116
resm-i otlak, 103
resm-i tütün, 111, 115
resm-i yatak, 110
sālāriye ***see*** *sālārlık*
sālārlık, 94, 96, 97, 100, 101, 114, 115
salgun, 113, 114
sheep-tax, 37, 83, 86, 92, 94, 95, 97, 98, 100, 103, 105, 106, 109, 110, 113, 115
sheepfold-tax, 101
suhrā, 37
tapu [-tax], 79; ***see also*** *tapu*
tax-evasion, 132
tax-exemptions, 30n, 36, 63, 73, 87, 115, 116, 135, 150, 151
tekālif-i 'örfīye, 36, 87, 135
tolls, 3, 26, 28–9, 62n, 91, 95, 97, 98, 105, 109, 110, 122n, 123, 124, 125, 130n, 133
tithe, 42, 59, 74, 86, 87, 93, 94, 95, 97, 100, 101, 102, 104, 105, 110, 111, 113, 114, 115, 116, 124, 125, 133, 134, 135, 152, 174; ***see also*** 'öşr
tradesmen, tax on, 93, 95
uncultivated land, 48, 95, 101, 118
widows, tax on, 56, 61, 96, 101, 108, 110, 137, 138
zakāt, 83, 86

Titles

ağa, 5, 16, 17, 21, 22, 23, 30, 31, 32, 33, 42, 43, 44, 45, 50, 51, 53, 69, 117
amīr al-mu'minīn, 8, 10, 11
ban, 167, 173
beg, 2, 5, 6, 8, 9, 10, 19, 20, 21, 31, 33, 34, 35, 36, 46, 49, 58, 63, 64, 67, 69, 75, 98, 130, 132, 143, 149, 150, 151, 152, 155, 160, 161, 162, 165, 166, 167, 169, 170
Caesar, 11, 172, 173
çelebi, 15, 16, 19, 20, 47, 60, 78, 79, 143, 155, 156, 162
emīr, 6, 7, 8, 9, 20, 35, 42, 46, 63, 104, 159, 160, 161, 164n, 166, 167
hākān, 7, 8, 10, 11, 12, 40, 167, 168, 169
hān, 1, 3, 5, 6, 7, 8, 9, 10, 11, 12, 14, 15, 20, 21, 22, 40, 42, 43, 45, 46, 48, 50n, 53, 92, 152, 165, 168
hüdavend, 97
hüdavendgār, 8, 14, 35, 66, 99n, 103, 107, 136, 151
hünkār, 8, 21
pādişāh, 2, 3, 5, 7, 8, 11, 12, 16, 17, 20, 21, 22, 23, 24, 29, 35, 40, 41, 42, 44, 45, 46, 47, 52, 53, 63, 67, 87, 88, 93, 98, 101, 106, 108, 110, 116, 127, 149, 150, 152, 153, 167, 168
paşa, 4n, 14, 15, 19, 20, 22, 23, 35, 39, 40n, 41, 47, 49, 50, 51, 52, 53, 65, 66, 68, 117n, 138, 139, 142, 143, 148, 162, 172
shāhinshāh, 9, 10

Troops and military auxiliaries

akıncı, 27, 48, 56, 59, 67, 127
'azab, 56, 59, 105, 117, 127, 128, 129, 131, 132, 133, 134
beşlü, 67
cānbāz, 107
cebelü, 64, 105, 106
Circassians, 117, 129
corsairs, 46n, 59, 60
ellici, 48
eşkinci, 48
garīb, 34, 125
gönüllü, 117, 129
hisār eri, 100, 117
Janissaries, 18, 19, 20, 21, 22, 23, 29, 30, 31, 32, 33, 34n, 42, 43, 44, 45, 47, 49, 50, 51n, 52n, 64, 67n, 95n, 98n, 117n, 125, 128, 133 n 59, 136, 152n
koyun-eri, 94
martolos, 128

müsellem, 30, 94, 103, 105, 107, 108
silihdār, 16, 18, 34, 34n, 53, 69, 125
sipāhī
  'of the Porte', 16, 18, 34, 45, 125
  timar-holding, 29, 30, 35, 44, 48, 56, 62, 66, 74, 86, 87, 92n, 94n, 100, 101, 102n, 103n, 105, 106, 107, 108, 110, 111, 112, 113, 114, 115, 116, 127, 128, 129, 130, 137, 167, 17; ***see also*** *su eri*
su eri, 92, 93, 94, 95, 96, 97, 106
'ulūfeci, 16, 34, 128
voynuk, 30, 92, 107, 115–16
yamak, 108, 115
yaya, 94, 103, 105, 107, 108

Viziers, statesmen and governors
Bāyezīd Paşa, 20
Çandarlı Ibrāhīm Paşa, (vizier of Mehmed I), 20
Çandarlı Ibrāhīm Paşa (vizier of Bāyezīd II), 138, 139
Ferhād Paşa, 139
Gedik Ahmed Paşa, 20
Hāccī 'Ivaz Paşa, 20
Halīl Paşa, 22
Hasan Paşa, 162
Ibrāhīm Paşa (vizier of Süleymān I), 47, 117n
Ibrāhīm Paşa (vizier of Mehmed III), 22
Ishāk Paşa, 15
Karamanī Mehmed Paşa, 4n, 20
Kāsim Paşa, 23
Lālā Mehmed Paşa, 52
Lutfī Paşa, 39–48
Mesīh Paşa, 41
Pīrī Paşa, 41
Sāhib, 5
Sinān Paşa, Cigalazāde, 52n
Sokolluzāde Hasan Paşa, 50
Timurtaş, 162
Tırnakçı Hasan Paşa, 51
Yemişçi Hasan Paşa, 50, 51, 52, 53–5

Weights and measures
arşun, 15, 80, 133
dirhem, 80, 119, 139, 140, 148
dönüm, 100, 101, 102, 106, 114, 149, 153
garbīl, 109
kantar, 50, 51, 98, 122
kīle, 62, 63, 74, 86, 94, 101, 109, 114, 146, 148
kırāt, 119
kulaç, 78
lidra, 94
medre, 97, 114
miskāl, 119
modio, 161
müd, 93, 94, 95, 101, 114
okka ***see*** *vukiyye*
vukkiyye, 148
zirā', 118

CPSIA information can be obtained
at www.ICGtesting.com
Printed in the USA
JSHW012209051021
19324JS00002B/4

9 781474 479370